AGING

Seventh Edition

Annual Editions
A Library of Information from the Public Press

Editor

Harold Cox
Indiana State University

Harold Cox, professor of sociology at Indiana State University, has published several articles in the field of gerontology. His paper "Priority Needs of Rural Elderly," coauthored by Gurmeet Sekhon, was part of the official proceedings of the 1981 White House Conference on Aging in 1981. He is a member of the Gerontological Society and the American Sociological Association—Occupation and Professions Section, and Youth and Aging Section.

Cover illustration by Mike Eagle

The Dushkin Publishing Group, Inc.
Sluice Dock, Guilford, Connecticut 06437

The Annual Editions Series

Annual Editions is a series of over fifty volumes designed to provide the reader with convenient, low-cost access to a wide range of current, carefully selected articles from some of the most important magazines, newspapers, and journals published today. Annual Editions are updated on an annual basis through a continuous monitoring of over 200 periodical sources. All Annual Editions have a number of features designed to make them particularly useful, including topic guides, annotated tables of contents, unit overviews, and indexes. For the teacher using Annual Editions in the classroom, an Instructor's Resource Guide with test questions is available for each volume.

VOLUMES AVAILABLE

Africa
Aging
American Government
American History, Pre-Civil War
American History, Post-Civil War
Anthropology
Biology
Business and Management
Business Ethics
Canadian Politics
China
Comparative Politics
Computers in Education
Computers in Business
Computers in Society
Criminal Justice
Drugs, Society, and Behavior
Early Childhood Education
Economics
Educating Exceptional Children
Education
Educational Psychology
Environment
Geography
Global Issues
Health
Human Development
Human Resources
Human Sexuality

Latin America
Macroeconomics
Management
Marketing
Marriage and Family
Microeconomics
Middle East and the Islamic World
Money and Banking
Nutrition
Personal Growth and Behavior
Psychology
Public Administration
Race and Ethnic Relations
Social Problems
Sociology
Soviet Union and Eastern Europe
State and Local Government
Third World
Urban Society
Violence and Terrorism
Western Civilization,
   Pre-Reformation
Western Civilization,
   Post-Reformation
Western Europe
World History, Pre-Modern
World History, Modern
World Politics

Library of Congress Cataloging in Publication Data
Main entry under title: Annual editions: Aging. 7/E.
        1. Gerontology—Periodicals. 2. Gerontology—United States—Periodicals. 3. Aged—United States—Periodicals. 4. Aging—Periodicals. I. Cox, Harold, comp. II. Title: Aging.
ISBN 0–87967–943–3   301.43 5′0973   78–645208

Seventh Edition

Manufactured by The Banta Company, Harrisonburg, Virginia 22801

To the Reader

In publishing ANNUAL EDITIONS we recognize the enormous role played by the magazines, newspapers, and journals of the *public press* in providing current, first-rate educational information in a broad spectrum of interest areas. Within the articles, the best scientists, practitioners, researchers, and commentators draw issues into new perspective as accepted theories and viewpoints are called into account by new events, recent discoveries change old facts, and fresh debate breaks out over important controversies.

Many of the articles resulting from this enormous editorial effort are appropriate for students, researchers, and professionals seeking accurate, current material to help bridge the gap between principles and theories and the real world. These articles, however, become more useful for study when those of lasting value are carefully *collected, organized, indexed,* and *reproduced* in a *low-cost format,* which provides easy and permanent access when the material is needed. That is the role played by *Annual Editions.* Under the direction of each volume's *Editor,* who is an expert in the subject area, and with the guidance of an *Advisory Board,* we seek each year to provide in each *ANNUAL EDITION* a current, well-balanced, carefully selected collection of the best of the public press for your study and enjoyment. We think you'll find this volume useful, and we hope you'll take a moment to let us know what you think.

The decline in the crude birth rate combined with an ever-improving medical technology, which is partly responsible for keeping most people alive and healthy well into their retirement years, has resulted in a shift in the age composition of the American population. Since 1900 there has been a gradual reduction in the number and percentage of young people in the total population; simultaneously, there has been a gradual increase in the number of older persons.

In 1900 approximately 4 percent of the total population was 65 years old or older. Currently, approximately 12 percent of the population is in the 65 and above age group. Demographic projections indicate that by the year 2000, the elderly will comprise 15 percent of the total population. The rapid growth in the number of older persons has made many of the problems of aging quite visible, and they have become widespread topics of concern.

Moreover, the aging of the population has not only become a phenomenon of the United States and the industrialized countries of Western Europe, but it is also occurring in the underdeveloped countries of the world. An increasing number and percentage of the world's population is now defined as aged.

Today almost all middle-aged people expect to live to retirement age and beyond. Both the middle-aged and the elderly have pushed for solutions to the problems confronting older Americans. Everyone seems to agree that granting the elderly a secure and comfortable status is desirable. Voluntary associations, communities, and state and federal governments have committed themselves to improving the lives of older persons. Many programs for senior citizens, both public and private, have emerged in the last 15 years.

The change in the age composition of the American population has not gone unnoticed by the media or the academic community. The number of articles appearing in the popular press and professional journals concerning the problems and opportunities confronting older Americans has increased dramatically over the last several years. While scientists have been concerned with the aging process for some time, in the last two decades there has been an expanding volume of research and writing on this subject. This growing interest has resulted in the seventh edition of *Annual Editions: Aging.*

This volume is representative of the field of gerontology in that it is interdisciplinary in its approach, including articles from the biological sciences, medicine, nursing, psychology, sociology, and social work. The articles are taken from the popular press, government publications, and scientific journals. They represent a wide cross section of authors, perspectives, and issues related to the aging process. They were chosen because they address the most relevant and current problems in the field of aging and present a variety of divergent views on the appropriate solutions to these problems. The topics covered include demographic trends, the aging process, longevity, social attitudes toward old age, problems and potentials of aging, retirement, death, living environments in later life, and social policies, programs, and services for older Americans. The articles are organized into an anthology useful for both the student and the teacher.

The goal of this edition was to choose articles that are pertinent, well-written, and helpful to those concerned with the field of gerontology. Comments, suggestions, or constructive criticism are welcomed to help improve future editions of this book. Please fill out the article rating form on the last page of this volume. Any anthology can be improved. This one will continue to be—annually.

Harold Cox

Harold Cox
Editor

Contents

Unit 1

The Phenomenon of Aging

Five selections examine the impact of aging on the individual, the family, and society.

Unit 2

The Quality of Later Life

Six selections consider the implications of living longer, as well as the physiological and psychological effects of aging.

The concepts in bold italics are developed in the article. For further expansion please refer to the Topic Guide and the Index.

Unit 3

Societal Attitudes Toward Old Age

Four selections discuss societal attitudes of discrimination toward the elderly, sexuality in the later years, and institutionalization.

Unit 4

Problems and Potentials of Aging

Six selections examine some of the inherent medical and social problems encountered by the aged, including the dynamics of poverty and elder abuse.

The concepts in bold italics are developed in the article. For further expansion please refer to the Topic Guide and the Index.

Unit 5

Retirement: American Dream or Dilemma?

Four selections look at the broad social implications of the continuing trend toward early retirement, and examine the necessity of reassessing and reshaping policies to keep valuable elderly employees in the work force.

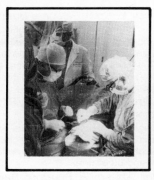

Unit 6

The Experience of Dying

Five selections discuss how increased longevity will affect support programs and the family, and consider the effects of death and terminal illness on the family.

Unit 7

Living Environments in Later Life

Four selections examine the problems of maintaining a positive living environment for the increasing number of elderly people.

The concepts in bold italics are developed in the article. For further expansion please refer to the Topic Guide and the Index.

Unit 8

Social Policies, Programs, and Services for Older Americans

Six selections consider the necessity of developing effective and positive support programs, policies, and services for older Americans.

The concepts in bold italics are developed in the article. For further expansion please refer to the Topic Guide and the Index.

Topic Guide

This topic guide suggests how the selections in this book relate to topics of traditional concern to students and professionals involved with gerontology. It is useful for locating articles which relate to each other for reading and research. The guide is arranged alphabetically according to topic. Articles may, of course, treat topics that do not appear in the topic guide. In turn, entries in the topic guide do not necessarily constitute a comprehensive listing of all the contents of each selection.

TOPIC AREA	TREATED IN:	TOPIC AREA	TREATED IN:
Abuse	15. The Vintage Years 20. The Prevalence of Elder Abuse 21. Aging: Can it be Slowed?	Family Relations (cont'd)	33. Aging, Generational Continuity, and Filial Support 34. Family Caregivers 40. Talkin' 'Bout My Generation
Autonomy	18. It's Never Too Late	Health Care/Health Problems	1. Why Do We Age? 4. The Graying of America 6. Older—But Coming on Strong 7. To Find a Way to Age 21. Aging: Can It Be Slowed? 37. Process, Politics, & Policy
Benefits of Aging	2. Meeting the Challenges 3. Old Age 4. The Graying of America 10. Starting Over at Midlife 12. Never Too Late		
Death and Dying	31. Options for Aging 32. Access to Health Care	Learning/Mental Ability	1. Why Do We Age? 11. Meet the People 16. Aging of the Brain
Definitions of Aging	4. The Graying of America 15. The Vintage Years	Life Expectancy/ Longevity	1. Why Do We Age? 2. Meeting the Challenges 4. The Graying of America 6. Older—But Coming on Strong 7. To Find a Way to Age 12. Never Too Late 17. Minorities Face Stubborn Inequities 20. The Prevalence of Elder Abuse
Demography	2. Meeting the Challenges 4. The Graying of America		
Discrimination	4. The Graying of America 18. It's Never Too Late		
Economic Status	5. Human Aging 17. Minorities Face Stubborn Inequities 22. Productive Aging and the Future 23. The "Unretired"—Seniors 24. Life-Care Contracts 26. The Many Faces of Grief 31. Options for Aging 35. A New Look at Companies 36. Staying in the Work Force 38. Roles for Aged Individuals	Minorities	12. Never Too Late 17. Minorities Face Stubborn Inequities 20. The Prevalence of Elder Abuse
		Physiology of Aging	1. Why Do We Age? 4. The Graying of America 7. To Find a Way to Age 12. Never Too Late 19. Actions of Alcohol and Drugs in Older People 21. Aging: Can It Be Slowed?
Education	11. Meet the People		
Employment	5. Human Aging 18. It's Never Too Late 23. The "Unretired"—Seniors 30. Kübler-Ross's Stages of Dying 35. A New Look at Companies 36. Staying in the Work Force 38. Roles for Aged Individuals	Politics	39. Generational Equity 40. Talkin' 'Bout My Generation
		Poverty	17. Minorities Face Stubborn Inequities
		Psychology of Aging	3. Old Age 10. Starting Over at Midlife 16. Aging of the Brain
Euthanasia	27. Health Technology vs. Death 28. Euthanasia 29. In Defense of the . . . Death Act	Religion	9. Religiosity, Aging, and Life 12. Never Too Late
Exercise	4. The Graying of America 6. Older—But Coming on Strong	Retirement	22. Productive Aging and the Future 23. The "Unretired"—Seniors 24. Life-Care Contracts 26. The Many Faces of Grief 30. Kübler-Ross's Stages of Dying
Family Relations	8. Marriage in Later Life 32. Access to Health Care		

TOPIC AREA	TREATED IN:	TOPIC AREA	TREATED IN:
Self Help Ethos	3. Old Age 4. The Graying of America 5. Human Aging 7. To Find a Way to Age 18. It's Never Too Late	**Sociology of Aging**	3. Old Age 5. Human Aging 8. Marriage in Later Life 10. Starting Over at Midlife 11. Meet the People 33. Aging, Generational Continuity, and Filial Support 34. Family Caregivers 38. Roles for Aged Individuals 40. Talkin' 'Bout My Generation
Sexuality	14. Age Stereotyping		
Social Policy	26. The Many Faces of Grief 33. Aging, Generational Continuity, and Filial Support 35. A New Look at Companies 36. Staying in the Work Force 37. Process, Politics, & Policy 38. Roles For Aged Individuals	**Stereotypes**	6. Older—But Coming on Strong 7. To Find a Way to Age 14. Age Sterotyping 15. The Vintage Years
Social Security	5. Human Aging 22. Productive Aging and the Future	**Understanding the Aged**	1. Why Do We Age? 2. Meeting the Challenges 4. The Graying of America 5. Human Aging 8. Marriage in Later Life 9. Religiousity, Aging, and Life 10. Starting Over at Midlife 13. Old Age as a Second Childhood 18. It's Never Too Late
Social Services	33. Aging, Generational Continuity, and Filial Support 34. Family Caregivers 37. Process, Politics, & Policy		
Social Status	2. Meeting the Challenges 15. The Vintage Years		

The Phenomenon of Aging

The process of aging is complex, and includes biological, psychological, sociological, and behavioral changes. Biologically, the body gradually loses the ability to renew itself. Various body functions begin to slow down, and the vital senses become less acute. Psychologically, aging persons experience changing sensory processes; perception, motor skills, problem-solving ability, and drives and emotions are frequently altered. Sociologically, they must cope with the changing roles and definitions of self imposed by society. For instance, the role expectations and the status of grandparents are different from those of parents, and the roles of the retired are unlike those of the employed. Because aging individuals are assuming new roles and are viewed differently by others, their attitudes about themselves, their emotions, and, ultimately, their behavior can be expected to change.

Those studying the process of aging often explain behavior using developmental theories of the life cycle—a sequence of predictable phases, beginning with birth and ending with death. A person's age, therefore, provides clues about his or her behavior at a particular phase of the life cycle, be it childhood, adolescence, adulthood, middle age, or old age. There is, however, greater variety of health and human development among older persons than among any other age group. While every three-year-old child can be predicted to experience certain developmental tasks, there is a wide variation in the behavior of 65-year-olds. Some are in good health, employed, and performing important work tasks. Others are retired and in good health. Still others are retired and in poor health, while some have died before reaching the age of 65.

The articles in this section are written from a biological, psychological, and sociological perspective. These disciplines attempt to explain the effects of aging, and the resulting choices in life-style, as well as the wider cultural implications of an older population.

In "Why Do We Age?" the author points out that while everyone will experience certain age-related changes, the age at which these changes occur can vary considerably. This allows each of us to have some degree of control over how we age. As is pointed out in "Human Aging: Usual and Successful," adjusting one's life-style through diet, exercise, and personal habits can affect not only longevity but the quality of one's life.

In "Meeting the Challenges of an Aging Nation" the concept of a shift in basic values is discussed. As the country moves away from a youth-oriented culture toward one of greater maturity, social and cultural traditions long taken for granted will change. Already, past stereotypes of old age are being refuted. In "Old Age Is Not What It Used to Be," the author emphasizes that old age is not simply a matter of chronological years, but is defined by the health and well-being of the individual.

Looking Ahead: Challenge Questions

What accounts for most behavior changes during the aging process—biological, psychological, or sociological factors?

Biological, psychological, sociological, and behavioral researchers usually work independently to explain the aging process. Could these disparate perspectives be combined into a single theory of aging?

Will it ever be possible to slow down the aging process? Would this be desirable?

What is meant by "successful aging"?

WHY DO WE AGE?

Ken Flieger
Ken Flieger is a free-lance writer in Washington, D.C.

In December 1987, Anna Williams died in a nursing home in Wales. At age 114, she was believed to be the oldest person on Earth. Scientists think that 115 to 120 years is probably the upper limit of human longevity. But why should that be? Why should the human body give out after 70, 80, or even 115 years? Why are older people more susceptible to disease, more inclined to have impaired vision and hearing, and likely to lose some of the physical and mental capacity they once enjoyed?

There are no fully satisfactory answers to these questions. No one knows exactly what the process of aging is or why it runs a different course in different people. Nor does anyone know how to increase human longevity, despite the often fraudulent and sometimes dangerous claims of the "life extension" hucksters and others who traffic in the fears and ills of the elderly.

What is known is that our bodies undergo more or less predictable changes with advancing age. Some—like hair turning gray or falling out, wrinkled skin, and reduced physical and mental vigor—are obvious. Others may not be visible, but they are happening nonetheless. Blood pressure usually rises with age; the ability to metabolize sugar decreases. There is a general decrease in lean body mass (primarily muscle and bone) as opposed to fat so that, although a person may weigh the same at age 70 as he or she did at 20, the body composition is considerably different. Medical tests will show that an older person's heart pumps less efficiently, the kidneys may not work as well, lung function is diminished, and bone density is reduced.

Gerontologists (scientists who study aging) stress, however, that these "common" age-related changes don't all happen to everyone or at predictable stages, and most definitely cannot provide a reliable picture of the individual's well-being. As one scientist observed, knowing that a 75-year-old man has diabetes and a history of heart disease doesn't provide a clue as to whether he's sitting in a nursing home or on the bench of the Supreme Court.

BY MISTAKE OR DESIGN?

Research is, however, beginning to piece together bits of the puzzle of aging. Scientists are exploring numerous theories that may help explain the changes that come with advancing age. "Error" theories speculate that with advancing age, we become less able to repair damage caused by internal malfunctions or external assaults to the body from, for example, pollutants, viruses, and cosmic and solar radiation. Much like an automobile, the human machine can sustain just so much damage until effective repair is no longer possible and it ceases to run.

"Program" theories of aging, on the other hand, suggest that an internal clock starts ticking at conception and is programmed to run just so long and no longer. These theories hold that genes carry specific instructions that facilitate not only growth and maturation, but decline and death as well.

Whichever broad concept turns out to offer a more satisfactory explanation of what aging is all about—and most authorities doubt that any single theory will account for all the complexities of the aging process—it seems clear that human beings age as a result of events that take place within cells. One "error" hypothesis, the "wear and tear" theory, suggests that cells gradually lose the ability to repair damaged DNA, the substance that passes genetic information from one cell to the next. As a consequence, cells become less efficient in carrying out vital functions, such as making proteins, and eventually they die. Other error theories relate aging to metabolic rate, the rate at which cells convert nutrients into the energy they need to live and reproduce. This view of aging implies that the faster an organism lives, the quicker it dies, which might explain why animals with short

Reprinted from *FDA Consumer*, October 1988, pp. 20-23, 25.

lifespans (compared to man's) usually have much higher metabolic rates than we do.

Studies done in the mid-1930s support this "rate of living" theory of aging. Investigators at Cornell University found that newly weaned rats fed a diet severely restricted in calories but nutritionally adequate lived extraordinarily long lives. Later studies demonstrated the same thing in mice and showed that undernutrition, as it is called, could lengthen lifespan even if it wasn't started until the animals had reached adulthood.

Caloric restriction is the only technique that has been repeatedly shown to alter the rate of aging of laboratory animals. Scientists speculate that reducing caloric intake may slow the animals' metabolism and thus reduce the rate of damage to cells or to DNA. There is little evidence to suggest that undernutrition will increase the human lifespan, although comprehensive studies have not been done.

Another theory attributes aging to damage caused by protein "cross-linking." With the passage of time, more and more protein molecules in cells and tissues become chemically bound to one another in ways that interfere with their normal functioning. When this happens to collagen—a protein that supports cells and tissues and is especially abundant in bone, cartilage, and tendons—it tends to become more rigid. The effect is all too apparent in the wrinkled skin that is virtually a cardinal sign of growing older. But whether "cross-linking" is at the root of the aging process is far from certain.

TICKING AWAY

Unlike error theories of aging, internal clock theories don't try to explain the process in terms of one particular biologic mechanism or defect. Instead, they view aging in terms of a genetically determined program. Support for this concept can be seen throughout our lives: the coming of adult teeth, and the onset of puberty and menopause all seem to confirm that human growth and development march to a built-in drummer. But an important scientific finding in the 1960s added even more powerful support to the evidence of simple observation.

A quarter century ago, Drs. Leonard Hayflick and Paul Moorehead at the Wistar Institute in Philadelphia found that embryonic human cells in tissue culture have an inherent capacity to divide only about 50 times. Once this limit is reached, cell division stops, and the cell line dies. If cultures are begun with cells taken from an adult rather than an embryo, the number of divisions they undergo is fewer than 50. The only exception seems to be abnormal cancer cells that can go on dividing indefinitely. (Human cells divide at widely different rates: tumor cells in tissue culture may divide as fast as once in every 18 hours; nerve cells, on the other hand, may never divide once nerve tissue has been formed.)

Why cells lose the ability to reproduce is not known, but apparently some element in the genetic code dictates how many times a cell can divide and then brings cell division to a halt. It's probably an oversimplification to say that the lifespan of an organism as complex as a human being is determined by how many times its cells can divide. Yet the "Hayflick phenomenon" rules out the view of earlier scientists working with tissue culture that, given the proper conditions, cells, tissues, organs and perhaps people could survive indefinitely.

If there is a genetically programmed clock at the heart of the aging process, how are its instructions communicated to cells and tissues? Both the endocrine (hormone) system and the immune system have been proposed as the medium through which those instructions are transmitted and carried out.

Most people have a fairly good notion of the role of hormones in sexual development and reproduction. Scientists, however, are learning a good deal more about hormones and aging. For example, we now understand that hormones in premenopausal women seem to protect against cardiovascular diseases and that the decline in estrogen levels after menopause is associated with bone loss and osteoporosis.

Another hormone, dehydroepiandrosterone (DHEA), produced by the adrenal glands, is present in extremely high levels in the blood of young adults and falls sharply with age. This has led to speculation that this hormone may play a role in aging. Laboratory studies seem to support this hunch. Mice given the hormone have lower breast cancer rates, increased survival, and a delayed loss of immune functions. They are more active and have a more youthful appearance (glossier coats) than untreated animals. But investigators have also noted that these mice don't gain weight as rapidly as untreated animals. Hence, as in other animal experiments, caloric restriction may be behind the apparent anti-aging effect of this hormone.

Products claiming to contain DHEA have been promoted for weight loss and life extension, but in 1985 FDA ordered a halt to their marketing because they have never been reviewed for safety and effectiveness. In fact, the agency warned at the time, risks from long-term use of such products were unknown. Furthermore, some of the products may have been made from human urine, and scientists had no idea what effect reintroducing into the body this bodily excess might have.

Such unproven products aside, the role of hormones is a busy and legitimate avenue of aging research.

Whether or not the immune system translates genetic information into programmed aging, scientists know that it is closely associated with the aging process. The thymus gland, located in the upper chest, is a major component of the immune system. It is present at birth, reaches its maximum size during adolescence, and is barely visible by age 50. The immune system itself runs along a somewhat parallel track. It is most efficient during childhood and young adulthood, but with advancing age, it is less able to recognize and counteract foreign substances, such as viruses, that enter the body. Nor is the aging immune system as efficient in recognizing the difference between normal and abnormal cellular components—in other words, between "self" and "non-self."

Some authorities believe that the gradual decline in the efficiency and effectiveness of the immune system explains not just the increased susceptibility to infection in older people, but also their increased rate of chronic diseases, such as cancer. They speculate that the body becomes progressively less able to recognize and destroy malignant cells, which then have the chance to become established and develop into tumors and other cancers. Similarly, the decline of the immune system may account for the so-called "autoimmune" diseases, such as rheumatoid arthritis, in which the body attacks its own cells. It is possible that a declining immune system may be associated with other factors related to the aging process, such as loss of the ability to repair damaged DNA.

DEFYING NATURE?

Living to a ripe old age has a certain appeal to most people, but it may in fact not be part of nature's plan. Wild animals don't survive much beyond the age of peak maturity. They tend to be killed

The Aging of America

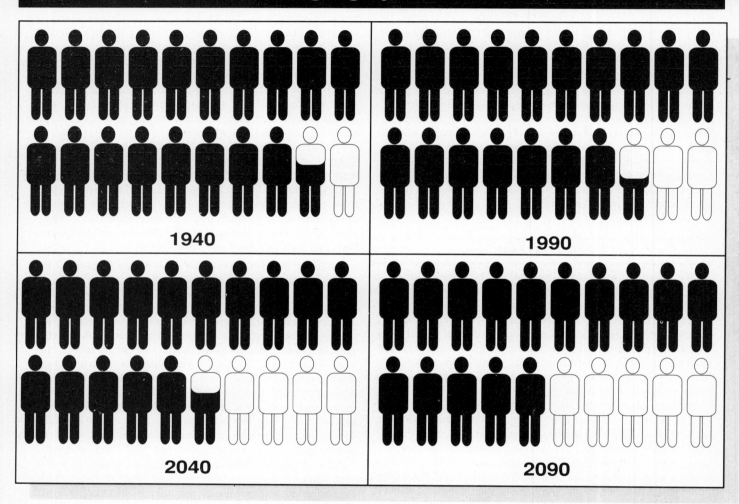

In 1940, 6.8 percent of the population was 65 or older. By 1990, 12.7 percent of us will have reached age 65; by 2040, 21.7 percent; and a century from now, nearly one out of four Americans will be 65 and older. An estimated 25,000 Americans now living are 100 years old or older.

Source: U.S. Bureau of the Census.

off by predators once their physical abilities start to decline or they become sick. For humans living in primitive societies, that peak comes at around age 30, at about the age when childbearing and child-rearing come to an end.

Whether or not we are defying Mother Nature, Americans are undoubtedly living longer, thanks in part to improved health care, more responsive social and public assistance programs, and better understanding of the importance of nutrition, exercise, and personal interactions in sustaining vitality in advancing age.

At the same time, the burden of illness and disability among older people is tragically heavy, and as more and more of us live to advanced years, the care of the elderly will impose an increasing demand on the nation's resources.

Much of the puzzle of aging remains to be solved. But the field of aging research, one of the youngest branches of the health sciences, has added a wealth of new information in just the last few decades. Spearheaded by the National Institute on Aging, one

of the National Institutes of Health in Bethesda, Md., aging studies are helping to dispel some myths—for example, that aging progresses rapidly as a result of an overwhelming event—and are enabling physicians to do a better job of caring for older patients. Knowing more precisely how older people absorb and excrete drugs can lead to better prescribing information for doctors who care for elderly patients. FDA is actively encouraging drug companies and others to make sure that, when appropriate, clinical studies of new investigational drugs do not arbitrarily exclude elderly persons, who may react to the drug very differently from younger patients.

Some people may be saddened by the realization that science doesn't hold the key to immortality (though the thought of a world in which no one ever died is rather alarming). But the goal of aging research is at once more realistic and more humane. It is to help people achieve the longest possible life with the least possible disability. Science just might be able to reach that goal.

Common Ailments in Older Americans

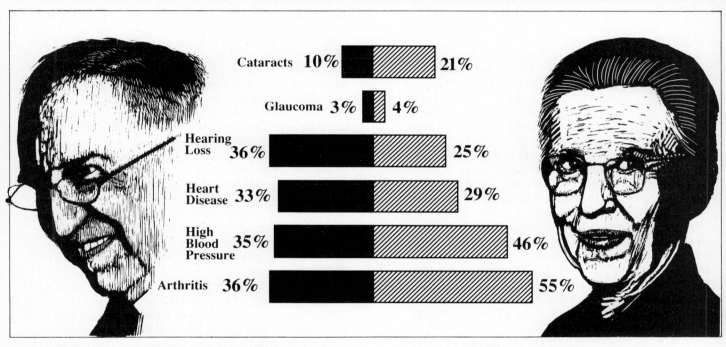

	Men	Women
Cataracts	10%	21%
Glaucoma	3%	4%
Hearing Loss	36%	25%
Heart Disease	33%	29%
High Blood Pressure	35%	46%
Arthritis	36%	55%

Percent of American men and women aged 65 or older who suffer from one or more of six common ailments.

Source: National Institute on Aging.

Men **Women**

Meeting the challenges of an aging nation

KEN DYCHTWALD WITH JOE FLOWER/*NEW AGE JOURNAL*

America is aging. The nation that was founded on young backs, on the strength, impetuosity, and hope of youth, is growing more mature, steadier, deeper—even, one may hope, wiser.

The Population Reference Bureau, a non-profit demographics study group in Washington, D.C., has projected that by the year 2025 Americans over age 65 will outnumber teenagers by more than two to one. According to the Census Bureau, by 2030 the median age is expected to have reached 41. By 2050, it's likely that as many as one in four Americans will be over 65. Many demographers consider these projections to be very conservative: By some estimates, the median age will eventually reach 50.

Three separate and unprecedented demographic phenomena are converging to produce the coming "Age Wave":

• *The senior boom.* Americans are living longer than ever before, and older Americans are healthier, more active, more vigorous, and more influential than any other older generation in history.

• *The birth dearth.* A decade ago, the birth rate in the United States plummeted to its lowest point ever. It has been hovering there since, and it's not likely to change. The growing population of elders is not being offset by an explosion of children.

• *The aging of the baby boom.* The leading edge of the boomer generation has now passed 40. As the boomers approach 50 and pass it, their numbers, combined with the first two demographic changes, will produce a historic shift in American life.

Our concept of marriage will change, as "till death do us part" unions generally give way to serial monogamy. In an era of longer life, some people will have marriages that last 75 years, while others will pick different mates for each major stage of life.

The child-centered nuclear family will increasingly be replaced by the "matrix" family, an adult-centered unit that spans generations and is bound together by friendship and circumstance as well as by blood and obligation.

More people will work at careers into their 70s and 80s. Many will "retire" several times during their lives—to raise a second (or third) family, enter a new business, or simply take a couple of years off to travel and enjoy themselves.

Even the physical environment will change. To fit the pace, physiology, and style of a population predominantly in the middle and later years of life, the type in books will get larger and traffic lights will change more slowly. Steps will be less steep, bathtubs less slippery, chairs more comfortable, reading lights brighter. Neighborhoods will become safer. Food might

In China, the highest achievement of Taoism was a long life.

be more nutritious.

But the aging of America will affect more than just our institutions, lifestyles, and surroundings. The demographic changes that rearrange our society will also touch our innermost thoughts, hopes, and dreams. The gift of longevity will make us rethink the tempo of our lives as well as the purposes, goals, and challenges we face in each stage of life.

Indeed, the cumulative effect of all these changes might be an entirely new perspective on the possibilities of old age. A compelling philosophy has recently emerged from the European tradition of adult education that provides a simple yet visionary look at this issue. Referred to as le troisième age—"the third age"—this theory proposes that there are three "ages" of human life, each with its own focus, challenges, and opportunities.

In the first age, from birth to approximately 25 years of age, the primary tasks of life center on biological development, learning, and survival. During the early years of human existence, the average life expectancy of most people wasn't much higher than 25, so the entire thrust of society was satisfying these most basic drives.

In the second age, from about 26 to 60, the concerns of adult life focus on starting and raising a family and on productive work. The second age is filled with social activity; the lessons learned during the first age are applied to the social and professional responsibilities of the second. Until several decades ago, most people couldn't expect to live much beyond 60 and most of society revolved around the concerns of the second age.

Now, however, we are in a new era of human evolution: the third age of humanity. The concerns of the third age are twofold. First, with children grown and many of life's basic adult tasks either well under way or already accomplished, this less pressured, more reflective period allows the further development of the intel-

---

"People in the third age should be the glue of society, not its ashes."

---

lect, memory, and imagination, of emotional maturity, and of one's spiritual identity.

The third age is also a period of giving back to society the lessons, resources, and experiences accumulated over a lifetime. From this perspective, the elderly are seen not as social outcasts, but as a living bridge between yesterday, today, and tomorrow—a critical evolutionary role that no other age group can perform. According to Monsignor Charles Fahey, who serves as director of Fordham University's Third Age Center, "People in the third age should be the glue of society, not its ashes."

Of course, this is not a new idea in human history, but it's one that modern society's intense focus on youth has obscured. In other cultures and other times, the elderly have been revered for their wisdom, power, and spiritual force. In ancient China, for example, the highest achievement in Taoism was long life and the wisdom

that came with the passing of years. According to writer and social historian Simone de Beauvoir, "Lao-tse's teaching sets the age of 60 as the moment at which a man may free himself from his body and become a holy being. Old age was therefore life in its very highest form."

Among the Aranda people, hunter-gatherers of the Australian forests, extreme old age brings with it a near-supernatural status: "The man whom age has already brought close to the other world is the best mediator between this and the next. It is the old people who direct the Arandas' religious life—a life that underlies the whole of their social existence."

In contemporary Japanese culture, a high value is placed on the unique opportunities for spiritual development offered by old age. According to Thomas Rohlen, an expert on Japanese culture, "What is significant in Japanese spiritualism is the promise itself, for it clearly lends meaning, integrity, and joy to many lives, especially as the nature of adult existence unfolds. It

---

By 2025 Americans over age 65 will outnumber teenagers by more than two to one.

---

recognizes the inherent value of experience. And for all its emphasis on social responsibility, discipline, and perseverance in the middle years, it encourages these as a means to a final state of spiritual freedom, ease, and universal belonging.... Here is a philosophy seemingly made for adulthood—giving it stature, movement, and optimism."

Even in the United States, before modernization shifted our interest from the old to the young, the elderly were the recipients of great reverence. In the early 1840s, the Rev. Cortlandt van Rensselaer said in one of his sermons, "What a blessed influence the old exert in cherishing feelings of reverence, affection, and subordination in families; in detailing the results of experience; in importing judicious counsel in Church and State and private life."

According to Calvinist doctrine, which was profoundly influential during the early 19th century, living to a great age was taken as a sign of God's special favor. The more spiritually evolved elder was considered one of the elect, and therefore worthy of veneration. The elderly were highly honored in all social rituals and on all public occasions. As influential leader Increase Mather commented in the late 17th century, "If a man is favored with long life . . . it is God that has lengthened his days." The soul, the Puritans believed, grew throughout our lives, reaching its highest earthly perfection in old age.

1. THE PHENOMENON OF AGING

A look at other eras and cultures offers a glimpse of the improvements in American life that can come with an aging population. But whether we can take advantage of this situation depends on whether our society can make the following changes:

• Uprooting ageism and gerontophobia and replacing them with a new, more positive view of aging;

• abandoning the limiting confines that come with viewing life as solely a linear progression and instead emphasizing the cyclical patterns of human existence, which is more appropriate to the shifting needs of an aging population;

• creating a new spectrum of family relationships that takes into account the sexual, companionship, and friendship needs of adults;

• improving the quality and availability of health care;

• providing products and services that will offer older men and women comfort, convenience, and pleasure;

• and achieving cooperation among Americans of all ages in creating a social system that is fair and equitable.

For us as individuals, whether an aged America turns out to be good or bad will depend on whether we can grow beyond the values and expectations of youth to discover a positive and expanded vision of who we might become in our later years.

Old Age Is Not What It Used to Be

Carol Tavris

Carol Tavris is a social psychologist and author of "Anger: The Misunderstood Emotion" Touchstone).

Age only matters when one is aging. Now that I have arrived at a great age, I might as well be 20.
—Pablo Picasso (at 80)

Adult life used to be fairly predictable, and so were theories of aging. It was simple: the older you got, the more you lost—sex drive, memory, brain cells, energy, intelligence. When psychologists first studied adult development, they would come around every few years and draw conclusions about the inevitable losses associated with age. Now they come around every few years and find that Grandma refuses to mind the grandchildren; she and Harry have bought a Winnebago and are camping in Yosemite. Aunt Sarah took up marathon running and local politics at the age of 73. And Uncle Fred retired at 58 from Amalgamated Teabiscuit & Muffins to become a jazz musi-

cian. Growing old is not what it used to be.

No one even agrees anymore on what "old" is. Not long ago, 30 was middle-aged and 60 was old. Now, more and more people are living into their 70's, 80's and beyond—and many of them are living well, without any incapacitating mental or physical decline. Today, old age is defined not simply by chronological years, but by degree of health and well-being.

I realized how my ideas of "old" had changed when I began looking for people to interview for this story. My friends who are in their 70's—such as Anne Louis, a 75-year-old realtor who worked night and day for months to find a house for my husband and me—were too young. Those in their 80's, like my mother, were busy working, exercising, traveling and fund raising; they didn't seem properly old either. And when I asked around for names of vigorous, interesting people in their 90's, I had more than I could manage within a day.

Until recently, people believed that all mental and physical functions declined with age. "Old" meant forgetful, senile

and feeble. But many researchers are now finding that some of the conditions thought characteristic of old age are a result of poor nutrition, lack of exercise or disease, such as Alzheimer's and other neurologically based dementias. According to Dr. T. Franklin Williams, director of the National Institute on Aging, even the heart and kidneys of a person over 65, if free of disease, can function as well as those of a young person.

In separating the biology of aging from its psychology, researchers have begun to realize that many of the presumed psychological deficits of old age would occur to people of any age who were deprived of loved ones, close friends, meaningful activity and intellectual stimulation.

When people don't lose these necessities, they often end up like Luba Kahan, who just turned 90 and has every marble she was born with. She did quit smoking last year because her children were pestering her about it, and she once took a "poison" prescribed by her doctor for a backache, but she continues to horrify her 73-

year-old son by eating what she likes rather than what she should. "My philosophy," she explains, "is that as long as you don't see a doctor, you'll stay healthy. When my son is as old as I am, he can tell me what to eat." Mrs. Kahan lives alone, walks to the local supermarket, reads all night when it suits her and continues to be busy and independent. "The only thing I need from my children," she says, "is love."

Many of the assumptions about mental and physical decline in old age were based on studies that compared several age groups and that did not distinguish between aging itself and the effects of illness, poverty, poor education or lack of intellectual stimulation. Although these studies found that some aspects of intelligence, such as reasoning ability, spatial ability and verbal comprehension, declined with age, more recent work, which followed the same people from middle age into old age, showed far less decline. This has led researchers to re-evaluate the earlier findings and question whether a decrease in mental abilities is natural to old age or whether it is specific to generational cohorts, people who have shared certain experiences and problems.

"Each aging group is different because of its particular history," says Dr. Jacqueline Goodchilds, associate professor of psychology at the University of California at Los Angeles and a researcher at the RAND Corporation. "Gerontology is a fascinating field because you know the findings will change every five years. For example, the average retirement age is now under 60. A whole generation is starting over at 59, finding new careers and interests." Dr. Goodchilds and her research associate, Leonie Huddy, even suspect that osteoporosis is a generational artifact—characteristic of a cohort of older women who, as young girls, rarely exercised and did not develop full bone strength.

According to Dr. Goodchilds, the generation now in their 40's and 50's "will be yet a different breed of old people—they are better educated, they have more skills."

"Many more of them are single and childless, and they worry about growing old on their own," she adds. "But we've found that in old age, never-married people report much higher life satisfaction than widowed people do, perhaps because they are used to doing things on their own. They do not experience the discontinuity that married people do when the spouse dies or the children move away."

"Old people in general feel psychologically better than young people," says Dr. Carin Rubenstein, a social psychologist and co-author, with Dr. Phillip Shaver, of "In Search of Intimacy," a study of loneliness in America. "They have fewer worries about themselves and how they look to other people; they have higher self-esteem; they aren't as lonely as people think they are." The loneliest people, Dr. Rubenstein says, are not the elderly, but teen-agers and young adults.

Young people just starting out in new careers and relationships are also under far more stress than older people, and have less experience in coping with it. This is one reason that many experts are now celebrating some of the benefits of aging: wisdom, a sense of humor, old-fashioned maturity.

THE EFFORT TO DIStinguish biological changes from psychological consequences has begun to erode many of the stereotypes of age. For instance, until recently it was assumed that the menopausal woman suffered from a syndrome that made her deeply depressed about losing her reproductive capacity, her sexuality, her femininity. This stereotype evolved chiefly from studies of women whose early menopause was brought on by surgery and from the assumption that women *naturally* become depressed when their reproductive capacity ends. Actually, most women go through normal menopause with no major psychological difficulties and very few physical ones.

Drs. Sonja McKinlay and John McKinlay, at the Cambridge Research Center in Cambridge, Mass., surveyed more than 8,000 menopausal women. Only 3 percent said they felt regret; the majority viewed menopause with relief, or had no particular feelings about it at all, apart from annoyance at such "temporarily bothersome symptoms" as hot flashes and menstrual irregularity. "If the truth were known," says Dr. Goodchilds, "we'd have to diagnose them as having P.M.F. — Post-Menstrual Freedom."

Certainly, aging produces physical limitations, as any 32-year-old "aging" athlete knows. The body generally reaches its peak condition at about age 30 and then slowly declines. Eyesight gets worse; it becomes more difficult, particularly for men, to hear tones in the higher registers; the sense of smell weakens after age 65 and drops sharply after age 80; the central nervous system processes information more slowly than it once did, and metabolism and reflexes slow down.

Yet aging does not inevitably mean the loss of intelligence or memory. Folklore has it that the brain loses brain cells the way the scalp sheds dandruff, but according to Dr. Marian Diamond, professor of anatomy at the University of California at Berkeley, normal human aging does not produce extensive brain cell deterioration until, perhaps, extreme old age. From her research with aged rats, and with vigorous, healthy people over the age of 88, Dr. Diamond is optimistic about the brain's "plasticity" — the ability of nerve cells to respond to stimuli — at any age. When people live in challenging environments, she argues, brain function does not naturally decay.

A case in point is Scott O'Dell, 89, who has written at least one book every year since 1966. His research has taken him to Bermuda, the Yucatan, Guatemala, Peru and the Pacific Northwest. He was 62 when his first children's book, "Island of the Blue Dolphins," was published.

Mr. O'Dell holds no truck with live-right-to-live-long theories. "There's no secret to being 89," he says. "No regimen, no trick, such as eating Wheaties, jogging 10 miles a day, drinking alcohol, not drinking alcohol. There is only the great, overriding secret: it all amounts to genes. My Irish great-great-grandfather died at 105. He was perfectly healthy at the time, but he fell off the porch. Drunk, I'm sure. He had 11 sons, and even counting the one who died at 36, their average age when they died was 96. Maybe I have a few of those genes."

Genes are helpful, Dr. Diamond agrees, but they are not sufficient. "A nerve cell is designed to receive stimuli," she explains. "Without stimuli, it shrivels and decays. This is true of the rat brain and the human brain, the young brain and the old brain. I've known many people with long-lived parents who died young, unhappy and unfulfilled. And I've known people whose genes were against them who have lived long, healthy lives."

It's not a matter of diet ver-

sus genes, or heredity versus environment, Dr. Diamond says; it's how they interact. "My father lived to be 93," she says. "He ate an egg every day, but he had low cholesterol. People scream about cholesterol without knowing their own levels. The important thing is to know yourself."

A HEALTHY OLD age, everyone agrees, depends on activity. Not only are older adults just as good as young ones at long-practiced abilities, they can also acquire new ones. In a study published in 1986, Dr. K. Warner Schaie, director of the gerontology center at Pennsylvania State University, and Dr. Sherry Willis of the department of human development at Penn State, were able to reverse the supposedly normal intellectual decline in a group of 60- to 80-year-olds by giving each of them five one-hour tutoring sessions in inductive reasoning and problem solving.

As for the universal fear of memory loss, it appears that memory plays tricks on everyone. I don't know one person over the age of 25 who hasn't complained about his or her lousy memory, or made nervous jokes about having Alzheimer's. The short-term memory of most older people — the ability to remember the name of a person they just met or a phone number they just looked up — is not much different from that of most younger people. It is long-term memory that tends to cause problems. But according to one recent study, years of schooling and current enrollment in school are better predictors of differences in memory ability than age is.

"Old people get bored taking boring tests," says Dr. Goodchilds. "A young person who is used to frequent school exams will sit still for four hours, counting numbers backward, if you ask him to. An older person will say, 'What the hell am I doing here?'"

As Dr. Robin West, a psychologist at the University of Florida at Gainesville, observes, most memory studies do not take place in the real world. It is important to remember to call your doctor or pay your bills, but it isn't important to remember nonsense syllables. When the material is relevant to them, older people can retrieve information as rapidly as younger people can. If they do have trouble remembering something, the reason seems to be slower reaction time, not impaired recall. In other words, we all eventually come up with the name of the actor who starred with Dustin Hoffman in "Midnight Cowboy"; it just takes some of us a little longer.

Perhaps the biggest difference between an old person and a young person who can't remember something is that the former can blame forgetfulness on old age. When my mother, who remembers more about my life than I do, can't think of a name immediately, she says, "Damn, I'm getting old." When my 19-year-old students can't remember the answer to a test question, they just say "Damn."

As with intelligence and memory, a decline in the frequency of sexual activity among older people is, researchers suspect, due less to biology than to social and psychological factors, including the *expectation* of such a decline.

Aging does cause some physiological changes in sexual response — women produce less vaginal lubrication, men take longer to reach full erection, and both sexes have fewer contractions at orgasm — but these changes do not necessarily affect frequency of sexual activity or pleasure. The main problem for most old people is lack of a partner, not lack of desire.

The frequency of a person's sexual experiences in early adulthood is the best predictor of his or her sexual activity in later life. According to Dr. Carole Wade, a psychologist and author of "Human Sexuality," "The greatest difference in sexual activity — or any other aspect of aging — is not between the old and the young, but between individuals."

This emphasis on individual development, and the corresponding move away from "stage-oriented" approaches, is perhaps the most dramatic change in theories of aging. "Unlike child development, which is powerfully governed by maturational and biological changes, adult development is more affected by psychology and experience," observes Dr. Orville Brim, a social psychologist and member of the MacArthur Foundation's Program on Successful Aging, a national committee of 15 experts from different fields. "This means that so-called adult stages cannot be as universal or as inevitable as childhood stages. Children go through a stage of babbling before they talk, they crawl before they walk. But as children mature, environmental factors take on greater impact. That's why you find far more variation among 80-year-olds than among 8-year-olds."

M ANY RE-searchers are now turning their attention to the transitions that mark adulthood. What matters, they say, is not how old you are, but what you are doing.

"Having a child affects new parents regardless of *when* they have a child," says Dr. Nancy Schlossberg, a developmental psychologist at the University of Maryland. "People facing retirement confront similar issues whether they are retiring at 40, 50 or 70. Adolescents may have identity problems, but so do adult auto workers who are laid off and divorced homemakers who must find new careers."

Unlike stage theories, which assume that life consists of a series of psychological crises that must be resolved before an individual can move on, transition theories assume that all human beings have certain psychological needs that can never be satisfied once and for all, but must be constantly renegotiated. To Dr. Schloss-berg, these needs include a reasonable degree of control over one's life, enthusiasm for one's activities and commitments to people and values. Most of all, she says, people need to feel that they *matter* to others.

To see Dr. Schlossberg's theory in the flesh, you should meet Benjamin Rosen, a 92-year-old musician who single-handedly runs a sheet music shop in Hollywood. Mr. Rosen turns every visiting questioner into a straight man. (*Do you still play?* No, I actively play. *What do you play?* Violin, viola, pinochle....) When I ask him how long he has had the store and whether he ever plans to retire, he says, "I don't have the store; the store has me. People rely on me. As a musician, I know what they need. Look at this picture of my kid brother. He's 65 and retired. I'm 92 and working. Who's better off?"

To Marian Diamond, there's no contest. "Having taught anatomy all these years," she says, "I always go back to the heart. It is designed by evolution to look after itself first, and then the rest of the body. This is not selfishness, but wisdom; when people feel good about themselves, they are able to give to others.

"I firmly believe that love is essential to a healthy old age — love of oneself and the ability to love someone besides oneself."

"Can a person change late in life?" I ask.

"You can change nerve cells at any age," says Dr. Diamond. "You just need the right environment."

The Graying of AMERICA

America has never seen anything like it. In the United States, an inescapable revolution is taking place. It has no leader or manifesto to give it direction. Rather, it is a quiet groundswell, rapidly gaining momentum, and there is absolutely nothing we can do to stop it: We are growing old. Individually, this fact is hardly remarkable. But we are growing old—and living longer—in such vast numbers that we will change the face of society forever.

Cheryl McLean

For the first time in its 200-plus years, the United States will have as many elderly citizens as teenagers. Lowered birth and death rates have brought about the aging of our population, the graying of America. At the turn of the century, just over 3 million individuals had reached the age of 65. Today nearly 30 million Americans thrive into their mid-sixties and well beyond.

As the 1945-57 "baby boomers" begin to move into their retirement years, the projections for the next century reveal even more startling figures: There will be over 50 million aged by the year 2020; add to that another 15 million by the next decade. At the time of the Big Crash of '29, only one in twenty people in America was over 65. In just a single century, that ratio will shrink to better than one in five.

Keep in mind, these projections are based on current mortality and birth rates. Advances in science and medicine, better education and health care, better preventive care, all promise to add years to our life expectancy in coming decades. The anticipations of some researchers seem to belong in the realm of science fiction—average individuals living 130 years or more. Whether we achieve such a life span or not, the reality remains that we are living longer, and we are healthier, than we have ever been.

A broad group of researchers at Oregon State University, representing a dozen or more disciplines, are addressing questions of how this gray revolution will shape American society in coming decades. The economic implications alone are staggering, ranging from predictions of the downfall of Social Security and Medicare to the augur of intergenerational warfare between younger workers paying burdensome taxes to support the nation's elders.

Above all, says Clara Pratt, director of OSU's Gerontology Program, how we survive such difficulties will depend in large measure on how we as a nation continue to view our elders. "I see the doomsday perspective and the Pollyanna perspective," she says. "If we continue to believe that productivity ends at 65, that old people have no value to society, then we are heading for some major crises."

Exploding the Myths

Sociologists and other professionals in gerontology, the study of aging, are pointing to some much more positive side effects of our aging: Slowly we are dismantling the myths and stereotypes surrounding old age in America. Because of sheer numbers, and in part because of the pedagogic efforts of gerontologists, we are beginning to change our perceptions of growing and being old.

Berneice Neugarten, a noted psychologist at Northwestern University and deputy chair of the 1981 White House Conference on Aging, argues

By Cheryl McLean. Reprinted by permission from *The Oregon Starter,* February 1988, pp. 11-17.

that we have become an "age-irrelevant" society, that knowing someone's chronological age tells us only how many years that individual has lived and nothing else. John Rowe, who heads the MacArthur Foundation Research Program on Successful Aging, told *Newsweek* magazine in 1986, "I can describe to you a 75-year-old man with a history of heart disease and diabetes, and you can't tell me with any confidence whether he will be sitting on the Supreme Court or in a nursing home."

The myths that depict all old people as decrepit and dying, shut up and alone in nursing homes, are exploded every day. We see men and women in their seventies and eighties running marathons, climbing mountains, working tirelessly within their communities. We see them striking out across the country in brand-new Winebagos. We see them as productive artists and scientists and politicians—Georgia O'Keefe, Pablo Picasso, Martha Graham, Linus Pauling, Armand Hammer, even Ronald Reagan.

Pratt, who has published widely in several areas of gerontological research, acknowledges that old stereotypes die slowly. "My favorite quote comes from Jonathan Swift: 'All men would live long but none would be old.' We all want to live as long as we can, but we don't want to be old, we don't

want to be sick, we don't want to be isolated. We don't want to be the stereotype of what old is."

Anthropologists and others often talk about a "golden age" or "golden place," where the elders of a given society were cherished and honored with gifts. That place never existed, says Pratt. Or if it did, others argue that it's easy to cherish and support elders when being old is unusual, but it's something else when they constitute 10 to 20 percent of the population.

A particularly pernicious image of old age in America depicts a skeletal figure, draped with sagging skin and baggy clothes, living in squalor and dining on dog food because the Social Security check barely covers the rent. Poverty and dependency as inevitable by-products of old age were soundly debunked by a U.S. Census special report released in 1983. The over-65 population showed a median discretionary income of $5,219, well above the national average.

Lest we establish a new myth—that all elderly are well-to-do—it's important to acknowledge those who clearly are not. While the percentage of elderly living in poverty has declined considerably in the last three decades—from 35 percent to around 14—there are still more than four million poor among the aged population today. Poverty is

Today, 2000, and Beyond

■ For the first time since 1776, the United States will have as many elderly—those 65 and older— as teenagers.

■ Elderly Americans number 30 million strong today, and will grow to nearly 65 million in 2030. By that time, they will comprise more than 20 percent of the population: one out of every five Americans will be over 65.

■ Octogenarians—those 80 years and older— are the fastest-growing segment of society. By 2000, their numbers will double. By 2050, one in twenty Americans will be over 85.

■ We will have more centenarians—people 100 or older—and they will be healthier than ever before. The latest census counted 32,000 Americans who were at least 100 years old.

■ Only 5 percent of the elderly population today are institutionalized, and while predictions indicate an increase in numbers, the percentage will remain fairly constant.

■ The median age of all Americans was just 28 in 1970. Today it's an all-time high, nearly 33. By the year 2030, the median age of the population will be over 40 years.

■ Approximately 4 million aged Americans live in poverty (some 14 percent), while the majority of the elderly population, as a group, enjoys a disproportionate share of discretionary income— higher per capita than the national average.

■ While many fear a minor spate of forgetfulness foreshadows the onset of Alzheimer's disease, in reality only 1 percent of the population is afflicted with this type of dementia. Concerns among physicians suggest that as people live longer, however, this percentage will increase.

■ The elders of tomorrow will be better educated than their parents or grandparents. Education correlates positively with longer and healthier lives.

■ Scientific discoveries of the powers of thymosin, a naturally produced hormone of the thymus, could increase our life span by a dozen or more years.

■ Among old people, women today outnumber men by three to two, as compared with a five-to-four ratio in 1960.

■ Social Security benefits go to 91.2 percent of the elderly and are almost the total income for one-fifth.

■ The average life expectancy in America has risen from just 47.3 years in 1900 to nearly 75 today.

particularly acute among widowed women, minorities, and the very old who make up a disproportionate share of the elderly poor.

The stereotype of universal deterioration among the aged has little basis in science, according to the National Institute on Aging (NIA). Researchers have discovered that physiological and mental changes are not always in the direction of decline, and that personal choices—such as regular exercise—can mediate some of the typical changes that occur with age. A study funded by the NIA revealed that, contrary to traditional beliefs, the majority of people maintain or actually improve their levels of intellectual competence as they age, barring problems such as cardiovascular disease or disadvantaged socioeconomic conditions.

One of the most damaging myths about old age, according to Pratt, is found in the cliche, "You can't teach an old dog new tricks." It's harmful, she says, "because people apply it to themselves, and they limit themselves severely. The research is so powerful in saying that physiologically and psychologically and socially we can make major changes in our lives, even into advanced age. While we're influenced by our earlier lives, we're not victims of them."

The perception that all old people end their days in nursing homes is also far from the truth. Only 5 percent of the elderly population reside in nursing homes or other instictions, and they are not generally abandoned by their children. Families in the United States provide more than 80 percent of the care of dependent elderly, according to Alexis Walker, OSU researcher in human development and family studies.

Nor do all elder Americans spend contented years sitting on the front porch in a well-worn rocking chair, a beloved Rockwellian view of old age. They confront more stresses than any other age group. Yet their ability to endure crises is remarkable. They are up and doing: The senior citizens of today have logged more travel miles, both national and international, than any other age group. Senior centers and clubs have sprouted throughout the United States like hamburger stands in the 1950s, offering activities from aerobic exercise to couples poker.

Speaking of couples, another myth plaguing the elderly is that they are asexual. Men and women who "flirt" with members of the opposite sex are told to "act their age." Yet NIA researchers have revealed that individuals who are sexually active in their youth and middle age remain relatively active in old age, providing the availability of a partner.

When Old is Young

What all of this really says, and what gerontologists have been saying for years, is that people over 65 are not all the same—no one description will serve to tell us what they are like.

This heterogeneity led Neugarten to coin the terms "young old" and "old old" to distinguish old people who are vigorous and healthy from old

people who are ill. The terms have since been used to differentiate on the basis of age, and a new term was added: "middle old." The "young old," therefore, are 65 to 74 years old; the "middle old" are 75 to 84; and the "old old" are those 85 and older.

Yet even these numbers—75, 85 years—are losing their meaning for the people who have lived them. A 1982 study by Cadwell Davis Partners found that most elders feel five to fifteen years younger than their chronological age might suggest. Other studies showed that many aged Americans feel they're in the prime of their lives, with some over 70 regarding themselves as "middle-aged."

These people are realizing that growing old doesn't bring only problems and losses. They're better educated than their predecessors, and they have higher expectations for their quality of life. Society has begun to relax its cultural expectations of the aged, and we're even approaching a redefinition of when old is old, based more on behavior than chronology. Today's older generation is finding no internal alarm clock sounding the hour at age 65 for pulling out the checker board and settling into a sedentary life.

A Fountain of Vitality

Despite a growing acceptance of aging, our cultural orientation still seems to hold youth in some mystical place of worship. Says Pratt, "The motive behind eating well and exercising regularly should be to stay *healthy* longer, not to try to be forever young. I have a hairdresser who, every time she cuts my hair, asks, 'Don't you want me to put a rinse on your hair?' because I'm getting more and more gray. But no, I really don't. I'm comfortable with the gray. In this culture we have some very schizophrenic attitudes about aging."

While the research shows that measured attitudes toward aging and being old are more positive, she explains, our behavior suggests just the opposite. "People have always looked for a fountain of youth, and they'll continue to look. But I don't like that idea. For most people, it really means they want to stay young, and that's not realistic."

"We've come closer to an understanding of how lifelong vitality is influenced by what happens in the social environment, what happens in the political environment, and what people do themselves to contribute to that sense of well-being—at whatever age they are. I'd be really happy to talk about a fountain of vitality," says Pratt, "where you can talk about being vital—not just physically always up—but vital and alive and *connected* from the time they're born until the time they die."

The over-65 crowd has begun to dip into that fountain of vitality, and the baby boomers will probably drink to excess. As those aged 30 to 50 look toward their golden years, they're perhaps the first generation to know—in scientifically documented terms—how their lives today will affect how they age.

All we have learned from preventive health care, medical advances, and lifestyle changes will mean even greater advantages for the baby boomers—just now beginning to gray—and the generations to follow. One of the major factors, say gerontologists, will be education: not just education gleaned from the broad scope of research within the profession, but education generally.

The boom generation will be better educated on the whole than their parents and grandparents. Education correlates positively with longevity, physical and mental well-being, and overall life satisfaction. People with good educations tend to get better, more satisfying jobs. Their jobs carry higher salaries, so they are plagued by fewer financial stresses, they can afford good preventive health care, and they can better plan for their retirement. Their adaptability helps keep them apace with the marketplace, and therefore more marketable in their professions.

The vestiges and afflictions of old age are still with us—wrinkles and gray hair, a loss of elasticity in the skin, arthritis, hypertension, faltering vision and hearing, varicose veins, receding hairlines, slowed metabolism, decreased lung capacity. Yet by no means are all of these changes inevitable, and very few of them have anything to do with our ability to function effectively.

Pratt insists that we don't have to let the usual harbingers of age change the way we live. "The fact that I have gray hair doesn't affect me *at all*," she says. "Wrinkles, by and large, don't affect us. There are changes in terms of fat distribution that are normal, age-related changes. And we get more susceptible to heat and cold. But in an environment that is at all supportive, that doesn't affect us. We can do all the things that we did before, we just have to wear a sweater."

Economic Implications

One of the most compelling questions facing the federal government today is how to continue paying for Social Security when nearly twenty percent of the population will be eligible for benefits? When Social Security legislation was enacted in 1935, its intent was not to assure adequate income for retirees. Rather, with the nation reeling from 25 percent unemployment, the system provided an incentive for older workers to leave their jobs, making room for the young.

The age 65, explains OSU economist Ken Patterson, was an arbitrary age chosen in part because the average life expectancy for American workers at that time was around 68. "The typical 'graduate' of the Social Security system drew pension benefits for about three years," says Patterson. "When you only had about three years of Social Security pension to pay out for someone, the contributions didn't have to be very large. Now that average nationally is about 12, and

that's changing with the increasing number of women retirees, who generally live longer than men."

To further compound the issue, the ratio of workers supporting nonworkers has declined drastically. When the system was established, approximately 22 workers made contributions into the system for every pension drawn out. Today, that ratio has narrowed to three workers for one retiree, and predictions of a two-to-one ratio early in the next century have everyone worried: Will the system bankrupt itself before *I* retire?

Concerns about an intergenerational civil war, sparked by burdensome FICA deductions, assume that except for the numbers, nothing will change. However, while the number of elderly is on the rise, the number of children born—the dependents at the other end of the age spectrum—has been declining. Population predictions indicate that the total dependency ratio of workers to nonworkers—child dependency plus aged dependency—will not change. The "burden" on society will simply shift from one age group to another.

Older Workers

Where once workers were forced to retire at 65—an age set more than 150 years ago by Germany's Otto von Bismarck and adopted in 1930s America—today mandatory retirement at 65 or even 70 has been set aside altogether. A Rand Corporation report predicts that a tighter labor market resulting from declining birth rates may combine with our improved health to reverse a 30-year trend toward earlier retirement. Congress recently added some of its own incentives by raising the age at which retirees become eligible for benefits—67 for those born after 1959—as a means of shoring up its fiscal outlook. Those who oppose this type of action claim that, in the short run at least, it will relegate younger workers to entry-level positions for an extended period of time, thus fueling resentment over excessive FICA taxes.

The U.S. Senate Special Committee on Aging, however, reported that the baby bust of the last three decades would yield a national shortage of younger workers, aged 16 to 44, as early as 1990. "So," the report concludes, "if our economy is to continue to grow it is clear that the expanding labor force needed to produce economic growth must be increasingly found among middle aged and older persons."

Some argue that technology and automation will take up the slack, but others maintain that technology will more likely reduce the emphasis on physical strength, thus opening opportunities for older workers who have a wealth of experience behind them.

A few American firms are beginning to realize the benefits of luring older workers back into the fold. Travelers Companies executive F. Peter Libassi reported company-wide savings of $1 million annually by reemploying experienced workers—often well into their 80s—through the Retiree Job Bank.

Not everyone wants or is able to continue working, though, and for some the financial consequences can be grave. When Social Security is the only source of income, the recipient is generally living below or hovering just above the poverty level. Although the percentage of poverty among the elderly has decreased steadily over the last few decades, the numbers are still unnecessarily large—more than six million if, by rights, we include those whose incomes rise only slightly above the official demarkation line.

The census report identifying the over 65s as better off financially than we realized has prompted some politicians to espouse means-testing for Social Security benefits—you don't get any if you're making a lot of money from other sources.

These types of changes will become increasingly difficult to instigate the older the population gets, Patterson predicts. "In many communities, the elderly have organized enough to be a major political force."

The Gray Panthers, inaugurated in the 1960s by Maggie Kuhn, heralded a new role for America's elderly as political activists. Sixty-nine percent of the population of 65-74 year olds exercised their right to vote in the last presidential election, second only to the 55 to 64-year-old group. The American Association of Retired Persons (AARP) is flexing unprecedented political muscle this year during the Iowa presidential campaign primary and elsewhere. And as the flower children of the 60s enter their sixties, this generation of rabble rousers will bring new meaning to the words "Gray Power."

How will the aging of our population affect public education in America? Some fear that older workers whose children have grown and gone and finished school will be unwilling to pay for the educations of others' children.

At the same time, continued low birth rates have begun to empty schoolrooms across the nation, and projections imply further declines. The implications for higher education, however, are harder to predict because of the rise in "older-than-average" students on American campuses. With the burgeoning of technology in the workplace, more people are returning to universities for retraining, some look to start second careers.

But a tighter labor market will mean increased competition for the traditional-age college student. Young people may be able to move directly from high school into good-paying jobs, and many employers, such as the vast IBM Corporation, are providing "colleges" of their own.

Even the most optimistic figures for gains among older students will not account for the losses among the young, so we can expect to see some shrinking in the size and number of colleges and universities across the country.

Higher education won't be the only industry affected. The military, too, will find it increasingly difficult to attract and retain recruits. One solution for both groups is to ease restrictions on immigration, according to a 1982 Rand Corporation report on demographic trends. Other options suggested for addressing the drain on the armed forces include enhancing educational opportunities for recruits, increasing privatization of certain tasks, or reinstating the draft.

How We Live

Virtually every aspect of American society will be affected by the aging of its members. Mass transit systems will cater increasingly to limitations sometimes imposed by age. Homes will be redesigned—no handrails in the bathrooms or elevator chairs for the stairways—but more high-rise condominiums and single-story apartments, smaller and easier to maintain.

Family structure will also be changed dramatically, as increased longevity means that some children will know not only their grandparents and great-grandparents, but conceivably their great-greats as well. These four-and five-generation families also face a growing dilemma, with two generations of elderly members who may be in need of health care.

"Ours is the first generation that's dealing with frail elderly on such a massive scale," observes OSU's Margaret Smith, gerontologist with the department of health. The over-85 group is the fastest-growing segment of the elderly population, and these are the people most likely to experience increasing needs for health care on some level.

"Dealing with the declining years of our parents I think will help us in framing social policy in this country because we really don't have a policy about aging," Smith adds. "We've got to come to grips with these very, very frail elderly—where do we put our resources? Social change doesn't generally come about because someone sits down and works out something theoretically on paper. Social change occurs when people have experienced something in their gut and therefore become very driven to make change."

"As the population of elderly grows, the issue of federal and state and local policy becomes very critical," says Jerome Hallan, director of OSU's Health Care Administration program. "We don't know yet how we're going to allocate resources and how we're going to train people. The policy implications are enormous."

Spiraling costs of long-term health care in nursing homes or skilled nursing facilities will affect far more than the 5 percent who are institutionalized at any one time, says Pratt: Twenty-five to 30 percent of us will spend some time in a nursing home before we die. "Nursing home care can literally devastate a family within two years," she says. "It can drive them right into poverty."

Medicare, available for everyone over the age of 65, does not yet cover the cost of long-term care, although this issue is being hotly debated in Congress right now. Patients are forced to "spend down" to a level of indigence, where Medicaid, the supplemental health insurance for the poor, takes over.

The health care industry as a whole is undergoing an evolution. It used to be that entering a nursing home meant you didn't expect to leave. Today, the people who check in to nursing homes are more likely to recover and check out again.

"We will have nursing homes that are more closely tied to hospitals," Hallan predicts. "I suspect that the fastest-growing type of facility will be a planned retirement community with a health care component attached—doctors or nurses available as needed for respite care, but not a major part of the living environment.

"We'll see a more service-driven industry to care for a home-bound population," he adds. "Home health care agencies and organizations are growing dramatically—a real investment opportunity. The industry is realizing that it can provide care for $40 a day or per week, much cheaper than keeping people in institutions."

Science: A Brave New Future

We are growing older, we are living longer, we are healthier. But scientists across the country are working to unravel the mysteries of the human organism in a search for more.

Several theories exist to explain the process of aging at the cellular level. The "free radical" theory argues that these highly reactive molecules, natural by-products of metabolism, most of them oxidizing agents, bombard our cells, subtly changing the DNA structure and causing cells to age.

Other scientists believe that the supercoiling of our DNA strands, coiled to form a helix then coiled again around beads of protein to form a superhelix, may function like a clock spring, slowly ticking away biological time. Some geneticists think this may be a sort of "genetic switch," which turns on the body's program for decline.

"The error theory is sort of like a Xerox machine," explains Smith. "You make a copy of something and you think it's an exact duplicate, but really it's enlarged about 2 percent. Then you take that copy and put it through the machine again and eventually, some 20 copies later, you have distorted your original image."

The Hayflick model, formulated in the 1960s by University of Florida researcher Leonard Hayflick, was among the more widely accepted theories. He hypothesized that the genes designed to keep us healthy and functional wear out, beginning to make mistakes that ultimately cripple the cell, bringing on those changes we associate with aging. His research centered on the notion that cells will only divide so many times—between 50 and 70—before they senesce, or age, and die.

The "Hayflick limit" was questioned in the early 1970s by a researcher who transplanted old mouse cells into young mice, and as they died, he took the cells and put them in new mice. He found that the old cells could live through several generations.

Now, an OSU scientist has made some discoveries that explode Hayflick's theory completely.

"An argument has been made for a long time—20 or 30 years—that you can reproduce some aging-related phenomena in a laboratory in cell culture," explains David Barnes, OSU cell biologist who recently received a $250,000 Career Research Development grant from the National Institutes of Health. "The idea is that you take a cell out of an animal or a human, put it in culture, and allow it to divide. The cell will only go through a limited number of divisions, and then it stops."

Using cells from mice, Barnes found that by manipulating the culture, he could get the cells to divide normally indefinitely. "Maybe that says we have overcome some aging phenomenon," says Barnes. "Maybe it says that the whole concept that aging can be reproduced in culture is incorrect."

Hayflick's work was done with human cells rather than mouse cells, yet Barnes' findings argue against the notion that cells simply wear out. Barnes favors one of the other major theories, that the mysteries of aging will be revealed in the endocrine or immune system.

"I think that kind of approach has a better chance of representing what's going on in the whole organism," Barnes explains. "It's easy to imagine how a single change in the level of a hormone can produce the kinds of whole-body effects that you see when an organism ages."

Allan Goldstein, chair of the biochemistry department at George Washington University, has been studying the thymus and its hormone, which he discovered is responsible for the production and functioning of white blood cells. His research found that an injection of thymosins can restore the immune systems of old animals, and it may do the same for humans. He predicts that within the next decade, we will be taking thymosin supplements as readily as we take vitamins.

Although not an "anti-aging" pill or a fountain of youth, the discovery of these hormones could well add a dozen or more years to our life expectancy because bolstered immune systems would protect our bodies from the ravages of disease for a much longer time.

William Simonson, OSU professor and a national leader in geriatric pharmacy, speaks of a recently released drug which "heralds a whole new series of drugs that may actually reverse hardening of the arteries.

"It's all very preliminary," says Simonson, "but if it does work this way—if we do see a 'roto-rooter' concept—it would be a miracle drug. It would rival such discoveries as penicillin. It would certainly be the drug of the decade, and there's evidence that might someday happen. That's really going to throw off all the predictions about old age and longevity."

Still, these promising gains in life expectancy have not yet altered the basic human life span, considered now to be a maximum of 115 years. Goldstein thinks that through manipulation of the body's hormones, we'll someday achieve a lifespan of 130 years or more. But that's not necessarily the goal, say most gerontologists.

"I don't think it's a search for a fountain of youth," says Simonson. "Most of the people I work with in the field of pharmacology never refer to eliminating the aging process. What we're trying to do is keep the quality of life as high as possible for as long as possible."

Almost daily advances in our understanding of the human organism promise great benefits for the future. Our social and political environment, still mired in a range of problems, will benefit from a broadening perspective, one that embraces old age as a culmination of living rather than as the tragic consequence of life.

"The situation for elderly individuals gets better every year," says Simonson. "I remember when I was in college in the mid-60s—it wasn't cool to be over 30. And now it's extremely cool to be over 30—not too far over 30, but very cool. And not too many years from now, it will be really cool to be 70 because a lot of people will be 70."

We all grow old. Barring miraculous discoveries by the scientists of longevity, it's an inescapable journey we all will make.

But look at it this way—we'll have an unprecedented amount of company along the way.

OSU

Rx for a Long and Healthy Life

Preventive maintenance helps keep your car running longer, so why not practice the same care on yourself? OSU's experts on aging have provided a prescription for living out your years in better health.

■ **Stop smoking.** Right now. No matter how long you've been smoking, as soon as you stop, your health starts improving. Heart disease, much of it the direct result of smoking, kills more than 2 million people every year.

■ **Eat well.** Good nutrition gives your body all the material it needs to function properly. Avoiding certain foods, such as sugar and animal fat, has also been found to improve overall health and to ward off certain conditions such as diabetes and atherosclerosis. But don't eat too much. Some research has found that by underfeeding laboratory animals, they've managed to increase the mouse lifespan by nearly 30 percent.

■ **Exercise regularly.** Scientists have proved that regular exercise improves heart and lung functioning and helps reduce stress, which may also affect our immune system. "Regular" means at least 30 minutes of activity that raises the heartbeat a bit, at least three times per week.

■ **Drink in moderation.** Actually, some research indicates that a little alcohol can have beneficial effects, but too much—more than three drinks a day—can be debilitating both physically and mentally.

■ **Stay active.** It may be purely anecdotal, but some studies indicate that people who are active socially, politically, in their communities, enjoy better health and longer lives than those who are more sedentary.

■ **Be politically aware and assertive.** Political institutions create much of the economic and social environment we live in as we age. The gains in economic well-being in past decades are the result of political actions. These gains can be lost through the same political process.

■ **Avoid excessive stress.** One of the best ways to manage stress is to have a confidant, or several, who can give you support when you feel the world is closing in. Research suggests that people who live alone tend to have more stress and an increased incidence of chronic illness. Good, quality relationships help keep your blood pressure down.

■ **Develop and maintain outside interests.** What are you going to do with yourself when you retire? Develop interests or hobbies now that will engage your body and stimulate your mind when you find yourself with time on your hands.

It's all part of a healthy lifestyle. "Basically," says Simonson, "It's all the things mom used to tell us to do—and still does."

Human Aging: Usual and Successful

JOHN W. ROWE AND ROBERT L. KAHN

J. W. Rowe is associated with the Charles A. Dana Research Institute and Harvard Thorndike Laboratory at the Beth Israel Hospital; the Joint Department of Medicine, Beth Israel Hospital and Brigham and Women's Hospitals; Brockton–West Roxbury Veterans Administration Medical Center; and Division on Aging, Harvard Medical School, Boston, MA 02115. R. L. Kahn is a research scientist at the Institute for Social Research and a professor in the Department of Psychology and School of Public Health, University of Michigan, Ann Arbor, MI 48109.

Research in aging has emphasized average age-related losses and neglected the substantial heterogeneity of older persons. The effects of the aging process itself have been exaggerated, and the modifying effects of diet, exercise, personal habits, and psychosocial factors underestimated. Within the category of normal aging, a distinction can be made between usual aging, in which extrinsic factors heighten the effects of aging alone, and successful aging, in which extrinsic factors play a neutral or positive role. Research on the risks associated with usual aging and strategies to modify them should help elucidate how a transition from usual to successful aging can be facilitated.

RESEARCH ON AGING HAS EMPHASIZED LOSSES. IN THE absence of identifiable pathology, gerontologists and geriatricians have tended to interpret age-associated cognitive and physiologic deficits as age-determined. We believe that the role of aging per se in these losses has often been overstated and that a major component of many age-associated declines can be explained in terms of life style, habits, diet, and an array of psychosocial factors extrinsic to the aging process.

Research on aging has also emphasized differences between age groups. The substantial heterogeneity within age groups has been either ignored or attributed to differences in genetic endowment. That perspective neglects the important impact of extrinsic factors and the interaction between psychosocial and physiologic variables. In this article we offer our perspective on the place of extrinsic factors in the aging process, the long-term consequences of extrinsically initiated changes, and the implications of our views for gerontological research.

The Concept of Normality in Studies of Aging

In recent decades, increasing interest in the medical problems of older people and in the process of aging itself has stimulated substantial growth in physiologic, psychologic, and sociologic research on aging in human populations. Investigators involved in such studies have from the beginning recognized the importance of separating pathologic changes from those that could be attributed to aging per se. Thus, for physiologic studies careful guidelines have been developed to exclude individuals whose age-determined responses and behaviors might be contaminated by specific disease processes (1, 2). Results on the population remaining after such exclusions have then been interpreted as representing "normal" aging, especially when the data came from longitudinal studies rather than cross-sectional comparisons of different age groups and were thus less confounded with cohort effects.

The concept of normality, explicit or implied, has served well in such research. During the past 30 years, numerous cross-sectional and longitudinal studies on populations carefully screened for disease have demonstrated major effects of age on such clinically relevant variables as hearing, vision, renal function, glucose tolerance, systolic blood pressure, bone density, pulmonary function, immune function, and sympathetic nervous system activity. More recently, related research has revealed characteristic changes with respect to cognitive and behavioral functions. Such nonpathologic changes are important not only as reflections of the aging process but also, in many cases, as precursors of pathology. They constitute the physiologic substrate for the influence of age on the subsequent presentation of disease, and perhaps on probable response to treatment and likelihood of complications.

Nevertheless, the division of populations into diseased versus normal and the division of research findings into disease-related and age-determined have serious limitations. Chief among these is the neglect of heterogeneity among older people in the nondiseased group with respect to many physiologic and cognitive characteristics, a heterogeneity that is important both within cultures and between cultures. A second limitation of the emphasis on normality is the implication of harmlessness or lack of risk. And a third limitation is the related implication that, risky or not, what is normal is somehow natural and therefore is or should be beyond purposeful modification. In short, the emphasis on "normal" aging focuses attention on learning what most older people do and do not do, what physiologic and psychologic states are typical. It tends to create a gerontology of the usual.

Successful and Usual Aging

Each of the foregoing limitations urges the development of an additional conceptual distinction within the normal category, which can be approximated by the contrast between usual on the one hand, and successful on the other. For example, while many important physiologic variables show substantial losses with advancing age on the average, an important characteristic of such age-grouped data is the substantial variability within groups (1–3). In many data sets that show substantial average decline with age, one can find older persons with minimal physiologic loss, or none at all, when compared to the average of their younger counterparts. These people might be viewed as having aged successfully with regard to the particular variable under study, and people who demonstrate little or no loss in a constellation of physiologic functions would be regarded as more broadly successful in physiologic terms. They, in combination with people who show the typical nonpathologic age-linked losses that we propose to designate usual, constitute the heterogeneous category of the normal (that is, nondiseased) in any age group.

A distinction between usual and successful is urged similarly by recent discoveries with respect to risk factors for specific diseases. We are learning, for example, that age-linked increases in blood pressure, body weight, and serum cholesterol levels, while they may be usual in the populations that have been most frequently studied, are risk factors for cardiovascular disease. Moreover, such changes, which had been interpreted as age-intrinsic, are turning out to be usual in prosperous industrial countries but not in pastoral and traditional agricultural societies (4).

It is at least a reasonable hypothesis, given such cross-cultural differences, that attributions of change to age per se may often be exaggerated and that factors of diet, exercise, nutrition, and the like may have been underestimated or ignored as potential moderators of the aging process. If so, the prospects for avoidance or even reversal of functional loss with age are vastly improved, and thus the risk of adverse health outcomes reduced.

The concept of successful aging does not, of course, replace the necessary concern with explicit diseases and their causes nor the need to know what the dominant patterns of aging are in our society, by whatever name (usual, average, or even normal) we designate them. The concept of successful aging, however, adds to these a focus on heterogeneity within age groups and on the elucidation of factors that explain success. We turn now to the research evidence that bears on the distinction between usual and successful aging, first for physiologic and then for psychosocial characteristics.

Aging and Carbohydrate Metabolism

It has been known for over 60 years that advancing age is associated with progressive impairments in the capacity to metabolize a glucose load (5). After exclusion of individuals with fasting hyperglycemia, which is indicative of diabetes mellitus, as well as those treated with medications known to alter glucose tolerance and those noted to have become diabetic during the course of longitudinal studies, results of oral or intravenous glucose tolerance tests show a remarkable increase in the mean 2-hour blood sugar level with advancing age. There is a substantial increase in the variability of results in successive age groups, however, with many older individuals metabolizing glucose as well as their average younger counterparts. Resistance to the effect of insulin on peripheral tissues appears to play a major role in the genesis of glucose intolerance among nondiabetic older people. As with other insulin-resistant states, the insulin resistance of aging is associated with progressive increases in postprandial insulin levels (6).

The carbohydrate intolerance of aging may carry substantial risk, even in the absence of disease. A recent report from the Honolulu Heart Program evaluated the 12-year risk of stroke in 690 diabetics and 6908 nondiabetics free of stroke at study entry (7). Diabetes was clearly associated with increased risk of stroke, as expected. Additionally, among nondiabetics the risk of stroke was markedly age-related and was significantly higher for those at the 80th percentile of serum glucose than for those at the 20th percentile.

Findings on the carbohydrate intolerance of aging as a risk factor in coronary heart disease are mixed. While some epidemiological studies suggested an increase in coronary heart disease risk with hyperglycemia in nondiabetics, an international collaborative group conducting a thorough review of the 15 available studies on this issue did not find consistent evidence for that effect (8). On the other hand, studies focusing on post-prandial hyperinsulinemia, a cardinal feature of the insulin resistance of aging, have shown increases in insulin levels to be a significant independent contributor to the incidence of coronary heart disease death (9–11). In addition to these direct effects, increases in insulin level are associated with increases in triglyceride levels and decreases in high density lipoprotein–cholesterol levels, both of which are known risk factors for heart disease (12–14).

Attempts have been made to determine which components of the age-associated alterations in carbohydrate intolerance are related to aging per se and which components might be related to factors such as diet, exercise, medications, and body composition. For example, in Italian factory workers aged 22 to 73 years, Zavaroni et al. (15) evaluated the relative contributions of obesity, physical activity, family history of diabetes, and the use of diabetogenic drugs to age-related increases in glucose and insulin levels after an oral glucose tolerance test. The initial strong statistical correlation between age and both post-prandial glucose and insulin levels became much weaker when the effects of exercise, diet, and drugs were taken into account, so that the correlation between glucose and age was limited to marginal statistical significance and there was no longer an effect of age on insulin levels. Hollenbeck et al. (16) showed a direct and statistically significant relation between physical fitness as reflected in maximal oxygen consumption and insulin-stimulated glucose metabolism in nonobese healthy older men. Seals and co-workers found the performance of older physically trained men on oral glucose tolerance tests was identical to that of young athletes and significantly better than that of untrained older men (17).

As pointed out by Reaven and Reaven (18), these findings clearly suggest that much of the observed carbohydrate intolerance of older people may be caused by factors other than biological aging per se, and that dietary or exercise modifications may substantially blunt the emergence with age of carbohydrate intolerance and insulin resistance. The latter view is supported by earlier studies demonstrating improvements in glucose tolerance in young adults and diabetics after exercise regimens (17, 19, 20), as well as recent studies suggesting that exercise programs also improve the glucose intolerance and insulin resistance of older people (21, 22).

Aging and Osteoporosis

Aging is associated with a progressive decline in bone density in both males and females after maturity. Losses in bone density so severe as to result in fractures after minimal trauma define the "disease" osteoporosis, which accounts for more than 1 million fractures in the United States each year. Osteoporosis is of staggering importance in the elderly—by age 65 one-third of women will have vertebral fractures and by age 81 one-third of women and one-sixth of men will have suffered a hip fracture, often a catastrophic, if not terminal, event (23).

Although it has long been recognized that osteoporosis is a process that has multiple possible causes and that varies a great deal among older people, aging itself has generally been considered a major factor in the loss of skeletal integrity. In their recent review of current information regarding involutional osteoporosis, Riggs and Melton (23) indicate that three separate components contribute to age-related bone loss. The first component—the effect of intrinsic aging—represents a decline in bone mass with advancing age in both men and women beginning in the 20s and 30s, and includes several identifiable physiologic processes. In women this bone loss occurs despite regular periods and intact ovarian function. The second component—a more rapid decline in bone mass in women after middle age—is accountable to the prominent effects of menopause. The third component, which is of major clinical importance, represents the net effect of "extrinsic" factors present to a variable degree in the population that contribute to the remarkable variance in bone density among the elderly. These preventable risk factors include cigarette smoking, heavy alcohol intake, and inadequate calcium intake (24–27).

In addition to identifying several potentially modifiable factors contributing to the emergence of osteoporosis, a number of studies suggest that bone loss can be blunted in advanced age by institution of moderate exercise programs (28–30). Thus, emergence of osteoporosis, a common, crippling, and expensive disorder previously considered to represent the "normal" aging process, is variable and influenced by aging and nonaging factors. The marked reductions in bone density associated with "usual" aging may be in large part preventable or modifiable.

Aging and Cognitive Function

Apparent age-related changes that further study suggests are not intrinsic to the aging process and may be modifiable have been found in cognitive domains as well (31). Schaie and his colleagues conducted an instructive series of cross-sequential studies on successive cohorts of individuals across the adult age range, thus permitting a comparison of cross-sectional and longitudinal data from the same study populations (32). Cross-sectional comparisons between age groups for subjects tested in 1963 showed significantly lower scores in many cognitive capacities for the older groups, a finding commonly interpreted as reflecting performance declines with advancing age. However, when the same subjects were retested 7 years later, they did not show the age-related declines that would have been predicted on the basis of the earlier cross-sectional comparisons. The longitudinal data suggested that declines in both verbal test scores (crystallized intelligence) and scores on reasoning and spatial tests (fluid intelligence) occurred at substantially later ages than the cross-sectional comparisons had implied. Such differences between cross-sectional and longitudinal comparisons exemplify a cohort effect, in which successive age cohorts score differently at the same chronological age. Differences of this kind cannot be explained in terms of factors intrinsic to the aging process, which are presumably constant from one age cohort to another. The explanation of cohort differences must be sought elsewhere—for example, in nutritional or educational differences between cohorts.

A clear demonstration of the influence of education on test performance commonly considered age-determined can be seen in Green's analysis of scores on the Wechsler Adult Intelligence Scale (33). Comparisons across age groups in a stratified random sample showed large age-related differences, of the kind usually interpreted as decrements caused by age. However, when similar comparisons were made between age groups limited to people of equal education, the "age effect" became insignificant.

These studies of Schaie and Green, taken together with similar findings by other investigators (31), indicate that much of the cognitive loss in late middle life that has been considered intrinsic to aging is caused in part by extrinsic factors and may therefore be preventable. That such losses may even be reversible once they occur is suggested by the recent studies of Schaie and Willis (34). These investigators divided participants in a longitudinal study into those with a clear pattern of decline in fluid intelligence (inductive reasoning and spatial orientation) with aging and those whose performance was stable. After five training sessions there was substantial and retained improvement among the individuals who were previously declining in cognitive function.

Psychosocial Factors in Health and Disease Among Older People

In the rest of this article we will focus on psychosocial factors, which constitute one category of the extrinsic variables that influence patterns of aging, both usual and successful. Most health-relevant psychosocial research on older people, however, has been concentrated on morbidity and mortality as the outcomes of interest with few if any distinctions made within the residual category of the nondiseased elderly. Despite this neglect of nonpathologic aspects of aging, this research provides a valuable backdrop for the research we call for, since it identifies extrinsic psychosocial properties that influence the well-being of older men and women. Psychosocial factors should be studied in their full range, not only in their negative aspects. Doing so is especially important to reveal their contributions to successful aging. Two dimensions that have been sufficiently studied to serve as examples of our views are autonomy (or control) and social support (or connectedness).

Autonomy and Control

A great deal of research has been done in the broad area of control or autonomy—that is, the extent to which individuals are able to make decisions regarding choice of activity, method and manner of engagement, timing, pace, and the like. Despite a discouraging scatter of measures, the research results show a remarkable convergence: lack of control has adverse effects—on emotional states, performance, subjective well-being, and on physiologic indicators.

The potential relevance of research on control, animal and human, for understanding the circumstances and well-being of older people was observed promptly by gerontological research workers. Older people commonly encounter reductions in autonomy and control for a variety of reasons—physical impairments, reduced economic capability as wages are replaced by retirement stipends, residential moves from separate households to combined or institutional living arrangements, and the like (35). In recent years a number of studies have been done on the effects, or at least the concomitants, of autonomy limitations of various kinds on older people. This considerable literature has been the subject of two recent summaries (36, 37), and we therefore limit ourselves to major examples.

The bulk of control-oriented research with older human populations is nonexperimental and more often cross-sectional than longitudinal, both of which facts urge caution in causal interpretation. Nevertheless, the substantive findings are encouraging in their consistency. For example, Wolk (38) compared the residents of two retirement settings, a low constraint retirement village and a relatively high constraint retirement home. Residents in the former setting were observed to be more in control of their own activities, they so perceived themselves, and they also scored higher in life satisfaction and adjustment.

Shupe (36) cites preliminary data from a longitudinal study of psychosocial events and health status (39) that provides a stronger basis for causal inference. Undesirable events over which the individual had full control did not correlate with the index of strain, whereas undesirable events over which the individual had no control were strongly correlated with strain. When the individual had partial control, the correlation with strain depended on a third variable, the predictability of the aversive stimuli, with low predictability heightening the relation between lack of control and strain, and high predictability suppressing the relation.

Perhaps the most persuasive data on the effects of control among older people come from the small number of field experiments in which the control of individuals over their own daily lives was systematically increased. These experiments have been done almost entirely with populations already in residential retirement facilities or nursing homes, or among people facing imminent relocation to such facilities.

Krantz and Schulz (40), following an earlier nonexperimental study (41) in which the negative health changes after admission to a nursing home were found to be moderated by the amount of individual control over the move, conducted an experiment in which prospective patients were given a choice about the timing of the move, which of several institutions they would move to, and some of the living arrangements after the move. Under these experimental conditions, there was little decline from the level of health and psychological well-being as assessed before the move.

Langer and Rodin (42) conducted an experiment in a nursing home in which residents on one floor were given a treatment that enhanced control consisting of a lecture from the nursing-home administrator about decisions that they could and should make for themselves. A comparison group, on another floor, heard a lecture of similar length that emphasized what the staff would do in taking care of such matters. During the first 3 weeks after the experimental treatment, people in the experimental group were happier and more active according to self-report and spent more time in social activities as reported by nurses, who also judged them to be generally more improved than those in the control group. These changes persisted and the differences between groups increased over an 18-month period.

A near replication of the Rodin and Langer experiment was conducted by Mercer and Kane (43). The experimental treatment was extended to include individual visits by the nursing-home administrator in which patients were invited to join a council of residents. The comparison group in this experiment came from a second nursing home. Again the experimental group showed increased activity, improvement in staff-rated patterns of eating and sleeping, and decreases in self-reported hopelessness.

A third field experiment in a nursing-home setting, similar in some respects, was conducted by Schulz and his colleagues (44, 45). Again the experimental treatment involved increased control, in this case over the timing and duration of student visits, and again enhanced control produced gains in positive affect, activity level, and general health status. The differences between the experimental

group (enhanced control) and two comparison groups, one of which received no student visits and one of which received visits on a random and unpredictable basis, were unambiguous. However, a fourth group, which had no control over the timing of the visits but was given advance information about their scheduling, showed improvements comparable to those of the enhanced control group. These findings suggest that the positive effects of enhanced control may be due at least in part to its making life more predictable; control confers predictability.

A more recent nursing-home experiment by Avorn and Langer (46) extends this line of work by comparing two experimental treatments, one of which is control-enhancing and the other control-reducing. Experimental subjects, a total of 72 with an average age of 78 years, were randomly assigned to three groups and given the task of completing individually a simple jigsaw puzzle. All subjects then had four 20-minute practice sessions. Subjects in the first group were given verbal encouragement during practice; subjects in the second group were given direct assistance, and subjects in the third group received no assistance or encouragement beyond the initial instruction. All subjects were rated for proficiency and speed both before and after the experimental treatments. The results showed significant improvement for subjects who had been encouraged, significant deterioration for subjects who had been directly assisted, and no change for subjects who had had no experimental treatment. The authors argue that the direct-assistance treatment is typical of approaches to older people that do for them what they could do or learn to do for themselves. The effect is infantilizing; the lesson is learned helplessness. We concur, and add that the essential difference between the two experimental studies is one of control: encouragement in this situation is control enhancing; assistance is control reducing.

On balance, these studies, all published within the past 10 years, represent an important line of field-experimental research. Their results reinforce earlier nonexperimental findings that suggested the importance of control for the well-being of older people. In our opinion, the extent to which autonomy and control are encouraged or denied may be a major determinant of whether aging is usual or successful on a number of physiologic and behavioral dimensions.

Aging and Social Support

Several lines of research on psychosocial factors and health converge around the concept of social support. Moreover, in spite of the definitional imprecision of the concept and the variety of measures that claim to assess it, empirical research has produced consistent if not often large associations between social support and various indicators of health and well-being (47). Some of this research has involved attempts to measure support directly, usually by report of the recipient but occasionally by report of the provider as well (48). Some has inferred support from less subjective data—marital status and household composition, for example, or proximity of family members. Most such research has neglected the variable of age and none shows systematically differentiated findings across the entire life course. A significant number of studies, however, are specific to older people or control appropriately for age, and it is those on which we rely for this review. We will consider first the evidence that social networks and support as persisting conditions affect mortality and morbidity among older people and next that support-disrupting life events have specific negative effects on both mortality and morbidity. Finally, we will consider some of the ramifications of this work for successful aging, including the relation to autonomy and control among older people.

Three epidemiological studies show that membership in a network of family and friends is associated with lesser mortality risk. In the Alameda County Study, Berkman (49) developed a social network index that included marital status, contacts with extended family and close friends, church group membership, and other group affiliations. Analyses based on this index showed age-adjusted relative risks of 2.3 for men and 2.8 for women over the 9-year period of the study, where relative risk refers to the likelihood of death among people at the bottom of the social network index in comparison with those at the top. The Tecumseh (Michigan) study (50), in similar multiple logistic analyses of social connectedness, found significant relationships to mortality over a 10-year period for both men and women, with age controlled. And the Durham County study (51), which included perceptions of social support as well as reported connectedness, and in contrast to the Alameda and Tecumseh studies was limited to men and women aged 65 years or more, showed relative mortality risks of 3.40 for impaired social support (self-perceived), 2.04 for impaired roles and attachments, and 1.88 for low frequency of social interaction.

The positive effects of social support have also been demonstrated by means of intervention studies, most of them involving supportive behaviors by professional or quasi-professional persons. Criteria include rate and completeness of recovery from injuries, heart attacks, cancer, and other physical illnesses (52–54). At least four intervention studies involve the introduction of social support by one or more informal sources (relatives, friends) to increase adherence to hypertensive regimens. Three of them showed significant increases in adherence, with some evidence that the involvement of people significantly related to the patient made an independent contribution to the outcome (55–57).

Bereavement and Relocation

If the presence of social support and its experimental introduction in times of stress are conducive to well-being and recovery from illness, it is plausible that support-disrupting events should have negative effects. Two such life events are especially common among older people—bereavement and relocation, which involve, respectively, the loss of one's spouse and the loss (or at least partial loss) of friends and neighbors. Both these events have been studied for their effects on mortality and morbidity, usually with some limitations in design and measurement. For example, losses of social support are typically inferred rather than measured directly.

The gross fact of higher age-specific mortality rates among widowed than among married people has been reported in studies for many years. In 1969, Parkes, Benjamin, and Fitzgerald (58) provided more precise prospective data from a 9-year follow-up of 4486 widowers aged 55 or more. Excess mortality in this group peaked during the first 6 months of bereavement (40% excess) and declined thereafter, so that in the fifth year the mortality rate for widowers was not significantly different from that for the married men who served as controls. Causes of death varied, but in almost half the cases death certificates showed heart disease as the cause.

The finding of excess mortality has been confirmed in three other longitudinal studies (59–61), although the most recent of them (61) does not show the peaking of mortality during the first 6 months, the concentrated reporting of heart disease as the cause of death, or the gradual return to nonexcessive mortality rates within 5 years. These studies, which included women as well as men, do show a significant gender effect. For reasons not fully understood, excess mortality after the loss of a spouse is more characteristic of men than women. Tentative explanations emphasize the different roles of men and women in nutrition and meal preparation and the greater reliance of men on emotional support from their wives (62).

The effects of bereavement have been studied in terms of morbidity as well as mortality, with varying results. Higher rates of reported symptoms have commonly been found, but without change in major diagnosed disease (63), physician visits, or rates of hospitalization (64). And one study (65) of elderly men and women (average age 74) found no differences between the married and widowed on any measure of health. Post facto explanation emphasized the expectation of people in the upper age range to encounter such losses and their consequent readiness to cope with them.

Next to bereavement, residential relocation is the network-disrupting event that has been most studied in elderly populations. In a review of this research, Minkler (66) distinguishes between moves within the community of private households and moves into or between nursing homes and other institutions. Moves of the latter kind have more consistently resulted in excess mortality, especially during the early months after the move (67), although not all studies show mortality effects. Moves of the former kind have not shown excess mortality, but they have showed increases in number of physician visits and nursing home admissions, with concomitant reductions in self-rated health (68). Kasl and Berkman (69) suggest that these differences in study results, especially those involving institutional residence, may depend on the manner of preparation and handling, as well as the relative quality of the two environments. This interpretation is consistent with findings on the effects of predictability and control described above.

Well-designed field experiments to test the effects of social support on morbidity and mortality changes after major life transitions are much needed and exceedingly rare. In one such study (70), 200 recently bereaved widows less than 60 years of age were assigned randomly to an experimental group that received support and encouragement during a 3-month period, or to a control group that received no treatment. Morbidity was significantly reduced in the experimental group during the 13-month post-intervention period. Apparently, social support can mitigate the ill effects of even this most painful relationship-disrupting event of later life. Its ability to facilitate successful aging in other ways has yet to be explored.

Support and Control

Social support and control have been studied separately as psychosocial factors affecting health, but they are almost certainly related. The interpersonal behaviors that are called supportive include, among others, the providing of material assistance, information, sick care, and expressions of respect and love. Support so defined, in our view, can either increase or decrease the autonomy and control of the recipient. Teaching, encouraging, enabling are autonomy-increasing modes of support. Constraining, "doing for," warning, and the like beyond the requirements of the situation may convey caring but they teach helplessness.

Some research findings are consistent with this line of speculation, which would predict greater positive effects for supportive behavior when it is also autonomy-enhancing. We referred earlier to the nursing-home experiment in which performance at a simple cognitive task was enhanced by encouragement but reduced by direct assistance (46). Pearlin et al. found that emotional support reduced depressive symptoms by the intervening process of increasing self-esteem and mastery (71). Bulman and Wortman found that paraplegic victims of severe accidents responded best to support that emphasized their control over their own lives, even in choosing the activity that led to the accident (72).

To realize the potential contributions of support to successful aging, we must establish a causal sequence that includes the individual's need for support (objective and perceived), the kind of support required (material, informational, emotional), and the effect of that support on other psychosocial predictors of success, of which autonomy and control are an important example.

Psychosocial and Physiologic Pathways

A further step in understanding the effect of psychosocial factors on health must be the integration of psychosocial causes with a broad array of biologic outcomes, including the full functional range instead of the conventional restriction to morbidity and mortality. Moreover, we must learn the pathways by which such causes and effects are linked. Berkman (73), in a review chapter on social networks, proposes four main possibilities for investigation:

1) Providing help, care, and material assistance may be directly health protective. For example, a person who is ill may receive care from family members and friends before and beyond the requirements of professional medical service.

2) Psychosocial resources may enable people to get better and earlier medical care. Antonucci et al. (74), in a study of early detection of cancer symptoms, found that the promptness with which individuals sought medical diagnosis was affected by the actions of their personal network members. Most consistent of these network factors was the direct intervention of friends or family members in making medical appointments, providing transportation, and the like.

3) Psychosocial influences may increase health-promoting and risk-reducing behaviors. For example, peer pressure may induce better nutritional practice, elimination of smoking, moderation in the use of alcohol, or adherence to medical regimens (55).

4) Psychosocial factors may also have direct physiologic effects. Research on cardiovascular disease, while by no means consistent, implies such a direct pathway, as do some animal experiments on neural, hormonal, and immunologic processes.

Epidemiological research on cardiovascular diseases suggests a direct link between psychosocial causes and physiologic effects mainly by a process of elimination: when the usual risk factors are statistically controlled, a direct physiologic pathway between supportive interpersonal relations and a specific disease is proposed as a plausible residual explanation. Interpretations of this kind have been offered to explain relations between sustained interpersonal bonds and coronary heart disease in widely diverse groups—Japanese Americans in California (75) and Hawaii (76), women clerical workers in the Framingham study (77), and Israeli civil servants (78). Such findings are intriguing but not conclusive, especially because they are inconsistent in several respects—in their generality across demographic subgroups, in their application of incidence as well as prevalence, and in their explanation of myocardial infarct as well as angina pectoris.

The direct effect of psychosocial factors on physiologic processes has been investigated more rigorously in animal research, with findings that link behavioral and environmental interventions to neural, hormonal, and immunologic processes and then to disease outcomes—alloxan diabetes in rats (79) and Marek's disease in chickens (80), for example. Studies of this kind with human populations are fewer, but increasing. Jemmott and Locke (81) describe 40 studies that link psychosocial factors, immunologic processes, and susceptibility to infectious diseases.

Few of these studies have yielded age-specific results or have been conducted with elderly populations. Two, however, have studied the effects of bereavement on lymphocyte function. Bartrop et al. (82) found lower lymphocyte response to mitogenic stimulation [with phytohemagglutinin (PHA) and concanavalin A (Con A)] among bereaved spouses as compared with controls matched by age, sex, and race, but no differences in T- and B-cell counts or in plasma cortisol. Schleifer et al. (83) reported a significant reduction in T-lymphocyte response to stimulation by one mitogen (PHA), a marginal reduction in response to another (Con A), and a significant reduction in B-lymphocyte response to pokeweed mitogen, which suggests that bereavement may affect humoral as well as cell-mediated immunity. Other studies, both animal and human, have demonstrated the effect of such stressors as novelty, unpredictability, and suspenseful anticipation on plasma cortisol secretion rates, especially among subjects with inadequate psychological defenses.

To the extent that older people are placed in situations where they lack control over their lives, and to the extent that the forms of support available to them are not control-enhancing, we would predict physiologic changes of the kinds reported in this research, with consequent increases in morbidity and passivity. The positive implications of such predictions are that increased predictability, control, and support that enhances both will be reflected in increased proactive behavior and resistance to disease. Research along these lines should help explain the great variability within the population of nondiseased elderly and thus increase our understanding of successful aging.

Directions for the Future

The central theme of this article is the distinction between usual and successful aging and the consequent need for interdisciplinary studies of the factors that determine the trajectory of function with advancing age. Most gerontological research, however, continues to concentrate on average tendencies within different age groups and to neglect the substantial heterogeneity within such groups. That heterogeneity, moreover, appears to increase with increasing age.

The emphasis on usual age-linked tendencies encourages an over-readiness to treat age as if it were itself a sufficient explanatory variable; the emphasis on heterogeneity within age groups compels a search for other explanations as well. Epidemiological research shows that age-extrinsic factors such as eating and exercise habits are prominent among such potential explanations. These habits are shaped and sustained by psychosocial influences—properties of the larger culture and behaviors of family members, friends, and professionals.

Our first recommendation, therefore, is that gerontological research should incorporate the distinction between usual and successful aging. That in turn means including the full functional range of the outcome variables under study. It also means undertaking the task of explaining the heterogeneity of older people with respect to those functions.

Our second recommendation is that gerontological research should concentrate on understanding transitions in later life, especially transitions that have functional significance. Some of these represent loss of function—from successful to usual, usual to diseased, diseased to impaired. But no less important and much less understood are the potentialities for transition in a positive function-expanding direction. Experimental results on the effects of exercise in increasing bone density and the effects of specialized training in improving cognitive functions demonstrate the possibility of positive reversals in older populations. To the extent that maintenance and recovery of function can be explained in terms of extrinsic factors, it becomes reasonable to think of increasing the proportion of the successful elderly.

Autonomy and social support were discussed as psychosocial factors relevant to understanding successful aging. Research on autonomy is reasonably interpreted as indicating that the role of the helpless elder is to a significant degree shaped by the immediate environment of the individual—its opportunities and constraints, and the specific behaviors of influential others who define them. Experiments with people showing extreme functional losses—residents and prospective residents of nursing homes—have shown that some of these losses are reversed by modest increases in autonomy and the encouragement to use them.

Social support, like autonomy, has positive effects on function and self-reported well-being. Support—defined to include the enhancement of material, informational, and emotional resources—seems to exert these effects both directly and by buffering the negative effects of stressors. The fact that behavior intended to be supportive has been shown in at least one situation to have negative effects on function suggests the importance of distinguishing between autonomy-enhancing and autonomy-reducing modes of support. This distinction is familiar in the field of child development but not in gerontological research, and it is only one example of a causal complexity that is almost certainly widespread.

Our third recommendation, therefore, is that extrinsic factors that influence successful aging should be studied in interdependent combinations as well as singly.

Finally, research that links the physiologic and psychosocial levels is suggested by the fact that both are implicated in the definition and explanation of successful aging. Recent experiments showing the effect of psychosocial interventions on physiologic indicators of stress and resistance to disease illustrate both the feasibility and the importance of such interdisciplinary efforts. Scientific work on aging requires both levels of explanation for completeness, and gerontological practice requires both for the development of effective interventions. Our fourth recommendation, therefore, is for aging research that links the psychosocial and physiologic levels.

These recommendations have in common a thrust toward health promotion and disease prevention in the elderly. A revolutionary increase in life span has already occurred. A corresponding increase in health span, the maintenance of full function as nearly as possible to the end of life, should be the next gerontological goal. The focus on successful aging urges that goal for researchers, practitioners, and for older men and women themselves.

REFERENCES AND NOTES

1. J. W. Rowe, *N. Engl. J. Med.* **312**, 827 (1985).
2. N. W. Shock *et al.*, *Normal Human Aging: The Baltimore Longitudinal Study of Aging* (U.S. Department of Health and Human Services, Washington, DC, 1984).
3. J. W. Rowe, *N. Engl. J. Med.* **309**, 1246 (1983).
4. I. Waldron *et al.*, *Soc. Sci. Med.* **16**, 416 (1982).
5. K. L. Minaker, G. S. Meneilly, J. W. Rowe, in *Handbook of the Biology of Aging*, C. E. Finch and E. L. Schneider, Eds. (Van Nostrand Reinhold, New York, 1985), pp. 433–456.
6. M. B. Davidson, *Metabolism* **28**, 688 (1979).
7. R. D. Abbott *et al.*, *J. Am. Med. Assoc.* **257**, 949 (1987).
8. International Collaborative Group on Asymptomatic Hyperglycemia and Coronary Heart Disease, *J. Chronic Dis.* **32**, 11/12 (1979).
9. P. Ducimetiere *et al.*, *Diabetologia* **19**, 205 (1980).
10. K. Pyorala, *Diabetes Care* **2**, 131 (1979).
11. T. A. Welborn and K. Kearne, *ibid.*, p. 154.
12. M. S. Greenfield *et al.*, *Metabolism* **29**, 1095 (1980).
13. L. A. Carlson and L. E. Bottinger, *Lancet* **1972-I**, 865 (1972).
14. I. Zavaroni *et al.*, *Atherosclerosis* **55**, 259 (1985).
15. I. Zavaroni *et al.*, *J. Am. Geriatr. Soc.* **34**, 271 (1986).
16. C. B. Hollenbeck, W. Haskell, M. Rosenthal, G. M. Reaven, *ibid.* **33**, 273 (1985).
17. D. L. Seals *et al.*, *J. Appl. Physiol.* **56**, 1521 (1984).
18. G. M. Reaven and E. P. Reaven, *J. Am. Geriatr. Soc.* **33**, 286 (1985).
19. D. E. James, E. W. Kraegen, D. J. Chisholm, *J. Appl. Physiol.* **56**, 1217 (1984).
20. J. B. Leblanc, A. Nadeau, M. Boulay, S. Rosseau-Migneron, *J. Appl. Physiol.* **46**, 235 (1979).
21. D. L. Seals *et al.*, *J. Am. Med. Assoc.* **252**, 645 (1984).
22. R. P. Tonino, W. H. Nedde, D. C. Robbins, E. S. Horton, *Clin. Res.* **34**, 557 (1986).
23. B. L. Riggs and L. J. Melton, *N. Engl. J. Med.* **314**, 1676 (1986).
24. E. Seeman, L. J. Melton, W. M. O'Fallon, B. L. Riggs, *Am. J. Med.* **75**, 977 (1983).
25. D. D. Bikle *et al.*, *Ann. Intern. Med.* **103**, 42 (1982).
26. M. A. Adena and H. G. Gallagher, *Ann. Hum. Biol.* **9**, 121 (1982).
27. H. Jick, J. Port, A. S. Morrison, *Lancet* **1983-I**, 1354 (1983).
28. J. F. Aloia, S. H. Cohn, J. A. Ostuni, R. Cane, K. Ellis, *Ann. Intern. Med.* **89**, 356 (1978).
29. B. Krolner, B. Toft, P. S. Nielson, E. Tondevold, *Clin. Sci.* **64**, 57 (1983).
30. E. L. Smith, W. Reddan, P. E. Smith, *Med. Sci. Sports Exercise* **13**, 60 (1981).
31. G. Labouvie-Vief, in *Handbook of the Psychology of Aging*, J. E. Birren and K. W. Schaie, Eds. (Van Nostrand Reinhold, New York, 1985), pp. 500–530.
32. K. W. Schaie and G. Labouvie-Vief, *Dev. Psychol.* **10**, 305 (1974).
33. R. F. Green, *ibid.* **1**, 618 (1969).
34. K. W. Schaie and S. Willis, *ibid.* **22**, 223 (1986).
35. T. H. Holmes and R. H. Rahe, *J. Psychosom. Res.* **11**, 213 (1967).
36. D. R. Shupe, in *Cognition, Stress, and Aging*, J. E. Birren and J. Livingston, Eds. (Prentice-Hall, Englewood Cliffs, NJ, 1985), pp. 174–197.
37. J. Rodin, *Science* **233**, 1271 (1986).
38. S. Wolk, *J. Consulting Clin. Psychol.* **44**, 420 (1976).
39. A. H. McFarlane *et al.*, *J. Health Soc. Behav.* **21**, 124 (1980).
40. D. Krantz and R. Schulz, in *Applications of Personal Control, Advances in Environmental Psychology*, A. Baum and J. E. Singer, Eds. (Erlbaum, Hillsdale, NJ, 1980), vol. 2, pp. 23–57.
41. R. Schulz and G. Brenner, *J. Gerontol.* **32**, 323 (1977).
42. E. J. Langer and J. Rodin, *J. Pers. Soc. Psychol.* **34**, 191 (1976).
43. S. Mercer and R. A. Kane, *Health Soc. Work* **4**, 90 (1979).
44. R. Schulz, *J. Pers. Soc. Psychol.* **33**, 563 (1976).
45. _____ and B. H. Hanusa, *ibid.* **36**, 1194 (1978).
46. J. Avorn and E. J. Langer, *J. Am. Geriatr. Soc.* **30**, 397 (1982).
47. J. S. House and R. L. Kahn, in *Social Support and Health*, S. Cohen and S. L. Syme, Eds. (Academic Press, Orlando, FL, 1985), pp. 83–108.
48. T. C. Antonucci, in *Handbook of Aging and the Social Sciences*, E. Shanas and R. H. Binstock, Eds. (Van Nostrand, New York, 1985), pp. 94–128.
49. L. Berkman, *Health and Ways of Living: Findings from the Alameda County Study* (Oxford Univ. Press, New York, 1983).
50. J. S. House, C. Robbins, and H. Metzner, *Am. J. Epidemiol.* **116**, 123 (1982).
51. D. Blazer, *ibid.* **115**, 684 (1982).
52. W. Gruen, *J. Consulting Clin. Psychol.* **43**, 223 (1975).
53. S. Bordow and D. Porritt, *Soc. Sci. Med.* **13A**, 251 (1979).
54. D. Spiegel, J. R. Bloom, I. Yalom, *Arch. Gen. Psychiatr.* **38**, 527 (1981).
55. R. D. Caplan *et al.*, *Social Support and Patient Adherence* (Institute for Social Research, Ann Arbor, MI, 1976).
56. J. L. Earp and M. G. Ory, *Prev. Med.* **8**, 155 (1979).
57. D. M. Levine *et al.*, *J. Am. Med. Assoc.* **241**, 1700 (1979).
58. C. M. Parkes, B. Benjamin, R. Fitzgerald, *Br. Med. J.* **1**, 740 (1969).
59. W. D. Rees and S. G. Lutkins, *ibid.* **4**, 13 (1967).
60. A. M. Ward, *ibid.* **1**, 700 (1976).
61. K. Helsing, G. W. Comstock, M. Szklo, *Am. J. Epidemiol.* **114**, 31 (1981).
62. R. L. Kahn, E. Wethington, B. Ingersoll-Dayton, in *Life-span Perspective and Social Psychology*, R. Abeles, Ed. (Erlbaum, Hillsdale, NJ, in press).
63. D. Maddison and A. Viola, *J. Psychosom. Res.* **12**, 4 (1968).
64. P. J. Clayton, *Arch. Gen. Psychiatr.* **30**, 747 (1974).
65. D. Heyman and D. Gianturco, *J. Gerontol.* **28**, 359 (1973).
66. M. Minkler, in *Social Support and Health*, S. Cohen and S. L. Syme, Eds. (Academic Press, Orlando, FL, 1985), pp. 199–216.
67. S. V. Kasl, *Am. J. Public Health* **62**, 379 (1972).
68. _____ and S. Rosenfield, in *Handbook of Mental Health and Aging*, J. Birren and B. Sloane, Eds. (Prentice-Hall, Englewood Cliffs, NJ, 1980), pp. 468–498.
69. S. V. Kasl and L. Berkman, in *Aging: Biology and Behavior*, J. L. McGaugh and S. B. Kiesler, Eds. (Academic Press, New York, 1981).
70. B. Raphael, *Arch. Gen. Psychiatr.* **34**, 1450 (1977).
71. L. J. Pearlin *et al.*, *J. Health Soc. Behav.* **22**, 337 (1981).
72. R. J. Bulman and C. B. Wortman, *J. Pers. Soc. Psychol.* **33**, 351 (1977).
73. L. F. Berkman, in *Social Support and Health*, S. Cohen and S. L. Syme, Eds. (Academic Press, Orlando, FL, 1985), pp. 241–262.
74. T. C. Antonucci *et al.*, *Cancer Symptoms in the Elderly: Support and Responses* (Institute for Social Research, Ann Arbor, MI, 1986).
75. J. G. Joseph and S. L. Syme, "Risk factor status, social isolation, and CHD," paper presented at the 21st Conference on Cardiovascular Disease Epidemiology, American Heart Association, San Antonio, TX, March 1981.
76. D. Reed *et al.*, *Am. J. Epidemiol.* **117**, 384 (1983).
77. S. Haynes and M. Feinleib, *Am. J. Public Health* **70**, 133 (1980).
78. J. Medalie and V. Goldbourt, *Am. J. Med.* **60**, 910 (1976).
79. R. Ader, A. Kreutner, H. L. Jacobs, *Psychosom. Med.* **25**, 60 (1963).
80. W. B. Gross, *Am. J. Vet. Res.* **33**, 2275 (1972).
81. J. B. Jemmott and S. E. Locke, *Psychol. Bull.* **95**, 78 (1984).
82. R. W. Bartrop *et al.*, *Lancet* **1977-I**, 834 (1977).
83. S. J. Schleifer *et al.*, "The influence of stress and other psychosocial factors on human immunity," paper presented at the 36th Annual Meeting of the Psychosomatic Society, Dallas, TX, 1979.
84. This work was supported by the MacArthur Foundation Research Program on Successful Aging. The authors are indebted to M. Albert, D. Featherman, G. Reaven, J. Nesslroade, and N. Resnick for stimulating discussions and helpful suggestions regarding this manuscript. This article was prepared while R.L.K. was a fellow at the Center for Advanced Study in the Behavioral Sciences. We are grateful for financial support provided in that connection by the Carnegie Corporation of New York and the William and Flora Hewlett Foundation.

The Quality of Later Life

Although one ages from the moment of conception to the moment of death, children are considered to be "growing and developing" while adults are thought of as "aging." Biologists concerned with the problems of aging focus their attention on what happens to individuals during the later part of adult life after maturity is reached. A common definition of senescence is "the changes that occur generally in the post-reproductive period and that result in decreased survival capacity on the part of the individual organism" (B. L. Shrehler, *Time, Cells and Aging*, New York: Academic Press, 1977).

As a person ages, physiological changes take place. The skin loses its elasticity, becomes more pigmented, and bruises more easily. Joints stiffen, and the bone structure becomes less firm. Muscles lose their strength. The respiratory system becomes less efficient. The metabolism changes, resulting in different dietary demands. Bowel and bladder movements are more difficult to regulate. Visual acuity diminishes, hearing declines, and the body is less able to resist environmental stresses.

Increases in life expectancy have resulted largely from decreased mortality rates among younger people, rather than from increased longevity after age 65. In 1900, the average life expectancy at birth was 47.3 years; in 1978, it was 73.3 years. Thus in 78 years life expectancy rose by 26 years. However, those who now live to the age of 65 do not have an appreciably different life expectancy than did their 1900 cohorts. In 1900, 65-year-olds could expect to live 11.9 more years, while in 1978, persons aged 65 could expect to live an additional 16.3 years—an increase of only 4.4 years. Although more people survive to age 65 today, the chances of being afflicted by one of the major killers of older persons is still about as great for this generation as it was for their grandparents.

While medical science has had considerable success in controlling the acute diseases of the young—such as measles, chicken pox, and scarlet fever—it has not been as successful in controlling the chronic conditions of old age, such as heart trouble, cancer, and emphysema. Organ transplants, greater knowledge of the immune system, and undiscovered medical technologies will probably increase the life expectancy for the 65-and-over population, resulting in longer life for the next generation.

Although persons 65 years of age today are living only slightly longer than 65-year-olds did in 1900, the quality of their later years has greatly improved. Economically, Social Security and a multitude of private retirement programs have given most older persons a more secure retirement. Physically, many people remain active, mobile, and independent throughout their retirement years. Socially, most older persons are married, involved in community activities, and leading productive lives. While they may experience some chronic ailments, most are able to live in their own homes, direct their own lives, and involve themselves in activities they enjoy. The articles in this section examine health, psychological, social, and spiritual factors that affect the quality of aging.

In this section the articles examine how one can increase the overall quality of later life. All of us are faced with the process of aging, and by putting a strong emphasis on health, both mental and physical, a long, quality life is much more attainable.

To prevent old age from being a period of sickness, senility, and sexlessness, the author of "Older—But Coming on Strong" focuses on the importance of exercise and life-style. Everyone has a choice in how well they live, and through selecting a positive and supportive life-style, age can be an enjoyable experience. The necessity of remaining in good health is also part of a long, quality life. In the article "To Find a Way to Age in Health" the author focuses on the importance of using medical science in a constructive way to live longer and remain in good health.

Emotional well-being has a direct effect on the "success" of aging. Marriage and religion are two very important factors in the emotional satisfaction formula. In "Marriages in Later Life" the author discusses the positive aspects of support as well as the negative tensions that must be put in perspective for a marriage to work. In "Religiosity, Aging, and Life Satisfaction," the role religion can play in providing social integration and a sense of community is examined.

Once an individual enters the middle years of life, a reevaluation of attitudes must take place to ensure a positive aging process. In "Starting Over at Midlife: Why There's More Satisfaction to Life After 40" the author offers a personal account of the changes he made that allowed him to enjoy the second half of his life. Another idea that must be refuted is that education stops when

one graduates from college. In "Meet the People Who Never Quit," the value of maintaining an active mind through continuing education is considered.

Looking Ahead: Challenge Questions

While medical science has increased life expectancy at birth by controlling diseases of the young, there has been relatively little success in controlling the diseases of old age and in increasing life expectancy after age 65. Can we expect new breakthroughs in medical technology that will increase the life expectancy of 65-year-olds?

While many people expect to live into their eighties and nineties, few imagine living to be 120. Do many Americans really want to live beyond their 100th birthday?

What changes in business, government, social services, and the economy will be produced by the increasing number of older Americans?

Older—but Coming on Strong

Aging no longer has to mean sickness, senility and sexlessness

 Doctors who specialize in treating old people delight in telling the story of a 90-year-old man named Morris who has a complaint about his left knee. Says his exasperated physician: "For heaven's sake, at your age what do you expect?" Rejoins Morris feistily: "Now look here, Doc, my right knee is also 90, and it doesn't hurt." It is an apocryphal tale with a pointed message. As long as anyone can remember, old age and disability have been paired as naturally and inevitably as the horse and carriage or death and taxes. After all, advancing years have been seen by most people as an inexorable slide into illness, impotence and immobility.

No longer. Nowadays America's seniors are giving the lie to that grim vision. Fully half of all people now 75 to 84 are free of health problems that require special care or that curb their activities, according to surveys. Says Sociologist Bernice Neugarten of Northwestern University: "Even in the very oldest group, those above 85, more than one-third report no limitation due to health." Declares Dr. Richard Besdine, director of the aging center at the University of Connecticut: "Aging doesn't necessarily mean a life that is sick, senile, sexless, spent or sessile."

That more cheerful view of growing old is gaining currency mainly because of the rapidly expanding scientific discipline of gerontology. Modern studies of the aging process involve everyone from laboratory researchers examining brain tissue to nutritionists interviewing nonagenarians to physicians specializing in treating the elderly. The goal of gerontology is not to extend the upper limit of human life— now about 115 to 120 years of age—but to make the lives of the elderly less burdensome physically and more rewarding emotionally. "The new focus," says Dr. John Rowe, director of the division on aging at Harvard Medical School, "is not on life-span but on health-span."

Although still in its infancy, gerontology has produced major revisions in doctors' understanding of how people grow old. Explains Dr. T. Franklin Williams, director of the National Institute on Aging: "It's the diseases that we acquire in later years that really cause the deterioration of functions." Or, as Dr. Robert Butler of Mount Sinai School of Medicine

in New York City puts it, "Disease, not age, is the villain." The good news is that in many instances, physical disorders that afflict the aging can be effectively treated. Today even multiple afflictions do not necessarily incapacitate a person. Citing the case of a man of 75 who has diabetes, heart disease and a history of cancer, Rowe points out, "You can't tell me whether that man is in a nursing home or sitting on the Supreme Court."

How long and how well one lives, of course, depend in part on heredity. The chances of blowing out 85 candles go up 5% with each parent or grandparent who has passed that milestone. A family history of certain ailments, such as breast or colon cancer, heart disease, depression or alcoholism, extends the risk of developing such problems. Increasingly, though, researchers believe personal habits and environmental influences may hold the key to why some people are more "successful" at aging than are others. "You find a tremendous variability between individuals," observes Rowe. "The older people become, the less alike they become."

Many of the fears people have about aging are greatly exaggerated. Senility is probably the most dreaded of all debilities, yet only about 15% of those over 65 suffer serious mental impairment. Alzheimer's disease, now considered the scourge of old age, accounts for more than half that total. For much of the remainder, mental impairment from conditions such as heart disease, liver or thyroid trouble and dietary deficiency is either reversible or preventable.

Another frequently overlooked culprit: overmedication. Nearly 80% of people 65 and older have at least one chronic condition (top four: arthritis, high blood pressure, hearing impairment, heart disease); about one-third have three or more. To combat their problems, they rely on a battery of over-the-counter and prescription drugs. The majority of people in this age group use more than five medications, and 10% take more than twelve. Interactions among drugs, as well as too much of some drugs, can cause a host of complications, from mental confusion to slowed blood clotting to disturbance of the heart's rhythm.

Depression, often mistaken for senility, or dementia, is by far the single most ignored disorder among the elderly. About 15% of older people suffer from the condition, double the figure for the general population; the elderly have the highest suicide rate of any age group. Drugs account for some of the high incidence of depression. But the old are also more vulnerable because they have suffered more major stresses, including the deaths of spouses or friends, living alone, retirement from a job, serious illness. The classic symptoms of depression—guilt, hopelessness, sleeplessness, lack of appetite, and suicidal thoughts—are more likely to be noticed in younger people because they are so out of character. But families and doctors too often overlook depression in the elderly. The warning signs may sometimes be subtle: headaches, stomach ailments, vague complaints of not feeling right. And there is always the tendency to dismiss the signals as normal aging, just old folks' crankiness. When depression is recognized, counseling and drugs successfully treat three-quarters of the cases.

Flagging libido and sexual ability have also been wrongly equated with advancing years. Women supposedly lose interest in sex after menopause; in fact, desire normally remains strong throughout life. The dampening of sexual urges often results from physical problems, such as hot flashes and vaginal dryness, which may be alleviated by estrogen therapy, lubricants and attention to nutrition and exercise. Older men, for their part, routinely accept continued impotence as normal. It is not. As a man ages, he does need more time to achieve an erection. But almost all impotence, whether psychological or physical, is reversible. Among the common physical causes: diabetes, heart disease and chronic alcohol abuse.

Yet another widely held fear is that wear and tear on the joints inevitably leads to painful and immobilizing arthritis. Yes, there is a wearing down of the cartilage pads that cushion bones, but less than half of those over 65 whose X rays show degenerative arthritic changes suffer symptoms. Many of the aches and pains attributed to acute arthritis, doctors say, have more to do with weakening muscles than creaky joints. People with some joint damage fare better when they engage in regular moderate exercise, such as walking or swimming.

Aging, however, is hardly a benign process. Acknowledges Dr. Christine Cassel of the University of Chicago: "By and large, the changes are decremental. Every organ is losing reserve capacity." That means a decline in the ability to recover from physical stresses. A 60-year-old and a 20-year-old who race around the block may start out with the same pulse rate, notes Vincent Cristofalo, director of the University of Pennsylvania's center for the study of aging. "Even when they stop," he notes, "their pulses may be only a little different. The big difference will be in how long it takes for each person's pulse rate to return to normal."

Slowed recovery has a profound impact when it comes to illness. With advancing years, bones take longer to knit, wounds to heal and infections to clear up. Ultimately, says Cassel, the difference is that a "healthy young person can lose a lung, a kidney and do fine. And so too an old person can be doing fine, but then he has a stroke, a heart attack, whatever. Because of the stress, it's much more likely that all the major organs will go one after the other."

There are some striking physiological changes that accompany age. Among them:

▶ The immune system starts to decline at around age 30. For instance, white blood cells that fight off invaders, such as viruses and bacteria, lose their effectiveness as a person gets older. The gradual weakening of the immune system makes it harder to stave off illness.

▶ Metabolism begins to slow at around age 25. For each decade thereafter, the number of calories required to maintain one's weight drops by at least 2%. Muscle mass gradually shrinks. As a result, people tend to get fatter. Kidneys may lose up to 50% of their efficiency between ages 30 and 80. Some of the liver's functions may decline. Thus alcohol remains in the body longer. So do drugs, a fact doctors are beginning to consider in deciding on dosages for older patients.

▶ Lungs lose on the average 30% to 50% of their maximum breathing capacity between ages 30 and 80. Blood vessels lose elasticity, though the heart stays astonishingly well preserved. Notes Cardiologist Jerome Fleg of the National Institute on Aging: "The heart of a normal 80-year-old can pump blood as effectively under stress as that of a normal 30-year-old."

▶ Bone mass reaches its peak in the 30s for both men and women, then begins to drop by about 1% a year. In women the rate surges for a few years after menopause. About 24 million Americans, the vast majority of them women, develop osteoporosis, a condition in which the bones become dangerously thin and fragile. Brittle bones are the major cause of the fractures, particularly of the hip, that cripple many of the elderly. Alcohol and tobacco use accelerates bone thinning.

Another reason to stop smoking: women who use tobacco reach menopause about two years earlier than women who do not.

▶ The senses flag. Taste diminishes as the nose loses its sense of smell (odor accounts for about 80% of overall flavor sensation). The loss of taste can lead to lack of appetite and sometimes to serious nutritional deficiencies. Hearing fades, particularly in the high-frequency range, and processing of information slows. Vision begins deteriorating at about 40. The pupil shrinks, reducing the amount of light reaching the retina. An 80-year-old's retina receives only about a sixth of the light that a 20-year-old's does. The lens hardens and clouds. More than half of those 60 and older have some cataract formation.

▶ Changes occur in the skin. The topmost layer, or epidermis, becomes dry and blemished. The middle layer, or dermis, thins dramatically, making the skin seem translucent, and becomes much less elastic and supportive. These changes, along with loss of fat from the underlying subcutaneous layer, cause the skin to sag and wrinkle. Drinking, smoking and suntanning speed up these processes. With less fat and a decline in the activity of sweat glands, the skin becomes a less efficient regulator of body temperature. The result: older people have a harder time staying warm and cooling off. Protective pigment-forming cells that absorb the sun's harmful rays are reduced by 10% to 20% for each decade of life, thus increasing susceptibility to skin cancers.

▶ The need for sleep gradually diminishes. Newborns sleep 16 to 18 hours a day; by age 65, three to six hours a night, perhaps with a nap during the day, is typically all that is necessary. The quality of sleep changes, becoming lighter and more fitful. Shorter, restless nights lead many who recall the easy slumber of youth to complain of insomnia. As a result, half of elderly women and one-quarter of elderly men take largely unneeded sleeping pills.

▶ The brain loses an average of about 20% of its weight, but as Neurologist David Drachman of the University of Massachusetts points out, "there is redundancy in the brain. It's like the lights in Times Square. Suppose you turn off 20% of the bulbs: you'll still get the message." Speed of recall and mental performance slow, but essential skills remain intact. Researchers speculate that memory loss among the elderly may be something of a self-fulfilling prophecy. Old people are supposed to have memory problems, so they may be more aware of, and bothered by, occasional lapses than are younger people.

So far, gerontologists have no surefire prescription for staying healthy longer, but they do make some strong recommendations: stay out of the sun, cut back on drinking and stop smoking. They stress that it is never too late to adopt better habits. A person of 70 who stops smoking immediately reduces the risk of developing heart disease. The elderly should follow general principles of a sound diet: avoid foods rich in cholesterol or saturated fat, such as eggs and beef, and eat more chicken and fish. Seniors should stress high-fiber foods, including whole-grain cereals and many fruits, and items rich in vitamins A and C, such as broccoli and cantaloupe.

Though some vitamin or mineral supplements may be beneficial, experts warn that taking excessive doses of nutrients is dangerous. Moreover, the combination of too much of a supplement and certain medications can cause trouble. For example, excessive vitamin E by itself can lead to diarrhea and skin rashes. Taken with certain blood-thinning drugs, large doses of vitamin E can trigger severe internal bleeding.

Exercise, at least half an hour three times a week, is an important aid to controling weight, keeping bones strong, building muscle strength, conditioning the heart and lungs and relieving stress. Declares Physiologist William Evans of the U.S. Department of Agriculture–Tufts University center on aging: "There is no group in our population than can benefit more from exercise than senior citizens. For a young person, exercise can increase physical function by perhaps 10%. But in an old person you can increase it by 50%." The advice is catching on: a Gallup poll taken at the end of last year found that 47% of those 65 and older regularly engage in some form of exercise.

Such seniors are living proof that aging is not synonymous with illness, that increasing years do not necessarily lessen desires or capabilities. That is a welcome surprise, particularly to the old. Muses Margaret Strothers Thomas, 72, a retired teacher from Philadelphia: "As a child I used to look at older people, and they were bent over, stooped and complaining. I can't believe that when you reach the age that you've feared you feel great." Achieving better health for longer requires a continual alertness to false assumptions about old age, whether they come from family, friends, doctors or the old. Declares Thomas: "I have lived so many years, but I'm not old. I have a very positive outlook on life."

More of such moxie is in order. Resignation exacts as heavy a toll on the road to old age as disease or poor habits, warn gerontologists, who stress the importance of cultivating new interests and staying mentally engaged. That view is shared by no less an authority than Comedian George Burns. "People practice to get old," he avers. "The minute they get to be 65 or 70, they sit down slow, they get into a car with trouble. They start taking small steps." Burns stays young by taking fearless strides. He plans to play the London Palladium on his 100th birthday—eight years from now. —*By Anastasia Toufexis*. *Reported by J. Madeleine Nash/Chicago and Dick Thompson/Washington*

To Find a Way to Age in Health

SUMMARY: Twentieth century amenities and, to a lesser degree, medicine have given the average American some three extra decades. But with this extension of life span has come a debate: Are the extra years to be spent in frailty and sickness? Some experts say the longer one lives, the more quickly one dies. Others say that with a greater number of older people comes a higher incidence of disability. No matter which camp is right, most everyone wants to live longer.

David Holzman

On the way to a banquet, two healthy doctors in their mid-80s were discussing how they might die. Both wanted the end to come as swiftly and painlessly as possible, Dr. Joseph D. Wassersug recounts in a recent essay in The Journal of the American Medical Association, and they extolled the virtues of massive heart attacks and strokes. Wassersug, then "a mere youngster of 74," was driving, and as he listened to their conversation, he began to worry. "The problem is, in a sense, that, for my age, I'm too healthy."

He explains that his blood pressure and cholesterol level were low, and he did not smoke. Coronary and cerebral hemorrhage were unlikely to strike him down, so "what else is left to terminate my existence? *Cancer?* How horrible! Perish the thought."

At the banquet, Wassersug writes, "I resolved to take a more active intervention in my destiny. I scanned the menu and order the thickest slab of rare roast beef. . . . If a fat-enriched, high-cholesterol gourmet diet can prevent death from cancer, I say it's worth it. Pass the butter, please."

"Anytime you have an advance that reduces early death from one pathology, you will see a later death from a different pathology," says Richard L. Sprott, associate director for biomedical research and clinical medicine at the National Institute on Aging. "This poses a very interesting ethical question. To what degree are we alleviating human misery and to what degree are we in-creasing it?" Are people living longer only to suffer more years of debility or a more painful death?

The policy implications of this question are huge. Billions of dollars are at stake. Disabling diseases, from arthritis to Alzheimer's, are the biggest concern, because their victims need long-term nursing care, whose costs are so great that authors of last year's federal catastrophic health care legislation did not even start to address them.

Consider Alzheimer's. For what it could cost the nation in dollars and misery, it has been called the disease of the 21st century. Already, caring for 2.5 million victims costs $45 billion a year, nearly 10 percent of what is spent annually on all health care, says Daniel Perry, director of the Alliance for Aging Research, a nonprofit advocacy organization. The incidence of this form of dementia, as of other diseases of old age, increases predictably with age. By 2040, when the baby boomers will be in their 80s and 90s, the portion of the population over 65 (now one in eight, for 31 million people) is expected to have doubled — over 85 to have quadrupled. "In sheer dollars, the health system could be overwhelmed by the needs of double and triple the population of very old."

Indeed, the average person over 65 uses $4,000 worth of health care a year, compared with the $1,100 worth for someone under 65, says Princeton University health care economist Uwe Reinhardt. Medical ethicist Daniel Callahan lobbed a grenade into the debate last year with the book "Setting Limits: Medical Goals in an Aging Society," in which he advocates the rationing of medical care to the elderly. The raising of the issue is a sign of the times.

Conversely, measures to reduce disability could save a fortune. "Each month's reduction in dependency for citizens over 85 means a $4 billion reduction in health care costs," former Health, Education and Welfare Secretary Joseph A. Califano noted recently.

But as to whether such people as Wassersug will necessarily die more painfully because they avoided a coronary, controversy rages. No, says Dr. James Fries, a professor of medicine at Stanford University. There is a genetically programmed limit on the life span, and the closer one approaches it, the more quickly and easily any disease will claim life. As all organ systems gradually decline, the entire system becomes increasingly vulnerable to milder and milder stresses. Although some pathology will probably trigger demise, simple and benign old age becomes the underlying cause of death.

But perhaps surprisingly, the question of whether old age, and not some pathology, can be the cause of death is one of the big controversies of gerontology. Fries's opponents assert that many of the diseases of old age, such as Alzheimer's, as well as arthritis, osteoporosis, and hearing and visual impairment, cause not death but merely disabilities that can lead to a painful, undignified and costly final few years. Gerontologists say their goal is no longer to increase life span but to increase health span.

The question then arises: Is the health and fitness movement merely going to populate the next century's nursing homes?

 From *Insight*, April 10, 1989, pp. 8-15. Copyright © 1989, Insight/David Holzman. Reprinted by permission.

Are millions of tax dollars wasted on the National Cholesterol Education Program of the National Heart, Lung and Blood Institute? Should the surgeon general shut up about smoking, already? Can Wassersug have his steak and eat it too?

In the last century, death came early. Mothers and small children were the first to go, and men who made it to adulthood were still likely to get knocked off from infectious disease before the end of middle age. People feared tuberculosis then as they fear cancer today, and as some fear AIDS. Infections that might develop from surgery or accidents could easily prove fatal. For those born at the turn of the century, the average life expectancy in the United States was 47.3.

Every industrialized nation has passed through this transition. "The first phase was reduction in infectious infant and maternal mortality," says Kenneth G. Manton, research professor of demographic studies at Duke University. The incidence of other infectious diseases also fell. "By 1900, tuberculosis had declined by about 70 percent since 1850," says Dr. Jacob A. Brody, dean of the school of public health at the University of Illinois at Chicago.

In the 1920s, life expectancy climbed to the late 50s, high enough to put many people at risk for the chronic killers. By 1930, heart disease had become the leading cause of death, followed closely by cancer.

It is a common misconception that medicine played an important role in this transition. "Half the gain in life expectancy [this century] had occurred by 1920, and medicine had nothing to do with it," says Brody. In fact, antibiotics were not widely available until the late 1940s. In the early 20th century, drugs were of questionable value, he says. "There was a famous saying by Oliver Wendell Holmes that if they threw all the drugs in the ocean, it would be better for people and worse for the fishes."

"The best evidence indicates that it is *social* interventions, rather than biomedical ones, that deserve the credit," Dr. Jerome L. Avorn, a Harvard University Medical School professor, writes in the recent anthology "Our Aging Society." He cites "the availability of adequate nutrition, of clean water free of sewage, of sufficient housing to prevent crowding and exposure to the elements, and the institution of rudimentary sanitation practices." Observers give education much of the credit as well. During the recent famine in Ethiopia, the best predictor of infant survival was the extent of the mother's education, says Brody.

In addition, he cites changes in work. "There were fewer coal miners, fewer people in heavy industry. The move toward a service economy started early this century."

The trend toward longer life continued after World War II. But in the mid-1950s, life expectancy hit a plateau for men at just under 67, though it continued to rise ever so slightly for women.

Changing Causes of Death

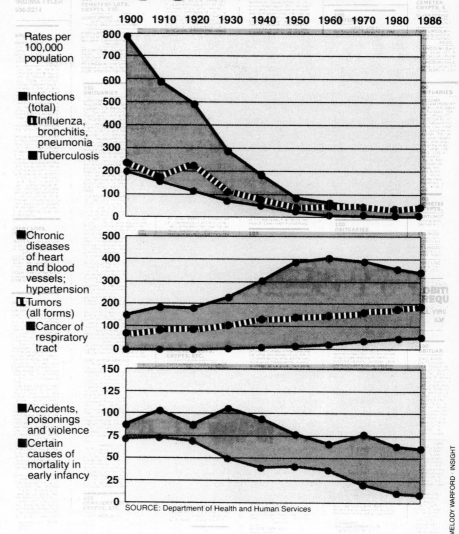

SOURCE: Department of Health and Human Services

MELODY WARFORD INSIGHT

"Many people were claiming we had reached the biological maximum in longevity," says Samuel H. Preston, chairman of demography at the University of Pennsylvania. Various social programs were planned accordingly. But in 1968, life expectancy began rising, fast. By 1986 it had reached 74.8 for both sexes, 71.3 for men.

To understand the plateau, it is important to note that the incidence of most chronic diseases in the population has been rising because, for the most part, increasing numbers of people have grown old enough to be at risk. But for the individual, the risk of, say, most cancers or arthritis was no greater for the 65-year-old (or for any specific age) in 1960 than it had been in 1920.

For coronary artery disease and lung cancer, the age-specific risk of death actually rose and then later declined. Demographers correlate the rise and decline with the beginning and end of the life expectancy plateau of the mid- 1950s to 1968.

Virtually nonexistent prior to 1930, respiratory tract cancers claimed 14 lives out of every 100,000 Americans by 1950, 22

by 1960 and nearly 33 by 1969. As to what was causing the cancers, the connections between the rate of smoking and lung cancer incidence are considered unambiguous.

Heart disease, a relatively minor cause of death compared with infectious disease before 1920, killed 230 per 100,000 in 1930. The toll climbed to 386 in 1950 but reached only 406 by 1969. More important, mortality from heart disease within each age group peaked in the mid-1960s and has since fallen by 30 percent, says Dr. Lee Goldman, vice chairman of the department of medicine for Brigham and Womens Hospital and Beth Israel Hospital in Boston. (Nonetheless, heart disease remains the premier killer.)

The decline of heart disease follows Americans' reduction of serum cholesterol in their arteries and fats in their diet, wrote Dr. Reuel A. Stallones in Scientific American in 1980. But he found no correlation between diet and the steep rise in coronary disease that began in the 1920s, nor was there any blip in that rise from the privations of the Great Depression.

The rise in heart disease from 1920 to the mid-1960s followed the decline of physical activity, as the percentage of those employed in agriculture plummeted and as the automobile made walking more a matter of a stroll than of necessity. But Stallones claimed that there had not been enough of a resurgence of physical activity to account for any of the later decline in heart disease. Such associations remain weak, says Dr. Richard W. Besdine, director of the Travelers Center on Aging at the University of Connecticut Health Center.

The rise and decline in smoking follows most closely that of heart disease, according to Stallones, but he concluded, "In no case is the fit as precise as one would like."

Undoubtedly one reason for this is that part of the decline is due to the intervention of modern medicine. In one study, which analyzed the trends from 1968 to 1976, researchers attributed 55 percent of the decline to diet and smoking reduction and 40 percent to coronary care units, bypass surgery and the like, says Goldman, the study's principal author. Adds Besdine, "Survival following first myocardial infarction is double what it was 25 years ago." Additionally, Besdine credits large-scale programs for detection of high blood pressure with much of the reduction.

Modern medicine has indeed played a dramatic but relatively minor role in reducing mortality, and that only recently. "Most of the modern medical interventions familiar to us today became widely available only after the midpoint of this century: antibiotics (in widespread use only after World War II), cardiac pacemakers (in the 1960s), hemodialysis (in the late 1960s), coronary artery surgery (in the 1970s), to name a few," writes Avorn. "With the exception of the birth-control pill, each of the medical-technology interventions developed since the 1950s has its most widespread impact on people who are past their fifties — the further past their fifties, the greater the impact."

"Medical intervention," he says, "is the intervention which causes more of the frailest old to survive."

Goldman's attribution of 40 percent of the decline in cardiac mortality to modern medicine is perhaps the most dramatic. More recently, flu vaccines and stimulants for the immune system, whose effectiveness declines steadily with age, have reduced flu and flu-related mortality among the elderly. Better drugs and surgery have added to the life span of diabetics, says Lois M. Verbrugge of the Institute of Gerontology at the University of Michigan.

But medical advances and preventive measures among adults are not the only things that make people live longer. It is important to note, researchers emphasize, that one generation lives longer than another because of the social and medical changes that took place when members of that generation were children.

"It used to be thought that if you lived long enough your sex drive would deteriorate and your mind would go."

This combination of civilizing influences and medical advances has bought the average American nearly three decades of extra life since the turn of the century, and it is continuing to buy additional years at the margin. But in making any purchase, informed consumers usually emphasize the importance of quality over quantity. What kind of years are we getting for our money?

The overall purchase has been a wise one, most would likely agree. The extra decades come with a modest increase in years of infirmity, says Besdine. And Fries of Stanford claims that as we live longer, we are approaching ever closer to the ideal of gerontologists, of living healthfully until we drop, all at once, like the one-hoss shay that Oliver Wendell Holmes extolled in his poem, "The Deacon's Masterpiece":

Have you heard of the wonderful one-hoss shay,
That was built in such a logical way
It ran a hundred years to a day.
And then . . . went to pieces all at once, —
All at once, and nothing first, —
Just as bubbles do when they burst.

Others dispute Fries's happy view of aging. "I love it, and I'm at the age where I want to believe it," says Dorothy P. Rice, 66, the former director of the National Center for Health Statistics. "But in my heart of hearts, I know it's not so."

"Fries is concentrating on fatal conditions and ignoring the age-dependent, nonfatal disabilities," says Brody. "We have no evidence that we have postponed the onset of arthritis, blindness, deafness, incontinence, osteoporosis and dementia."

These diseases are considered unpreventable and are difficult to treat. Their incidence rises quite predictably with age, and the chance of being in a nursing home, which is something of an index for level of disability, rises from 5 percent at age 65 to 22 percent at 85, says Rice.

Thus, increasing disability is the inevitable consequence of an aging population. And in fact, the data, which researchers caution are soft, suggest that of late, gains in life expectancy are being purchased at the cost of a lot of disability.

One study of the matter looked at life expectancy gains and disability in Canada from 1951 to 1978. "Very crudely, we had something like a six-year gain in life expectancy in that period," says Russell Wilkins, a senior analyst in the health division of Statistics Canada, a national record-keeping agency. "About half the gain in life expectancy appears to have been gains in disability expectancy." He cautions that the term disability does not necessarily mean wheelchair-bound. Many people labeled disabled "can't work but can do a lot of other things," and with that in mind, Wilkins suggests that it might be better to say that Canadians had purchased 4½ good years at the expense of 1½ bad years.

A similar study for the United States, from 1966 to 1976, a period when life expectancy was growing rapidly, found only a slight increase in disability-free life expectancy, says Wilkins. Brody maintains that for every four years of life bought at the margin, three are plagued by disability.

According to Verbrugge's figures, of the 46.4 million Americans 45 to 64, 18 percent of men and 31 percent of women have arthritis; 20 percent of men and 22 percent of women have hypertension; 16 percent and 21 percent respectively are plagued by chronic sinusitis; heart disease afflicts 13 percent of each; for hearing impairments, the figures are 15 percent and 9 percent. For people 65 and over, these impairments rise precipitously. For example, 36 percent of such men and 50 percent of such women have arthritis. To be sure, severe limitations occur in only a fraction of these cases; from arthritis, for example, in 8 percent of men and 13 percent of women.

But Verbrugge's statistics suggest that the percentage of disabled people within each age group is increasing. This is happening for three reasons, she says. Since more people are surviving heart attacks and strokes, more people are living with vascular disease. The same goes for other chronic killers, such as diabetes. Also, more people are willing to classify themselves as disabled because of "increased monetary incentives by the government to be disabled and more liberal views of disability."

Paradoxically, some of Fries's opponents — such as Rice, who teaches at the University of California at San Francisco's Institute for Health and Aging, Dr. T. Franklin Williams, director of the National Institute on Aging, and Avorn — assert that the number of people who are achieving a healthy old age and exiting quickly, like the one-hoss shay, is increasing, even along with the population of infirm elderly.

In his essay, Avorn explains this apparent paradox: "Large numbers of people [are] coming into their sixties and seventies healthier than their grandparents were at the same age. These seemingly different phenomena are in fact both offshoots of the same process. It is as if the health of older

Americans has been ratcheted up a notch or two in recent decades. While on the one hand, this results in an improvement in health for the non-ill elderly, on the other hand, this ratcheting up will cause many chronically ill people, who otherwise would have died, to remain one notch below death. 'The rising tide lifts all ships equally,' including those that might otherwise be resting at the bottom of the harbor."

And a variety of research suggests that disease is neither the inevitable consequence of aging nor the inevitable cause of death. "It used to be thought that if you lived long enough, your sex drive would deteriorate, your arteries would clog and your mind would go," says Dr. Robert N. Butler, chairman of the department of geriatrics and adult development at Mount Sinai Medical Center in New York. "We are beginning to see a much different portrait of old age."

"Textbooks say people lose muscle as they age," notes Jeffrey B. Blumberg, assistant director of the Department of Agriculture's Human Nutrition Research Center on Aging at Tufts University. "But we find that people who maintain higher activity levels don't lose lean body mass, and more importantly, we can exercise old people and have them gain muscle mass and strength. We took a 90-year-old from a nursing home, put him on physical training, and he increased his muscle mass by 400 percent."

At the same time, Blumberg and his colleagues have found that certain changes in diet and exercise can arrest and even reverse the development of glucose intolerance, which is closely related to diabetes and was thought to be an inevitable consequence of aging. Immune declines can be reversed with vitamin E supplements.

Moreover, even centenarians can be healthy. At the Sanders-Brown Center on Aging at the University of Kentucky, David R. Wekstein and his colleagues have performed detailed examinations of about one-third of all Kentuckians 100 or older. Thirty-five to 40 percent of them had dementia, he says, but among those who did not, CAT scans showed little loss of brain tissue and a brain chemistry no different from that of younger individuals. Those who are healthy lead active lives, he continues, describing how one woman camped with her son the night before she was scheduled to be examined at the center.

Furthermore, when they check out, the centenarians don't waste time about it, says Wekstein. "We have no information on any centenarian developing a prolonged illness. They get sick and die in the space of about a week." As to cause of death, it is usually reported as heart attack, stroke, pneumonia or old age, he says, cautioning that he cannot vouch for the accuracy of death certificates from all over the state.

Some would say that simple old age is killing the centenarians. In a study published in The Journal of the American Medical Association in 1982, Dr. Robert R. Kohn made the first case for accepting senescence as an underlying cause of death. Kohn examined autopsies of 200 persons who died past the age of 84 that had been performed by his colleagues at the Case Western Reserve University Institute of Pathology and found that in 26 percent of the cases, there were no apparent significant pathologies. Similarly, autopsies of experimental rats that lived exceptionally long showed that many died without apparent cause, says Edward J. Masoro, professor of physiology at the University of Texas Health Science Center in San Antonio.

The meaning of the Kohn data is controversial, but the debate degenerates into a fight over definitions. "If you look at the autopsy results, there was a large range of pathological changes, and the problem was assigning priorities from among them," says Manton. But these pathologies would not have harmed a younger person, says Dr. Vincent M. Monnier of Case Western, a collaborator on other research with Kohn, who died in 1984.

All this suggests that the one-hoss shay model of aging, though not current reality, is an attainable goal. But subsidiary questions remain unanswered: To what relative degree do medical interventions — drugs, surgery and the like — vs. today's changing habits toward diet, exercise, tobacco and alcohol contribute to keeping people alive into impaired old age? This question has important policy implications, says Dr. Joseph S. Cassells, chief of a study on aging being done for the Institute of Medicine of the National Academy of Sciences. "Medicare does not cover preventive services generally. It may be that some of these preventive services ought to be reimbursable."

More than 95 percent of the $500 billion the nation spends on health care goes to treatment rather than prevention, according to Dr. J. Michael McGinnis, director of the office of disease prevention and health promotion at the Department of Health and Human Services.

Indeed, there is some slim evidence to suggest that prudent habits may lead to a net reduction of disabilities later in life. Seventh-day Adventists who follow their faith's more rigid proscriptions live longer and have less disability in old age than the general population, says Jan Kuzma, biostatistics director at Loma Linda University, an Adventist institution in California. Not all Adventists shun meat, nor do they all exercise regularly. And some converts are former smokers. These differences within the population made it possible for Loma Linda researchers to compare Adventists to each other, as well as to Californians at large. This comparison among the Adventists was important, because two of the strongest predictors of longevity are higher education and socioeconomic level, and Adventists outstrip their fellow Californians in both.

Adventists live nearly a decade longer than other residents. Exercise made the greatest contribution to their life expectancy, adding nearly five years among men; vegetarianism added more than 3½; having never smoked added 1½ years; and obesity subtracted two years, says Kuzma.

As for quality of life in old age, "I constructed a quality of life index," he says, "which measures how well people are able to function physically and mentally in old age. The most predictive variable of quality of life is the number of health practices people follow."

The Kentucky centenarian study also suggested that today's norms for good health habits can make a difference in the quality of later years. "It's almost as if they have read the guidelines of good health from the American Heart Association and the American Cancer Society," says Wekstein. "Very few of them smoke, none have ever been obese, nor do they consume significant quantities of alcohol."

All this is not surprising. "The same measures that reduce heart attacks lower the incidence of certain cancers and diabetes," says Brody.

Moreover, those who would eschew prevention on the theory that the alternative is an old age fraught with disability and a painful death ignore the fact that neither painful death nor disability in old age is a certainty. In a new study of dying patients in a hospital, researchers found that only 12 percent were in severe pain the day before they died, while another 12 percent were in moderate pain, according to Dwight B. Brock, chief of the Aging Institute's biometry office. People whose habits prevent a massive heart attack at 68 may still die of a worn-out heart at 85, says Brody. Says Avorn: "Each of us has no way of knowing whether our terminal event is going to be heart attack, Alzheimer's disease or stroke, and wouldn't it be ironic if your destiny had been to live to 90 with mind intact, but because you didn't eat wisely, you died of a heart attack at 68?" On the other hand, the average person 70 to 74 years old, who has a life expectancy of 13.6 more years, can expect to be disabled for more than five of those years.

Much more equivocal is the question of the effect that medical interventions are having on the quality of old age. "Some medical interventions can add a tremendous amount to quality of life and disability-free life, whereas other high-technology interventions can prolong life in a disabled state," says Dr. Jack M. Guralnik, senior staff fellow at the National Institute on Aging.

In the face of this uncertainty, Besdine is quick to defend access to medical intervention by the disabled aged. "Everyone a horror story," he says. "But my clinical sense, from over 17 years exclusively in geriatrics, is that in the vast majority of cases of medical interventions that keep disabled people alive for more than a matter of a few weeks, be it the stroke victim who is paralyzed on one side and whose speech is thick or the person in a wheelchair, the bulk of these people prefer living, thank you very much." Physicist Stephen Hawking, 47, is probably doing more than anyone today to figure out how the world began, Besdine notes, despite total paralysis from a genetic disease.

But time and the rapid advance of medicine are probably on the side of easing old age, which would give people further reason to take preventive measures. For example, "we are making remarkable progress in understanding Alzheimer's disease," says Avorn. "It is not implausible to suggest that within 10 years we may have a much better understanding of what causes it, how to treat it and how to prevent it."

"The promise of the new molecular biology is that it will tell us more about how the molecular components of cells work," says Sprott. "It will be easier to understand what goes wrong and find ways to prevent breakdown." Additionally, the project for mapping all the genes in the human genome will make it possible to discover whether age-dependent diseases have genetic components, as Alzheimer's and osteoporosis almost certainly do. Combined with an understanding of environmental triggers, such knowledge might make it possible to develop preventive measures for those most at risk, he says.

Geriatricians would love to prevent all the chronic disabilities of aging, but if they could just stave off their onset for "as little as five years, people would die before they became disabled, and you could cut the incidence of many diseases in half," says Perry of the Alliance for Aging Research.

How best to extend the health span? Two studies just under way at the Institute of Medicine seek to set priorities in medicine and in research. One will study 13 causative and risk factors, such as nutrition, osteoporosis, physical inactivity and social isolation, to learn which interventions are most effective in reducing dependency on other people. The other will try to develop a research agenda on the science of aging.

It might seem that the best way to extend the health span would be through direct research on the age-dependent diseases of disability. But Sprott says that an understanding of the underlying aging process would provide a much better handle on alleviating some of its consequences.

Exactly what aging is is one of the great mysteries of biomedical science. Researchers do not even know whether organisms wear out or whether senescence is programmed into the genes. One wear and tear theory holds that free radicals, highly reac-

tive compounds which are inevitable products of metabolism (as well as of smog and smoking) rend the fabric of life. Or perhaps the myriad biochemical and physiological systems get out of sync, triggering secondary events that lead to visible aging. Program theories include the notions that decline of the immune or endocrine systems somehow triggers aging. Probably more than one process is at work.

But inevitably, these theories raise more questions than they might answer. For example, what causes the decline of the immune or endocrine systems in the first place, or the desynchronization of physiology? The whole problem of aging is like a Russian Matrioski doll that holds another doll inside of it that has another doll inside of it and so on, and researchers are no further than opening the second doll.

The closest anyone has come to gaining an insight on the fundamental process of aging is with the observation that the accepted maximum life span of laboratory animals can be breached. Among humans, although the average life span has been climbing steadily since the dawn of industrialization, the oldest old live no longer today — to a little more than 100 years — than they did 100 years ago.

The technique for extending the lives of lab animals, the only one that has worked, is diet restriction. Limit intake to about 60 percent of what they would eat if left to their own devices, and rats will live to the equivalent of 150 to 180 in human years. It is as if aging happens in slow motion; all the usual age-related diseases occur later.

The living conditions of laboratory rats, consuming as much as they like, are hardly natural, say critics. Not unlike the conditions of industrialized humans, counters Roy L. Walford of the University of California at Los Angeles, one of the leading researchers on diet restriction. In any case, the National Institute on Aging is experimenting with the technique on primates.

To penetrate the mysteries of aging and assuage the miseries of old age, researchers and their supporters on Capitol Hill are united in a quest for a lot more money. Compared with the Heart, Lung and Blood Institute and the Cancer Institute, which receive $1 billion and $1.5 billion a year respectively, with a similar amount going to AIDS research, "the Aging Institute gets a mere $229 million," says Perry, far below what it deserves in terms of its potential impact on human welfare. Likewise, the newly created arthritis and deafness institutes, which are important to those concerned about aging, "are at the bottom of the heap." At a recent news conference, the Alliance for Aging Research, backed by Sens. Pete V. Domenici, a New Mexico Republican, and David Pryor, an Arkansas

Democrat, as well as Califano, called for an additional $1 billion in research funds annually. Within 15 years, such an investment would reap a 300 to 400 percent return, said Domenici.

"The picture of aging is grim," says Brody. "But the prospect is not so grim." Says Guralnik, "We are all less interested in longevity for its own sake. Nobody is in the business of trying to increase longevity without trying to increase active life expectancy."

With luck, such research will alleviate the disabilities of aging. But in the foreseeable future, large numbers of people will continue to die of cancer, and for these terminal patients, managing their final pain is the most important issue. The problem is not so much a lack of effective medication as it is a squeamish attitude on the part of doctors toward the use of narcotics, according to Dr. C. Stratton Hill, director of the pain service at the University of Texas M. D. Anderson Cancer Center in Houston. Doctors apparently fear anything that can be associated with illicit drug use, and many simply accept pain as an unavoidable consequence of terminal illness — all to the detriment of patients. The National Committee for the Treatment of Intractable Pain, an advocacy group, has collected hundreds of letters from the loved ones of terminal patients, railing against the horrors of agonizing last days and a lack of compassion on the part of doctors and nurses.

But except in cases of extreme pain, few want to see the end come. "The person who wants to live to be 95 is the 94-year-old," says Brody. Existentialists rail against what they see as the absurdity of doom, but to Dr. Leon R. Kass, author of "Toward a More Natural Science," mortality is what makes us human.

"To be mortal means that it is possible to give one's life, not only in one moment, say, on the field of battle, . . . but also in the many other ways in which we are able in action to rise above attachment to survival," writes Kass, alluding to the ancient Greeks, whose bored gods looked on from Olympus while the mortals performed noble deeds and made the best of their flesh and blood while it lasted.

Kass retells the story of how Odysseus declined the immortality proffered by the nymph Calypso, who would have had the hero tarry for eternity on her island paradise: "What I want and all my days I pine for," responds Odysseus, "is to go back to my house and see the day of my homecoming. And if some god batters me far out on the wine-blue water, I will endure it, keeping a stubborn spirit inside me, for already I have suffered much and done much hard work on the waves and in the fighting."

"For this nobility, vulnerability and mortality are the necessary conditions," writes Kass. "The immortals cannot be noble. . . . Immortality is a kind of oblivion — like death itself."

Marriages in Later Life

ROSALIE GILFORD

Rosalie Gilford, Ph.D., is a professor, Department of Sociology, and the coordinator of gerontology programs, California State University, Fullerton. This work was supported by a research grant from California State University, Fullerton.

IT IS GENERALLY assumed that older married persons, whether survivors in long-lived intact marriages or newlyweds in old age, are among the most fortunate of the older population. Because they still have a life partner, presumably providing emotional support and integration into social networks, and also because they generally have higher incomes and social status, older husbands and wives are thought to be less vulnerable to personal and social breakdown than are their widowed or divorced counterparts. However, despite these advantages, older marriages also encounter unique challenges that may undermine their positive tenor and stability. For example, personal developmental processes may unfold over the life course to lead spouses in opposite directions, causing marital discord and dysfunction (Troll et al., 1979). Further, the socially structured role losses that frequently accompany aging may exert pressures on couples as the marital relationship becomes a primary source of social reinforcement in the face of shrinking social networks (Rosow, 1973). Thus, while marriage may function as a resource to older couples, marriage also sustains particular tensions that may strain the marital bond in later life. Given current longevity projections, it is estimated that spouses in one out of every five marriages will survive to celebrate a 50th wedding anniversary (Glick and Norton, 1977). The growth in the number of older couples in our society calls for systematic study of the dynamics of these long-lived marriage relationships.

This paper reviews selected literature on older marriages for the purpose of identifying their special strengths and strains. The evidence is examined from the perspective of three broad questions:

1. What are the strengths of older marriages? What power has the relationship to enrich and enhance the quality of spouses' later lives?

2. What strains do older marriages endure? How do the personal and social events of later life impinge upon the relationship?

3. What insights can service providers and planners gain from an understanding of long-lived marriages? What opportunities exist for systematic interventions that increase the solidarity of the marital bond?

MARITAL STATUS & QUALITY

Despite rising divorce rates and changing attitudes, marriage continues to occupy a central place in the lives of most Americans; the vast majority — 95 percent — marry at least once, and most who divorce, particularly at young ages, tend to marry again (Skolnick, 1981). While the ranks of aging marriage cohorts become depleted over the years as the result of death and divorce, more than half of the approximately 26 million Americans over the age of 65 are married and living with a spouse in an independent household. However, this finding is more true of men than women because women outlive men. At ages 55-64, 81 percent of men and only 67 percent of women are married. By age 75 and over, this gender discrepancy in marital status has widened; 70 percent of men and only 22 percent of women still have a spouse (U.S. Senate Special Committee on Aging, 1984). Moreover, the probability of having a spouse in old age differs by race and ethnicity as well as by gender. More older whites than Hispanics and more Hispanics than blacks are married.

Marriages are quite stable and divorce is rare among the elderly. Only about 1 percent of all divorces granted during 1975 involved a husband or a wife age 65 years or over (Uhlenberg and Myers, 1981). However, the number of divorced persons in the older population is projected to increase as a result of the rising divorce rate at earlier ages; more individuals who enter old age will have experi-

From *Generations*, Journal of the American Society on Aging, Vol. X, No. 4, Summer 1986, pp. 16-20. Copyright © 1986 by The American Society on Aging.

divorce at an earlier point in
...es.

While some marriages take place in old age, they are rare and more likely to be remarriages of widowed and divorced persons than first-time marriages. It is estimated that older persons constitute only about 1 percent of all brides and 2 percent of all grooms (Treas and VanHilst, 1976). Again, older men are favored; they are twice as likely to marry as older women because they have a larger pool of eligible people from which to select a mate, particularly given the tendency among men to marry women younger than themselves (Atchley, 1985). Moreover, the remarriage interval is only half as long for men as for women. For blacks, the remarriage probabilities for both sexes are lower and the remarriage interval is longer (Brubaker, 1985). In other words, marriage and remarriage rates in later life favor white men.

Older spouses appear to be quite happy in their marriages. They report higher levels of marital satisfaction than do middle-aged spouses, although not as high as youthful newlyweds (Rollins and Feldman, 1970; Gilford and Bengtson, 1979; Markides and Hoppe, 1985). Many older spouses report their marriages to have improved over time (Skolnick, 1981), with the aging years among the happiest periods of the entire family life cycle (Sporakowski and Hughston, 1978). Again, gender differences are observed; men are frequently more satisfied with marriage and the degree to which their emotional needs are fulfilled than are women (Stinnett et al., 1972; Rhyne, 1981; Gilford, 1984), while older women are less hopeful that the warmth and intimacy they seek will be forthcoming in their marriages (Lowenthal et al.,1975). Despite the greater prominence of the marital role for men after midlife (Tamir, 1982), men's happiness may be less dependent than women's upon events within marriage (Rollins and Feldman, 1970), with the likelihood that marriage is more satisfying to men because they need it less.

These same life-course and gender differences in marital satisfaction are found in Hispanic families as well (Markides and Hoppe, 1985). Less is known about older black couples than about whites; data are rare and do not distinguish between middle-class and lower-class couples (Troll et al., 1979). Black couples who are poorly fortified by income, education, and family solidarity against the stresses of late life (Gibson, 1982) might be less likely to report the close, harmonious marital relations (Parron, 1982) enjoyed by their counterparts with greater resources. Regardless of spouses' race or ethnicity, social and personal hardship might be expected to have a negative influence on marital interaction.

Another indication of the quality of older marriages is the desire of older persons to remarry after experiencing marital disruption, usually death of a spouse. Following a mourning period during which attempts at adaptation to the dramatic role-shifts associated with this transition are made, widows and widowers may seek companionship, social roles, and emotional support in a new marriage. Judging by spouses' evaluations and the low divorce rate, later-life remarriages are likely to be successful, especially for couples who have known each other well over a period of years, whose children and peers approve of the marriage, and who have good health, finances, and living conditions (McKain, 1972; Vinick, 1978).

Thus, marriage is a popular status in old age, and if a "happy marriage" is ranked among the most important aspects of life by adult Americans (Campbell et al., 1976), then older spouses are indeed favored, for, as a group, most older husbands and wives appreciate each other and are satisfied with their marriages. What are the special qualities of the marriage relationship that make it so highly valued?

STRENGTHS

Marriage appears to enhance the quality of life for spouses in important ways; married persons, regardless of age, appear to be happier, healthier, and longer-lived than widowed or divorced persons of the same ages (Gove et al., 1983). Older spouses report greater general happiness (Glenn, 1975) and more satisfaction with finances, family life, and friendships (Uhlenberg and Myers, 1981) than any age category of unmarried persons. Satisfaction with marriage is the strongest predictor of life satisfaction for older women and for men is second only to good health (Lee, 1978). Moreover, marriage is said to minimize the potentially disruptive impact of such events as retirement, reduced income, and declining physical capacity that characterize later life for many persons.

These positive effects may emanate from three major functions that marriage, according to Atchley (1985), performs for older couples: intimacy, interdependence, and sense of belonging.

Intimacy, including sexual intimacy, involves mutual affection, regard, trust, and loving (Atchley, 1985). Indeed, a close intimate relationship is a goal for a majority of older couples (Atchley and Miller, 1983), and being in love is considered by older spouses to be the most important factor contributing to the success of their marriages (Stinnett et al., 1972; Sporakowski and Hughston, 1978). These spouses value the marriage relationship for the opportunity to freely express respect, honesty, and their true feelings for one another (Stinnett et al., 1972; Parron, 1982). Sexual interest and activity remain an integral part of marriage, although many older husbands and wives tend to report a decline in frequency of coitus, which they generally attribute to the husband's physiological limitations (Newman and Nichols, 1970). Fortunately, sexual expression in old age takes many forms other than sexual intercourse, including cuddling, touching, exchanging fond looks, dating, dining, and being a couple — all of which continue to be an important source of gratification to older couples.

Interdependence involves sharing of housework, income, and other resources (Atchley, 1985). Spouses are important sources of help to each other and they appear to value the postparental period of marriage for the opportunities that it presents for give and take (Sporakowski and Hughston, 1978; Parron, 1982). Older wives tend to give advice, personal and nursing care, and meal preparation, while husbands help with transportation, and both spouses com-

Despite advantages, older marriages also encounter unique challenges that may undermine their positive tenor and stability.

monly share household tasks (McAuley et al, 1984). Couples who divide responsibility for tasks along nontraditional gender role lines tend to report higher morale and marital satisfaction (Lipman, 1962), but because of women's greater longevity, wives tend to engage in more caregiving than do husbands (Lopata, 1973).

A *sense of belonging* involves identification with couplehood, sharing of values and perspectives, and a routine source of comfortable interaction and socializing (Atchley, 1985). To older spouses, the very meaning of the word marriage denotes a joining of two people as a family (Sporakowski and Hughston, 1978). Such a feeling of unity appears to signal marital success; for long-married couples who value close ties with each other, family, and children tend to enjoy high levels of marital satisfaction (Atchley and Miller, 1983; Gilford, 1984), and couples who have marked the golden wedding milestone claim that a harmonious blending of values and togetherness has continued throughout their marital lives (Parron, 1982).

While the marriage relationship at all stages of its evolving career is far from trouble-free — and long-established marriages are no exception — intimacy, interdependence, and belonging appear to provide meaning and support to partners. Interpersonal support may constitute the special strength that links marital status to the superior well-being of married over unmarried individuals (Gove et al.,1983), and in later life may take on even greater salience as a source of identity and stability of life style. While realization of their greater interdependence in old age draws many couples closer together (Nye and Berardo, 1973), others may find that their marital situation grows worse as they age. What are the conditions that test the strength of the marital bond in later life?

STRAINS

It might seem obvious that older spouses are happy in their long-term marriages; otherwise, it is reasonable to assume, they would have divorced along the way. However, these couples exchanged marriage vows at a time when social pressures ruled out divorce as an alternative to an unhappy marriage. While some unhappy marriages may have been terminated, on the whole the present cohort of "golden-era" couples saw marriage as a lifetime commitment governed by obligation. But commitment is not synonymous with happiness, and obligation may not be the route to marital success.

For example, while older husbands and wives as a group may report moderate to high levels of marital satisfaction (Gilford and Bengtson, 1979), their positive feelings about their marriages do not necessarily persist throughout the remainder of the marital careers. In fact, spouses at the younger and older extremes of old age (ages 55-62 and 70-90) report considerably lower marital satisfaction than do spouses at the mid-state of old age (age 63-69) (Gilford, 1984). Furthermore, over the years of marriage, a decline in spouses' joint participation in activities (Orthner, 1975) and in the amount of love and commitment they express to each other (Swensen et al., 1981; Swensen and Trahaug, 1985) suggest diminished feelings of marital intimacy and belongingness. Declines in marital quality are also indicated in lack of mutual interests, differing values, inability to express true feelings, and frequent disagreements, which a substantial proportion of older spouses freely mention as troublesome aspects of their marriages (Stinnett et al., 1972).

It is also possible that marriage does not play the central integrative role attributed to it. In fact, the widowed, particularly women, who tend to have social skills may be more integrated into informal social networks than are their married counterparts (Kohen, 1983). For older men, a close relationship with a confidant and voluntary participation in an organization contribute more to overall life satisfaction than does marital status (Mouser et al., 1985). And widowed persons who have a confidant frequently have higher morale than married persons without such a close relationship (Lowenthal and Haven, 1968).

Marital conflict may also arise when personal development of husbands and wives follows noncomplementary paths over the life course (Troll et al., 1979; Swensen et al., 1981). The paths are determined by different sets of external demands such as family, work, and community, as well as personalities of the spouses. Developmental trajectories lead men to become more nurturant and women to become more aggressive and assertive (Neugarten, 1968) as they age. These changes in spouses' personal and behavioral orientations may lead to alterations in their expectations and performance of domestic roles. In turn, disagreement over role performance in everyday married life is associated with feelings of inequity and depression in older spouses (Keith and Schafer, 1985) that may impair marital harmony.

Retirement and ill health of one or both spouses are events that most long-lived marriages confront sooner or later. While retirement in and of itself may have no negative effect on the quality of most couples' lives (Atchley and Miller, 1983), the role adjustments that retirement requires can bring out the negative aspects of a marriage, particularly for women. Women appear to benefit less from husbands' retirement than do the retiring husbands, at least in working-class families. The husbands anticipate and enjoy retirement more than their wives do (Kerckhoff, 1964). The wives, particularly those who are older and in poor health, tend to be sorry their husbands retired and to regret it more the longer they are retired (Heyman and Jeffers, 1968). Even with good health and adequate finances, retirement can be problematic. Many wives consider it their responsibility alone to negotiate the couple's transition into retirement. This perception of responsibility may make the wives overly solicitous in planning activities for their husbands, which husbands frequently resent (Keating and Cole, 1980). With the current increase in women's labor force participation, more couples are

*Service providers in the range of community settings
are in a position to strengthen the ties that bind older spouses.*

now called upon to accommodate to the multiple interactive changes in life style associated with retirement of both spouses. Research is needed on the effects of retirement on two-worker marriages.

About 47 percent of all older persons suffer some limitation of activity because of chronic conditions (U.S. Senate Special Committee on Aging, 1984), and their primary source of help is a spouse (Shanas, 1979). Accordingly, care-giving to an ill spouse, usually a husband, is a commonplace role in later life — one which is becoming more prevalent with the dramatic surge occurring in the size of the old-old population. Wives who care for disabled husbands suffer poor health, social and emotional isolation, anger, and frustration (Crossman et al., 1981). The limited data on older husbands who give care indicate that they, too, report strain, though less of it, and use more formal community supports than do wives (Johnson, 1985). Regardless of which spouse gives care, the attendant burdens on both spouses have consequences that severely test the social and emotional resources that maintain the marital bond. Caregiving couples may express satisfaction with their marriages but their responses have a muted quality, with evidence of underlying anger and tension (Johnson, 1985).

In sum, long-lived relationships are a contemporary phenomenon; never in history have the lives of husbands and wives remained interwoven in intact marriages so long as to encounter the constellation of life-changing events that the last stages of the marital career now bring. Earlier socialization and emergent role models do not adequately prepare marital partners to take on the combined stresses, vulnerabilities, and potentials of this new stage of life. Although some couples may have built reserves of intimacy and belongingness on which to draw, other couples may find their interdependency in late life to be inequitably distributed, burdensome, and a source of conflict. These dynamics point to older marriages as a potential focus

for the supportive interventions of social-service providers.

IMPLICATIONS FOR PRACTICE

Older spouses have few outlets for deflecting the tensions that arise in their marriages. They generally have fewer kin, friends, and co-workers with whom to discuss personal and marital issues, and they are reluctant to violate the norm of marital confidentiality between the generations by discussing problems with their children. Few older spouses seek professional help for marital problems. When older adults do see social-service providers, the elders more commonly present problems of anxiety, individual adjustment and family relationships, physical illness and medical planning, finances and housing. However, the association of these problems with alterations in the marriage relationship is seldom explored or moderated because professional counseling is available in only a minority of community-service agencies, and when it is available, it is in high demand (Lowy, 1980).

Service providers in the range of community settings are in a position to strengthen the ties that bind spouses in older marriages. In situations where providers customarily gather information from married clients, providers should inquire into the quality of the marital relationship, assess the types of help that client and spouse exchange, and understand the history of the relationship and its perceived strengths and weaknesses. This procedure allows older clients an opportunity to express their concerns and provides the practitioner with information to guide interventions and referrals. The procedure is particularly important for older women on whom the consequences of their spouses' retirement and illness tend to have a deleterious effect and who may need to express and reconcile their feelings concerning altered patterns of marital interdependence.

Practitioners in social contact settings such as senior centers and congregate meal sites can assist older couples in the development of larger

social networks and renewed social skills suitable to this stage of the marital career. Meaningful volunteer, leadership, and recreational opportunities that these programs offer can replace lost work and other instrumental roles as a source of validation of aspects of the self that may be lacking in spouses' interaction. At the same time, these programs can provide the occasion for socialization and enrichment experiences that renew and reaffirm the spouses' sense of belonging to a couple, a dimension of their lives they may have neglected during the earlier family life-cycle stages so heavily invested in work and parental identities. Task-oriented activity groups offer couples instruction in new skills, for example, cooking, sewing, household repairs, car maintenance, and consumerism, that can introduce and support a more flexible balance of interdependence in household responsibilities. Education programs prepare spouses for the common experiences that may be expected in an aging marriage, helping to reduce strain and improve understanding within couples.

Social services, quite appropriately, have traditionally tended to focus on the remedial needs of the frail, dependent, and deteriorated elderly, who comprise from 5 to 20 percent of people over the age of 65. But there is also need for social programs that increase opportunities for adequate functioning and contribution of the well elderly, who constitute the majority of the older population (Hartford, 1985). Social programs have appeared to overlook well, older couples as a consumer population, possibly on the common assumption that their marital status protects them from distress. Yet older husbands and wives may need social and professional support as they undertake to redefine the marital relationship and reestablish the bases of mutuality that bind them. For better or for worse, the marital bond represents the last major primary relationship in later life. Service providers have the knowledge, skills, values, and capacity to strengthen this relationship with programs that support older spouses in accomplishing the developmental tasks that enable marriages to survive and thrive.

REFERENCES

Atchley, R., 1985. *Social Forces and Aging,* 4th ed., Belmont, Calif.: Wadsworth.

Atchley, R. and Miller, S., 1983. "Types of Elderly Couples." In T. Brubaker, ed., *Family Relationships in Later Life.* Beverly Hills, Calif.: Sage Publications.

Brubaker, T., 1985. *Later Life Families.* Beverly Hills, Calif.: Sage Publications.

Campbell, A., Converse, P. and Rodgers, W., 1976. *The Quality of American Life.* New York: Russell Sage Foundation.

Crossman, L., London, C. and Barry, C., 1981. "Older Women Caring for Disabled Spouses: A Model for Supportive Services." *Gerontologist* 21(5):464-70.

Gibson, R., 1982. "Blacks at Middle and Late Life: Resources and Coping." *The Annals* 464(November):79-90.

Gilford, R., 1984. "Contrasts in Marital Satisfaction Throughout Old Age: An Exchange Theory Analysis." *Journal of Gerontology* 39(3):325-33.

Gilford, R. and Bengtson, V., 1979. "Measuring Marital Satisfaction in Three Generations: Positive and Negative Dimensions." *Journal of Marriage and the Family* 41(2):387-98.

Glenn, N., 1975. "The Contribution of Marriage to the Psychological Well-Being of Males and Females." *Journal of Marriage and the Family* 37(3):594-601.

Glick, P. and Norton, A., 1977. "Marrying, Divorcing, and Living Together in the U.S. Today." *Population Bulletin* 32:1-39.

Gove, W., Hughes, M. and Style, C., 1983. "Does Marriage Have Positive Effects on the Psychological Well-Being of the Individual?" *Journal of Health and Social Behavior* 24(June):122-31.

Hartford, M., 1985. "Understanding Normative Growth and Development in Aging: Working with Strengths." *Journal of Gerontological Social Work* 8(3/4):37-54.

Heyman, D. and Jeffers, F., 1968. "Wives and Retirement: A Pilot Study." *Journal of Gerontology* 23(4):488-96.

Johnson, C., 1985. "The Impact of Illness on Late-Life Marriages." *Journal of Marriage and the Family* 47(1):165-72.

Keating, N. and Cole, P., 1980. "What Do I Do With Him 24 Hours a Day? Changes in the Housewife Role After Retirement." *Gerontologist* 20(1):84-89.

Keith, P. and Schafer, R., 1985. "Equity, Role Strains, and Depression Among Middle Aged and Older Men and Women." In W. Peterson and J. Quadagno, eds., *Social Bonds in Later Life.* Beverly Hills, Calif.: Sage Publications.

Kerckhoff, A., 1964. "Husband-Wife Expectations and Reactions to Retirement." *Journal of Gerontology* 19(4):510-16.

Kohen, J., 1983. "Old But Not Alone: Informal Social Supports Among the Elderly by Marital Status and Sex." *Gerontologist* 23(1):57-63.

Lee, G., 1978. "Marriage and Morale in Later Life." *Journal of Marriage and the Family* 40(1):131-39.

Lipman, A., 1962. "Role Conceptions of Couples in Retirement." In C. Tibbitts and W. Donahue, eds., *Social and Psychological Aspects of Aging.* New York: Columbia University Press.

Lopata, H., 1973. *Widowhood in an American City.* Cambridge, Mass.: Schenkman.

Lowenthal, M. and Haven, C., 1968. "Interaction and Adaptation: Intimacy as a Critical Variable." *American Sociological Review* 33(1):20-30.

Lowenthal, M., Thurnher, M. and Chiriboga, D., 1975. *Four Stages of Life.* San Francisco: Jossey-Bass.

Lowy, L., 1980. "Mental Health Services in the Community." In J. Birren and R. Sloane, eds., *Handbook of Mental Health and Aging.* Englewood Cliffs, N.J.: Prentice-Hall, Inc.

Markides, K. and Hoppe, S., 1985. "Marital Satisfaction in Three Generations of Mexican Americans." *Social Science Quarterly* 66(March):147-54.

McAuley, W., Jacobs, M. and Carr, C., 1984. "Older Couples: Patterns of Assistance and Support." *Journal of Gerontological Social Work* 6(4):35-48.

McKain, W., 1972. "A New Look at Older Marriages." *Family Coordinator* 21(1):61-69.

Mouser, N., Powers, E., Keith, P. and Goudy, W., 1985. "Marital Status and Life Satisfaction: A Study of Older Men." In W. Peterson and J. Quadagno, eds., *Social Bonds in Later Life.* Beverly Hills, Calif.: Sage Publications.

Neugarten, B., 1968. "Toward a Psychology of the Life Cycle." In B. Neugarten, ed., *Middle Age and Aging.* Chicago: University of Chicago Press.

Newman, G. and Nichols, C., 1970. "Sexual Activities and Attitudes in Older Persons." In E. Palmore, ed., *Normal Aging.* Durham, N.C. Duke University Press.

Nye, I. and Berardo, F., 1973. *The Family: Its Structure and Interaction.* New York: Macmillan.

Orthner, D., 1975. "Leisure Activity Patterns and Marital Career." *Journal of Marriage and the Family* 37(1):91-102.

Parron, E., 1982. "Golden Wedding Couples: Lessons in Marital Longevity." *Generations* 7(2):14, 15, 34.

Rhyne, C., 1981. "Bases of Marital Satisfaction Among Men and Women." *Journal of Marriage and the Family* 43(4):941-55.

Rollins, B. and Feldman, H., 1970. "Marital Satisfaction Over the Family Life Cycle." *Journal of Marriage and the Family* 32(1):20-28.

Rosow, I., 1973. "The Social Context of the Aging Self." *Gerontologist* 13(1):82-87.

Shanas, E., 1979. "The Family as a Social Support System in Old Age." *Gerontologist* 19(2):169-74.

Skolnick, A., 1981. "Married Lives: Longitudinal Perspectives on Marriage." In D. Eichorn, J. Clausen, N. Haan, M. Honzik and P. Mussen, eds., *Present and Past in Middle Life.* New York: Academic Press.

Sporakowski, M. and Hughston, G., 1978. "Prescriptions for Happy Marriage: Adjustments and Satisfactions of Couples Married for 50 or More Years." *Family Coordinator* 27(4):321-27.

Stinnett, N., Carter, L. and Montgomery, J., 1972. "Older Persons' Perceptions of Their Marriages." *Journal of Marriage and the Family* 34(4):665-70.

Swensen, C. and Trahaug, G., 1985. "Commitment and the Long-Term Marriage Relationship." *Journal of Marriage and the Family* 47(4):939-45.

Swensen, C., Eskew, R. and Kohlhepp, K., 1981. "Stage of Family Life Cycle, Ego Development, and the Marriage Relationship." *Journal of Marriage and the Family* 43(4):841-53.

Tamir, L., 1982. "Men at Middle Age: Developmental Transitions." *The Annals* 464(November):47-56.

Treas, J. and VanHilst, A., 1976. "Marriage and Remarriage Rates Among Older Americans." *Gerontologist* 16(2):132-36.

Troll, L., Atchley, R. and Miller, S., 1979. *Families in Later Life.* Belmont, Calif.: Wadsworth.

Uhlenberg, P. and Myers, M., 1981. "Divorce and the Elderly." *Gerontologist* 21(3):276-82.

U.S. Senate Special Committee on Aging/American Association of Retired Persons, 1984. *Aging America: Trends and Projections,* 2nd ed., Washington, D.C.

Vinick, B., 1978. "Remarriage in Old Age." *Family Coordinator* 27(4):359-63.

Religiosity, Aging, and Life Satisfaction

Harold Cox, PhD
André Hammonds, PhD

Harold Cox and André Hammonds are affiliated with the Department of Sociology and Social Work, Indiana State University, Terre Haute, IN 47809.

ABSTRACT. A review of the past studies of religiosity and aging indicates that a number of common patterns of church attendance, belief in God, life satisfaction and personal adjustment can be found. Past research indicates that church attendance hits a low point between 18 and 24, remains relatively stable between 25 and 54, rises slightly after 54 and drops slightly after 80. Thus for most of one's adult life up to age 80, church attendance is fairly stable with a slight rise in the later years. The data indicated that a majority of all age groups express a belief in God but that the older one becomes the more likely he/she is to express a belief in God. There is a tendency for a higher percentage of older age groups to believe that religion is important in one's life and to believe in immortality. All of the past studies that looked at religiosity and life satisfaction came to the same conclusion—those persons who attend church experience greater life satisfaction and are better adjusted than those who do not. A plausible explanation for the positive value that religious participation has on the lives of the elderly is that the church becomes a focal point of social integration and activity for the elderly, providing them with a sense of community and well-being. This concept of the positive functions the church serves in the lives of the elderly is analogous to Durkheim's discussion of the church as a moral community.

INTRODUCTION

When reviewing the past articles and research reports that address the subject of religion and aging, one cannot help but notice the dearth of materials that exist on this topic. On occasion, sociology of religion textbooks will refer to religious participation over the life cycle, to age and religious participation or to differences in religious participation by men and women. In examining research articles in the various gerontology journals, one will find a few articles dealing with religion and aging but this clearly is not a topic that has caught the imagination and attention of large numbers of gerontologists. Given the fact that the great majority of older persons profess some religious belief and when questioned will assert that religion is very important in their lives, the sparsity of scientific writing on this subject is surprising. Assuming that a knowledge of the relationship between religion and aging should provide us with greater insight into the beliefs, values, and attitudes of a very large percent of the older American population, this paper will attempt to review the past research on this topic, to summarize the more significant findings of these studies, and to suggest future directions for researchers interested in this field.

CHURCH ATTENDANCE

While researchers have devised a variety of methods to measure a person's religiosity, perhaps one of the quickest and best indicators of religious commitment is church attendance. Several studies have examined church attendance to determine what pattern was most prevalent over the life cycle. The early studies done in the 1950s and 1960s had indicated a slightly higher church attendance among older people than among younger people.[1] Later studies done in the 1970s did not indicate this pattern of church attendance.[2] The research findings on church attendance throughout the life cycle are inconclusive and subject to a variety of interpretations. One major problem of interpretation is that most of these were cross-sectional studies based on interviews and questionnaires given to younger and older persons at a single point in time. Thus, in the cross-sectional studies it is impossible to determine whether these differences show changes over time or whether the recent generations are simply less religious than earlier ones.

Bahr reviewed the earliest studies of church attendance and developed four different models based on the findings of these studies.[3] These models are:

1. The traditional model which reveals a steady drop in church attendance from ages 18-35 with the lowest point for most people being between 30 to 35 after which church attendance increases until old age.
2. The stability model asserts that there is no relationship between aging and church attendance and that the pattern of church attendance remains stable throughout one's lifetime.
3. The family cycle model indicates that church attendance is altered by stages of the family cycle. Families peak in church attendance when the children reach Sunday school age. As the children grow up and leave home, the church attendance of the parents begins to drop.
4. The disengagement model assumes that like many other areas of social participation after middle age, church attendance declines.

The pattern of religious belief and church attendance found by most of the more recent studies tends to indicate a stability of religious belief and church attendance over the life cycle, the only exception being a decline in church attendance among the very old. Blazer and Palmore report that religious beliefs and attitudes remain fairly stable over the life cycle with no significant increase or decrease.[4] They did however find a gradual decrease in religious activity during the later years. Similarly Riley and Foner, in their inventory of research on religion, observed that church attendance tends to decrease rather than increase in old age.[5] Moberg also observed a pattern of declining church attendance among older persons.[6]

The 1975 Harris poll (see Table 1) indicates a low in church attendance between ages 18-24 and a fairly stable attendance pattern over the life cycle with a slight increase after the age of 55 and a slight decrease after the age of 80.[7]

The Harris findings confirmed the earlier findings of Havighurst and Albreckt[8] that women attend church more frequently and maintain a higher degree of religious participation for a longer period of time than men do.

From *Journal of Religion and Aging*, Vol. 5, Nos. 1/2, 1988, pp. 1-21. Copyright © 1989 by The Haworth Press, Inc.

TABLE 1

Attendance at a Church or Synagogue in Last Year or So

	Attended in Last Year %	Within Last Week or Two %	A Month Ago %	More Than 3 Months Ago %	Not Sure %	%
	When Attended Last					
Total Public	75	71	13	7	9	*
18 to 64	74	70	14	7	9	*
65 and over	77	79	9	5	7	*
18 to 24	67	60	18	8	14	*
25 to 39	73	72	11	7	10	*
40 to 54	78	70	15	8	7	--
55 to 64	81	79	11	4	6	--
65 to 69	80	79	9	5	6	1
70 to 79	78	79	10	4	7	*
80 and over	68	76	10	6	8	*

*Less than 0.5 per cent.
Source: Louis Harris and Associates, The Myth and Reality of Aging in America, Washington, D.C.: National Council on the Aging, 1975, p. 181.

Lazerwitz found that among persons 65 and over, 66 percent of the Catholics, 46 percent of the Protestants, and 25 percent of the Jews attended church regularly.[9]

While the diverse research findings on age and church attendance do not entirely support any of Bahr's four models, there appear to be some common trends. Other than for 18-24 year olds, the pattern of church attendance over the life cycle is fairly stable with a slight increase after age 55 and a slight decrease after age 80. The low point in church attendance for 18-24 year olds can perhaps best be explained by the fact that this is a period of transition in their lives from teenage to adult status. They are frequently moving away from their home communities to go into the service, attend college or to take a job. It takes time to become established in the new community and reestablish the same religious ties and commitments they had in their home community. The drop in church attendance and activity noted in many of the studies among the very old was probably related to poor health and a lack of available transportation to attend church services.

BELIEF IN GOD

Crandall argues that a person's commitment to religious beliefs is important because it tends to shape his/her attitudes, beliefs, opinions and values.[10] Simultaneously it provides the individual a framework with which to see and interpret events in the world for himself/herself and others.

Riley and Foner indicated that the older the person was, the more likely he/she was to express a belief in God.[11] In every age category from the 18-24 to the 65 and over group, the proportion expressing a belief in God increases.

These results were obtained, however, from cross-sectional data and it is impossible to determine if this reflects an increase in religious belief as one ages or merely generational differences in belief. Some would argue that this is a reflection of the increasing secularization of society by which each succeeding age cohort is somewhat less religious than their predecessors.

Whether these differences are a result of generational differences in religious belief or of a gradual shift in religious belief over the life cycle, it does appear that the current group of older persons is more likely to believe in God and to consider religion more important than those persons under 65.

It is interesting to note a similar pattern of response by age when inquiring about the importance of religion in one's life.[12] According to Harris' data, only 34 percent of those persons 18-24 indicate that religion is "very important" but 73 percent of those 80+ do so (Table 2).

BELIEF IN IMMORTALITY

The belief in immortality may have special significance for older persons since they must recognize that at some point they will die. Moreover the older they become, the more they must realize and accept the fact that death for them will occur sometime in the not too distant future. Past studies have indicated that most older persons have come to accept the reality of their own death and are not unduly worried about the termination of their lives.

While one's degree of religious faith and commitment apparently remains fairly stable over the life cycle, Stark hypothesized that because of its special relevance for the elderly, belief in immortality would increase systematically with age.[13] The data clearly indicate that this is the case for Protestants whether liberal, moderate, or conservative, but not for Catholics for whom the data are ambiguous and difficult to interpret (Table 3).

In a study of the psychology of religion, Pratt had observed that in the modern secular world, religion had lost much of its sacred and supernatural status and the most important pragmatic value of religion was the belief in a personal future life.[14] In a similar view, Riley and Foner conclude after a review of the research on religion that belief in God and immortality is firmly ingrained in most older people and the public as well.[15]

ORTHODOX RELIGION

Stark attempted to determine if people were more orthodox in their religious belief as they aged.[16] Orthodox religious beliefs were presumed by Stark to be the most conservative beliefs and he felt that older persons might be more likely to hold these beliefs. The four measures of orthodox belief which Stark measured were a firm belief in a personal God, a belief in the divinity of Jesus Christ, a belief in the authenticity of biblical miracles and a belief in the existence of the devil. As Table 4 indicates, Stark did not find a gradual shift toward orthodox religious beliefs as one ages but rather a lower percentage of orthodox believers for those post-World War II generations. The meaningful shift for both moderate

TABLE 2

The Importance of Religion in Your Life

	18-64	65+	18-24	25-39	40-54	55-64	65-69	70-79	80+
Very important	49	71	34	45	58	65	69	71	73
Somewhat important	33	21	40	35	29	25	22	21	19
Hardly important at all	17	7	25	20 o	12	10 o	8	8 o	6
Not sure	1	1	1		1		1		

o
 Less than 0.5 percent.
SOURCE: Louis Harris and Associates, The Myths and Realities of Aging 1975.

TABLE 3

Age and Belief in Life after Death

Percentage who think it "completely true" that
"there is a life beyond death"

Age:	Liberal Protestants		Moderate Protestants		Conservative Protestants		Roman Catholics	
Under 20	38%	(21)	56%	(16)	87%	(15)	90% a	(10)
20-29	41	(95)	62	(99)	90	(89)	84	(93)
30-39	47	(249)	65	(205)	92	(105)	78	(145)
40-49	44	(278)	69	(251)	90	(103)	77	(122)
50-59	51	(169)	75	(149)	99	(68)	80	(87)
60-69	75	(91)	86	(92)	96	(45)	81	(47)
70 and over	70	(52)	87	(59)	100	(20)	78	(18)

aToo few cases for a stable percentage, presented for descriptive interest only.
Source: Rodney Stark, "Age and Faith: A Changing Outlook or an Old Process?" in Religion in Sociological Perspective: Essays in the Empirical Study of Religion, edited by Charles Y. Glock. Belmont, CA: Wadsworth.

and conservative Protestants came between the prewar generations who were above 50 in age and the 40-year olds who were considered by Stark to be the postwar generations. The postwar generations were less likely to hold orthodox religious beliefs. The Catholics remained fairly orthodox throughout the life cycle. The liberal Protestants were relatively nonorthodox in religious belief throughout the life cycle.

Stark concluded that post—World War II America was a more urban and a considerably more secular society and as a result less accepting of orthodox religious beliefs. Stark states:

World War II was a watershed between the new world and the older America of parochial small-town and rural society. While all the persons in this sample live today in this new America, those past fifty did not grow up in it. This data strongly suggests that in new America traditional Christian orthodoxy is less powerful.[17]

Wingrove and Alston noted a similar trend toward secularization of society when they concluded that all cohorts reached their peak in religious service attendance between 1950 and 1960.[18] They found that after 1965 all cohorts showed a decline in religious attendance.

RELIGIOUS RITUALISM AND PRIVATE DEVOTIONALISM

Stark examined the relationship between age and both religious ritual involvement and private devotionalism.[19] The relationship which Stark found between ritual involvement and private devotionalism can be seen in Table 5.

The only noticeable pattern for Protestants was for those persons 70 and over to be more inclined to ritual commitment than those under 70. There seems to be no distinct pattern for those under 70 except that those under 20 are a bit less likely to become involved in ritual than are those over 20. It should be noted, however, that there are so few respondents under 20 that one should be careful in drawing any conclusions. Other than the under 20 group being less involved in ritual than the rest, there appears to be no noticeable relationship between ritual involvement and age of Roman Catholics.

The most notable result of Stark's research can be seen in the bottom half of Table 5 where it seems apparent that private devotionalism increases noticeably with age. Only 34 percent of the liberal Protestants in their 20s scored high on private devotionalism, whereas 48 percent of those in their 50s and 68 percent of those 70 and over did so. For moderate Protestants, the figures indicate that private devotionalism was practiced by 35 percent for those in their

TABLE 4

Age and Orthodoxy

===

Percent High on Orthodoxy Index

Age:	Liberal Protestants	Moderate Protestants	Conservative Protestants	Roman Catholics
Under 20	5 (19)	29 (15)	a (12)	a (9)
20-29	10 (91)	26 (95)	75 (89)	64 (89)
30-39	10 (243)	27 (203)	79 (101)	66 (141)
40-49	9 (262)	28 (244)	78 (102)	48 (124)
Postwar generations				

Prewar generations				
50-59	11 (157)	40 (134)	94 (67)	61 (83)
60-69	14 (80)	49 (79)	89 (43)	73 (41)
70 and over	27 (40)	45 (51)	100 (19)	64 (15)

----

a Too few cases for stable percentages

SOURCE: Rodney Stark, "Age and Faith: A Changing Outlook or an Old Process?" in Religion in Sociological Perspective: Essays in the Empirical Study of Religion, edited by Charles Y. Glock. Belmont, CA: Wadsworth.

20s, 58 percent for those in their 50s and 81 percent for those 70 and over. The proportions of conservative Protestants who engaged in private devotionalism were 62 percent for those 70 and older. Among Roman Catholics the same pattern is found going from 56 percent for 20-year olds to 74 percent for 50-year olds to 75 percent for those 70 and above.

Moberg[20] and Hammond[21] both found a similar pattern of private devotionalism and age and concluded that although church attendance or "external" religious practices decline with increasing age, internal religious practices such as reading the Bible at home, praying, and listening or watching religious programs on radio and television all increase.

This turning inward to very private and personal religious practices as confirmed by several researchers would seem to be consistent with the psychological studies of personality changes in later life which indicate a closure of personality in old age and less need for group support and external sanctions for one's behavior.

RELIGIOSITY AND LIFE SATISFACTION

A number of scientists have observed the potentially positive value that religious faith and activities can have on the lives of older Americans. Barron notes some of the psychological supports that religion provides for older persons which include helping them: (1) face impending death; (2) find and maintain a sense of meaningfulness and significance in life; (3) accept the inevitable losses of old age; and (4) discover and utilize the compensatory values that are potential in old age.[22] Socially the church provides a number of functions which can be particularly useful for older Americans. The church provides a variety of different social activities which bring people of all ages and backgrounds together. The social interaction that ensues tends to pull the individual into an active social involvement and to reduce social isolation. These activities can involve the older persons in community concerns and the current issues of the day, whatever they may be, since they will inevitably be discussed on such occasions. Moreover, the interest shown the individual by others involved in the activities becomes a source of social support. In addition, they draw the older person's attention away from himself/herself and to the problems and concerns of others. All of these things have positive consequences for the older person and are likely to improve the overall morale and outlook on life. Wolff observed that religious belief, prayer, and faith in God all helped the aged to overcome many of the common problems of old age such as loneliness, grief and unhappiness.[23]

A number of studies have attempted to determine if there was a positive relationship between religion and life satisfaction for older Americans. Moberg and Taves made a study of church participation and life adjustment in old age.[24] They questioned 5000 persons over 65 in four midwestern states. They found that church members had higher personal adjustment scores than nonmembers and that church leaders and officers had higher adjustment scores than the church members. They concluded that their evidence convincingly indicated church participation was related to good personal adjustment in later life. Moberg and Taves did observe that the direction of this relationship was difficult to determine. Do those who are

TABLE 5

Public Ritual Involvement, Private Devotionalism, and Age

==

Percent High on Index of Public Ritual Involvement

Age	Liberal Protestants		Moderate Protestants		Conservative Protestants		Roman Catholics	
						a		a
Under 20	19	(21)	38	(16)	36	(14)	30	(10)
20-29	23	(97)	40	(99)	73	(89)	46	(92)
30-39	38	(247)	45	(208)	73	(107)	47	(146)
40-49	28	(282)	46	(258)	75	(104)	46	(129)
50-59	24	(168)	41	(146)	83	(65)	43	(94)
60-69	24	(95)	47	(90)	75	(43)	54	(46)
70 and over	54	(54)	53	(60)	90	(21)	41	(22)

Percent High on Index of Private Devotionalism

Age	Liberal Protestants		Moderate Protestants		Conservative Protestants		Roman Catholics	
						a		a
Under 20	37	(19)	29	(14)a	64	(14)	56	(9)
20-29	34	(90)	35	(97)	62	(87)	58	(93)
30-39	41	(237)	43	(204)	75	(105)	63	(142)
40-49	35	(268)	46	(246)	79	(104)	62	(125)
50-59	48	(163)	58	(148)	88	(68)	74	(91)
60-69	51	(94)	71	(93)	93	(45)	77	(47)
70 and over	68	(53)	81	(57)	96	(21)	75	(20)

a
    Too few cases for stable percentages, presented for descriptive purposes only.

Source: Rodney Stark, "Age and Faith: A Changing Outlook or an Old Process?" in Religion in Sociological Perspective: Essays in the Empirical Study of Religion, edited by Charles Y. Glock. Belmont, CA:Wadsworth.

well adjusted choose to engage in many religious activities or does engaging in many religious activities lead one to be well adjusted?

Studies by both Edwards and Klemmeck[25] and Spreitzer and Snyder[26] came to the same conclusion regarding the positive value of religious participation for older persons. Their evidence indicated that religiosity was related to life satisfaction and other measures of well-being for older persons. Similarly, Blazer and Palmore found that happiness and a sense of usefulness and personal adjustment are significantly related to religious activity and attitudes.[27]

Guy, in a study of religion and life satisfaction, found that the group which scored highest on the measure of life satisfaction was the one which reported attending church more frequently today than fifteen years ago.[28] They were closely followed by the group whose church attendance pattern had remained relatively stable. Respondents attending church less today than fifteen years ago score lower than the other two groups (on life satisfaction) with the lowest (on life satisfaction) scores being made by those who never attended church. Similarly, Markides, in a study of church attendance, self-rated religiosity, and practice of private prayer and life satisfaction, found only church attendance was significantly related to life satisfaction.[29] Markides concluded that apparently the integrative function of religion was the crucial determinant of life satisfaction rather than the spiritual function.

Ortega, Crutchfield and Rushing's findings, in a study of race differences and personal well-being of the elderly, would tend to support Markides' argument with a respect to the integrative function of the church.[30] Ortega et al. found elderly blacks reporting higher life satisfaction scores than elderly whites. After introducing a multitude of control variables to explain the race differences in life satisfaction scores, they concluded:

that control with friends mediates the relationship only where friendships have the church as their locus. It appears that the

association between race and life satisfaction is due, at least in part, to greater church related friends among the black elderly.[31]

One possible explanation of their findings which they suggest is that the black church in the South forms a focal point of the community, serving as a pseudo-extended family, particularly for the aged. As noted, this argument is very similar to Markides' hypothesis of the integrative function of religion.

The past studies then overwhelmingly support the fact that there is a positive relationship between religious belief, religious participation and life satisfaction in later life. While as Moberg observed, it is not possible at this time to determine the direction of this relationship, it is clear that older church members score higher on tests of personal adjustment, maintain a healthier outlook on life and express a greater degree of life satisfaction. Markides and Ortega et al. argue that the church serves as a focal point for individual and community integration of the elderly and that this is crucial to their sense of personal well-being.[32]

CONCLUSION

The subject of religion and aging has not been one of the more widely researched areas of gerontology. Admittedly there may be a degree of scientific bias here since scientists are somewhat less likely to be religious than the general public and simultaneously may reflect the more secular attitudes of a society that is becoming more urbanized.

Regardless of the limited and sometimes dated nature of studies of religion and aging, some trends and patterns can be located. Church attendance hits a low point between 18 and 24, remains relatively stable between 25 and 54, rises slightly after 54 and drops slightly after the age of 80. Most researchers concluded that the drop in church after age 80 is a reflection of the declining health of older persons and the fact that many of them don't drive and frequently have no way of getting to church. For most of one's adult life up to age 80 then, church attendance is fairly stable with a slight rise in the later years. Stark has estimated that this pattern of church attendance may not remain true for future generations of old persons since he felt that the post-World War II generations were on the whole somewhat less likely to attend church than their elders had been. Blazer and Palmore, in one of the few longitudinal studies of religious attitudes and participation, found that religious attitudes are fairly constant over time but that religious activities do decline with age.

In terms of the individuals believing in God, past research had indicated that a majority of all age groups express a belief in God, but that the older one becomes, the more likely he/she is to express belief in God. Similar patterns were found with regard to the importance of religion in a person's life, and a belief in immortality. Once again, a majority of all age groups believe that religion is important in life and believe in immortality. There is a tendency for a higher percentage of the older age groups to believe that religion is important in one's life and to believe in immortality. Since these studies of church attendance and religious beliefs have, for the most part, been cross-sectional, the interpretation of the results and any conclusions drawn must be made with considerable caution.

Stark, in examining whether persons became more orthodox and conservative in their religious beliefs as they aged, did not find this to be the case. He felt that his most significant finding was that the post-World War II generations were less likely to be orthodox in their religious beliefs.

In terms of their involvement in private devotions several studies found that older persons were more likely to engage in private devotions than younger age groups. Apparently older persons compensate for some of their decline in religious activity which Blazer and Palmore found by engaging in private devotions. Perhaps the psychological studies which indicate a closure of personality and a turning inward on the part of older persons are true and can explain the increase in private devotionalism on the part of the older persons.

All of the past studies that looked at religion and life satisfaction came to the same conclusions: those persons who attend church experience greater life satisfaction and are better adjusted than the average church member. This relationship may, in part, be explained by Crandall's[33] observation that faith in religion provides the individual with a philosophy of life as well as a whole series of attitudes, values and beliefs which help him interpret and understand the world around him. Moreover, persons with strong religious beliefs are likely to attend church services and social functions which are comprised of others who share their beliefs and views of reality and thereby receive group support for their convictions. Markides'[34] and Ortega's[35] studies indicated that the church provides for individuals a sense of social and community integration which is highly correlated with their sense of personal well-being. This integrative function of the church described by Markides and Ortega is very similar to Durkheim's discussion of the church as a moral community.[36]

Religious activities tend to provide useful roles for older persons during the retirement years. They can become deacons, elders, or Sunday school teachers and thus assume leadership roles in religious activities which they may have been deprived of in work activities at the time of their retirement. Since the work of the church in ministering to the needs of the community is a never ending task, there are always a great variety of volunteer activities the older person can become involved in from visiting the homebound, to working with counseling services, to directing a recreational program for young people. The church does provide for its older members a wide range of social activities which tend to pull the older person into contact with other people and to reduce the possibility of social isolation and loneliness. Regardless of the reasons, older church members tend to be happier and better adjusted than non-members.

A critical unanswered question which researchers in this field should address is whether Stark is correct that post-World War II generations are less religious and less orthodox in their religious views than those born prior to this time.

ENDNOTES

1. Joseph H. Fichter, "The Profile of Catholic Religious Life," *American Journal of Sociology*, 1952, 58:145-149; Geoffry Gorer, *Exploring English Character* (London: Cresset, 1955); Charles Y. Glock, Benjamin Ringer, and Earl Babbie, *To Comfort and to Challenge* (Berkeley: University of California Press, 1967).

2. C. Ray Wingrove and Jon P. Alston, "Age and Church Attendance," *The Gerontologist*, 1971, 4:356-358.

3. Harvard M. Bahr, "Aging and Religious Disaffiliation," *Social Forces*, 1970, 49:57-71.

4. Dan Blazer and Erdman Palmore, "Religion and Aging in a Longitudinal Panel," *The Gerontologist*, 1976, 16:82-85.

5. Matilda White Riley and Ann Foner, *Aging and Society, Vol. 1: An Inventory of Research Findings* (New York: Russell Sage, 1968).

6. David O. Moberg, "Religiosity in Old Age," *The Gerontologist*, 1965, 5:80.

7. Louis Harris and Associates, *The Myth and Reality of Aging in America* (Washington, DC: National Council on the Aging, 1975).

8. Robert J. Havighurst and Ruth Albreckt, *Older People* (New York: Logmans Green, 1953), pp. 202-203.

9. Bernard Lazerwitz, "Some Factors Associated with Variations in Church Attendance," *Social Forces*, 1961, 39:301-305.

10. Richard C. Crandall, *Gerontology: A Behavioral Science Approach* (Reading, MA: Addison Wesley, 1980).

11. Op. cit.

12. Op. cit.

13. Rodney Stark, "Age and Faith: A Changing Outlook or an Old Process?" in *Religion in Sociological Perspective: Essays in the Empirical Study of Religion*, edited by Charles Y. Glock (Belmont, CA: Wadsworth, 1973), p. 4.

14. James B. Pratt, *The Religious Consciousness* (New York: Macmillan, 1928).

15. Op. cit.

16. Stark, p. 51.

17. Ibid.

18. Op. cit.

19. Stark, p. 55.

20. Op. cit.

21. Philip E. Hammond, "Aging and the Ministry," in *Aging and Society, Vol. 2, Aging and the Professions*, edited by Matilda White Riley, John W. Riley, Jr., and Marilyn E. Johnson (New York: Russell Sage, 1969) pp. 293-323.

22. Milton L. Barron, *The Aging: An Introduction to Social Gerontology and Geriatrics* (New York: Thomas Y. Crowell, 1961), p. 166.

23. Kurt Wolff, "Group Psychotherapy with Geriatric Patients in a State Hospital Setting: Results of a Three-Year Study," *Group Psychotherapy*, 1959, 12:218-222.

24. David Moberg and Marvin J. Taves, "Church Participation and Adjustment in Old Age," in *Older People and Their Social World*, edited by Arnold M. Rose and Warren A. Peterson (Philadelphia, PA: F. A. Davis, 1956).

25. J. N. Edwards and D. L. Klemmach, "Correlates of Life Satisfaction: A Reexamination," *Journal of Gerontology*, 1973, 28:497-502.

26. Elmer Spreitzer and Eddon E. Snyder, "Correlates of Life Satisfaction Among the Aged," *Journal of Gerontology*, 1974, 29:454-458.

27. Op. cit.

28. Rebecca Faith Guy, "Religion, Physical Disabilities, and Life Satisfaction in Older Age Cohorts," *International Journal of Aging and Human Development*, 1982, 15:225-232.

29. Kyriakos S. Markides, "Aging, Religiosity, and Adjustment: A Longitudinal Analysis," *Journal of Gerontology*, 1983, 38:621-625.

30. Suzanne T. Ortega, Robert D. Crutchfield, and William A. Rushing, "Race Differences in Elderly Personal Well Being, Friendship, Family and Church," *Research on Aging*, 1983, 5:101-118.

31. Ibid., pp. 110-111.

32. Op. cit.

33. Op. cit.

34. Op. cit.

35. Op. cit.

36. E. Durkheim, *The Elementary Forms of Religious Life*, translated by J. W. Swain (New York: The Free Press, 1915).

Starting over at midlife: Why there's more satisfaction to life after 40

MARK GERZON

More than 50 years ago, psychologist Carl Jung wrote that "the elements of the psyche undergo in the course of life a very marked change—so much so, that we may distinguish between a psychology of the morning of life and a psychology of its afternoon." The afternoon of my life began at the age of 38. It was then that I began to discover both a darkness and light within me that I never before knew existed.

On the one hand was pain, which I had been blocking out and denying for years. On the other hand was joy, a deep serenity and profound aliveness that I did not know existed. The first half of my life, as rich and rewarding as it had felt at the time, now seemed as if it had been limited to a narrow band of experience. Outside of the reality of my earlier life were parts of myself that I had barely even glimpsed.

I entered midlife under the influence of our culture's widespread belief that one of two things happen to us at that age: Either we remain solid, stable, fixed, serious, and "grown-up," or we have a "midlife crisis" and all hell breaks loose. A midlife crisis is viewed as a sign of mental, and often marital instability; it is something to be ashamed of. When friends and relatives refer to it, the comments are often punctuated with snickers—and sometimes laced with anger.

I was determined not to become one of those people whose life suddenly turns upside-down. I was so busy avoiding the midlife crisis that I risked missing what I've come to look on as "the midlife quest."

The quest awaits us all. We may ignore it, postpone it, resist it, or embrace it. But we cannot avoid it. Physically, socially, economically, psychologically, sexually—in every respect—the agenda of the second half of our life varies greatly from the agenda of the first. We turn midlife into a "midlife crisis" by pretending that everything is supposed to stay the same. But it isn't.

Based on my own experiences, the lives of others, and a review of fiction and scholarship about midlife, I am convinced that the second half of human lives is a profound opportunity for transformation. It is a chance to live by new rules, and to catch a second, and deeper, wind.

The second half is an extraordinary opportunity because, quite literally, it has not been ordinarily available until now. For most of humanity, and throughout most of history, the forties were on the far horizon of the human lifespan. Many men and women died of illness long before then; those who reached their forties had lived "full lives." Some, blessed with exceptional resistance to disease and a vigorous constitution, lived longer. But it is only quite recently that entire generations have lived long enough to experience midlife as a transition, not an end. Nowadays, people live into their seventies, eighties, and beyond. If we are reasonably healthy, we are eventually going to have to face midlife.

Sadly, we are often unprepared for this critical transition to the second half of our lives. Neither our workplaces nor other social institutions recognize and respect the necessity of midlife change and renewal. So it is up to each of us to draw our own map, and to find our own path. The real crisis may hit those who do *not* change at midlife.

When we begin the midlife quest, we enter another time zone. You may be only 30 and already deeply engaged in the midlife quest; you may be 50 and still resisting it. This is because your chronological age is based on clock time, while you are actually moving through "soul time." Getting old turns out to have less to do with calendars than with fear; less to do with wrinkles than with truth; and less to do with death itself than with the deepest dimensions of life.

The first half of my life now seemed as if it had been limited to a narrow band of experience.

From *Utne Reader,* January/February 1990, pp. 70-77. Excerpted from *Act Two: The Midlife Quest* by Mark Gerzon. Copyright © 1989 by Mark Gerzon. Reprinted by permission of the author.

In this new time zone of midlife, the world is turned upside down. Our old compasses no longer work. No matter how clear the directions we have inherited from previous generations may be, getting lost is part of the process. In truth we discover lies; in love, hate; in meaning, hollowness; in passion, boredom; and in dreams, a deeper reality.

T rained by our culture to value youth over age, we tend to view aging in terms of our bodies. Like a general preparing for battle, we all search for weapons in the war against time. We fortify our immune system with vitamins, our digestive system with acidophilus and bran, our skin with collagen. We strengthen our muscles with weight lifting and our cardiovascular system with aerobics. Armed with Pritikin and papaya extract, Jane Fonda workout tapes and alfalfa sprouts, we prepare to spend the next several decades of our life in an unending battle against the most cunning and ruthless of our enemies—the Grim Reaper.

I have no quarrel with those who want to live a long and healthy life. Indeed, I count myself among them. But if this legitimate concern is compounded by

The second half of our life is a profound opportunity for transformation.

an unconscious yearning for immortality, it can be dangerous. It can lead to frenzy and fear, to obsessive diets and frenetic workouts, and to a narrow cult of youthfulness that denies the rhythms of life.

Men may worry about their receding hairlines and their expanding waistlines, their failing bladders and their failing memories, but we may still actually fool ourselves into thinking that we have held the aging process at bay. For women, however, this illusion is much harder to sustain. Their bodies are sending them messages that they simply cannot deny.

For most women, menopause is a painful reminder of loss of youth, fertility, and sexual attractiveness. Shrouded in silence and fear, it has been approached, like pregnancy, primarily in biological terms—not in terms of the psychological and spiritual unfolding of women in midlife. Yet in some cultures, women in their post-childbearing years are highly esteemed. Anthropologist Margaret Mead, who was more productive in the second half of her life than most of us are in our entire lives, called such women "the most creative force in the world."

Why is the same physical process a source of zest for one woman, and a cause of dread for another? Does menopause mean that the feminine well has run dry? Or is it a path to a deeper wellspring than fertility, a deeper purpose than procreation? Do men's weakened bladders and expanding waistlines mean

the machine is breaking down? Or are they signals that it is time to discover that this "machine" has not only an engine, but a soul? These intriguing riddles can be solved only when we allow ourselves to consider how the aging process ends.

I began exploring this subject before my midlife quest was fully under way. Death was still the "D-word" to me, something I did not talk about or think about much. As important as the subject was, I decided to write about much more upbeat subjects first: health, fitness, and longevity. I read everything I could find about the physiology and psychology of aging, including advice about diet, exercise, attitude, etc. But I could not help but be struck that virtually none of these books about health and longevity used the "D-word" at all. There were eloquent paragraphs about living longer, endless pages about vitamins and aerobics, elaborate chapters about cholesterol and bran. But death? Not a word!

This is a big mistake. If fear of death lurks behind our choosing bran cereal for breakfast and jogging several miles a day, the fiber and exercise may help us live longer. But the fear will remain. There comes a time in our midlife quest when we can no longer eat and exercise away the fear. We must confront it.

Even if we somehow manage to ignore our own aging bodies, we cannot ignore our parents'. When we are in midlife, they are nearing life's end. Just when we are confronting the rumblings of our own mortality, they make things worse by actually dying. We must confront not only the death of our own parents, but those of our mate's and friends' parents as well. And so, after years with few, if any, funerals to attend, we find ourselves unable to avoid them any longer. And at their funerals, we envision our own.

Not long after my close friend Ken's father died, Ken visited and met my father. He saw the love between us, but he also saw the distance. I knew that his seeing me with my father made him miss his, and I asked him if he had any advice. "Don't wait," he said. "If you have something to say, say it now."

I pondered his advice, but did not embrace it. I was healthy; my parents were healthy; I felt I had said

Our bodies can be our wisest teachers.

everything I needed to. And besides, I rationalized, we still have plenty of time. I did not want to confront the reality of their death because I was still not ready to confront the reality of my own. Even watching my wife's and one of my best friend's parents die was not enough. I simply could not yet take it in.

Death finally broke through my defenses at the most unexpected time and in the most unexpected

Tolstoy's bicycle: The best is yet to come

Leo Tolstoy finished his epic Anna Karenina *at age 49. At 67 he had his first bicycle lesson. This sampling of achievements should dry the alligator tears of any moping midlifer.*

40—In 610 A.D., Muhammad receives a vision that he is to be the messenger of God and begins preaching. After his death at 62, his teachings were collected to form the Koran.

41—Henry Rousseau retires from the French Customs and Excise service and starts his painting career.

42—Joyce Smith is the first woman to finish the Tokyo Marathon; at 43 she is the first woman in the London Marathon.

43—Niccolò Machiavelli loses his civil service job in Florence, is imprisoned and tortured, and over the next 13 years in exile writes *The Prince* and *The Art of War*.

44—Louis Pasteur resigns from administrative duties and returns to the lab to look at the causes of decay in fresh food.

45—Richard Strauss composes *Der Rosenkavalier*, one of his best-known operas, all composed in his 40s.

46—Empress of Russia Catherine the Great takes the first of 15 lovers between then and her death at 67; they are always men between 22 and 25.

47—Margot Fonteyn dances as Juliet with Rudolf Nureyev, then 28, as Romeo.

48—Philosopher George Santayana leaves Harvard: It is said he is in the middle of a philosophy class, suddenly sees the futility of it all, and walks out.

49—Leadbelly's first concert after being "discovered" in prison by a visiting folk-music historian.

50—Katsushika Hokusai says, "I was born at the age of 50." His best-known work—paintings of mountains with huge waves in the foreground—was published at age 63.

51—Confucius leaves private life to enter government office. Unpopular, he loses office and gains fame only later through books written about him by his disciples.

52—Gail Bordon invents condensed milk; his first career as a surveyor made him interested in easy-to-carry food.

53—Alfred Kinsey's landmark study *Sexual Behavior of the Human Male* is published; at 44, Kinsey stumbled onto the topic of sex as a professor researching wasps.

54—Cary Grant takes LSD for the first time; says "I have just been born again."

55—Rachel Carson completes *Silent Spring*.

56—Cézanne has his first solo show and attracts fame.

57—Anna Sewell's *Black Beauty* is published; the disabled author had long been dependent on horses for transportation.

58—James Counsilman swims the English Channel—21 miles in 13 hours.

59—C.G. Jung's *The Archetypes of the Collective Unconscious* is published; despite a severe heart attack at 68, many consider work done in his 70s and 80s his best.

60—After lobbying for nearly 15 years, British feminist Emmeline Pankhurst's "Representation of the People Act" passes in 1918, giving women the right to vote.

—Jeremy Baker

company. Death came when I was on vacation, and it came with love.

I was heading home on the freeway at the end of a quick vacation away from our children that my wife, Shelley, and I had managed to take. We had found a deeper, closer love than we had ever before believed possible; and we knew the pain of losing it as the pressures of our everyday lives approached. We had spent two blissful days in a little cabin by a river surrounded by towering sequoias, but now, driving back toward Los Angeles, we were profoundly aware of our fear that we would lose our love again once we returned to the big, dirty city, with work and bills and car repairs and arguing children and responsibilities—the reality of midlife.

With love in our hearts but fear in our bellies, we asked ourselves more honestly than ever before: Could we sustain this love we had found? When we lost it again—as we most certainly would—how would we regain it?

As the questions lingered in the air, I realized that what made sustaining love so hard for me is that I was afraid that it could be sabotaged at any moment by our history. After being married for 15 years, we had, like most couples, hurt each other often. If we weren't careful, even the smallest hurt could trigger a memory chain reaction, reminding us of earlier pain.

In the car, I began thinking of a book I had read recently, *Who Dies?* by Stephen Levine. He writes movingly about the need to "come clean" with each other as death approaches. He includes a "self-forgiveness meditation" in which a person tells another a simple phrase: "Whatever you have done to hurt me, I forgive you; whatever I have done to hurt you, I ask to be forgiven."

In the car, I told Shelley of my need to feel that we start again with a clean slate, forgiving each other for the past. Maybe, I said, this would give us the strength and the courage to stay true to our love. In fact, I realized, there were a host of people—family, children, friends—against whom I still held grudges for one thing or another, people whom I blamed for contributing to my pain—or the world's. Although intellectually I had told myself that I should take responsibility for my own life, I was amazed at how much I blamed others. When I asked Shelley to wipe clean our marital slate, it became clear that a surprising number of the marks on it were mine.

As I thought of the many people I'd hurt and who had hurt me, I began to cry. And I also realized

---

The real crisis may hit those who do not change at midlife.

---

that beneath all those biographical grudges had been another deeper and more timeless grudge. I had resented Life for ending in Death. I had resented God for making us mortal. It had seemed unfair, unkind, unjust,

and unnecessary. With these tears, I was forgiving Life, and God, and allowing their cosmic forgiveness to flow into my soul.

Shelley reached out her hand and held mine. I had asked her to forgive me, but had ended up forgiving myself. After we returned home, I recognized that this encounter on Highway 101 was about our deeper and more universal relationship with death. By becoming more accepting of death I could finally accept myself. It was about the pain and the pleasure of aging deeply.

If we do not accept death, and the aging that precedes it, we do not accept ourselves. Until we accept ourselves, our own souls will be strangers to us. To become friends with our souls, and to accept death as our companion, is the challenge—and the gift—of midlife.

A growing number of people have told researchers of having "near-death experiences" (NDEs) after undergoing medical emergencies or accidents that brought them perilously close to death. Those who have undergone NDEs report dramatic changes of values in their lives. They begin to place greater emphasis on intimacy and authenticity in personal relationships; they have a deeper appreciation for nature and the beauty and interconnectedness of all life; decreased interest in material rewards and professional ambition; and a generally heightened awareness of the spiritual dimension of life.

These are also the most commonly reported transformations of the midlife quest. This is not coincidence. Unless our eyes and our hearts are shut tightly in denial, midlife is a nearer-death experience. In midlife, a part of us dies. Without the actual physical trauma of near-death experiences, many of us experience the psychological and spiritual death of the self that governed the first half of our lives, and the birth of something new.

A colleague told me the story of a doctoral candidate in her late thirties who was working on a book about midlife. She had finished a draft of her dissertation and was flying home for the holidays with it in her briefcase. She died in a plane crash. It turned out that her "midlife" was, in fact, the end of her life. By the time we reach our forties, all of us know at least one person for whom this was the case. In this sense, slowing the aging process is not only meaningless, but an illusion. Death can come at any time.

It was with this in mind that I decided to write to my own parents about my encounter with Shelley about forgiveness and death. I wrote a letter and mailed it right away because I knew that if I didn't I never would. Like any family, ours has had its bitterness as well as its joy, its distance as well as its intimacy. It seemed time to begin "finishing business," not because someone was about to die, but because I needed to live more deeply. So I sent them Stephen Levine's meditation and a letter that expressed my "hope that, within the circle of our family, we can reduce the fear and resentment that exists between us and within us and find a greater measure of forgiveness for each other and ourselves."

This is the first lesson I have allowed death to

If we do not accept death, we do not accept ourselves.

teach me. During the second half of life, I expect there will be many more.

During midlife, our bodies can weigh us down, like old cars that need constant repair. But they can also teach us, and enlighten us, in ways that a robust 20-year-old body simply cannot. By midlife, each of us discovers that certain patterns of stress, strain, and often pain, have taken hold in our bodies. By taking a "biography" of our body, we can learn to know it better than we did when we were younger. Perhaps it is a headache or backache, slumping shoulders or chest pain, failing eyes or constipated bowels. Almost always, hidden in our wound, is something that will enrich and deepen our lives.

Our bodies can be our wisest teachers, our most enlightened gurus. They will teach us more than we can imagine, if only we will listen. My teacher was my back. Like more than seven million Americans who are in treatment for chronic back pain, and many millions more who suffer without treatment, a sometimes dull, sometimes sharp pain followed me for years. I assumed it was simply part of my life. Occasionally I would have it examined by a physician, or adjusted by a chiropractor. I would also try stretching exercises and vitamin therapies. But the pain remained.

Then a friend who was a gifted muscular therapist agreed to work on my back where it hurt most—in the middle right between my shoulder blades. "The place where it hurts is a very common source of pain," she explained as I lay on her massage table, feeling her fingers dig into muscle and ligament that had turned hard as gristle. "It is the place where we hold anger."

Anger—and grudges, resentment, hostility, and bitterness. Suddenly it struck me that this was where I held all my anger at all the people (including myself) whom I refuse to forgive. I had talked about "holding on" to anger, or "bearing" grudges, or not being able to get something "off my back." But I never took my own words seriously. I never connected my own unfinished business to my back pain.

The source of my pain was not only my flesh, but my own soul. The wound was so deep that it cut through all the divisions (physical, psychological, spiritual) by which we split ourselves. As my physician confirmed, muscle was actually hardening in that area, and pressure was being exerted on the spinal disc. If it had continued, it could have turned into arthritis or a degenerative condition of the spine. It was not something I could cure through diet (although the right nutrients would help) or through exercise (although certain stretching exercises would limit the pain). It would heal only if, in the second half of my life, I changed the way I live.

Since then, by working on the feelings I had stored in that part of my back for almost 40 years, the pain has decreased. I cannot report an overnight change. I came to consider myself in training, not for boxing or basketball, but for wholeness—and my health depended on it.

ALMOST CERTAINLY YOUR PRESCRIPTION for health includes something about food—and it should. But your first challenge should not be to change what you eat, but to deepen your understanding of your relationship with food.

Some have spent their lives being afraid of food, terrified of becoming fat and therefore eating little, burdened with anxiety and obsessive control. In such lives, becoming more whole at midlife means breaking through those inhibitions and finding a lifestyle in which the pleasures of eating can truly be enjoyed.

In my case, the problem was just the opposite. The evidence that I was overeating was not my waistline but my energy level and state of mind. I had eaten to fill an emptiness, a void inside me. I had overeaten as a child to make myself feel "taken care of" in ways my parents could not. I had overeaten in college to compensate for feelings of loneliness and confusion. I had eaten to chase away the feelings that I did not want to encounter yet. It was as if every mouthful was ingested to disprove the notion that I did not deserve to be loved, or to be alive. But each mouthful only filled my stomach; it did not nourish my soul.

As I finally broke those old patterns, my eating habits changed and my energy increased. I needed less sleep. I was quicker to rise in the morning. And so in my fortieth year, occasional fasting and generally eating less became part of my journey, and part of my definition of fitness.

To truly nourish ourselves, to find our deepest sources of energy, to express sincerely our whole selves—these are not overnight accomplishments. They are not the results of six-week crash diets or miracle fitness programs. On the contrary, they are part of our ongoing midlife quests.

A vibrant, healthy body is a blessing and a joy. It will allow us to journey to far regions, descend deeply to the most verdant valley, and climb the highest peaks. It will enable us to carry enough belongings to care for ourselves, and to share with others. It will also give us the strength to work along the way. But before all this can happen, we must still decide in which direction to turn. We must ask ourselves where we are going.

Meet the people who never quit learning

You name it. You can learn it. No age limit. Sound exciting? Read on!

The average man who retires at age 65 today is apt to live to be 80, and the average woman to be 84. As Dr. John Merritt, chief of geriatric medicine at the Hospital of Saint Raphael says, ''That's a lot of life to do a lot of things with. If it's approached positively, it can be a great experience.'' Lifelong learning is one of the ways older people can keep growing.

Learning isn't just ''the three R's.'' And it's not just teachers, textbooks, and tests. Learning can take place on a nature trail, at an overseas resort, in a classroom, or in a favorite armchair.

But wherever it happens—and whatever its subject—learning is strong medicine.

According to Dr. Harvey Rubin, a member of Saint Raphael's attending staff in psychiatry, lifelong learning can lead to long life.

''The more you do, the better you'll feel and the longer you'll live,'' he says.

Dr. Rubin points out that continuing learning can ''counteract depression, the number-one problem among the elderly. It also counteracts anxiety, boredom, and a preoccupation with physical complaints.''

David A. Goldberg, 82, says, ''When I'm driving home from my classes at Southern Connecticut State University (SCSU), I see men and women, 65 and older, sitting on the bench, depressed, without a mission, without hope, without a goal. And it's sad. There's so much available to take advantage of, and they miss that.''

Mr. Goldberg has firsthand knowledge of the value of lifelong learning: Next May he will receive his B.A. degree in political Science from SCSU.

''Education promotes social interaction,'' explains Dr. David Peterson, professor of gerontology at the University of Southern California. ''Usually you get educated in groups, and, for older people, getting out and seeing other people seems to be about as important as the particular content of the course. Just by participating in an activity, you're likely to be more social, happier, and better integrated.''

Keeping in touch. Opportunities for social contact are especially important for older persons, who may feel cut adrift due to age-related changes. ''Some societal structures drop away after age 65,'' explains Dr. Carol Dye, a gerontologist at the Veterans' Administration Medical Center in St. Louis, Missouri. She adds that, as older family members and friends die, additional social support networks are lost. Declining physical powers or ill health may also necessitate a change in activities. ''Continuing education programs can lessen the negative impacts of these changes,'' Dr. Dye says.

Diane Gibralter, 74, is a case in point. Before beginning art classes at SCSU seven years ago, Mrs. Gibralter was sure she could never be an artist. But now she has two paintings displayed in her grandson's dorm at Yale University, with a commission to complete a third.

Her art work has become so important to her that when she underwent open-heart surgery and was told the operation had not gone as well as expected, she ''sat down and started painting, and I got so involved, I didn't even think about it.''

Physical health can even get a boost from learning that involves activities such as folk dancing, tennis, walking, or anything else that, as one retiree puts it, ''gets the old body moving.''

Lifelong learning can be found in many places, though it's not always officially labelled as such. Churches and synagogues, public school systems, community organizations such as the Red Cross and the YMCA — all sponsor classes for adults.

Many colleges and universities have developed special programs for adults beyond typical college age. In Connecticut, for example, the state university system offers tuition-free classes for those 62 and older. Another notable college-based program for older people is the Elderhostel program.

There's a continuing-education topic to suit just about everyone's taste. A small sampling includes:
- Self-protection
- Money management
- Exercise
- Preventive health care
- Modern languages
- Yoga
- Macrame
- Cooking
- American history
- Needlepoint

MedTerms

Activity theory: The theory that older people should remain as active as they can as long as they can. When certain activities and associations must be given up (employment, for example), substitutes should be found.

Health: According to the World Health Organization, health is a state of physical, mental, and social well-being, *not* merely the absence of disease or infirmity.

Life expectancy: The number of years of life expected for an individual or a group. Life expectancy is rising rapidly in most countries.

Life span: The biological limit to the length of life. Each species has a characteristic average life span. For humans, it is over 100 years.

Reprinted by permission from *St. Raphael's Better Health*, November/December 1988, pp. 27-32.

- Mathematics
- Art appreciation
- Speed-reading
- Folk music
- Chess
- Car care and repair.

Today, adult learners are one of the fastest-growing segments of the population.

One reason is that people are living longer. Another is the growing number of people in the United States who have completed high school or college.

By 1990, an estimated 50 percent of the population over 65 will be high school graduates. And that, says Dr. Peterson, is one of the most important factors influencing a person's participation in continuing education.

But that doesn't mean only high-school or college graduates are eager to learn. Many older people who had to forgo an education due to the Depression or World War II are making up for lost time. So are women who interrupted or postponed their education because of childrearing responsibilities.

Aliss Cunningham, for example, was unable to attend college in her youth because of family finances, but enrolled at SCSU under its tuition-free program for senior citizens. She'll receive her B.A. degree in English next spring — at the age of 82. "Should I survive after I graduate, and if I'm on my feet, I'll probably audit some more classes," she says.

Unfortunately, getting older doesn't automatically lead to knowing the facts about aging. Many older people believe that loss of their learning ability is inevitable. They interpret the physical signs of aging, such as fatigue or failing vision, as indications that their intelligence is deteriorating as well. Popular culture — with its stereotypes and jokes about the elderly — reinforces these beliefs.

When surveyed, old and young people alike are apt to agree with the myth that "You can't teach an old dog new tricks." The idea that older people lose their ability to learn is one of the most pervasive — and harmful — myths about older people.

Even worse, the myth is self-perpetuating: Younger people assume that older people can't learn, and relegate them to insignificant roles on the sidelines, where there are few opportunities to learn.

According to Saint Raphael's Dr. Merritt, there is no basis for the myth that older people can't learn. "Except for people who have strictly neurological problems, an older person can assimilate as much overall as a younger person can in the same situation," he says.

In a Duke University Medical Center study of people aged 60 to 94, there was no demonstrable decline in overall ability to learn. The primary change in learning capacity noted in older people is that they take longer to learn something new, compared with their own ability when they were younger or with that of younger people.

According to Dr. Dye, "the hallmark of aging is the slowing of function. The brain is less responsive and less retentive as you grow older. Some of the best memories we have are old memories, because they were put into the brain at a

The Elderhostel program

Outer space. Watercolor techniques. Pioneer life. Computer technology. These are just a few of the subjects offered by Elderhostel, a continuing education program for people age 60 or older.

In all, Elderhostel offers over 3,500 programs, ranging from "Fun with the Dictionary" to "Predicting the Weather" to "Exploring the Okefenokee Swamp."

In 1987 the program had 142,000 enrollments—two of whom were Ruth and Wolfgang Wenten, a Fairfield couple who have participated in Elderhostel programs for more than nine years.

"It's a great thing because you learn something that you haven't learned before," says Mr. Wenten. "And the speakers are always experts in their fields.

"It's not just 'high-brow' courses, either. It could be tennis, it could be golf, it could be folk dancing," adds Mrs. Wenten. She says people shouldn't be afraid they'll have to face "really scholarly things. It runs the gamut." The Wentens, for instance, recently chose courses on art appreciation and on the politics of the family. Last year they traveled to Brazil to study its culture and history.

In the U.S. and Canada, Elderhostelers live on the campus of one of 1,200 colleges and universities for a week or more while participating in up to three classes. International programs in more than 40 foreign countries last two to four weeks, each week at a different institution.

According to Mrs. Wenten, the programs provide a "fantastic low-cost vacation." The average cost in the U.S. is $225 per program, which includes tuition, room, board, recreational facilities, and extracurricular activities. Courses abroad include these features as well as airfare and land travel to and from the host country. Prices vary according to destination and place of departure; a trip to Great Britain and Ireland is listed in the current Elderhostel at $1,689 to $2,100. Some scholarships are available.

No prior knowledge or training in the subject is required. Some participants have advanced degrees; others never graduated from high school. "We all have something to contribute," says Renee Dubina of New Haven. Now almost 80, she started working toward an associate degree while in her early 70s, and has participated in the Elderhostel program for more than five years.

Though Elderhostel traditionally uses university campuses and other educational facilities, programs are also held in national parks and environmental education centers. In the far north, for instance, hostelers at Arctic College in the Canadian Northwest Territories can study Indian and Inuit cultures while taste testing partridge and caribou. Elderhostel also sponsors rafting excursions in Oregon and cruises of Alaskan waterways.

The program is open to anyone over age 60 and spouses or companions age 50 or older. Three new intergenerational Elderhostel programs are now available at Warren Wilson College in North Carolina, the University of Michigan at Flint, and the University of Southern California at Catalina. In these programs elders participate with their own grandchildren or with high school students from the community.

Depending on the facility, Elderhostel accommodations range from the luxurious to the spartan, with shared bathroom facilities and cafeteria food the norm. But dedicated hostelers seem to be more concerned about their mental environment than their physical comforts. And when it comes to mental stimulation, Elderhostel gets an A + .

As Renee Dubina says, "It keeps the brain from getting rusty."

time when it was operating better. As you get older, the things that you put into the brain aren't kept there as well and they're more difficult to get to.

"But that doesn't mean older people can't learn," Dr. Dye hastens to add.

Older people *can* learn, and specific conditions can make learning easier for them.

For one thing, learning is a matter of "using it or losing it," Dr. Dye says. "If you have a lifestyle in which learning and reading and keeping up with current events is the norm, then your ability to learn will be much better than that of a person whose lifestyle is more mentally passive."

Dr. Dye suggests the following practical strategies for older learners:

● Take your time learning the information.
● Take your time "retrieving" or remembering information.
● Break learning into small parts. Learn a little, practice what you've learned, then learn a little more.
● Create a stress-free setting for learning.
● Allow yourself time to sit and think about what you've just learned, without interruptions or distractions.
● Participate actively in learning. Allow time to practice what you've learned. Repeat what you've just heard, and repeat the steps you've just been shown.
● Use rhymes or slogans to help jog the memory.
● Organize what you've learned in ways meaningful to you — through outlines, for example.
● Take notes on what you've heard or read and leave yourself notes about things to do or where to go.

Natalie Felske can attest to the value of these suggestions. Mrs. Felske's hopes for a college education were stymied first by the Depression, then by the beginning of World War II, and then again by her husband's illness. A determined lifelong learner, she is now working toward a degree in English at SCSU.

But first she has to complete a language requirement. Her slight hearing impairment has made it difficult to understand her language instructor and, at age 68, she finds that her retention of new information isn't as sharp as it once was, which makes it difficult to learn new vocabulary words in a foreign language. To conquer these problems, she has devised a system of flash cards for vocabulary words, and she fully intends to receive her degree in 1990.

These learning aids are important not just for older people themselves, but for people who interact with older people in a professional capacity.

For example, physicians who take their fast-paced, stressful work for granted may be frustrated when older patients can't remember information about medications when it's been given to them hurriedly in a busy clinic and without time to ask questions. But the same individual might have little or no trouble remembering instructions if he received them in a quiet room, was given written notes, allowed to repeat back the information, and encouraged to practice carrying out the instructions with supervision.

Because of the differences in their learning styles, many older learners prefer what is known as "age-segregated" learning where participants are about the same age, and the specific needs of adult learners can be addressed. Others deliberately seek the challenge of an age-integrated setting.

One such learner is Martha Caesar, who in 1978 became one of the first to take advantage of the free tuition program at SCSU. Mrs. Caesar finds that "one of the really exciting aspects of taking courses is the young people." At 81, Mrs. Caesar boasts, "some of my best friends are 18."

Like many older learners, Mrs. Caesar has found learning is more fun the second time around. She finds that "today, the classroom is freer. There's more give and take. I remember my professors as very austere, maybe because I was young and revered them. Now they are much more approachable."

Lack of pressure is another bonus from learning in later life, since courses can be audited without exams or grades. Mrs. Caesar had vowed, "never, as long as I lived, would I write another paper." She now takes classes that strike her fancy, starting off with geography classes and now exploring Asian religions.

Some older learners find that learning is in some ways easier later in life. David Goldberg notes, for example, that older people may be able to pay more attention in class because they aren't looking at classmates and thinking, "Am I going to be dating her?" or worrying about the college football team. Finding a job after graduation also needn't be a concern, although Mr. Goldberg teases his younger classmates that "when I graduate, you better watch out!" since he might look for a job as a political scientist.

Of course, it's not just the older learners who benefit from "age-integrated" learning. Young students benefit from their older colleagues' years of experience.

Frank Trangese, who has taken classes at SCSU since 1980, finds that, at 73, he can offer a unique perspective in history courses, since he has actually lived many of the events being discussed.

Having resolved that "when I retire, I'm not going to let my brain go blank," Mr. Trangese now takes classes at SCSU, is a coordinator for the campus Elderhostel program, and helps register others in the free-tuition program.

In a similar way, Natalie Felske thinks her age allowed her to serve as a "catalyst for discussion" in her creative writing class. Being older, she could "let her hair down" and share personal stories about her life and family, something the younger students were reluctant to do until she served as a role model.

By sharing ideas, strengths, and experiences, lifelong learners end up teaching as well as learning. And that's an important lesson in itself.

Melanie Scheller
Melanie Scheller, of Durham, North Carolina, frequently writes about health and wellness.

Societal Attitudes Toward Old Age

There is a wide range of beliefs regarding the social position and status of the aged in American society today. Some people believe the best way to understand the problems of the elderly is to regard them as a minority group, faced with difficulties similar to those of other minority groups. Discrimination against older people, like racial discrimination, is believed to be based on a bias against visible physical traits. Since the aging process is viewed negatively, it is natural that the elderly try to appear and act younger. Some spend a tremendous amount of money trying to make themselves look and feel younger.

The theory that old people are a minority group is weak, however, because too many circumstances prove otherwise. The United States Congress, for example, favors senior members of Congress and senators, and delegates considerable prestige and power to them. The leadership roles in most religious organizations are held by older persons. Many older Americans are in good health, have comfortable incomes, and are treated with respect by friends and associates.

Perhaps the most realistic way to view the aged is as a status group, like other status groups in society. Every society has some method of "age grading," by which it groups together individuals of roughly similar age. ("Pre-teens" and "senior citizens" are some of the age grade labels in American society.) Because it is a labeling process, age grading causes members of the age grade, as well as others, to perceive themselves in terms of the connotations of the label. Unfortunately, the tag "old age" often has negative connotations in American society.

The readings included in this section illustrate the wide range of stereotypical attitudes toward older Americans. Many of society's typical assumptions about the limitations of old age have been refuted. A major force behind this reassessment of the elderly has been the simple fact that there are so many people living longer and healthier lives, and in consequence playing more of a role in all aspects of our society. This important point is driven home in the article "The Vintage Years," in which the authors contend that the activities and attitudes of a 70-year-old today are equivalent to those of a 50-year-old a decade ago. Older people can remain productive members of society for many more years than has been traditionally assumed.

Such standard stereotypes of the elderly as senility, lack of sexuality, and limited employment abilities are topics discussed in other articles in this section. In "Never Too Late," the authors find that the difference between the sexual activity of younger and older people is very little. In "Another Stereotype: Old Age as a Second Childhood," the misdirected tradition of seeing older persons as infants is discussed. The stereotype of the elderly not being employable is examined in the article "Age Stereotyping."

Looking Ahead: Challenge Questions

Do most people see older persons as sexually inactive?

Do Americans generally look upon old age as a desirable, or an undesirable status?

How do the attitudes of children toward older persons differ from those of adults?

How are attitudes toward old age likely to change as older persons become a larger segment of the total population?

Never Too Late

*SINGLE PEOPLE OVER 65 WHO ARE DATING
AND SEXUALLY ACTIVE BELIE THE NOTION THAT
PASSION AND ROMANCE ARE ONLY FOR THE YOUNG.*

KRIS BULCROFT AND
MARGARET O'CONNER-RODEN

Kris Bulcroft is a sociologist at St. Olaf College in Northfield, Minnesota. Margaret O'Conner-Roden is a sociology doctoral candidate at the University of Minnesota in Minneapolis.

What is the age of love? The star-crossed lovers Romeo and Juliet were teenagers; Anthony and Cleopatra's torrid affair occurred at the prime of their health and beauty; Lady Diana Spencer was barely 20 when she married her Prince Charming. How old is too old for the sparkle in the eye and the blush in the cheek?

The message our culture often gives us is that love is only for the young and the beautiful—people over 65 are no longer interested in or suited for things such as romance and passion. Few of us imagine older couples taking an interest in the opposite sex other than for companionship—maybe a game of bridge or conversation out on the porch. But, in fact, there are quite a few older single people who not only date but are involved sexually with someone.

Statistically there are good reasons for older people to be dating. At the turn of the century only about 4 percent of the total American population was 65 years of age or older. Today that number has soared to approximately 11 percent, with the total expected to increase to about 20 percent by the year 2050. In addition, older people are living longer and staying healthier, and they are less likely than before to have children living at home. And an increasing number of divorces among the elderly is casting many of these older people back into the singles' pool. All of these factors create an expanded life stage, made up of healthy and active people looking for meaningful ways to spend their leisure.

The question of whether older people date, fall in love and behave romantically, just as the young do, occurred to us while we were observing singles' dances for older people at a senior center. We noticed a sense of anticipation, festive dress and flirtatious behavior that were strikingly familiar to us as women recently involved in the dating scene. Although our observations indicated that older people dated, when we looked for empirical research on the topic we found there was none. We concluded this was due partly to the difficulty in finding representative samples of older daters and partly to the underlying stereotype of asexual elders. So we decided to go out and talk to older daters ourselves. Once we began looking, we were surprised at the numbers of dating elders who came forward to talk to us. We compared their responses to those from earlier studies on romance and dating, in which the people were much younger.

Dating, as defined by our sample of older people, meant a committed, long-term, monogamous relationship, similar to going steady at younger ages. The vast majority of elderly daters did not approach dating with the more casual attitude of many younger single people who are "playing the field." All respondents clearly saw dating as quite distinct from friendship, although companionship was an important characteristic of over-60 dating.

One of our major findings was the similarity between how older and younger daters feel when they fall in love—what we've come to call the "sweaty palm syndrome." This includes all the physiological and psychological somersaults, such as a heightened sense of reality, perspiring hands, a feeling of awkwardness, inability to concentrate, anxiety when away from the loved one and heart palpitations. A 65-year-old man told

us, "Love is when you look across the room at someone and your heart goes pitty-pat." A widow, aged 72, said, "You know you're in love when the one you love is away and you feel empty." Or as a 68-year-old divorcée said, "When you fall in love at my age there's initially a kind of 'oh, gee!' feeling . . . and it's just a little scary."

We also found a similarity in how both older and younger daters defined romance. Older people were just as likely to want to participate in romantic displays such as candlelight dinners, long walks in the park and giving flowers and candy. Older men, just like younger ones, tended to equate romance with sexuality. As a 71-year-old widower told us, "You can talk about candlelight dinners and sitting in front of the fireplace, but I still think the most romantic thing I've ever done is to go to bed with her."

A major question for us was "What do older people do on dates?" The popular image may suggest a prim, card-playing couple perhaps holding hands at some senior center. We found that not only do older couples' dates include the same activities as those of younger people, but they are often far more varied and creative. In addition to traditional dates such as going to

the movies, out for pizza and to dances, older couples said they went camping, enjoyed the opera and flew to Hawaii for the weekend.

Not only was the dating behavior more varied, but the pace of the relationship was greatly accelerated in later life. People told us that there simply was "not much time for playing the field." They favored the direct, no-game-playing approach in building a relationship with a member of the opposite sex. As one elderly dater commented, "Touching people is important, and I know from watching my father and mother that you might just as well say when lunch is ready . . . and I don't mean that literally."

Sexuality was an important part of the dating relationship for most of those we spoke to, and sexual involvement tended to develop rapidly. While sexuality for these couples included intercourse, the stronger emphasis was on the nuances of sexual behavior such as hugging, kissing and touching. This physical closeness helped fulfill the intimacy needs of older people, needs that were especially important to those living alone whose sole source of human touch was often the dating partner. The intimacy provided through sex also contributed to self-

esteem by making people feel desired and needed. As one 77-year-old woman said, "Sex isn't as important when you're older, but in a way you need it more."

A major distinction we found between older and younger daters was in their attitudes toward passionate love, or what the Greeks called "the madness from the gods." Psychologists Elaine Hatfield, of the University of Hawaii in Manoa, and G. William Walster, of Los Gatos, California, have similarly defined passionate love as explosive, filled with fervor and short-lived. According to their theory of love, young people tend to equate passionate love with being in love. Once the first, intense love experience has faded, young lovers often seek a new partner.

For older daters, it is different. They have learned from experience that passionate love cannot be sustained with the same early level of intensity. But since most of them have been in marriages that lasted for decades, they also know the value of companionate love, that "steady burning fire" that not only endures but tends to grow deeper over time. As one older man put it, "Yeah, passion is nice . . . it's the frosting on the cake.

But it's her personality that's really important. The first time I was in love it was only the excitement that mattered, but now it's the friendship . . . the ways we spend our time together that count."

Nonetheless, the pursuit of intimacy caused special problems for older people. Unlike younger daters, older people are faced with a lack of social cues indicating whether sexual behavior is appropriate in the dating relationship. Choosing to have a sexual relationship outside of marriage often goes against the system of values that they have

WHEN MY GIRLFRIEND SPENDS THE NIGHT SHE BRINGS HER CORDLESS PHONE, JUST IN CASE HER DAUGHTER CALLS.

followed during their entire lives.

Older couples also felt the need to hide the intimate aspects of their dating relationship because of a fear of social disapproval, creating a variety of covert behaviors. As one 63-year-old retiree said, "Yeah, my girlfriend (age 64) lives just down the hall from me . . . when she spends the night she usually brings her cordless phone . . . just in case her daughter calls." One 61-year-old woman told us that even though her 68-year-old boyfriend has been spending three or four nights a week at her house for the past year, she has not been able to tell her family. "I have a tendency to hide his shoes when my grandchildren are coming over."

Despite the fact that marriage

WHO'S WHO IN THE SAMPLE

For our study we interviewed 45 older people in a Midwestern metropolitan area who were widowed or divorced and had been actively dating during the past year. Fifty-four percent were men and 46 percent were women; all were white. The age of the subjects ranged from 60 to 92; the average age was 68. Although most of the group was middle-class, some were affluent and others lived solely on Social Security. Names were obtained through a variety of methods, including a membership list of a singles' club for older persons, senior citizens' centers, newspaper ads and word of mouth. The face-to-face interviews were, for the most part, conducted in the home of the older person. We asked people questions about how they met, what they did on a date, how important sexuality was in their relationship and what family and friends' reactions were to their dating.

would solve the problem of how to deal with the sexual aspects of the relationship, very few of these couples were interested in marriage. Some had assumed when they began dating that they would eventually marry but discovered as time went on that they weren't willing to give up their independence. For women especially, their divorce or widowhood marked the first time in their lives that they had been on their own. Although it was often difficult in the beginning, many discovered that they enjoyed their independence. Older people also said they didn't have the same reasons for marriage that younger people do: beginning a life together and starting a family. Another reason some elders were reluctant to marry was the possibility of deteriorating health. Many said they would not want to become a caretaker for an ill spouse.

Contrary to the popular belief that family would be protective and jealous of the dating relative, family members tended to be supportive of older couples' dating and often included the dating partner in family gatherings. The attitude that individuals have the right to personal happiness may be partially responsible for families' positive attitudes. But more importantly, many families realize that a significant other for an older person places fewer social demands on family members.

Peers also tended to be supportive, although many women reported sensing jealousy among their female friends, who were possibly unhappy because of their inability to find dating partners themselves and hurt because the dating woman didn't have as much time to spend with them.

Our interviews with older daters revealed that the dating relationship is a critical, central part of elders' lives that provides something that cannot be supplied by family or friends. As one 65-year-old man told us, "I'm very happy with life right now. I'd be lost without my dating partner. I really would."

Our initial question, "What is the age of love?" is best answered in the words of one 64-year-old woman: "I suppose that hope does spring eternal in the human breast as far as love is concerned. People are always looking for the ultimate, perfect relationship. No matter how old they are, they are looking for this thing called love."

Another Stereotype: Old Age As A Second Childhood

Arnold Arluke Ph.D.
and Jack Levin Ph.D.

Dr. Jack Levin is a professor of sociology at Northeastern University in Boston and is the co-author of Ageism: Prejudice and Discrimination Against the Elderly. *Dr. Arnold Arluke is Associate Professor of Sociology, also at Northeastern University, and is co-author of the forthcoming book,* Division of Labor As Marketplace: Rehabilitation Medicine, 1890-1980.

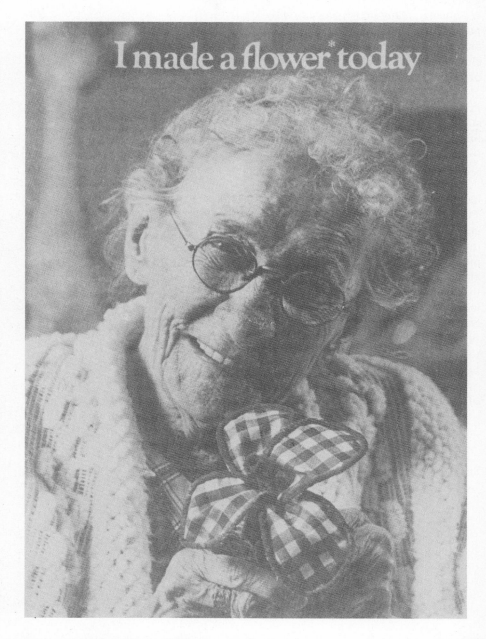

I made a flower* today

Stereotypes are more than privately held "pictures in our heads." They are more often culturally shared and institutionalized negative images which are used to justify unequal treatment, or discrimination, directed against minority groups, ranging from perpetrating, petty indignities in everyday life to slavery and genocide.

One common and particularly damaging stereotype, "infantilization," reduces minority group members to the status of children, ranging from infants to adolescents, who lack moral, intellectual, or physical maturity. According to this image, they are typically depicted as "irresponsible," "impulsive," "fun-loving," and "immature." In sum, they are seen as dependent on the "more mature" dominant group for guidance to accomplish the tasks to which they are assigned or even to survive.

The antebellum South provides an appropriate example. The "Little Black Sambo" image was extensively applied to sell the ideology of a "white man's burden," whereby slaves would actually perish if denied the paternalistic "protection" of their masters who administered corporal punishment and withheld rewards to assure that tasks were accomplished. To this day, the epithet "boy" remains as a vestige of the infantilization of the slave (Blassingame, 1972). In the same manner, women before the liberation movement of the 1960's were often called "baby," "girl," "honey," and "sweety." Their fashions were made to reflect the fashions of children, frequently imitating the clothing worn by infants or teenagers of a previous generation (Lurie, 1982).

Similarly, many stereotypes currently portray old age as a time of second childhood. This dim view of the elderly suggests that they are losing, or have lost, the very things a growing child gains. It implies a backward movement to earlier developmental stages, with no recognition of the lifetime of experience that unquestionably separates the elderly from children (Gresham, 1973).

The image of old people as childlike has been with us for a long time. Tuckman and Lorge (1953) asked graduate students in psychology to indicate their agreement or disagreement with a number of statements about old people. Despite the fact that the students were well acquainted with psychology and enrolled in a course involving the aging process, there was a high level of agreement that old people are unproductive, have to go to bed early, need a nap every day, are in the "happiest" period of their lives, cannot manage their own affairs, and are in their second childhood.

More recent research indicates that stereotyping continues to be an integral part of public images of the aged, and that one of the major stereotypes still perpetuates the second childhood image. McTavish (1971) found considerable acceptance for an image of old people that is distinctly reminiscent of the view of toddlers during the stage known as "the terrible two's." Many of his subjects

felt that old people are likely to be annoying, obstinate, and unreasonable. In 1975, the National Council on the Aging reported the results of a survey of 4,254 adult Americans (Harris, 1975). Old people were generally thought of as useless and inactive by participants in the survey. They viewed the elderly as spending most of their time watching television or "doing nothing," in the true spirit of directionless adolescence.

Viewing the Old as Childlike

The ubiquitousness of the "second childhood" stereotype becomes apparent when we examine its common forms.

First, old people are given the personality and moods of children. It

is common, for example, in prescription drug ads to describe senility in terms normally associated with children. An ad for a tranquilizer "for the agitated geriatric" shows an elderly man angrily waving his fist. "TANTRUMS" is printed large across the page. Other tranquilizer ads use terms such as "nuisance," "disruptive," and "obstreperous" to describe the actions of elders. Even in a recent children's book, which was written to acquaint children with old age, the elderly woman who is explaining to a young girl what it is like to be old describes herself as sometimes "cranky," a word usually reserved for children. Television shows and movies characterize the personality of older people as childlike whether it is "Mother Jef-

ferson's" cantankerousness, the silliness of Johnny Carson's "Aunt Blabby," or the impulsiveness and recklessness of Ruth Gordon in the film, *Harold and Maude*.

Second, old people are given the dress and appearance of children. On the cover of one birthday card is a blackboard with "You're only young once!" chalked on it along with various doodles. Inside, an overweight, unshaven elderly man smoking a cigar is wearing a summer camp tee shirt, shorts, sneakers and cap and is playing with a yo-yo and a baseball bat. Above his grinning face the card says "Happy Birthday Playboy." In addition to its other connotations, the card suggests that when you get old, you are at liberty to play like a child again. One of the worst examples of attributing childlike qualities to the elderly is the appearance of an older man—dressed in pajamas and a birthday hat and blowing a noisemaker—in an advertisement for a "geriatric highchair." On the chair's tray is a birthday cake.

Third, old people are given the physical problems of children. One ad for catheters, which appears in a geriatric nursing journal, shows the forearms and hands of a baby as its model instead of an elder. A prescription drug ad for a stool-softener features a smiling bifocaled older woman. The text reads: "Minnie moved her bowels today. The day started right for Minnie. That young doctor feller gave her a stool softener to take last night. And it worked!. . .Minnie figures she's got the smartest doctor in town." It is not too farfetched to imagine that Minnie's smile not only expresses her physical relief but also her pride at being told she moved her bowels.

Fourth, old people are given parties in the spirit of children's parties. In a suburban smalltown newspaper, a recent article reported that the patients at a local nursing home "held their very own Christmas party." The article went on to indicate that patients "planned the party, made the invitations, decorated the cookies

made by the chef, and took part in the entertainment, which included a group singing of Christmas Carols." The article thanked a local drugstore for supplying "Santa's gifts." The intentions were admirable, but the message rang loud and clear: Old people are like big children.

Posters in a popular chain of fast-food restaurants urge customers to "Have a Senior Birthday Party." For the "birthday kid" who is "young at heart," the fast food chain offers to provide the cake, hats, and party favors. Also consider a telephone company ad for custom phones which can be given as gifts to "celebrate any occasion." One such occasion is "Gertrude's" retirement party, complete with colorful ribbons and balloons. In honor of her retirement, Gertrude is shown receiving her own Snoopy phone from her co-workers. A similar ad shows an elder receiving a Mickey Mouse phone at a party.

Fifth, old people are encouraged to pursue the activities of children. In an article called "The Fun Life for Young and Old," a major city newspaper provided "a guide to August activities for senior citizens and children." Pictures were shown of a puppet show and a magic act. Even the "Kiddies' Menu" of a popular Massachusetts ice cream parlor portrays an older man walking hand-in-hand with a young boy. As clearly stated on the face of the menu, "for all kids under 10 and over 65," the bill of fare consists of a "hot doggie," "kiddie burger," and "peanut butter and jelly samwhich."

Advice books for the elderly often treat them as children by advising them to reduce the work-related activities associated with adulthood (Arluke, et al., 1984). Programs in nursing homes and hospitals intended to make life more interesting for elderly patients also become infantilizing at times (Levin at al., 1983). One handbook of activities and recreational programs for nursing homes recommends discussing such topics as "growing things," "boys," "sunshine," "stones," and "favorite story."

Kiddies' Menu

For all kids under 10 and over 65 offers the following Bill of Fare

HOT DOGGY .99
KIDDIE BURGER .99
PEANUT BUTTER &
JELLY SAMWHICH .75

all of the above served with Steak Fries

Sixth, old people are given the playthings of children. A department store ad in *TV Guide* shows an elderly man riding a child's three wheeler. The caption reads: "Wish they had Hot Cycles when I was a kid. . .Yep, kids sure are lucky today. Hey, maybe when no one's around. . ."

A prescription drug used to treat symptoms associated with organic brain syndrome, claims in an ad that it "Usually leaves the disturbed elderly patient in the nursing home more alert, more responsive." In the ad, the photograph of an elderly woman shows her smiling limply and holding a large red and white checked cloth flower. Above her is the caption: "I made a flower today." A similar arts-and-crafts portrayal of the aged appears in an ad for a drug used to improve circulation. Three elders who are "deficient in peripheral circulation" but "proficient in the 'home'" are shown hard at work making ceramics—which is evidently considered to be a higher level activity in the nursing home. A major newspaper recently ran an article entitled "Latest Trends from Toyland," in which the reporter suggests that dolls can be a "companion to the elderly as they are to children."

Implications

"Infantilization" justifies the paternalistic treatment of minority group members with the consequence that they may be "kept in their place" as dependent inferiors. Forms of discrimination supported by infantilization include slavery, forcing women to stay at home and various forms of institutionalization.

Casting old people as children has detrimental effects on old and young alike. The "second childhood" stereotype tends to make young people feel distant from their elders. Having just graduated from childhood, what adolescent wants to endure it again by associating with the old? The stereotype may well also encourage gerontophobia, the neurotic fear of old age. How many adults want to be thought of one day as a six-year-old who isn't toilet trained?

For old people, the second-childhood stereotype creates a self-fulfilling prophecy. Many elderly people come to accept the second-childhood stereotype and play the role with enthusiasm. But is that because they fail to see any alternative? Our society has traditionally offered certain rewards to those elderly citizens who are willing to "stay in their place." Riding on a special bus for senior citizens, or dancing with other seniors to the tune of Yankee Doodle, may isolate elderly people. But it may be preferable to watching re-runs of "Marcus Welby."

Acting like children has three negative consequences for old people.

First, such behavior lowers their social status because their individual responsibility has been diminished, while their dependency has increased. Secondly, the perception of infantile behavior in the elderly may allow certain things to be done to them that would otherwise not be considered: the prescription of psychoactive medications, institutionalization, and declaration of legal incompetency. Thirdly, infantilization robs the "gray power" movement of adults who might otherwise work for political change and social betterment.

Not all old people buy the second-childhood stereotype. A large number of elderly Americans are thoroughly offended by infantilization and seek to avoid the consequences of the stereotype. For many, this means making efforts to "pass" for middle-age by dying hair, lying about their age, and using youth-oriented cosmetics. A positive form of avoidance is reengagement, whereby old people seek to become either re-employed or remarried after the loss of a job or spouse.

On the damaging side, an unknown number of cases of apparent senility may actually represent a refusal to accept the second-childhood syndrome. Rather than comply, some elders may retreat into a more comfortable, more secure psychological state which ironically has the appearance of infantile behavior. So, for example, we might see lack of sexual interest, giddiness, forgetfulness, inability to maintain a stable relationship, and lack of control over bodily functions.

A Warning

In contemporary America, stereotyped images of the elderly may one day include less emphasis on infantilization and more emphasis on dehumanization. There is a tendency to view some aged people as mere "vegetables" —totally beyond the age of productivity and usefulness. They are viewed as no longer alive in the sense that we understand what it means to be human and therefore not worthy of the medical and social services available to those who are younger—such as expensive dialysis or lengthy rehabilitation for fractures, stroke, and other problems.

Another aspect of this dehumanization of the elderly may be "to color them all gray" and see them as a group that presents a threat. In periods of economic retrenchment, a large and growing elderly population may to an increasing extent be regarded as a major threat to the economic well-being of younger Americans. Those Americans who feel especially frustrated may look for a justification to reduce the power of their older competitors. Substantial reductions in social security and health benefit payments might be a first step.

Stereotypical or dehumanizing views of the elderly (or any age group) damage the social fabric of our nation even though they may not be held by all Americans. Much is being done currently to counter these views through education and advocacy in the public and private sectors. As the examples in this article illustrate, however, much remains to be done.

REFERENCES

Arluke, A., Levin, J., and Suchwalko, J. "Sexuality and Romance in Advice Books for the Elderly." *Gerontologist.* In press, 1984.

Blassingame, J. *The Slave Community.* New York: Oxford University Press, 1972.

Gresham, M. "The Infantilization of the Elderly." *Nursing Forum* 15, 1976, pp. 196-209.

Harris, L., and Associates. *The Myth and Reality of Aging in America.* New York: National Council on Aging, 1975.

Helmreich, W. *The Things They Say Behind Your Back.* New York: Doubleday, 1982.

Levin, J., and Arluke, A. "Our Elderly's Fate?" *New York Times,* September 29, 1983, p. A31.

Levin, J. Arluke, A., and Cheren, C. "The Challenge of Ageism." *American Health Care Association Journal* 9, March 1983, pp. 47-50.

Lurie, A. *The Language of Clothing.* New York: Random House, 1982.

McTavish, D. "Perceptions of Old People: A Review of Research Methodologies and Findings." *Gerontologist* 11 (4, Part 2), 1971, pp. 90-101.

Tuckman, J. and Lorge, I. "Attitudes Toward Old People." *Journal of Social Psychology* 37, 1953, pp. 249-260.

Age Stereotyping
College Student Evaluations

WILLIAM C. LEVIN
Bridgewater State College

William C. Levin is Professor in the Department of Sociology/Anthropology at Bridgewater State College in Bridgewater, Massachusetts. He is particularly interested in age prejudice and is currently working on a monograph on the subject of ageism.

College students from California, Tennessee, and Massachusetts evaluated 19 characteristics of a 25-, 52-, or 73-year-old stimulus person on semantic differential scales. Results revealed significantly more negative evaluations of the person when he was older than when he was either middle-aged or younger and were consistent for all three regions of the country.

Since Barron's (1953) proposal that the elderly have some of the characteristics of a minority group, researchers have attempted to document empirically the extent to which this group has been subjected to discrimination and prejudice. This is an especially important question today given the suggestion by some social gerontologists that the existence of age stereotypes in America has been exaggerated (Kogan, 1979; Schonfield, 1982) and by others that attitudes toward the elderly have become increasingly positive (Tibbitts, 1979; Austin, 1985).

While it is possible that age stereotyping has declined, it is also possible that it has merely become more difficult to document. That is, given the public attention that "ageism" received in the 1970s, it may be that respondents have become unwilling to express such stereotypes publicly, and that they can now be better uncovered by experimental methods than by those of survey research. There is precedent from the study of racism for this phenomenon. After the great increase in attention to issues of race in the 1950s and 1960s, a number of studies reported declines in racist attitudes in the culture (Karlins, Coffman and Walters, 1969; Taylor, Sheatsley, and Greeley, 1978). However, it was also suggested by some research that attention to issues of race had made the expression of racial stereotypes socially unacceptable and that measured declines in stereotyping may have been the result of "a little fading and a little faking" (Sigall and Page, 1971).

Many of the studies reporting age stereotyping in the culture have been criticized for their employment of survey research techniques (McTavish, 1971; Cochran, 1977; Green, 1981, Braithwaite, Gibson, and Holman, 1986). Among the problems raised are (1) the transparency and social desirability effect of asking respondents to express negative attitudes toward the elderly (Green, 1981), (2) the inaccuracies inherent in evaluating a group of people as heterogeneous as the elderly by the use of generalized stimuli such as "older people" (Braithwaite, Gibson, and Holman,

1986), and (3) the creation of unrealistic contexts in which evaluations are made (Green, 1981).

To deal with these problems some research has employed experimental methods (Bell and Stanfield, 1973; Crockett, Press, and Osterkamp, 1979; O'Connell and Rotter, 1979; Levin and Levin, 1981; Banziger and Drevenstedt, 1982; Puckett et al., 1983). Experimental designs allow the researcher to deal with (1) transparency and social desirability effect, by concealing from subjects the intent of the study to test for the existence of age stereotypes; (2) generalized targets, by presenting a specific "stimulus person" about whom evaluations are made; and (3) unrealistic or absent, contexts by presenting the stimulus person in a concrete, realistic setting in which he or she might be found and evaluated.

The criticisms of the contexts in which evaluations of older persons have been measured present a particularly difficult problem. For example, Green (1981) has contended that where evaluations are made of old people as a general category, negative perceptions have been found. However, when individual targets are rated, no such stereotyping is found. In addition, Wingard, Heath, and Himelstein (1982) examined the effects of procedural context and reported that when subjects are asked to evaluate the characteristics of old versus young people, significantly more negative attitudes toward the elderly are discovered than when evaluations are made of old people only.

To deal with these problems, the present study consisted of a series of experimental sessions in which each subject was presented at random with one of three photographs taken of the same person, each photograph having been taken at a different age in his life (25, 52, and 73: see photographs). Subjects were then asked to read the resume data of the person whose photograph they had received (this information was bogus and was held constant for the three conditions) and, after looking at the photograph, to make evaluations of his characteristics on a series of dependent variable measures. It was expected that the problems of generalized evaluation and context would be resolved since (1) each subject received only one photograph to evaluate, (2) the evaluations were of the individual and not made in comparison with any other individual or age group, and (3) the simulation of a job candidate's evaluation would be seen as concrete and realistic. That is, it was hoped that the context in which age-related judgments were being made would be like the real world.

It was hypothesized that the older "stimulus person" would be more negatively evaluated than he would be in either his middle-aged or younger photographs. It was further hypothesized that since age stereotyping is a characteristic of the overall culture, such differences would be found in all three samples and that male and female evaluations would not differ by age of the stimulus person.

AUTHOR'S NOTE: This research was supported in part by grants from the Bridgewater State College Faculty Research Program and the Alumni Foundation.

Method

SUBJECTS

The subjects for this study were three samples (approximately 170 each sample) of undergraduate students enrolled in introductory courses in economics and management at San Francisco State University, East Tennessee State University, and Salem State College (Massachusetts). Subjects at each of the campuses

Figure 1

did not differ by mean age (X = 20.83, X = 21.16, X = 21.28, p < .381). Participation was voluntary and anonymous.

MATERIALS AND PROCEDURE

In each experimental session during regular class meetings, subjects were told the following by the researcher:

There have recently been some studies conducted in social psychology that have identified some very successful managers who displayed an uncanny ability to accurately evaluate the qualities of job candidates on the basis of very little information. A number of personnel officers were shown photographs of job candidates and given a few facts from the candidates' resumes. They then made guesses about the characteristics of the people in the photographs. Surprisingly, the individuals who made the most accurate evaluations (and some, as I said, were amazingly accurate), were not necessarily the most experienced in personnel;

that is, years on the job. It may be, then, that this skill in making judgment from a first impression is acquired earlier in life, before entering a career in business.

Each subject was then given an envelope in which there was "a picture of a person to be evaluated and a few facts from his resume." Subjects were asked to open the envelopes, read the resume data (a few sentences stating that the person in the photograph "was born in Springfield, Illinois, currently lives in Boston, and is interested in marketing and sales"), and look at the picture for 15 seconds. They then responded to 19 seven-point semantic differential items that served as dependent variable measures of a range of personal characteristics of the stimulus person. The last three items measured were (1) the age of the evaluator, (2) their estimation as to how accurate they had been in their evaluations, and (3) as a check on the manipulation, their guess as to the age of the person in their photograph.

After each experimental session, the subjects were asked to discuss the study in which they had just participated. To discover whether they had "seen through" the manipulation, they were asked how accurate they thought they had been in their guesses and whether they thought it was possible to make evaluations on the basis of so little information. In their verbal responses most said they could not tell how accurate they had been, but only two subjects from the three sessions said that the task was impossible. Analysis of the responses to the evaluation accuracy question revealed a mean estimate of accuracy of 4.96, with 7.0 being the most accurate and 1.0 being the least accurate. In other words, the subjects believed that they could in fact "tell a book by its cover" with some accuracy.

In addition, subjects expressed interest in how they had done. They wished to be informed of the results, especially the comparison of their accuracy of evaluation with those of students from the other campuses studied. When told that the true purpose of the study was to look at attitudes toward age, the subjects were consistently surprised. (After the study, the subjects were of course reassured that the results were anonymous and were given a talk on the literature of ageism and the problems and dangers of making such "face" evaluations.)

STIMULUS PHOTOGRAPH

The key to this study was the acquisition of photographs to serve as stimulus. A photograph from a 1940 college yearbook of a 25-year-old male was found in which the clothes, hairstyle, and photography did not reveal that this was an old picture. The male in the photograph was located and agreed to provide a later photograph of when he was 52 that matched the first photograph for clothing, lighting, head and body position, facial expression, and hairstyle. (This particular man had held some prominent executive positions and had many photographs from which we could choose.) He was then rephotographed at age 73 in the appropriate clothing, lighting, and position to match the first two pictures. All three photographs were then professionally reproduced to equalize their tone qualities and screening counts.

CHECK ON THE MANIPULATION

Analysis of the scores for the evaluators' estimates of the age of their target person provided a check on the effectiveness of the manipulation. Results revealed that those in the "young" condition (photograph at age 25) had a mean age estimation of 25.1, those in the "middle-age" condition estimated the age of the photographed person at 49.1, and those in the "old" condition estimated the age at 68.7 (F = 1,294, p < .001).

Beliefs about the characteristics of the target person were measured on 19 seven-point semantic differential items ranging, for each characteristic, from 7 for the most positive evaluation to 1 for the most negative. For example:

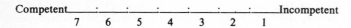

Competent____:____:____:____:____:____:____Incompetent
       7   6   5   4   3   2   1

Such semantic differential measures have been used successfully in a number of studies on attitudes toward age (Ross and Freitag, 1976; O'Connell and Rotter, 1979; Decker, 1983).

The 19 characteristics measured were the following:

(1) activity—active vs. passive
(2) competence—competent vs. incompetent
(3) intelligence—high I.Q. vs. low I.Q.
(4) power—powerful vs. weak
(5) health—healthy vs. sickly
(6) security—secure vs. insecure
(7) creativity—creative vs. uncreative
(8) speed—fast vs. slow
(9) attractiveness—attractive vs. ugly
(10) pleasantness—pleasant vs. unpleasant
(11) reliability—reliable vs. unreliable
(12) energy—energetic vs. lazy
(13) calm—calm vs. irritable
(14) flexibility—flexible vs. rigid
(15) education—educated vs. uneducated
(16) generosity—generous vs. selfish
(17) wealth—wealthy vs. poor
(18) memory—good memory vs. poor memory
(19) social Involvement—involved vs. socially isolated

These characteristics were selected from lists of age stereotypes included in Robert Butler's (1975, p. 6) summary description of the cultural image of the elderly in America and the National Council on the Aging report of the results of a Louis Harris (1975) survey of American adults. From the extensive lists of characteristics that were available, only those that seemed appropriate for the evaluation of a job candidate were chosen.

Results

A 3 × 2 analysis of variance (age of stimulus person × sex of subject) was conducted on scores for each of the 19 dependent variable characteristics. The results revealed that, as hypothesized, the older target person was more negatively evaluated for a wide range of characteristics than either the middle-aged or younger person and that this was the case in all three regions of the country in which data were collected. These results occurred among both male and female evaluators.[1] In the San Francisco sample, the older target was evaluated significantly more negatively on 14 of the 19 characteristics, in the Tennessee sample on 17 of the 19, and in the Massachusetts sample on 15 of the 19. (See Tables 1-3 for summary of results.)

On 12 of the dependent variable measures, the older target person was evaluated significantly more negatively by the subjects from all three samples. Of the 19 dependent variable measures, only one characteristic, generosity, failed to produce significant differences by age in any of the three samples. The dependent variable, wealth, produced significant differences by age in only one of the three samples, with the older person evaluated as significantly less wealthy. And five more dependent variables, creativity, flexibility, security, pleasantness, and degree of calm, produced significant differences by age in two of the three samples. In each of these cases, again, the older person was more

TABLE 1
Means and F Scores for Effect of Age of Target on Evaluations
for 19 Characteristics (D.V.s), San Francisco Sample (N = 173)

Dependent Variable Characteristics	Mean Evaluations: (Lower scores indicate more negative evaluations)			F-Score	Significance (P. < .05)
	Young (N=57)	Middle (N=64)	Old (N=52)		
Activity	4.74	4.09	3.31	16.01	Sig.
Competence	5.26	5.19	4.29	10.41	Sig.
Intelligence	5.18	5.27	4.50	6.95	Sig.
Power	4.72	4.56	4.08	4.26	Sig.
Health	5.61	4.75	3.71	29.30	Sig.
Security	4.75	4.86	4.37	2.91	N.S.
Creativity	4.47	4.06	3.69	4.82	Sig.
Speed	4.65	4.39	3.17	21.83	Sig.
Attractiveness	5.04	3.44	2.77	43.94	Sig.
Pleasantness	4.75	4.55	4.48	.62	N.S.
Reliability	5.02	5.36	4.75	3.60	Sig.
Energy	4.67	4.36	3.54	12.84	Sig.
Calm	5.02	5.30	4.85	2.84	N.S.
Flexibility	4.46	4.20	3.87	3.75	Sig.
Education	5.54	5.83	5.27	4.52	Sig.
Generosity	4.47	4.34	4.77	1.68	N.S.
Wealth	4.91	4.89	4.75	1.02	N.S.
Memory	4.70	5.16	3.98	14.86	Sig.
Social Involvement	5.07	4.47	4.19	6.42	Sig.

negatively evaluated as less creative, flexible, secure, pleasant, and calm.

MULTIPLE MEANS COMPARISON

Since this study employed the evaluation of a person at three different ages, a significant main effect for age merely indicated that at least one age was evaluated significantly differently from one of the others. That is, it is possible that a significant F value was created by the difference in the evaluation of the young and middle-aged person, in which case age stereotyping of older persons would not have been shown. To establish that in each analysis the older person was judged significantly more negatively than at least one of the other ages, Dunnett's procedure for comparing treatment means with a control was employed (Winer, 1962). It was found that in every instance in which the age of the "target person" was significant, the evaluation of the older person was significantly more negative than at least one of the other ages and, in most cases, was significantly different from both.

Conclusions and Implications

These results indicate strong and consistent age stereotypes by college students against a specific male target. He was evaluated in the concrete context of application for a job and in the absence of comparison with younger applicants. Thus the evaluation procedure was uncontaminated by generalized evaluation of "older people," noncontextual or unrealistic context evaluation, or invidious comparison with younger people.

The present research was designed to deal with some of the methodological problems in measuring age stereotypes, but it has also raised some further ones. For example, care was taken to

TABLE 2
Means and F Scores for Effect of Age of Target on Evaluations for 19
Characteristics (D.V.s), East Tennessee State University Sample (N = 151)

Dependent Variable Characteristics	Mean Evaluations: (Lower scores indicate more negative evaluations)			F-Score	Significance (P. < .Ø5)
	Young (N=42)	Middle (N=52)	Old (N=57)		
Activity	5.Ø7	3.9Ø	3.57	18.14	Sig.
Competence	5.17	5.29	4.7Ø	4.14	Sig.
Intelligence	5.21	5.31	4.56	7.16	Sig.
Power	5.Ø5	4.52	3.83	9.33	Sig.
Health	5.93	5.19	4.Ø2	41.19	Sig.
Security	5.28	4.98	4.44	6.Ø7	Sig.
Creativity	4.55	3.98	3.56	5.75	Sig.
Speed	4.76	4.15	3.29	17.11	Sig.
Attractiveness	5.Ø2	3.65	2.93	33.41	Sig.
Pleasantness	4.98	4.67	4.19	3.67	Sig.
Reliability	5.41	5.62	4.88	5.54	Sig.
Energy	5.1Ø	4.39	3.61	17.15	Sig.
Calm	5.31	5.29	4.68	2.49	N.S.
Flexibility	4.86	4.Ø8	3.72	6.8Ø	Sig.
Education	5.91	5.81	5.ØØ	9.34	Sig.
Generosity	4.45	4.54	4.26	.58	N.S.
Wealth	5.33	4.81	4.68	5.38	Sig.
Memory	5.43	5.29	4.35	14.98	Sig.
Social Involvement	5.83	4.37	4.12	22.Ø3	Sig.

make the stimulus photographs equivalent on a variety of qualities (even in the age 73 photograph the stimulus target had a full head of hair and no glasses), but there was no way to hold constant the attractiveness of the person in the three conditions. This was because attractiveness is strongly related to age in our culture. Expert judges could not be expected to find the same person equally attractive as a young, middle-aged, and old man. In addition, it was impossible to find three comparison photographs of a female target person. Clothing, hairstyles, and photographic "fuzzing" of females' portraits made photographs from the 1940s "dated looking." Consequently, results of this study may not be generalized to females. Lastly, though post-manipulation interviews with the respondents suggested that they

TABLE 3
Means and F Scores for Effect of Age of Target
on Evaluations for 19 Characteristics (D.V.s),
Salem State College (Massachusetts) Sample (N = 163)

Dependent Variable Characteristics	Mean Evaluations: (Lower scores indicate more negative evaluations)			F-Score	Significance (P. < .Ø5)
	Young (N=53)	Middle (N=55)	Old (N=55)		
Activity	5.17	4.16	3.8Ø	19.31	Sig.
Competence	5.42	5.4Ø	4.58	12.9Ø	Sig.
Intelligence	5.11	5.35	4.38	14.68	Sig.
Power	5.15	4.38	3.95	11.43	Sig.
Health	5.89	5.ØØ	3.95	41.83	Sig.
Security	5.Ø2	5.13	4.58	3.17	Sig.
Creativity	4.15	4.ØØ	3.86	.63	N.S.
Speed	4.66	4.2Ø	3.51	11.82	Sig.
Attractiveness	4.93	3.53	3.33	25.5Ø	Sig.
Pleasantness	4.93	4.51	4.Ø6	6.94	Sig.
Reliability	5.26	5.75	4.8Ø	11.15	Sig.
Energy	5.ØØ	4.49	3.93	11.21	Sig.
Calm	5.ØØ	4.89	4.35	3.Ø6	Sig.
Flexibility	4.49	4.15	3.91	2.9Ø	N.S.
Education	5.49	5.87	5.2Ø	6.44	Sig.
Generosity	4.64	4.49	4.51	.24	N.S.
Wealth	5.Ø9	4.86	4.93	.69	N.S.
Memory	5.38	5.13	4.Ø4	19.82	Sig.
Social Involvement	5.38	4.46	3.51	3Ø.13	Sig.

had thought it reasonable to evaluate total strangers on the basis of a bit of resume information and photograph, the task was not as realistic as an actual job interview.

Though these results seem strong and consistent across samples, there is a need for further data to show whether the same sorts of stereotypes are held toward older females and by subjects of different ages.

THE DILEMMA OF STEREOTYPES VERSUS PROBABILISTIC EVALUATIONS

One of the most powerful differences in age evaluations uncovered in this study is that the same man was judged to be much less attractive in later life (to both male and female evaluators) than he was when younger. This seems to provide clear evidence of a negative attitude toward age in our culture. However, what about the attitudes toward age that seem to be based on data about the realities of biological aging? The data supporting the notion of inevitable decline with age are widely accepted in the American culture. Therefore, if a respondent in this study guesses that the energy or health levels of a 70-year-old person are low, is that respondent expressing a negative stereotype of the elderly or merely a probabilistic evaluation for which there is widespread evidence?

This issue has already been dealt with in the study of race and gender stereotyping. Some years ago, racist and sexist stereotypes were based on relatively unchallenged, if unsound, biological evidence (Gould, 1981). Today, such arguments are rare. It is not that there are no data at all that can be cited to support stereotypes, but that the relationship between data and stereotyping has been made clear.

Stereotypes are exaggerations of reality that are applied to entire groups of people. It is virtually unavoidable that there be a kernel of truth on which a stereotype may be based. For example, there are certainly some emotional women, some musical Blacks, and some clannish Jews. What makes for stereotyping is the extension of such characteristics to all members of a given group and to any individual who belongs to the group. In the area of race stereotyping, the evidence that Black Americans score lower than white Americans on standard tests of intelligence does not prevent us from labeling as a stereotype the belief that Blacks are naturally less intelligent than whites.

Clearly, there is evidence that qualities such as activity and health do decline over time for some people. But, as every text in social gerontology is careful to point out, the elderly are still the most heterogeneous stratum in the age spectrum. The data presented here, however, affirm that older people continue to be lumped together and negatively evaluated, even on characteristics for which there is no evidence, or poor evidence, for decline. For example, the older person was more negatively evaluated for intelligence though it is increasingly clear from the evidence that intelligence does not decline in everyone or in every area of intelligence with age (Baltes and Labouvie, 1973).

Though gerontologists have continued to collect data to the contrary, older Americans are still judged to be of lower competence, activity, intelligence, attractiveness, health, and so on, than their younger counterparts. Senescence may be a fact, but the extent to which it occurs can surely be exaggerated and its effect accelerated by excessive acceptance of its role in later life. In addition, to the extent that the elderly are stereotyped, there will seem to be evidence that justifies denying them opportunities for employment and other varieties of social involvement that contribute vitally to social integration (Butler, 1975; Levin and Levin, 1980; Binstock, 1983).

3. SOCIETAL ATTITUDES TOWARD OLD AGE

NOTE

1. In the 57 analyses (3 samples with 19 dependent variables each), there were only 4 significant first-order interactions between age of target and sex of evaluator, approximately the number of significant interactions one might expect by chance alone (type I error).

REFERENCES

Austin, D. R. 1985. "Attitudes Toward Old Age: A Hierarchical Study." *Gerontologist* 25:431-434.

Baltes, P. and G. Labouvie. 1973. "Adult Development of Intellectual Performance: Description, Explanation and Modification." In *The Psychology of Adult Development and Aging,* edited by C. Eisendorfer and M. Lawton. Washington, DC: American Psychological Association.

Banziger, G. and J. Drevenstedt. 1982. "Achievement Attributions by Young and Old Judges as a Function of Perceived Age of Stimulus Person." *Journal of Gerontology* 37:468-474.

Barron, Milton L. 1953. "Minority Group Characteristics of the Aged in American Society." *Journal of Gerontology* 8:477-482.

Bell, B. D. and G. G. Stanfield. 1973. "The Aging Stereotype in Experimental Perspective." *Gerontologist* 13:341-344.

Binstock, R. H. 1983. "The Aged as Scapegoat." *Gerontologist* 23:136-143.

Braithwaite, V., D. Gibson, and J. Holman. 1986. "Age Stereotyping: Are We Oversimplifying the Phenomenon?" *International Journal of Aging and Human Development* 22:315-325.

Butler, Robert N. 1975. *Why Survive? Being Old in America.* New York: Harper & Row.

Cochran, W. A. 1977. "Comment on Survey Research in Aging. *Gerontologist* 18:64-66.

Crockett, W. H., A. N. Press, and M. Osterkamp M. 1979. "The Effect of Deviations from Stereotyped Expectations upon Attitudes Toward Old People." *Journal of Geron-tology* 34:368-374.

Decker, W. H. 2983. "Stereotypes of Middle-Aged and Elderly Professionals." *Psychology* 20:60-67.

Gould, S. J. 1981. *The Mismeasure of Man.* New York: Norton.

Green, S. K. 1981. "Attitudes and Perceptions About the Elderly: Current and Future Perspectives." *International Journal of Aging and Human Development* 13:99-119.

Louis Harris and Associates. 1975. *The Myth and Reality of Aging in America.* New York: National Council on Aging.

Karlins, M., T. Coffman, and G. Walters. 1969. "On the Fading of Social Stereotypes: Studies in Three Generations of College Students." *Journal of Personality and Social Psychology* 13:1-16.

Kogan, N. 1979. "Beliefs, Attitudes and Stereotypes About Old People: A New Look at Some Old Issues." *Research on Aging* 1:11-36.

Levin, J. and W. C. Levin. 1980. *Ageism: Prejudice and Discrimination Against the Elderly.* Belmont, CA: Wadsworth.

Levin, J. and W. C. Levin. 1981. "Willingness to Interact with an Old Person." *Research on Aging* 3:211-217.

McTavish, Donald G. 1971. "Perceptions of Old People: A Review of Research, Methodologies, and Findings." *Gerontologist* 11:90-101.

O'Connell, A. N. and N. G. Rotter. 1979. "The Influence of Stimulus Age and Sex on Person Perception." *Journal of Gerontology* 34:220-228.

Puckett J. M., R. E. Petty, J. T. Cacioppo, and D. L. Fischer. 1983. "The Relative Impact of Age Attractiveness Stereotypes on Persuasion." *Journal of Gerontology* 38:340-343.

Ross, R. F. and C. B. Freitag. 1976. "A Comparison of Adolescent and Adult Attitudes Toward the Aged." *Educational Gerontology* 1:291-295.

Schonfield, D. 1982. "Who Is Stereotyping Whom and Why?" *Gerontologist* 22:267-272.

Sigall, H. and R. Page. 1971. "Current Stereotypes: A Little Fading, a Little Faking." *Journal of Personality and Social Psychology* 18:247-255.

Taylor, D., P. Sheatsley, and A. Greeley. 1978. "Attitudes Toward Racial Integration." *Scientific American* 238:42-49.

Tibbitts, C. 1979. "Can We Invalidate Negative Stereotypes of Aging?" *Gerontologist* 19:10-20.

Winer, B. J. 1962. *Statistical Principles in Experimental Design.* New York: McGraw-Hill.

Wingard, J. A., R. Heath, and S. A. Himelstein. 1982. "The Effect of Contextual Variations on Attitudes Toward the Elderly." *Journal of Gerontology* 37:475-482.

The Vintage Years

THE GROWING NUMBER OF HEALTHY, VIGOROUS OLDER PEOPLE HAS HELPED OVERCOME SOME STEREOTYPES ABOUT AGING. FOR MANY, THE BEST IS YET TO COME.

Jack C. Horn and Jeff Meer

Jack C. Horn is a senior editor and Jeff Meer is an assistant editor at the magazine.

Our society is getting older, but the old are getting younger. As Sylvia Herz told an American Psychological Association (APA) symposium on aging last year, the activities and attitudes of a 70-year-old today "are equivalent to those of a 50-year-old's a decade or two ago."

Our notions of what it means to be old are beginning to catch up with this reality. During the past several decades, three major changes have altered the way we view the years after 65:

• The financial, physical and mental health of older people has improved, making the prospect of a long life something to treasure, not fear.

• The population of older people has grown dramatically, rising from 18 million in 1965 to 28 million today. People older than 65 compose 12 percent of the population, a percentage that is expected to rise to more than 20 percent by the year 2030.

• Researchers have gained a much better understanding of aging and the lives of older people, helping to sort out the inevitable results of biological aging from the effects of illness or social and environmental problems. No one has yet found the fountain of youth, or of immortality. But research has revealed that aging itself is not the thief we once thought it was; healthy older people can maintain and enjoy most of their physical and mental abilities, and even improve in some areas.

Because of better medical care, improved diet and increasing interest in physical fitness, more people are reaching the ages of 65, 75 and older in excellent health. Their functional age—a combination of physical, psychological and social factors that affect their attitudes toward life and the roles they play in the world—is much younger than their chronological age.

Their economic health is better, too, by almost every measure. Over the last three decades, for example, the number of men and women 65 and older who live below the poverty line has dropped steadily from 35 percent in 1959 to 12 percent in 1984, the last year for which figures are available.

On the upper end of the economic scale, many of our biggest companies are headed by what once would have been called senior citizens, and many more of them serve as directors of leading companies. Even on a more modest economic level, a good portion of the United States' retired older people form a new leisure class, one with money to spend and the time to enjoy it. Obviously not all of America's older people share this prosperity. Economic hardship is particularly prevalent among minorities. But as a group, our older people are doing better than ever.

In two other areas of power, politics and the law, people in their 60s and 70s have always played important roles. A higher percentage of people from 65 to 74 register and vote than in any other group. With today's increasing vigor and numbers, their power is likely to increase still further. It is perhaps no coincidence that our current President is the oldest ever.

Changing attitudes, personal and social, are a major reason for the increasing importance of older people in our society. As psychologist

Bernice Neugarten points out, there is no longer a particular age at which someone starts to work or attends school, marries and has children, retires or starts a business. Increasing numbers of older men and women are enrolled in colleges, universities and other institutions of learning. According to the Center for Education Statistics, for example, the number of people 65 and older enrolled in adult education of all kinds increased from 765,000 to 866,000 from 1981 to 1984. Gerontologist Barbara Ober says that this growing interest in education is much more than a way to pass the time. "Older people make excellent students, maybe even better students than the majority of 19- and 20-year-olds. One advantage is that they have settled a lot of the social and sexual issues that preoccupy their younger classmates."

Older people today are not only healthier and more active; they are also increasingly more numerous. "Squaring the pyramid" is how some demographers describe this change in our population structure. It has always been thought of as a pyramid, a broad base of newborns supporting successively smaller tiers of older people as they died from disease, accidents, poor nutrition, war and other causes.

Today, the population structure is becoming more rectangular, as fewer people die during the earlier stages of life. The Census Bureau predicts that by 2030 the structure will be an almost perfect rectangle up to the age of 70.

The aging of America has been going on at least since 1800, when half the people in the country were younger than 16 years old, but two factors have accelerated the trend tremendously. First, the number of old people has increased rapidly. Since 1950 the number of Americans 65 and older has more than doubled to some 28 million—more than the entire current population of Canada. Within the same period, the number of individuals older than 85 has quadrupled to about 2.6 million (see "The Oldest Old," this article).

Second, the boom in old people has been paired with a bust in the proportion of youngsters due to a declining birth rate. Today, fewer than one American in four is younger than 16. This drop-off has been steady, with the single exception of the post-World War II baby boom, which added 76 million children to the country between 1945 and 1964. As these baby boomers reach the age of 65, starting in 2010, they are expected to increase the proportion of the population 65 and older from its current 12 percent to 21 percent by 2030.

The growing presence of healthy, vigorous older people has helped overcome some of the stereotypes about aging and the elderly. Research has also played a major part by replacing myths with facts. While there were some studies of aging before World War II, scientific

> A man over 90 is a great comfort to all his elderly neighbours: he is a picket-guard at the extreme outpost; and the young folks of 60 and 70 feel that the enemy must get by him before he can come near their camp.
> —Oliver Wendell Holmes, *The Guardian Angel.*

BY THE YEAR 2030 MORE THAN 20 PERCENT OF THE POPULATION IS EXPECTED TO BE 65 OR OLDER.

interest increased dramatically during the 1950s and kept growing.

Important early studies of aging included three started in the mid or late 1950s: the Human Aging Study, conducted by the National Institute of Mental Health (NIMH); the Duke Longitudinal Studies, done by the Center for the Study of Aging and Human Development at Duke University; and the Baltimore Longitudinal Study of Aging, conducted by the Gerontological Institute in Baltimore, now part of the National Institute on Aging (NIA). All three took a multidisciplinary approach to the study of normal aging: what changes take place, how people adapt to them, how biological, genetic, social, psychological and environmental characteristics relate to longevity and what can be done to promote successful aging.

These pioneering studies and hundreds of later ones have benefited from growing federal support. White House Conferences on Aging in 1961 and 1971 helped focus attention on the subject. By 1965 Congress had enacted Medicare and the Older Americans Act. During the 1970s Congress authorized the establishment of the NIA as part of the National Institutes of Health and NIMH created a special center to support research on the mental health of older people.

All these efforts have produced a tremendous growth in our knowledge of aging. In the first (1971) edition of the *Handbook of the Psychology of Aging,* it was estimated that as much had been published on the subject in the previous 15 years as in all the years before then. In the second edition, published in 1985, psychologists James Birren and Walter Cunningham wrote that the "period for this rate of doubling has now decreased to 10 years...the volume of published research has increased to the almost unmanageable total of over a thousand articles a year."

Psychologist Clifford Swenson of Purdue

University explained some of the powerful incentives for this tremendous increase: "I study the topic partly to discover more effective ways of helping old people cope with their problems, but also to load my own armamentarium against that inevitable day. For that is one aspect of aging and its problems that makes it different from the other problems psychologists study: We may not all be schizophrenic or neurotic or overweight, but there is only one alternative to old age and most of us try to avoid that alternative."

One popular misconception disputed by recent research is the idea that aging means inevitable physical and sexual failure. Some changes occur, of course. Reflexes slow, hearing and eyesight dim, stamina decreases. This *primary aging* is a gradual process that begins early in life and affects all body systems.

But many of the problems we associate with old age are *secondary aging*—the results not of age but of disease, abuse and disuse—factors often under our own control. More and more older people are healthy, vigorous men and women who lead enjoyable, active lives. National surveys by the Institute for Social Research and others show that life generally seems less troublesome and freer to older people than it does to younger adults.

In a review of what researchers have learned about subjective well-being—happiness, life satisfaction, positive emotions—University of Illinois psychologist Ed Diener reported that "Most results show a slow rise in satisfaction with age. . .young persons appear to experience higher levels of joy but older persons tend to judge their lives in more positive ways."

Money is often mentioned as the key to a happy retirement, but psychologist Daniel Ogilvie of Rutgers University has found another, much more important, factor. Once we have a certain minimum amount of money, his research shows, life satisfaction depends mainly on how much time we spend doing things we find meaningful. Ogilvie believes retirement-planning workshops and seminars should spend more time helping people decide how to use their skills and interests after they retire.

A thought that comes through clearly when researchers talk about physical and mental fitness is "use it or lose it." People rust out faster from disuse than they wear out from overuse. This advice applies equally to sexual activity. While every study from the time of Kinsey to the present shows that sexual interest and activity diminish with age, the drop varies greatly among individuals. Psychologist Marion Perlmutter and writer Elizabeth Hall have reported that one of the best predictors of continued sexual intercourse "is early sexual activity and past sexual enjoyment and frequency. People who have never had much pleasure from sexu-

WHILE THE OLD AND THE YOUNG MAY BE EQUALLY COMPETENT, THEY ARE DIFFERENTLY COMPETENT.

ality may regard their age as a good excuse for giving up sex."

They also point out that changing times affect sexual activity. As today's younger adults bring their more liberal sexual attitudes with them into old age, the level of sexual activity among older men and women may rise.

The idea that mental abilities decline steadily with age has also been challenged by many recent and not-so-recent findings (see "The Reason of Age," *Psychology Today*, June 1986). In brief, age doesn't damage abilities as much as was once believed, and in some areas we actually gain; we learn to compensate through experience for much of what we do lose; and we can restore some losses through training.

For years, older people didn't do as well as younger people on most tests used to measure mental ability. But psychologist Leonard Poon of the University of Georgia believes that researchers are now taking a new, more appropriate approach to measurement. "Instead of looking at older people's ability to do abstract tasks that have little or no relationship to what they do every day, today's researchers are examining real-life issues."

Psychologist Gisela Labouvie-Vief of Wayne State University has been measuring how people approach everyday problems in logic. She notes that older adults have usually done poorly on such tests, mostly because they fail to think logically all the time. But Labouvie-Vief argues that this is not because they have forgotten how to think logically but because they use a more complex approach unknown to younger thinkers. "The [older] thinker operates within a kind of double reality which is both formal and informal, both logical and psychological," she says.

In other studies, Labouvie-Vief has found that when older people were asked to give concise summaries of fables they read, they did so. But when they were simply asked to recall as much of the fable as possible, they concentrat-

The pleasures that once were heaven Look silly at sixty-seven.
—Noel Coward, *"What's Going to Happen to the Tots?"*

Old age consoles itself by giving good precepts for being unable to give bad examples.
—La Rochefoucauld, *The Maxims.*

THE OLDEST OLD: THE YEARS AFTER 85

Every man desires to live long, but no man would be old," or so Jonathan Swift believed. Some people get their wish to live long and become what are termed the "oldest old," those 85 and older. During the past 22 years, this group has increased by 165 percent to 2.5 million and now represents more than 1 percent of the population.

Who are these people and what are their lives like? One of the first to study them intensively is gerontologist Charles Longino of the University of Miami, who uses 1980 census data to examine their lives for the American Association of Retired People.

He found, not surprisingly, that nearly 70 percent are women. Of these, 82 percent are widowed, compared with 44 percent of the men. Because of the conditions that existed when they were growing up, the oldest old are poorly educated compared with young people today, most of whom finish high school. The average person now 85 years and older only completed the eighth grade.

Only one-quarter of these older citizens are in hospitals or institutions such as nursing homes, and more than half live in their own homes. Just 30 percent live by themselves. More than a third live with a spouse or with their children. There are certainly those who aren't doing well—one in six have incomes below the poverty level—but many more are relatively well-off. The mean household income for the group, Longino says, was more than $20,000 in 1985.

What of the quality of life? "In studying this group, we have to be aware of youth creep," he says. "The old are getting younger all the time." This feeling is confirmed by a report released late last year by the National Institute on Aging. The NIA report included three studies of people older than 65 conducted in two counties in Iowa, in East Boston, Massachusetts, and in New Haven, Connecticut. There are large regional differences between the groups, of course, and they aren't a cross-section of older people in the nation as a whole. But in all three places, most of those older than 85 seem to be leading fulfilling lives.

Most socialize in a variety of ways. In Iowa, more than half say they go to religious services at least once a week and the same percentage say they belong to some type of professional, social, church-related or recreational group. More than three-quarters see at least one or two children once a month and almost that many see other close relatives that often.

As you would expect, many of the oldest old suffer from disabilities and serious health problems. At least a quarter of those who responded have been in a hospital overnight in the past year and at least 8 percent have had heart attacks or have diabetes. In Iowa and New Haven, more than 13 percent of the oldest old had cancer, while in East Boston the rate was lower (between 7 percent and 8 percent). Significant numbers of the oldest old have suffered serious injury from falls. Other common health problems for this group are high blood pressure and urinary incontinence. However, epidemiologist Adrian Ostfeld, who directed the survey in New Haven, notes that "most of the disability was temporary."

Longino has found that almost 10 percent of the oldest old live alone with a disability that prevents them from using public transportation. This means that they are "isolated from the daily hands-on care of others," he says. "Even so, there are a surprising number of the oldest old who don't need much in the way of medical care. They're the survivors.

"I think we have to agree that the oldest old is, as a group, remarkably diverse," Longino says. "Just as it is unfair to say that those older than 85 are all miserable, it's not fair to say that they all lead wonderful lives, either."
—*Jeff Meer*

ed on the metaphorical, moral or social meaning of the text. They didn't try to duplicate the fable's exact words, the way younger people did. As psychologists Nancy Datan, Dean Rodeheaver and Fergus Hughes of the University of Wisconsin have described their findings, "while [some people assume] that old and young are equally competent, we might better assume that they are differently competent."

John Horn, director of the Adult Development and Aging program at the University of Southern California, suggests that studies of Alzheimer's disease, a devastating progressive mental deterioration experienced by an estimated 5 percent to 15 percent of those older than 65, may eventually help explain some of the differences in thinking abilities of older people. "Alzheimer's, in some ways, may represent the normal process of aging, only speeded up," he says. (To see how your ideas about Alzheimer's square with the facts, see "Alzheimer's Quiz" and "Alzheimer's Answers," this article.)

Generalities are always suspect, but one generalization about old age seems solid: It is a different experience for men and women. Longevity is one important reason. Women in the United States live seven to eight years longer, on the average, than do men. This simple fact has many ramifications, as sociologist Gunhild Hagestad explained in *Our Aging Society*.

For one thing, since the world of the very old is disproportionately a world of women, men and women spend their later years differently. "Most older women are widows living alone; most older men live with their wives...among individuals over the age of 75, two-thirds of the men are living with a spouse, while less than one-fifth of the women are."

The difference in longevity also means that among older people, remarriage is a male prerogative. After 65, for example, men remarry at a rate eight times that of women. This is partly a matter of the scarcity of men and partly a matter of culture—even late in life, men tend to marry younger women. It is also a matter of education and finances, which, Hagestad explains, "operate quite differently in shaping remarriage probabilities among men and women. The more resources the woman has available (measured in education and income), the less likely she is to remarry. For men, the trend is reversed."

The economic situations of elderly men and women also differ considerably. Lou Glasse, president of the Older Women's League in Washington, D.C., points out that most of these women were housewives who worked at paid jobs sporadically, if at all. "That means their Social Security benefits are lower than men's, they are not likely to have pensions and they are less likely to have been able to save the kind of money that would protect them from poverty during their older years."

Although we often think of elderly men and women as living in nursing homes or retirement communities, the facts are quite different. Only about 5 percent are in nursing homes and perhaps an equal number live in some kind of age-segregated housing. Most people older than 65 live in their own houses or apartments.

We also think of older people as living alone. According to the Census Bureau, this is true of 15 percent of the men and 41 percent of the women. Earlier this year, a survey done by Louis Harris & Associates revealed that 28 percent of elderly people living alone have annual incomes below $5,100, the federal poverty line. Despite this, they were four times as likely to give financial help to their children as to receive it from them.

In addition, fewer than 1 percent of the old people said they would prefer living with their children. Psychiatrist Robert N. Butler, chairman of the Commonwealth Fund's Commission

AMONG OLDER PEOPLE TODAY, REMARRIAGE IS STILL LARGELY A MALE PREROGATIVE, DUE TO THE SEX DIFFERENCE IN LONGEVITY.

on Elderly People Living Alone, which sponsored the report, noted that these findings dispute the "popular portrait of an elderly, dependent parent financially draining their middle-aged children."

There is often another kind of drain, however, one of time and effort. The Travelers Insurance Company recently surveyed more than 700 of its employees on this issue. Of those at least 30 years old, 28 percent said they directly care for an older relative in some way—taking that person to the doctor, making telephone calls, handling finances or running errands—for an average of 10 hours a week. Women, who are more often caregivers, spent an average of 16 hours, and men five hours, per week. One group, 8 percent of the sample, spent a heroic 35 hours per week, the equivalent of a second job, providing such care. "That adds up to an awful lot of time away from other things," psychologist Beal Lowe says, "and the stresses these people face are enormous."

Lowe, working with Sherman-Lank Communications in Kensington, Maryland, has formed "Caring for Caregivers," a group of professionals devoted to providing services, information and support to those who care for older relatives. "It can be a great shock to some people who have planned the perfect retirement," he says, "only to realize that your chronically ill mother suddenly needs daily attention."

Researchers who have studied the housing needs of older people predictably disagree on many things, but most agree on two points: We need a variety of individual and group living arrangements to meet the varying interests, income and abilities of people older than 65; and the arrangements should be flexible enough that the elderly can stay in the same locale as their needs and abilities change. Many studies have documented the fact that moving itself can be stressful and even fatal to old people, particularly if they have little or no influence over when and where they move.

AGING HAS ITS PLACE: THE ANDRUS CENTER

There are impressive facilities for research on aging throughout the country. Duke University's Center for the Study of Aging and Human Development, the National Institute on Aging's Gerontology Research Center in Baltimore and the Institute of Gerontology at the University of Michigan are just three well-known examples. The Ethel Percy Andrus Gerontology Center at the University of Southern California combines the multidisciplinary research and teaching on aging found at many such facilities with an extraordinarily comprehensive community outreach program.

With research associates and more than 40 faculty members who have joint appointments in other academic disciplines, Andrus has a strong research base. "I think it is unique in terms of the disciplines it spans," says Eileen Crimmins, a sociologist and demographer. "Where else do you see linguists discussing problems of aging with neuroscientists?" Even the building in which the Center is housed was designed specifically to increase contact between the people who work there. According to James Birren, a psychologist who is also director of the Center's Institute for Advanced Study, "We regard interpersonal distraction as an element of our fertility."

The Andrus Center is not an inaccessible ivory tower, but a mecca for students. At least 400 undergraduates take courses in gerontology every year, including about 10 to 15 gerontology majors. The Center also supports a program of continuing education on aging for practitioners and the general public. Some doctoral-level students who earn their degrees in disciplines such as psychology, sociology and economics do the bulk of their work at the Center.

The Center's master's-level students, who usually number about 80, specialize in client services, administration, health planning or policy. They must either complete a thesis or a comprehensive examination. Whichever they choose, most of the students also work part-time at Andrus, helping the Center achieve the third part of its mandate—to bring the fruits of research to the community. "The mission of a place such as Andrus," Birren says, "is not nearly as monastic as it used to be. Instead of placing information in a bottle and setting it adrift in the intellectual sea, hoping someone will find it and make use of it, we try to place the bottle directly in the hands of those who can use the information."

The Center cosponsors the Andrus Older Adult Center (AOAC), located just a block from the Andrus Center itself. There, older people and their families can obtain low-cost mental-health care and referrals from a student and professional staff on problems ranging from depression and memory loss to the stress confronting people who care for patients with Alzheimer's disease.

The counseling, which is priced on a sliding scale based on ability to pay, is done almost exclusively by Andrus graduate students. According to psychologist Margaret Gatz, who directs the clinical psychology training program, "My research shows that the increased sensitivity that the trainees gain toward the aging gets transmitted to other graduate students, even if they aren't themselves involved in the program. It's a ripple effect."

ONE OF OUR ACCOMPLISHMENTS HAS BEEN TO BREAK DOWN STEREOTYPES. WE ARE TRYING TO BE ROLE MODELS FOR OTHER PEOPLE TO COME OUT AND GET INVOLVED.

The Center's strongest link with the community is the Andrus Volunteers program. Under the guidance of Polly McConney, community members ranging in age from their early 60s to their late 80s volunteer one or more days each week. They collaborate with the faculty on research projects and informational-literature projects, sponsor community seminars and visit local senior-citizen centers in Los Angeles. "One of our main accomplishments has been to break down stereotypes," McConney says. "Most of us are extremely healthy and some have chronic disabilities, but we are all trying to be role models for other people to come out and get involved."

—Jeff Meer

This matter of control is important, but more complicated than it seemed at first. Psychologist Judith Rodin and others have demonstrated that people in nursing homes are happier, more alert and live longer if they are allowed to take responsibility for their lives in some way, even in something as simple as choosing a plant for their room, taking care of a bird feeder, selecting the night to attend a movie.

Rodin warns that while control is generally beneficial, the effect depends on the individuals involved. For some, personal control brings with it demands in the form of time, effort and the risk of failure. They may blame themselves if they get sick or something else goes wrong. The challenge, Rodin wrote, is to "provide but not impose opportunities. . . . The need for self-determination, it must be remembered, also calls for the opportunity to choose not to exercise control. . . ."

An ancient Greek myth tells how the Goddess of Dawn fell in love with a mortal and convinced Jupiter to grant him immortality. Unfortunately, she forgot to have youth included in the deal, so he gradually grew older and older. "At length," the story concludes, "he lost the power of using his limbs, and then she shut him up in his chamber, whence his feeble voice might at times be heard. Finally she turned him into a grasshopper."

The fears and misunderstandings of age expressed in this 3,000-year-old myth persist today, despite all the positive things we have learned in recent years about life after 65. We don't turn older people into grasshoppers or shut them out of sight, but too often we move them firmly out of the mainstream of life.

In a speech at the celebration of Harvard

> *If I had known when I was 21 that I should be as happy as I am now, I should have been sincerely shocked. They promised me wormwood and the funeral raven.*
>
> —Christopher Isherwood, letter at age 70.

University's 350th anniversary last September, political scientist Robert Binstock decried what he called The Spectre of the Aging Society: "the economic burdens of population aging; moral dilemmas posed by the allocation of health resources on the basis of age; labor market competition between older and younger workers within the contexts of age discrimination laws; seniority practices, rapid technologi-

ALZHEIMER'S QUIZ

Alzheimer's disease, named for German neurologist Alois Alzheimer, is much in the news these days. But how much do you really know about the disorder? Political scientist Neal B. Cutler of the Andrus Gerontology Center gave the following questions to a 1,500-person cross section of people older than 45 in the United States in November 1985. To compare your answers with theirs and with the correct answers, turn to the next page.

		True	False	Don't know
1.	Alzheimer's disease can be contagious.			
2.	A person will almost certainly get Alzheimer's if they just live long enough.			
3.	Alzheimer's disease is a form of insanity.			
4.	Alzheimer's disease is a normal part of getting older, like gray hair or wrinkles.			
5.	There is no cure for Alzheimer's disease at present.			
6.	A person who has Alzheimer's disease will experience both mental and physical decline.			
7.	The primary symptom of Alzheimer's disease is memory loss.			
8.	Among persons older than age 75, forgetfulness most likely indicates the beginning of Alzheimer's disease.			
9.	When the husband or wife of an older person dies, the surviving spouse may suffer from a kind of depression that looks like Alzheimer's disease.			
10.	Stuttering is an inevitable part of Alzheimer's disease.			
11.	An older man is more likely to develop Alzheimer's disease than an older woman.			
12.	Alzheimer's disease is usually fatal.			
13.	The vast majority of persons suffering from Alzheimer's disease live in nursing homes.			
14.	Aluminum has been identified as a significant cause of Alzheimer's disease.			
15.	Alzheimer's disease can be diagnosed by a blood test.			
16.	Nursing-home expenses for Alzheimer's disease patients are covered by Medicare.			
17.	Medicine taken for high blood pressure can cause symptoms that look like Alzheimer's disease.			

Alzheimer's Answers — National Sample

	True	False	Don't know
1. False. There is no evidence that Alzheimer's is contagious, but given the concern and confusion about AIDS, it is encouraging that nearly everyone knows this fact about Alzheimer's.	3%	83%	14%
2. False. Alzheimer's is associated with old age, but it is a disease and not the inevitable consequence of aging.	9	80	11
3. False. Alzheimer's is a disease of the brain, but it is not a form of insanity. The fact that most people understand the distinction contrasts with the results of public-opinion studies concerning epilepsy that were done 35 years ago. At that time, almost half of the public thought that epilepsy, another disease of the brain, was a form of insanity.	7	78	15
4. False. Again, most of the public knows that Alzheimer's is not an inevitable part of aging.	10	77	13
5. True. Despite announcements of "breakthroughs," biomedical research is in the early laboratory and experimental stages and there is no known cure for the disease.	75	8	17
6. True. Memory and cognitive decline are characteristic of the earlier stages of Alzheimer's disease, but physical decline follows in the later stages.	74	10	16
7. True. Most people know that this is the earliest sign of Alzheimer's disease.	62	19	19
8. False. Most people also know that while Alzheimer's produces memory loss, memory loss may have some other cause.	16	61	23
9. True. This question, like number 8, measures how well people recognize that other problems can mirror Alzheimer's symptoms. This is crucial because many of these other problems are treatable. In particular, depression can cause disorientation that looks like Alzheimer's.	49	20	30
10. False. Stuttering has never been linked to Alzheimer's. The question was designed to measure how willing people were to attribute virtually anything to a devastating disease.	12	46	42

	True	False	Don't know
11. False. Apart from age, research has not uncovered any reliable demographic or ethnic patterns. While there are more older women than men, both sexes are equally likely to get Alzheimer's.	15	45	40
12. True. Alzheimer's produces mental and physical decline that is eventually fatal, although the progression varies greatly among individuals.	40	33	27
13. False. The early and middle stages of the disease usually do not require institutional care. Only a small percentage of those with the disease live in nursing homes.	37	40	23
14. False. There is no evidence that using aluminum cooking utensils, pots or foil causes Alzheimer's, although aluminum compounds have been found in the brain tissue of many Alzheimer's patients. They may simply be side effects of the disease.	8	25	66
15. False. At present there is no definitive blood test that can determine with certainty that a patient has Alzheimer's disease. Accurate diagnosis is possible only upon autopsy. Recent studies suggest that genetic or blood testing may be able to identify Alzheimer's, but more research with humans is needed.	12	24	64
16. False. Medicare generally pays only for short-term nursing-home care subsequent to hospitalization and not for long-term care. Medicaid can pay for long-term nursing-home care, but since it is a state-directed program for the medically indigent, coverage for Alzheimer's patients depends upon state regulations and on the income of the patient and family.	16	23	61
17. True. As mentioned earlier, many medical problems have Alzheimer's-like symptoms and most of these other causes are treatable. Considering how much medicine older people take, it is unfortunate that so few people know that medications such as those used to treat high blood pressure can cause these symptoms.	20	19	61

cal change; and a politics of conflict between age groups."

Binstock, a professor at Case Western Reserve School of Medicine, pointed out that these inaccurate perceptions express an underlying ageism, "the attribution of these same characteristics and status to an artificially homogenized group labeled 'the aged.'"

Ironically, much ageism is based on compassion rather than ill will. To protect older workers from layoffs, for example, unions fought hard for job security based on seniority. To win it, they accepted mandatory retirement, a limitation that now penalizes older workers and deprives our society of their experience.

A few companies have taken special steps to utilize this valuable pool of older workers. The Travelers companies, for example, set up a job

GREAT EXPECTATIONS

If you were born in 1920 and are a ...

	...white man	*..white woman*
your life expectancy was ...		
at birth	*54.4 years*	*55.6 years*
at age 40	*71.7*	*77.1*
at age 62	*78.5*	*83.2*

If you were born in 1940 and are a ...

	...white man	*...white woman*
your life expectancy was ...		
at birth	*62.1 years*	*66.6 years*
at age 20	*70.3*	*76.3*
at age 42	*74.7*	*80.7*

If you were born in 1960 and are a ...

	...white man	*...white woman*
your life expectancy was ...		
at birth	*67.4 years*	*74.1 years*
at age 22	*73.2*	*80.0*

bank that is open to its own retired employees as well as those of other companies. According to Howard E. Johnson, a senior vice president, the company employs about 175 formerly retired men and women a week. He estimates that the program is saving Travelers $1 million a year in temporary-hire fees alone.

While mandatory retirement is only one example of ageism, it is particularly important because we usually think of contributions to society in economic terms. Malcolm H. Morrison, an authority on retirement and age discrimination in employment for the Social Security Administration, points out that once the idea of retirement at a certain fixed age was accepted, "the old became defined as a dependent group in society, a group whose members could not and should not work, and who needed economic and social assistance that the younger working population was obligated to provide."

We need to replace this stereotype with the more realistic understanding that older people are and should be productive members of society, capable of assuming greater responsibility for themselves and others. What researchers have learned about the strengths and abilities of older people should help us turn this ideal of an active, useful life after 65 into a working reality.

Problems and Potentials of Aging

Viewed as part of the life cycle, aging might be considered a period of decline, poor health, increasing dependence, social isolation, and—ultimately—death. It often means retirement, decreased income, chronic health problems, and the death of a spouse. In contrast, the first 50 years of life are a period of growth and development.

For a young child, life centers around the home, and then the neighborhood. Later, the community and state become a part of the young person's environment. Finally, as an adult, the person is prepared to consider national and international issues—wars, alliances, changing economic cycles, and world problems.

During the later years, however, life space narrows. Retirement may distance the individual from national and international concerns, although he or she may remain actively involved in community affairs. Later, even community involvement may decrease, and the person may begin to stay close to home and the neighborhood. For some, the final years of life may once again focus on the confines of home, be it an apartment or a nursing home.

Many older Americans try to remain the masters of their own destinies for as long as possible. They fear dependence and try to avoid it. Many are successful at maintaining independence and the right to make their own decisions. Others are less successful, and must depend on their families for care and to make critical decisions.

Most older persons are able to overcome the difficulties of aging and lead comfortable and enjoyable lives. The articles in this section address mental abilities, minority problems, the effects of alcohol and drugs on the aging body, elder abuse, maintaining health in later life, and older persons as entrepreneurs.

In "Aging of the Brain: How Can We Prevent It?" the author emphasizes that significant cognitive impairment is the result of disease, not normal aging; intellectual decline is not inevitable in later years. "Minorities Face Stubborn Inequities" examines the reasons for poverty among older minority group members. Today, a disproportionate number of the older minority population still live below the poverty line. As a person ages, their body's ability to dispose of drugs and alcohol lessens. The risk of suffering adverse effects from alcohol and other drugs is examined in "Actions of Alcohol and Drugs in Older People." The risk of abuse to the elderly is often from a spouse. In "The Prevalence of Elder Abuse: A Random Sample Survey," the authors examine the dynamics of elderly abuse. Individuals who have aged in good health and the ways that the aging process can be slowed are topics of the article "Aging: Can It Be Slowed?" In "It's Never Too Late" the ability of many seniors to become successful business entrepreneurs is discussed. The elderly can indeed belie the many assumptions about their lack of ability by simply not accepting the role in which society places them.

Looking Ahead: Challenge Questions

Which aspects of life after 65 are desirable and should be anticipated with pleasure?

Which aspects of life after 65 are undesirable and should be a cause of concern to people of all ages?

What steps might be taken by both business and the local community to assist the elderly in overcoming the problems of aging?

How does drug abuse among young people differ from drug abuse among the elderly?

Aging of the Brain: How Can We Prevent It?

The distinction between normal and abnormal aging of the brain changes as data emerge
which identify as pathology what had previously been considered the norm. Forty years of
research have yielded some facts: That intellectual decline is not inevitable after age 60; that
neuropsychological test performance is related to survival and to development of dementia;
and that dementia is associated with chromosome loss, and may result from an inherent defect
in microtubules. The mysterious human brain, by its own inquisitive nature, leads the search
to discover its secrets.
Key Words: Alzheimer disease, Microtubules, Neuropsychology,
Philothermal response, Twins

Lissy F. Jarvik, MD, PhD

Psychogeriatric Unit, West Los Angeles Veterans Administration Medical
Center, Brentwood Division; and the Department of Psychiatry and Biobe-
havioral Sciences, Neuropsychiatric Institute, University of California, Los
Angeles, 760 Westwood Plaza, Los Angeles, CA 90024-1759.

How can we prevent aging of the brain? There is a
simple answer, of course: Die young! But it is not an
answer we like. It certainly was not the answer for me
when I first began to concern myself with the question: Why do some people become senile in old age
whereas others maintain their mental faculties until
the day they die? That question was not of interest
either to researchers or to the public back in the
1940s, when hardly anyone knew anything about
cognitive changes in old age. Neuropsychology did
not exist, neurochemistry was in its infancy (indeed,
an argument was raging about whether nerve transmission was electrical or chemical), and neuroimaging was 25 years in the future. Nursing homes were a
rarity, and no one spoke of extended care facilities.
The elderly were a disenfranchised group in those
days before the first White House Conference on
Aging (1950), the American Association of Retired
Persons (1958), and the Gray Panthers (1970).

In the 1940s old age was considered synonymous
with decrepitude and senility. From the literature to
the dictionary, Shakespeare's view reigned supreme; some 400 years after his death, it was still
generally accepted that the last, seventh age of man
was "second childishness and mere oblivion, sans
teeth, sans eyes, sans taste, sans everything" (*As You
Like It*, II, vii, 139). A major text of abnormal psychology (Landis & Bolles, 1947) taught that "the behavior
of the old man in his 'second childhood' or of the old

woman in her 'dotage' is not regarded as abnormal,
since it appears so regularly and has been accepted
as part of the usual course of human life'' (p. 149).
Webster's Universal Dictionary (1936) defined senility as "old age" with the alternate definition of
"weakness or infirmity due to old age." Indeed, only
a *senile psychosis* was considered an *abnormal* mental condition, occurring during the period of old age.

That was the spirit of the times when, through
newspaper announcements, social agencies, fraternal organizations, Social Security records, churches,
clubs, and word of mouth, we began to collect information on twins living in or near New York State. Our
sample (Jarvik et al., 1962) included 134 same-sexed
English-speaking pairs in which both partners survived to at least age 60 and were living in the community (not institutionalized). Most of them were native
born, many from old Yankee stock, and many from
rural areas that were hard to reach in days when
roads were poor, cars capricious, and research funds
scarce. We enjoyed remarkable hospitality and cooperation: These twins opened their homes and hearts
to us and shared their family Bibles, albums, and
other keepsakes (Figures 1 and 2). They spent numerous hours with us providing information about themselves and their families, going back for two or three
generations.

Over a 20-year period, we learned much more
from the twins than I can even summarize. Hence, I
have selected only four major findings that pertain to
the aging of the brain. They are (1) Intellectual decline after age 60 is not necessary; (2) Decline on
certain tests predicts mortality; (3) Low scores on
certain tests predict dementia; (4) Dementia of the
Alzheimer type is associated with chromosome loss.

Intellectual Functions Do Not Necessarily Decline After Age 60

In the 1940s, there were no data for old adults:
Wechsler's oldest standardization group was 55–59
years old (Wechsler, 1944). The observation that,
during the first 10 years of our longitudinal study,

Presented as the Robert W. Kleemeier Lecture at the Annual Meeting of
the Gerontological Society of America on November 20, 1987. The work was
supported in part by PHS grants HD-01615 and MH-36205, State of California
grant 84-84560 and the Veterans Administration. The opinions expressed
are those of the author and not necessarily those of the Veterans Administration. The author extends her thanks to the many collaborators in this
work, with special mention of the late Drs. Kallmann and Sander, who
initiated the study of aging twins at New York State Psychiatric Institute;
Drs. June E. Blum, Arthur Falek, Tsu-ker Fu, Asenath LaRue, and Steven S.
Matsuyama, whose contributions have been central; and particularly to the
research participants without whose cooperation the studies could not
have been done.

Figure 1. Identical, or monozygotic, twin brothers at the ages of 4, 16, 52, and 68 years.

Figure 2. Four sisters whose parents had a set of identical, or monozygotic, twins and were so traumatized by the event that they waited 10 years before risking another child. They then had another set of twin girls — fraternal, or dizygotic, this time!

none of the test scores changed significantly was surprising. During that time, the average age of the twins had increased from 64 to 73 years; and yet, scores for tests on which speed was *not* a factor, showed an average *gain* rather than loss (Jarvik, 1967). That was the first finding to emerge from our twin study: Intellectual decline is *not* necessary after age 60.

We continued to follow our twins, and during the next decade all of the average scores went down, whether the test had a speed component or not (Blum et al., 1970). If that finding comes as a surprise

now, we gerontologists are to blame; we have done so good a job of debunking the myth of senility as the symbol of old age, that we have created the myth of intellectual stability throughout late life. Unfortunately, it is a myth, although there are some people who do hold their own. For example, the verbal scores of one of our twins were better at age 82 than they had been 20 years earlier (Jarvik, 1973). Even her performance scores showed little change between age 62 and 82 (less than 15% except for the last Block Designs test) although performance on speeded tasks is well-known to decline with advancing age. This twin's stable performance, however, is not representative of the total sample.

Another way of looking at these data is presented in Table 1. We compared the weighted scores of our twins to those of normal adults on four subtests of the Wechsler Adult Intelligence Scale (the only subtests we used from that battery), including only those twins who had completed the tests at least three times. At an average age of nearly 76 years, our twins

Table 1. Comparative Mean Weighted Scores[a]

Test	Longitudinal twin data Mean age (in years)			Wechsler data Age group
	67.5	68.4	75.7	55–59
Digit span	7.8	8.0	8.0	7.5
Digit symbol	7.2	7.0	6.4	5.9
Similarities	8.2	8.4	8.2	7.9
Block designs	7.6	7.8	6.8	6.7
Number of subjects	48	48	48	50

[a]Adapted from Jarvik et al., 1962.

were at least as smart as Wechsler's oldest standardization group (age 55 to 59 years). Their average score was higher on every one of the four tests. By age 85, however, most of the scores of those who survived to be retested showed a statistically significant decline, as shown in Table 2. Both men and women manifested the same trend (Blum et al., 1970).

This decline cannot be dismissed as an aberration of our twin sample as is evident from examination of the revised Wechsler Adult Intelligence Scale (WAIS-R; Wechsler, 1981). If a 30-year-old and a 70-year-old were to have the identical test results, that is, the identical raw scores on every single subtest of the WAIS-R (e.g., sum of scaled scores = 53), the 70-year-old could fall into the group of low *average* intelligence, whereas the 30-year-old would be classified as mentally *retarded*; that is, *not* borderline, but retarded. Furthermore, the highest standardization group for the WAIS-R was age 70–74, more than 10 years *younger* than the age at which the marked declines were documented in our twins.

Thus, although we brand as agist anyone who associates old age with intellectual decline, we quietly add bonus-points-for-years to the scores of those past their prime! Having thus magically restored equality in achievement, we can now comfortably

Table 2. Mean Raw Scores for 35 Twins Tested in 1947, 1955, and 1967[a]

Test	Male				Female			
	N	1947	1955	1967	N	1947	1955	1967
Vocabulary	10	27.10	27.20	24.30[b]	22	29.05	29.14	27.82
Similarities	11	10.09	10.18	6.73[b]	21	10.00	10.33	8.71[b]
Digits forward[c]	12	6.25	6.58	5.67[b]	23	5.96	6.39	5.74[b]
Digits backward[c]	11	4.91	4.45	4.09[b]	19	4.21	4.37	3.89[b]
Tapping	11	64.73	58.18	40.27[b]	22	72.91	60.46	49.95[b]
Block design	7	13.29	13.00	6.29[b]	18	15.33	14.72	10.72[b]
Digit symbol substitution	10	27.75	23.30	13.25[b]	18	33.83	30.53	20.17[b]
Mean ages	12	66.3	74.6	85.7	23	64.5	73.4	84.6

[a]Adapted from Blum et al., 1970.
[b]Difference within group (male or female) significant at $p < 0.05$.
[c]Digits forward and digits backward together make up Digit Span test.

deny the existence of differences between young and old. That is one way to prevent aging of the brain, or at least its consequences. If we adopt the statistical norm, then the masquerade is complete, and only psychologists know that it is normal for a 70-year-old to be retarded, or rather, de-mented, having presumably declined from a previously higher level of intellectual achievement. That is agism gone underground, agism more subtle, more sophisticated and more dangerous than Wechsler's (1944) definition of senescent decline as "normal mental deterioration after maturity with the natural increase in age" (p. 54).

Why is agism gone underground more dangerous than agism openly expressed? If there is no intellectual decline in old age, then we need not look for its causes. If today's attitude had prevailed 40 years ago, we would not have done the twin study, we would not have asked why mental deterioration was considered normal after maturity, and we would not have detected the relationship between cognitive decline and mortality.

Decline on Certain Tests Predicts Mortality

Part-way through our twin study, we realized that a decline in test scores seemed to be relatively frequent in those twins who failed to survive to the next test round (Jarvik et al., 1957). Retrospectively, we derived an empirical Critical Loss Ratio from our data, requiring two of the following: Annual decrement in score of at least 2% on Digit Symbol Substitution, annual decrement of at least 10% on Similarities, and any decline on Vocabulary (Jarvik, 1962). We then waited for the completion of the 5-year follow-up to confirm that Critical Loss would predict mortality. It did, as shown in Figure 3. Of the 41 twins alive 5 years or more, 37 had no Critical Loss, whereas 7 of the 11 who died did have a Critical Loss.

Several other longitudinal studies of aging individuals (not twins) have since been reported, and all of them confirmed the relationship between intellectual decline and mortality (see Blum et al., 1973; LaRue & Jarvik, 1986). One study done about the same time was that of Robert W. Kleemeier, the man

in whose honor this lecture is named. In 1961, he reported that there was an acceleration of intellectual decline prior to death (Kleemeier, 1961). He had been studying retired men at Moosehaven in Orange Park, Florida, members of the Loyal Order of the Moose. On periodic re-testing, he noted a sharp decline in their intellectual performance a few months to several years before they died, and he postulated an "imminence of death" factor.

The remarkable aspect of Critical Loss in our twin study, however, was not that it confirmed Kleemeier's observation of *terminal drop* (as it became known), but that Critical Loss predicted differential mortality even in monozygotic twins, or those who shared identical heredity. In every one of the identical twin pairs discordant for Critical Loss (i.e., one twin had a Critical Loss, the other did not), the twin with the Critical Loss died first (Jarvik & Blum, 1971).

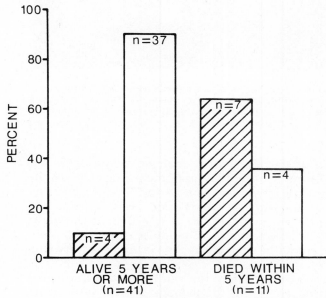

Figure 3. Critical Loss and survival in 26 twin pairs. ☐ Critical Loss, ▨ No Critical Loss. Adapted from Jarvik & Blum, 1971.

Low Scores on Certain Tests Predict Dementia

Our third finding was that an initially low level of performance on the Critical Loss tests predicted the development of dementia some two decades later (LaRue & Jarvik, 1980). Asenath LaRue and I examined the original 1947 test scores of the 65 twins who were still alive and retested in 1967. We discovered that 66.7% of those scoring in the lowest quartile on the Digit Symbol Substitution test in 1947 had received a psychiatric diagnosis of dementia by 1967, compared to only 18% of those who had scored in the highest quartile 20 years earlier. For the Vocabulary test, the results were 75% compared to 23%, and for Similarities, 84.6% versus 16.7%, as shown in Figure 4. Analyses of covariance with dementia status as the independent variable and with variance due to age and education removed showed that the effect of dementia status remained significant (LaRue & Jarvik, 1980, 1986).

This finding suggested two conclusions. First, it may be possible to utilize standardized cognitive tests to distinguish older persons who will subsequently develop dementia from those who will not, and, second, dementia may develop much more slowly than we generally assume: 15, 20, or 25 years prior to diagnosis is well within the realm of possibility. These conclusions can only be confirmed after the accumulation of longitudinal data specifically designed to follow individuals in *pre*symptomatic phases of dementia, and several groups (including our own) are currently collecting such data. If the extended presymptomatic period is confirmed, it will allow ample time for intervention and prevention once we know what to do. Meanwhile, there are some leads we can follow, such as the relationship between dementia and chromosome loss.

Dementia of the Alzheimer Type Is Associated With Chromosome Loss

In the 1960s, techniques became available for examining and reliably counting human chromosomes using lymphocytes, a type of white blood cell. Not long thereafter, it was reported that aging women had an increased frequency of chromosome loss (reviewed in Jarvik & Kato, 1970). When we looked at the chromosomes of our twins (Jarvik et al., 1971), we found that those twins with a diagnosis of dementia (we called it organic brain syndrome then) had a higher frequency of chromosome loss, or hypodiploidy, than did those without dementia, as shown in Figure 5. Without the modern technology of CT scanning, MRI, PET, or SPECT, we had to rely on clinical judgment and psychometrics, but we excluded vascular and other causes of dementia as best we could to identify the twins with dementia of the Alzheimer type. In several other studies in the literature the significant increase in aneuploidy in patients with dementia of the Alzheimer type has since been confirmed, although in a few it was not (cf. review Matsuyama et al., 1985).

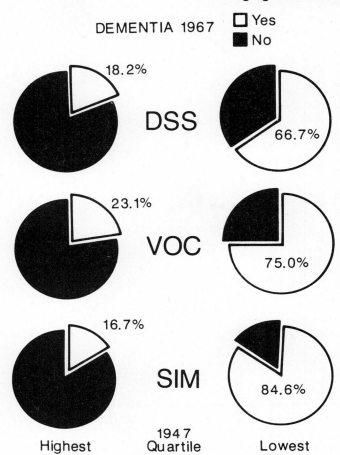

Figure 4. Psychometric predictors of dementia: 20-year follow-up. Presence of dementia in 1967 for twins whose 1947 scores were in the lowest and highest quartiles on three WAIS subtests: Digit Symbol Substitution (DSS), Vocabulary (VOC), and Similarities (SIM). Adapted from LaRue & Jarvik, 1986.

What is the meaning of this increased chromosome loss in dementia of the Alzheimer type? It was puzzling that the increased aneuploidy was found in lymphocytes (white blood cells), because Alzheimer disease is considered a disease of the brain. Our finding led us to postulate that Alzheimer disease is not a disease of the brain alone, and that lymphocytes could serve as a model for other cellular systems, including neuroglial cells in the brain. Indeed, by now, numerous systems have been reported as affected in Alzheimer disease, as shown in Chart 1. Now, I will discuss only the one system with which our laboratory is currently concerned (i.e., the microtubular system in white blood cells).

Microtubules, in a very oversimplified way, are subcellular structures that make up the cell skeleton; an intact microtubular system is also needed for directed cell motion (Malech et al., 1977), for spindle formation during cell division (Dustin, 1984; LaFountain, 1975; Taylor, 1965), and for the transport of a variety of substances in the central nervous system (Gan et al., 1986; Johnston et al., 1986). Indeed, Heston (1976) proposed more than a decade ago that a microtubular abnormality might explain the increased incidence of Down syndrome among the

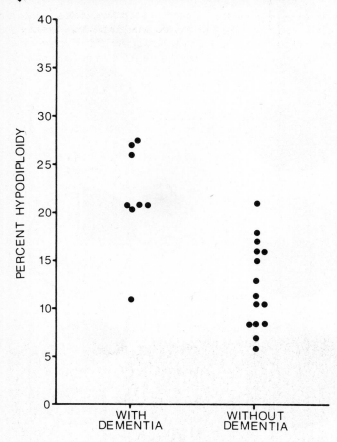

Figure 5. 23 aged female twins (cerebral atherosclerosis clinically excluded). Adapted from Jarvik et al., 1971.

Chart 1. Abnormalities Reported in Nonneural Cells in Dementia of the Alzheimer Type[a]

Tissue	Abnormality
Red blood cells	Increased choline
	Decreased cholinesterase
	Increased choline efflux
	Altered ESR signal
	Increased Na-Li countertransport
	Increased ouabain binding
Lymphocytes	Increased acentric fragments
	Increased aneuploidy
	Increased mutagen sensitivity
	Increased radiosensitivity
	Increased suppressor cells
	Decreased killer T-cell activity
Polymorphonuclear leukocytes	Altered philothermal response
Platelets	Increased monoamine oxidase
	Decreased phosphofructokinase activity
	Decreased polarization
Fibroblasts	Microtubular defect
	Decreased phosphofructokinase activity
	Decreased interferon response
	Decreased calcium transport
	Impaired DNA repair
	Hypersensitivity to X-rays
	Decreased glutamine oxidation
	Decreased lactate production

[a]Adapted from Blass et al., 1985.

relatives of Alzheimer patients (see also Ford, 1984), as well as the fact that patients with Down syndrome who live long enough (until about age 35 or so) show the characteristic Alzheimer changes in their brains, neuritic plaques and neurofibrillary tangles (Jervis, 1948). According to Heston's hypothesis, microtubules are involved in both the formation of neurofibrillary tangles and the error in cell division responsible for the extra chromosome number 21 in Down syndrome (by means of their role in spindle formation). Moreover, an error in cell division also may be responsible for the increased frequency of chromosome loss observed in Alzheimer disease. Thus, we have come full circle, back to our initial observation of increased chromosome loss in white blood cells of twins with Alzheimer-type dementia.

Microtubules, however, have yet another function, and that concerns goal directed cellular motion. We decided to study the migration of white blood cells taken from patients with Alzheimer disease (primarily those participating in our ongoing Family Study of Alzheimer-Type Dementia). This group of families, collected during the past decade, does not include any of the twins in the twin study discussed earlier. The specific migratory response which we are investigating takes place along a temperature gradient, the cells migrating from colder to warmer temperatures. We have called this migration

the "philothermal response" (Fu et al., 1982; Jarvik et al., 1982).

Philothermal Response and Microtubules

Briefly, our test system utilizes peripheral white blood cells (polymorphonuclear leukocytes, or PMNs). We obtain a blood sample, prepare the cell suspension, expose it to a temperature gradient for 3 hours, and analyze photomicrographs. To measure the philothermal response, we place a grid with graded arc segments over a photomicrograph, count the cells nearest the origin (proximal) and the cells that have migrated furthest from the origin (distal); we divide the number of proximal cells by the number of distal cells to obtain the ratio R, as shown in Figure 6. Our analysis of data from the first dozen Alzheimer patients, all diagnosed with state-of-the-art technology, indicated that an R value of 11 or more distinguished the patient group from the control group. In other words, patients had significantly fewer distantly migrated cells. Our analyses showed that R was not related to age, sex, medications, duration, or severity of illness.

Because the philothermal response technique is tedious, time-consuming, and laborious, it does not lend itself to large scale surveys: to date, we have completed 53 Alzheimer patients, 43 normal controls, and 39 patients in other diagnostic categories. Of the 53 Alzheimer patients, 29 have since died, and about half of them have come to autopsy. We have

PHILOTHERMAL RESPONSE

DAT

CONTROL

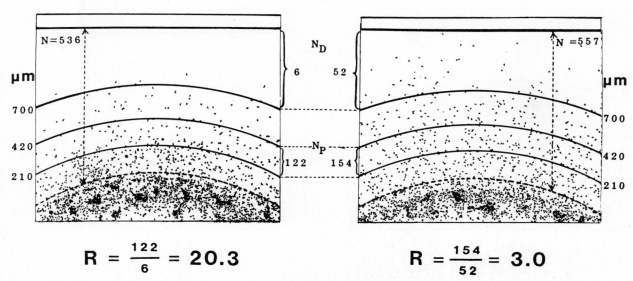

$$R = \frac{122}{6} = 20.3 \qquad\qquad R = \frac{154}{52} = 3.0$$

Figure 6. Comparison of philothermal response (R value) of one patient with dementia of the Alzheimer type (DAT) (left) and one person without psychiatric disorder (right).

results from the first 15 autopsies: For 13 patients (87%) the clinical diagnosis of Alzheimer disease was confirmed, one was diagnosed as Pick disease, and one as dementia of unknown etiology.

An abnormal R was present in 49% (25/51) of the Alzheimer patients but only 12% (5/43) of the controls, statistically a highly significant difference. Of the 39 patients with other diagnoses (multi-infarct dementia, dementia with history of alcoholism, and major depressive disorder), only four (10%) had an abnormal response. For the 13 autopsy confirmed Alzheimer patients, 46% (6/13) had an abnormal R. Both patients who received other neuropathological diagnoses had normal R values (Pick, 8.3; unknown, 5.9). Thus, all the evidence we have collected so far points to a subgroup of Alzheimer patients with an abnormal philothermal response.

The evidence, however, is indirect. We are simply describing an event (i.e., the spatial distribution of migrated cells). Because we postulated that the reason for the difference between patients and controls might be an impaired microtubular system, we tested that hypothesis. Our premise was that if the abnormal philothermal response were due to an impaired microtubular system, then we should be able to reproduce it by taking cells from normal individuals and damaging their microtubules. Colchicine, an old remedy for gout, specifically disrupts the microtubule system. We, therefore, added colchicine to cells taken from normal persons; the result mimicked the abnormal philothermal response seen in some of our Alzheimer patients.

As shown in Figure 7, the control preparation (cells without colchicine) has a normal R of 3.5; the colchicine-treated preparation an abnormal R of 18.7, well above our cut-off point of 11. We also derived a dose response curve with cells from 12 normal volunteers, one man and one woman for each age decade from the 20s through the 70s. As the colchicine concentration increased so did R (Fu et al., 1986).

Taken together, we feel that the evidence argues in favor of an important role for a microtubular defect in Alzheimer disease. Further, the brain is the organ with the greatest concentration of microtubules (Dustin, 1984), and in the brain, microtubules have functions beyond the basic ones related to skeletal structure of the cell, cell division, and goal-directed cell motion. Specifically, microtubules are involved in the transport of a variety of substances from the cell body to the end of the cell processes and the other way around (DeBrabender, 1982; Dustin, 1984). This axonal transport, as it is called, is a complex organized transportation system with traffic moving to and fro in both fast and slow lanes.

Because microtubules are part of so vital a system, it is not surprising that the effects of microtubular impairment would be observed throughout the body: Further, it is to be expected that the brain would be a particularly vulnerable target organ. In terms of chemistry and anatomy, we already know that Alzheimer disease causes widespread brain damage. It impairs multiple neurotransmitter systems (e.g., cholinergic, aminergic, somatostatin), affects disparate brain regions (temporoparietal and frontal cortex, olfactory, hippocampus, nucleus basalis, locus ceruleus) and impairs a variety of higher

PHILOTHERMAL RESPONSE

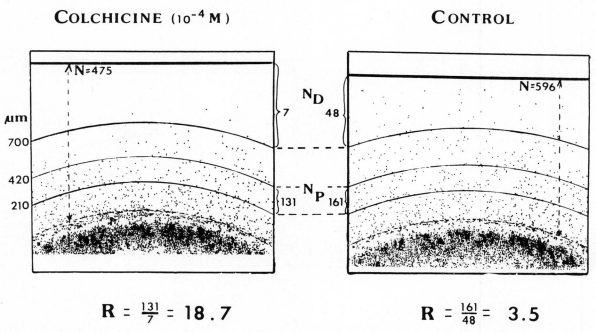

$$R = \frac{131}{7} = 18.7 \qquad\qquad R = \frac{161}{48} = 3.5$$

Figure 7. Comparison of philothermal response (R value) in cells from a normal healthy individual: Experimental cell preparation treated with colchicine (10^{-4} M) (left); untreated control preparation (right).

mental functions (memory, language, mathematical skills, spatial orientation, personality). Indeed, by definition, Alzheimer disease causes global mental impairment and diffuse, not localized, brain damage.

Genetic Research in Alzheimer Disease

Although it is being vigorously pursued by numerous researchers (see Matsuyama, 1988; Matsuyama et al., 1985; Tobin, 1987), definition of the role of genetic factors in Alzheimer disease remains elusive. Essential data from longitudinal studies are accumulating, but the work is slow. For example, in our 20-year study of normal aging twins, there were only seven surviving pairs in whom at least one of the twins developed dementia of the Alzheimer type (Jarvik et al., 1980; see Table 3). Six of the seven pairs were identical (monozygotic), and half of them were concordant, i.e., in half of them, both twins developed the disease. The one fraternal (dizygotic) pair happened to be discordant (i.e., only one of the twins developed the disease). The numbers are much too small to allow us to draw any conclusions. The first reported twin study of the three in the world literature (Table 3), however, identified 108 twins as having senile psychosis. Most of them would be diagnosed today as having Alzheimer disease. Kallmann (1956) found that 43% of the monozygotic twins but only 8% of the dizygotic pairs were concordant. These pairs were not followed longitudinally, so it is possible that some discordant pairs might

Table 3. Dementia of the Alzheimer Type Twin Studies[a]

	Twin pairs	MZ/DZ[b]	Percent concordant MZ/DZ
Kallmann, 1956	—[c]	—[c]	43/8
Jarvik et al., 1980	7	6/1	50/0
Nee et al., 1987	22	17/5	41/40

[a]Plus case reports: 5 MZ pairs, 3 concordant.
[b]MZ = monozygotic, DZ = dizygotic.
[c]No information except 108 twin index cases.

have become concordant (co-twin developing the disease later). In large enough samples statistical corrections can be applied for the latter. A much more sophisticated prospective investigation than the two just mentioned is the study reported by Nee and associates (1987). This NIH study included neuroimaging data as well as autopsies when feasible. Nonetheless, the 41% concordance rate for monozygotic twins observed in that study is strikingly similar to the 43% reported by Kallmann and the 50% found in our small sample. By contrast, the 40% concordance in dizygotic pairs found by the NIH group is much higher than that observed in Kallmann's sample. Because it is essentially indistinguishable from that for monozygotic pairs, one might conclude that genes do not play a vital role in Alzheimer disease. That conclusion is not warranted, however, because the report includes only five dizygotic pairs. A larger sample is needed. Nevertheless, the fact that in three separate studies monozygotic twins showed only 40% to 50% concordance for Alzheimer disease indicates that non-genetic influences also have a major role, at least in determining the manifestation of the disease.

Although great excitement and more evidence for a genetic influence in Alzheimer disease was generated by the recent reports of a gene for familial Alzheimer disease localized to chromosome #21 (see editorial by Tobin, 1987), more work is needed before the ramifications of this finding can be fully assessed. The familial Alzheimer gene has been found only in families with early-onset (diagnosed before age 60 years) Alzheimer disease (St. George-Hyslop et al., 1987; Tanzi et al., 1987; Van Broeckhoven et al., 1987), and early-onset familial Alzheimer disease is rare. But even if the entire human genome with its 3 billion base pairs were mapped, and the location of one or more other genes associated with Alzheimer-type dementia determined, we would still have to discover their actions. The Huntington gene was mapped to chromosome #4 four years ago, and its actions still remain to be defined. We cannot wait for gene mapping; we need to find out in other ways what causes the mental impairment characteristic of Alzheimer disease. Nevertheless, the location of the familial Alzheimer disease gene on chromosome #21 is a tantalizing piece of evidence, because chromosome #21 also plays a part in Down syndrome, the common form of mental retardation which has been associated with Alzheimer disease as mentioned earlier.

How Is Alzheimer Disease Relevant to the Aging Brain?

The topic of this paper is how to prevent the untoward consequences of the aging of the brain, and yet, a substantial portion of the discussion has dealt with Alzheimer disease. Are they synonymous? I do not think so, although there are some who espouse the view that Alzheimer disease can be considered premature aging of the brain. The question will remain open until more data become available. In contrast to the premature aging theory, however, I believe that the normal aging brain, free of disease, may well function as effectively and efficiently as the normal younger adult brain, except for speed. Our twin studies provided evidence favoring this view inasmuch as some of our twins failed to show intellectual deterioration despite far advanced ages. I believe that significant cognitive impairment is due to disease and not to normal aging. As we get older, we face an increased frequency of disease; most individuals over age 65 suffer from one or more chronic diseases or disabilities. One of these diseases is Alzheimer disease which is estimated to affect 1% to 2% of those below the age of 65 but 20% or more of those over the age of 75.

Alzheimer disease, therefore, is relevant to the aging of the brain in that it affects a large proportion of the aging population, and changes due to Alzheimer disease may be attributed to aging. Alzheimer disease is also relevant to the aging of the brain because it may represent a final common pathway for a variety of different etiological factors ranging from genetic determinants to environmental toxins, nutritional deficiencies, and infectious agents, as well as combinations of one or more such factors. All these factors together with the individual's life style and life-long experiences may be responsible for what we consider age-associated brain changes. Even the slowing down, so characteristic of the aging individual, may be a function of life style, nutrition, and inactivity with advancing chronological age. Because we have documented stability in intellectual functioning for some individuals, it should be possible to achieve such stability for most individuals whether by means of genetic engineering or environmental manipulation.

Conclusion

An increased vulnerability to a variety of diseases is recognized as characteristic of the aging organism, and modern medicine has taken on that challenge. One by one, diseases of the major organ systems are yielding their secrets as we study individuals in whom such vital organs as kidneys, liver, pancreas, and even the human heart have been replaced. So far, the brain has been an exception; we have not as yet found a way to transplant a brain or substitute an artificial one. The human brain may be the last organ to yield its secrets, but using ever more sophisticated techniques together with the brain's own capacities, we should be able to uncover the mechanisms responsible for its diseases and their detrimental consequences. We will then have a new view of normal aging.

References

Blass, J. P., Hanin, I., Barclay, L., Kipp, U., & Reding, M. (1985). Red blood cell abnormalities in Alzheimer disease. *Journal of the American Geriatrics Society, 33,* 401–405.

Blum, J. E., Clark, E. T., & Jarvik, L. F. (1973). The New York State Psychiatric Institute Study of Aging Twins. In L. F. Jarvik, C. Eisdorfer, & J. E. Blum (Eds.), *Intellectual functioning in adults.* New York: Springer Publishing Company, Inc.

Blum, J. E., Jarvik, L. F., & Clark, E. T. (1970). Rate of change on selective tests of intelligence: A twenty-year longitudinal study of aging. *Journal of Gerontology, 25,* 171–176.

DeBrabender, M. (1982). Microtubules, central elements of cellular organization. *Endeavor (New Series), 6,* 124–134.

Dustin, P. (1984). *Microtubules,* 2nd rev. ed. New York: Springer-Verlag.

Ford, J. H. (1984). Spindle microtubular dysfunction in mothers of Down syndrome children. *Human Genetics, 68,* 295–298.

Fu, T-K., Kessler, J. O., Jarvik, L. F., & Matsuyama, S. S. (1982). Philothermal and chemotactic locomotion of leukocytes: Method and results. *Cell Biophysics, 4,* 77–95.

Fu, T-K., Matsuyama, S. S., Kessler, J. O., & Jarvik, L. F. (1986). Brief communication: Philothermal response, microtubules and dementia. *Neurobiology of Aging, 7,* 41–43.

Gan, S-D., Fan, M-M., & He, G-P. (1986). The role of microtubules in axoplasmic transport in vivo. *Brain Research, 369,* 75–82.

Heston, L. L. (1976). Alzheimer's disease, trisomy 21, and myeloproliferative disorders: Associations suggesting a genetic diathesis. *Science, 196,* 322–323.

Jarvik, L. F. (1962). Biological differences in intellectual functioning. *Vita Humana, 5,* 195–203.

Jarvik, L. F. (1967). Survival and psychological aspects of ageing in man. *Aspects of the Biology of Ageing, Symposium of the Society for Experimental Biology, 21,* 463–481.

Jarvik, L. F. (1973). Discussion: Patterns of intellectual functioning in the later years. In L. F. Jarvik, C. Eisdorfer, & J. E. Blum (Eds.), *Intellectual functioning in adults.* New York: Springer Publishing Company, Inc.

Jarvik, L. F., Altshuler, K., Kato, T., & Blumner, B. (1971). Organic brain syndrome and chromosome loss in aged twins. *Diseases of the Nervous System, 32,* 159–170.

Jarvik, L. F., & Blum, J. E. (1971). Cognitive declines as predictors of mortality in twin pairs: A twenty-year longitudinal study of aging. In E. Palmore & F. C. Jeffers (Eds.), *Prediction of life span.* New York: D. C. Heath and Co.

Jarvik, L. F., Kallmann, F. J., & Falek, A. (1962). Intellectual changes in aged twins. *Journal of Gerontology, 17,* 289–294.

Jarvik, L. F., Kallmann, F. J., Falek, A., & Klaber, M. M. (1957). Changing intellectual functions in senescent twins. *Acta Genetica et Statistica Medica, 7,* 421–430.

Jarvik, L. F., & Kato, T. (1970). Chromosome examinations in aged twins. *American Journal of Human Genetics, 22,* 562–573.

Jarvik, L. F., Matsuyama, S. S., Kessler, J. O., Fu, T-K., Tsai, S. Y., & Clark, E. O. (1982). Philothermal response of polymorphonuclear leukocytes in dementia of the Alzheimer type. *Neurobiology of Aging, 3,* 93–99.

Jarvik, L. F., Ruth, V., & Matsuyama, S. S. (1980). Organic brain syndrome and aging. *Archives of General Psychiatry, 37,* 280–286.

Jervis, G. A. (1948). Early senile dementia in mongoloid idiocy. *American Journal of Psychiatry, 105,* 102–106.

Johnston, K. M., Connolly, J. A., & van der Kooy, D. (1986). Inhibition of axonal transport 'in vivo' by a tubulin-specific antibody. *Brain Research, 385,* 38–45.

Kallmann, F. J. (1956). Genetic aspects of mental disorders in later life. In O. J. Kaplan (Ed.), *Mental disorders in later life* (2nd ed.). Stanford, CA: Stanford University Press.

Kleemeier, R. W. (1961). Intellectual changes in the senium, or death and the I.Q. Presidential address, Division on Maturity and Old Age, American Psychological Association, September 1, 1961.

LaFountain, J. R., Jr. (1975). What moves chromosomes, microtubules or microfilaments? *BioSystems, 7,* 363–369.

Landis, G., & Bolles, M. M. (1947). *Textbook of abnormal psychology.* New York: MacMillan.

LaRue, A., & Jarvik, L. F. (1980). Reflections of biological changes in the psychological performance of the aged. *Age, 3,* 29–32.

LaRue, A., & Jarvik, L. F. (1986). Toward the prediction of dementias arising in the senium. In L. Erlenmeyer-Kimling & N. E. Miller (Eds.), *Life-Span research on the prediction of psychopathology.* NJ: Lawrence Erlbaum Associates, Inc.

Malech, H. L., Root, R. K., & Gallin, J. I. (1977). Structural analysis of human neutrophil migration: Centriole, microtubule, and microfilament orientation and function during chemotaxis. *Journal of Cell Biology, 75,* 666–693.

Matsuyama, S. S. (1988). Editorial — the year in review. *Alzheimer Disease and Associated Disorders — An International Journal, 2,* 1–3.

Matsuyama, S. S., Jarvik, L. F., & Kumar, V. (1985). Dementia: Genetics. In T. Arie (Ed.), *Recent advances in psychogeriatrics.* London: Churchill Livingstone.

Nee, L. E., Eldridge, R., Sunderland, T., Thomas, C. B., Katz, D., Thompson, K. E., Weingartner, H., Weiss, H., Julian, C., & Cohen, R. (1987). Dementia of the Alzheimer type: Clinical and family study of 22 twin pairs. *Neurology, 37,* 359–363.

Shakespeare, W. (1937). "As You Like It." In *The complete works of William Shakespeare* (Classics Club Edition). New York: Walter J. Black.

St. George-Hyslop, P. H., Tanzi, R. E., Polinsky, R. J., Haines, J. L., Nee, L., Watkins, P. C., Myers, R. H., Feldman, R. G., Pollen, D., Drachman, D., Growdon, J., Bruni, A., Foncin, J-F., Salmon, D., Frommelt, P., Amaducci, L., Sorbi, S., Piacentini, S., Steward, G. D., Hobbs, W. J., Conneally, P. M., & Gusella, J. F. (1987). The genetic defect causing familial Alzheimer's disease maps on chromosome 21. *Science, 235,* 885–890.

Tanzi, R. E., St. George-Hyslop, P. H., Haines, J. L., Polinsky, R. J., Nee, L., Foncin, J-F., Neve, R. L., McClatchey, A. I., Conneally, P. M., & Gusella, J. F. (1987). The genetic defect in familial Alzheimer's disease is not tightly linked to the amyloid-B protein gene. *Nature, 329,* 156–157.

Taylor, E. W. (1965). The mechanism of colchicine inhibition of mitosis. *Journal of Cell Biology, 25,* 145–160.

Tobin, A. J. (1987). Guest Editorial — Alzheimer disease: Enter molecular biology. *Alzheimer Disease and Associated Disorders — An International Journal, 1,* 69–71.

Van Broeckhoven, D., Genthe, A. M., Vandenberghe, A., Hosthemke, B., Backhovens, H., Raemaekers, P., Van Hul, W., Wehnert, A., Ghuens, J., Cras, P., Bruyland, M., Martin, J. J., Salbaum, M., Multhaup, G., Masters, C. L., Beyreuther, K., Gurling, H. M. D., Mullan, M. J., Holland, A., Barton, A., Irving, N., Williamson, R., Richards, S. J., & Hardy, J. A. (1987). Failure of familial Alzheimer's disease to segregate with the A4-amyloid gene in several European families. *Nature, 329,* 153–155.

Webster, N. (1936). Webster's universal dictionary of the English language. New York: The World Syndicate Publishing Co.

Wechsler, D. (1944). *The measurement of adult intelligence.* Baltimore: Williams & Wilkins.

Wechsler, D. (1981). *Wechsler Adult Intelligence Scale — Revised.* New York: The Psychological Corporation.

Minorities Face Stubborn Inequities

FRANKIE M. FREEMAN AND COQUESE L. WILLIAMS

FRANKIE M. FREEMAN (Left) practices law in St. Louis, Mo. She is First Vice Chair of NCOA's Board of Directors and chairs its Minority Concerns Committee. She served for 16 years on the U.S. Civil Rights Commission and is active on the boards of a number of organizations, including the Girl Scouts of the USA, Howard University, and National Association for the Advancement of Colored People.

COQUESE L. WILLIAMS is Management Systems Manager for the National Council on the Aging's Senior Community Service Employment Program Division (SCSEP), and is responsible for developing and coordinating program management systems, directing special projects, and serving as the Division's liaison with other NCOA Divisions. She is also one of the staff liaisons to the NCOA Board Committee on Minority Concerns.

Twenty-five years ago Michael Harrington's book, *The Other American,* declared that racism undergirded an economic underworld in the wealthiest nation the world has ever known. Black people and other minorities, the historic manifesto continued, would never really be emancipated until a massive assault upon all inequities—slums, inferior education, inadequate medical care, discrimination and all the rest—was successfully pursued.

A partial federal response in the 1960s did bring a watershed in social policy. Demands for social equity caused, in fact, *a redefinition of public responsibility for the poor.* But the nation must face up to the fact that the longstanding job market problems that blight entire lifetimes are still very much with us.

For minorities, employment problems are especially severe. For older minorities, they become even more so. Their difficulties are ingrained because of widespread discrimination, shortcomings in education and a general failure to provide them with the tools to compete in many of today's work places.

This article, while recognizing the severe handicaps facing older minorities, will nevertheless report on significant, if limited, progress that can be made if there is a will to do so. It will also make suggestions to accelerate such progress.

But first, a challenge must be made to the common tendency to group all "minorities" into one cohesive group. Diversity, a characteristic of our society, is even more pronounced among the many kinds of people with which this article deals.

Older Blacks look back over decades of discrimination—in jobs, in education, in all areas that affect their current status.

Many older Hispanics have been poorly educated in English. Their peak earning years were often limited to part-time or menial jobs not covered by Social Security or private pensions. It should be remembered that variety among Hispanics is great; they may be **Mexican-Americans, Puerto Ricans, Cubans, and those of Central or South American and European origin.**

The Native American elders often live in remote rural areas, and they may also be bereft of so-cial insurance and pension coverage. Their employment experience, if any, has primarily consisted of service and hard labor since many have had little or no formal education.

Groups represented in the Asian elder population have had varying employment experiences and related problems. For example, English language skills tend to be excellent for Filipino natives and Japanese-American elders, but poor for other groups. Chinese and Korean older women sometimes have little education and no work experience. Many of the groups cling to cultural traditions and experience difficulties integrating into the broader society. Asian Americans also include Pacific Islanders and Vietnamese, increasing the diversity even more.

Different as their characteristics and experiences have been, older minorities face similar obstacles because of age and race. For example, older Blacks typically have an unemployment rate that is two to three times the level for aged whites. Bureau of Labor Statistics show that for *all* displaced older workers, only 41 percent of persons 55-64 years of age and 21 percent of those 65 years or older return to the work place. This is staggering. The data suggest that the earnings of workers returning to the labor force after displacement are very often so low that the older worker becomes totally discouraged and completely drops out of the labor force.

Many minority older workers turn to part-time work or service jobs in small businesses. And, some turn to federally-funded employment programs such as the Senior Community Service Employment Program (SCSEP) funded through Title V of the Older Americans Act or the Job Training Partnership Act (JTPA).

SCSEP provides part-time employment and training opportunities for low-income workers aged 55 and over and is operated by eight national sponsors (including NCOA) and the 50 states and the Territories, through grants from the U.S. Department of Labor. An examination of the SCSEP minority participation rates for the program year ending June 30, 1986, reveals that minorities are being employed through SCSEP at levels higher than for the rate for the total 55-plus population or for the poor 55-plus population.

Blacks account for 8.4% of the 55-plus population and 20.5% of the poor 55-plus. Yet, 23.1% of the SCSEP enrollees were Black. Hispanic SCSEP enrollees comprise 8.1%, while accounting for only 3% of the 55-and-over population, and 5.2% of all persons living in poverty. Asian Americans, while representing 1% of the aged population and 0.9% of the poor aged, participated in SCSEP at a rate of 2.8%. The Native American elderly, representing 0.3% of those 55-plus and 0.8% of the poor elderly, represented 1.5% of all SCSEP participants. In all, 35.5% of the 63,700 authorized positions under Title V were filled by minorities. This represents an exceptional record on the part of SCSEP sponsors to provide employment services to aged minorities.

The other source of employment and training for older minorities is JTPA. Funded by the Department of Labor, and administered by state and local governmental entities, this program enables older workers to participate in skill training, on-the-job training and many other activities. The JTPA legislation also has

How many persons age 55+ are minority group members—and poor?

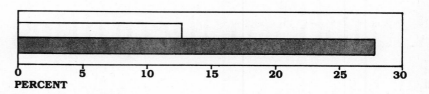

PERCENT

More than nine million persons, 13% of the population over age 55, were reported in the 1980 census as poor. A disproportionate number, 27.4%, are members of minorities. Are job programs aimed at older workers reaching minority participants?

Minority Participation in SCSEP (Title V) Programs

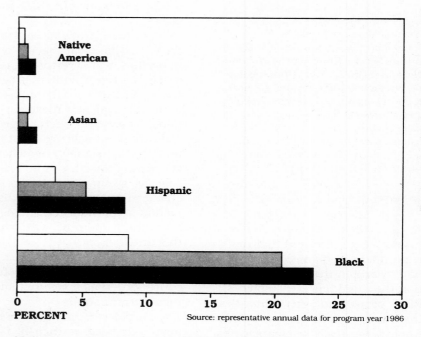

PERCENT   Source: representative annual data for program year 1986

Minorities are being employed by SCSEP at rates higher than their percentage of the general 55+ population and the poor 55+ population. The total number of SCSEP positions authorized in the year from which these figures are taken was 63,700.

☐ In the *general* population over age 55, % who are minority members
▨ In the *poor* population over age 55, % who are minority members
■ Among SCSEP participants, % who are minority members

a special older worker set-aside provision. Information available through December 1986, for program year 1986-87, indicates that of the 373,400 persons served under the main JTPA program, 2% were 55 or older. Minorities represented 46% (171,800) of all program participants, but only 1% of those were 55-plus, with Blacks and Hispanics accounting for almost all of the 1,700 older minority participants. Unfortunately, data were not available on minority participation rates in the JTPA older worker set-aside program. However, the low participation rates of older minorities in JTPA, particularly when compared to SCSEP data, is a cause for concern, and indicates a need for further examination of existing public policies.

It is recognized that the federal government cannot be the cure for all problems, and that many local governments and private organizations have begun to address the employment needs of older minorities. However, a partnership is still needed to insure that those persons most in need are being served.

Here are some strategies that have made a difference:

- A Native American service organization in Arizona received funding from JTPA to develop an entrepreneurial program for older residents on four reservations. The program has a two-fold purpose—it enables the older workers to make and market their native crafts, while at the same time allowing them to teach the craft work to other residents (young and old) participating in other JTPA- or SCSEP-funded activities.
- An SCSEP project in West Palm Beach, Florida, sponsored by an Hispanic service organization, found itself deluged by Central and South American immigrants who spoke little or no English. Although the project's

We must get the story across that federal programs work ... but it is premature to declare victory.

staff is bilingual, job placements were extremely difficult.

In cooperation with the local school system and the JTPA Program, a special English-as-a-Second Language program was developed. Many of these immigrants had been professionals or skilled craftsmen in their homelands, and through the combined efforts of SCSEP and JTPA they have been able to return to their trades.

- The National Caucus and Center on Black Aged (NCBA) has sponsored a housing management training program for older workers for the last three years. Funding for the program has come from both Title V and JTPA resources, and the majority of the participants have been Black. The program, which was piloted in Washington, D.C., trains older workers in all facets of managing apartment buildings—tenant/landlord relationships, security, maintenance, upkeep, etc. The success of the D.C. pilot was such that the program was expanded to Chicago, Pittsburgh, Baltimore, Tampa/St. Petersburg, Clearwater, and Puerto Rico. Many success stories tell of persons who entered the program with zero income and are now employed fulltime as apartment managers at $16,000 annually plus a free apartment.
- A Pennsylvania-based older worker program undertook a home safety survey for older

residents in selected communities. In order to assure access to the homes, the project recruited older workers and volunteers from each racial and ethnic group to be surveyed. These surveyors were able to put the residents at ease and, when necessary, overcome language barriers.

- A California SCSEP project that serves a large number of Asian-Americans discovered that it was having problems "relating" to members of a particular ethnic group. After a bit of research, the project concluded that assistance from within the ethnic community was needed and solicited guidance from its leaders. Through community meetings, training sessions with project staff, and a general sensitization to the group's culture and mores, the project has been able to better meet the needs of this older worker population.

It is important to devise such strategies to defend the core interests of Blacks, Hispanics, Native Americans, the Asian elderly and the poor in general. There should be no compromise on fundamental issues. There must be an all-out effort to preserve housing programs, affirmative action, school desegregation, strict enforcement of civil rights laws, and important employment and social services programs.

It is the duty of our federal government to bring about social change. It is our duty as citizens to be vigilant in working for a better nation and world—we must get the story across that federal social programs work. Food stamps have done much to wipe out hunger in America. Head Start programs have helped children do better in school. Great progress has been made in fighting poverty among the elderly. But it is premature—and for minorities, especially embittering—to declare victory for older Americans in the struggle for income security.

It's Never Too Late

Carmen Jones' life did not have enough pizzazz, so she turned back to pizza. The mother of two and grandmother of seven had worked in the frozen pizza business her husband, Jess, had founded, and she went into retirement with him when he sold it in 1967. Not once did she dream, at the time, that entrepreneurship was in her future.

In the next 10 years, Jess and Carmen did a lot of golfing and traveling. Then, says Carmen, "I just got bored. I needed something to keep me busy." She talked to Jess about opening a pizza shop in Wausau, Wis., where they lived, but Jess did not want to come out of retirement. So she went ahead on her own, taking out a loan and renting a site on a corner. By 1979 she was selling franchises. Today the business has grown to more than 30 stores—most of them franchised—in four Midwestern states.

With operators avoiding the headaches of running restaurants—Kids Korner Fresh Pizza, Inc., purveys an unfrozen product that it calls "we make 'em, you bake 'em" pizzas—Carmen thinks the number of outlets will double by mid-1987. She will be 71 then.

Thomas Duck says he has drawn paychecks in 26 different occupations. Though he spent 30 years selling insurance, Duck found time to be a toy manufacturer, automobile upholstery repairman and converter of buses into mobile homes during a long career.

But an idea that came to him while he was looking out the window one afternoon in retirement is making him the most money by far, as well as providing a lot of satisfaction. Five cars were lined up in the two-acre front yard of his Tucson, Ariz., home—they included vehicles belonging to his son and daughter, who then lived with their families on the 12-acre property. Duck joked that since the yard looked like a car lot, he ought to rent out cars.

He thought about it some more and decided there could be a lot of money in buying used cars, cleaning them up and

By Nancy L. Croft

"This pizza business brings out the kid in me," says Carmen Jones, 70. Bored with retirement, she founded Kids Korner Fresh Pizza, Inc., in

Wausau, Wis., when she was 61. Today her company stores and her franchise operation are worth millions.

PHOTOS: T. MICHAEL KEZA

More and more senior citizens, bitten by the be-your-own-boss bug, are starting businesses these days. They face some special pitfalls—but they also have some special advantages.

renting them out at half the cost of what big-name auto rental companies charge for the cars they buy new. Enter the Ugly Duckling Rent-A-Car System, Inc., which purchases last year's models and further cuts costs by keeping them twice as long as most rental firms keep their cars. Duck says he has also reduced expenses by forming his own insurance brokerage to act as a middleman between his company and insurance firms.

In the years since its founding in 1977, Tom Duck's Ugly Duckling has become the fifth largest auto rental firm in the United States, with over 500 franchises. Duck is 72.

Thomas Murray says he never really planned to start a company. Forced to retire from a 29-year career of managing investments for a real estate investment firm, under a company policy that made 65 the retirement age for everyone, Murray spent two years selling his knowledge as a consultant.

Then a mutual friend persuaded him to go into business with an energetic young man who wanted to start a real estate investment and development firm. Murray saw this as a chance to put his experience to work in helping an entrepreneur get started. It was a good business opportunity for himself, too.

In eight years, American Continental Properties Group, of New York City, has become a 40-employee corporation with over $300 million in assets. Murray is 75.

Entrepreneurship, Murray, Duck and Jones argue, has no age limit. Enjoying excellent health and bountiful energy, they are part of a growing group that is redefining the time of life the business world has traditionally considered to be rocking chair years.

A desire to build a larger nest egg to pass on to children prompts many older people to launch their own enterprises. Others see taking the plunge as a refreshing alternative to what can be an empty retirement. Most agree that starting a business heralds a fuller life.

According to the Bureau of Labor Statistics, more than a million people over 60 were self-employed in nonagricultural occu-

pations in 1985.

Although small business experts believe that the be-your-own-boss bug typically bites between ages 27 and 35, "there definitely is a trend toward older entrepreneurs," says Jeffry A. Timmons, professor of entrepreneurial studies at Babson College, in Babson Park, Mass. He adds: "I think we're going to see it continue."

Over-65s, the country's most rapidly growing age bracket, have increased twice as fast as the rest of the population in the last 20 years. The American Association of Retired Persons estimates that 2 million people celebrated their 65th birthdays in 1984 alone—an average of 5,500 a day.

In many cases the odds for success tip in favor of older entrepreneurs, says Ian C. MacMillan, professor of entrepreneurship and director of the Sol C. Snider Entrepreneurial Center at the University of Pennsylvania's Wharton School. Financially, they often can cope with temporary reverses better than their juniors can. Older entrepreneurs, says MacMillan, "don't have those fixed expense commitments they had in earlier years, like bringing up children or paying on mortgages."

Conversely, when a business is doing well, older entrepreneurs often are able to freely invest more money. Says Frank Johnson, professor of psychiatry in human development and aging at the University of California at San Francisco: "People who are very productive usually have provided well for themselves for retirement."

J.R. "Red" Uldrick, 72-year-old owner of a travel agency and a weekly newspaper in Sun City and Sun City West, Ariz., does not rely on his businesses for his livelihood, though they are doing quite well. "If the truth were known, and I'm not fudging on this, I don't take a salary," he says. Uldrick prefers to plow earnings back into the businesses, drawing instead on investments and Social Security.

Experts say people of retirement age often have an edge in finding financing, too. "They have a tremendous secret weapon in their rich experience and

their contacts," says Timmons. "If they have been good at all, they have built up a reputation for credibility and reliability. That's the stuff that really gets you collaboration from investors."

Monetary gain for themselves is at the bottom of the list of motivators for older entrepreneurs, Johnson says, though gain for the benefit of children is a frequent motive.

Tom Duck says that one reason he quit selling insurance to get into entrepreneuring was that "in the insurance business, there wasn't much for a child to inherit." Tom and his wife, Junia, who is vice president, plan to pass on Ugly Duckling Rent-A-Car to their son and daughter.

Their son, Thomas, Jr., currently serves as chief executive officer. Their daughter, Carolynn, heads a division that sells auto accessories embossed with the company logo to franchisees. Her son, Christopher, is also involved in the company. He is learning the printing business at the corporate print shop, which produces rental and franchise agreements, brochures and franchise information.

Most people who start a business instead of living in retirement try to make their second career less pressured than their first, though some may put in as many—or more—hours. J.R. Uldrick owned and ran a golf course in Hawaii for several years before he decided to quit at 58. "Both my parents died in their early 60s of cerebral hemorrhages, and I had a feeling that I was going the same way," he recalls. "I thought: If I'm going to have a cerebral hemorrhage when I'm 61, I want to get out and smell the flowers a little." Uldrick and his wife moved back to the mainland and settled in Sun City. That was in 1972.

After four years, Uldrick, at 62, felt healthier than ever. He thought it would be the perfect time to sign a new lease on life on his own terms. He started by rejuvenating a foundering travel agency that he originally had invested in as a silent partner. After two years, he bought his partner out and expanded to three other offices in Sun City and Sun City West.

At these communities outside Phoenix, developed by Del E. Webb Communities, Inc., people of retirement age are encouraged to lead active, vigorous lives. Businesses run by people over 60 flourish. Residents also do a lot of traveling, says Uldrick, who several times a year leads tours in exotic countries.

On a typical day, Uldrick rises before dawn to spend a few hours working on the *Wester*, the newspaper he founded a year ago to report goings-on in Sun

City West. Then he puts in a full day at his Thunderbird Travel agency.

Some older entrepreneurs seek a more relaxed work schedule. Walter Ewing, 66, started a woodworking business in Peoria, Ariz., when he retired two years ago. "You have to retire to something, you can't just retire to retirement," he says. Previously an aeronautics field engineer, Ewing planned his retirement for nine years. He wanted to establish a company at which he could put in flexible hours and be under little stress.

Woodworking had always been his hobby, so he decided to turn it into a business. He came up with a way to camouflage unsightly rooftop air-conditioning units on houses in the Phoenix area by constructing picket or lattice fences around the units. He achieves his goals of flexible hours and little stress by turning down or postponing jobs when he feels like it.

Ewing says his new career keeps his wife sane. "She says she married me for better or worse, but not for lunch," he jokes.

Turning a hobby into a business is a way to recuperate from the depression that can accompany retirement, says Mike Parker, 79, founder of New Career Opportunities, Inc., in Glendale, Calif. "All of a sudden you're not very important to the world," he says. Eight years ago, he started a service to help retirees like himself adjust to their newfound freedom. "In retirement you're primarily directing yourself for the first time," says Parker.

After a 24-year career of raising funds and organizing programs for Junior Achievement—a business-funded organization in which business volunteers help youngsters gain a working knowledge of the free enterprise system—Parker decided to apply J.A.'s learning-by-doing method to adults. He set up a school to instruct retirees on how to turn hobbies or other interests into businesses. Funded by the Los Angeles Rotary Club, New Career Opportunities is a nonprofit, 11-week program with guest lectures by local business leaders. It has graduated more than 400 students.

People who have been active all their lives often find it difficult to resign themselves to lives of leisure during retirement. In 1984, a 65-year-old man could expect to live 14.5 more years, and the life expectancy of a woman the same age was 18.7 years, according to the National Center for Health Statistics. "People are living a lot longer than they expected," observes Ian MacMillan. So, he says, retirees "are saying to

PHOTO: T. MICHAEL KEZA

Thomas Duck, 72, buys last year's car models, keeps them spruced up for twice as long as most auto rental firms and rents them at half the cost.

His nine-year-old Ugly Duckling Rent-A-Car Systems, Inc., of Tucson, Ariz., is the fifth largest auto rental firm in the country.

themselves, 'Why should I sit in a rocking chair when there are interesting and exciting things to do?' "

To Samuel Hachtman, the answer was easy. "When you work, and your mind is occupied, you keep healthy, and you don't get lazy," says Hachtman, who at 63 left a long career as a corporate lawyer to start Sugarless Candy Corporation, in Chicago. Though Hachtman, now 85, sold the business in January, he is staying on as a consultant, working six days a week as he always has. "You'd be surprised how many aches and pains you get just sitting at home in a chair," he says. "I never get tired."

Frank Bauer does not have much leisure time now, either, but he says he may hang up his corporate hat in nine years—at 95. He has worked 71 consecutive years, with only five weeks of unemployment during that stretch.

Bauer, who looks like a trim Col. Sanders, started his Sun City-based Portable Diesel Power, Ltd.—a diesel construction equipment leasing business—when he was 60. He says he has no hobbies, he just loves to work.

"I don't think anybody enjoys work-

ing more than I do," he says, tapping the brim of his white, flat-top hat. But some of his employees are in the running. Bauer's accountant, George Brierley, is 73, and one secretary, May Rau, is 75. The other secretary, Eleanor Wagnild, 86, has worked for Bauer for 22 years. "She's a real live wire," Bauer says.

Pizza franchisor Carmen Jones was raised on a Wisconsin farm during the Depression and learned from her parents that being energetic and innovative would get her ahead in life. She had several direct selling jobs and, in the 1950s, she owned a Merle Norman cosmetics and gift shop in Oshkosh, Wis.

In her late 40s she married Jess, and she became more than his wife and companion. She became his marketing director, peddling his frozen pizzas (then, in the mid-1960s, a new food discovery) to Midwestern supermarkets. She remembers sashaying up to supermarket managers' offices and, with no appointment, announcing her arrival. "I was much smaller then and wore big hats," Carmen recalls. After two years of continual travel and hectic schedules, she grew weary of her job. She was ready for retirement. Jess was ready, too, so they sold the business.

When Carmen became weary of retirement 10 years later, she surprised Jess by announcing that she wanted to start a pizza shop and hoped he would join in the venture. Jess, four years older than Carmen and recovering from a heart attack and stroke, declined. He did, however, help her clean up the shop she had selected for her new enterprise.

She recalls: "One day a longtime friend stopped by to see what we were up to and said, 'I thought you had retired. What do you think you are, a couple of kids?' And I said, 'Yeah, this is kids' corner.'"

The joke not only became the name of her business, which features the same secret Northern Italian sauce recipe used in Jess' old business, but it also had another significance. Working with franchisees and expanding Kids Korner Fresh Pizza, Inc., keeps her young, Jones says.

"If I don't have anything to do, I get ornery. I have to put my mind on something. I have to keep learning."

Jack Fenimore built a business around the love of learning, but he had to wait 40 years to do it. When he went into World War II as a fighter pilot, Fenimore was trained audiovisually with slide shows and motion pictures. He realized then that audiovisuals had potential as an effective teaching aid for the general public, but he could not see a business opportunity.

Nevertheless, he made a career for himself in an allied field—photography and film production. In 39 years with various production companies and advertising agencies, Fenimore produced everything from corporate training films to television commercials. It wasn't until video cassette recorders became popular that he finally saw his chance to sell the idea of instructional videos for use in the home.

At 60, Fenimore took early retirement from an ad agency and founded Mid-Com, Inc., based in Evansville, Ind., to produce how-to video cassettes on more than 150 subjects, ranging from watercolor painting and foreign languages for adults to lessons for children on how to become a magician or cartoonist.

Today, the three-year-old company's cassettes are distributed nationwide. To Fenimore, starting a business during his retirement years was "an opportunity to do what I thought I was going to do when I got out of the service in 1945. But the industry wasn't ready for me until the 1980s."

You might think that health would be more of a problem for older entrepreneurs than for their younger counterparts. Not necessarily. In addition to living longer, the over-60 generation is enjoying better health, say experts. Improvements in diet and medical science mean that older people less frequently succumb to debilitating diseases and infirmities.

Good health and the older entrepreneur seem to be synonymous, says Karl H. Vesper, professor of business administration at the University of Washington, Seattle. "You could surmise that only a person in good health would start a business, or you could surmise that when someone is starting a business it is such an exciting activity that they don't have time not to be healthy," he says. "If it is the latter, then I think it is a tremendous thing for older people to do."

Starting a company at any age causes stress, says psychiatrist Frank Johnson. Johnson says warning signs of too much stress—such as insomnia, increased alcohol consumption or gastrointestinal disorders—"would not be any different for older people than the signs that would appear when they were younger."

If Tom Duck is having a bad day, you will find him playing the piano. A self-taught musician, Duck says that when the demands of his multimillion-dollar auto rental franchise operation get the best of him, he closes his office door and serenades himself on his Baldwin spinet until he cannot remember what his last conversation was about. "It's my Valium," he jokes.

Duck has also built a health spa—complete with hot tub, weight-lifting equipment, sauna and massage room—for his employees at his new corporate headquarters in Tucson. The object is "to ensure the durability of yours truly and the rest of the company," he says.

Calisthenics at 7 a.m. are a daily routine for developer Thomas Murray, who finds respite in his weekly bowling game and in the golf games he plays three times a week. Murray can afford the luxury of so much time on the links because his partner holds the reins when he is away. Taking on a partner is a good idea for the older entrepreneur, says Murray, "because if you're like me, you may not want to work full time."

Carmen Jones visits a chiropractor regularly and takes vitamins to keep herself as energetic as ever. Her 14-year-old granddaughter, Sarah, who has worked after school at a number of the pizza shops since she was 7, attests to her grandmother's energy. "I don't even have to be out of bed before she

runs me ragged!"

Keeping fit and full of energy does not prevent older entrepreneurs from experiencing the frustration of typical problems that come with running a small business. And they realize that age can at times present special pitfalls.

Jones says one problem older women entrepreneurs encounter is that "some younger men have the idea that they can pat an old lady on the back, be nice to her and then do what they want." She recently had to let a young supervisor go. "I kept finding out that things were not being run according to our company rules," she says. "I talked to him three times, but he would go ahead and do what he wanted."

Crime can be a particular concern for businesses run by the elderly. The Cheese House, of Sun City, has several workers over 60 and is owned by Roland Schlueter, 65, and his wife, Mary, 51. Criminals "prey on the elderly," Mary says. She remembers the terror she felt when a man robbed the store last year. "I was the one who was staring down the barrel of the gun," she says. "I gave him $1,000. I would have given him anything."

Another pitfall for older entrepreneurs is the temptation to bypass precautions that anyone going into business should take, says New Career Opportunities' Mike Parker. It is a mistake, he tells retirees thinking of starting businesses, to feel that years of experience are an automatic safeguard against errors in judgment.

Planning the business thoroughly and doing adequate preliminary research are essential, he says. The next step, he says, is to start out small: "You can't afford to start big and risk your nest egg, because you don't have enough time to recoup it if things go wrong."

Hazel Oates, 57, and her husband, James, 66, found out the hard way that research can be vital. Although their faltering business poses no real economic tragedy for them, the Oateses are saddled with a lease on a self-service laundry that sees few dirty clothes.

When James retired, and the Oateses moved to Sun City West from England, Hazel—vivacious and outgoing—wanted to keep on working. She found a job with a Sun City corporation, but it didn't have enough challenge for her. A friend in San Francisco suggested that she start a business and offered to finance it. After talking to neighbors in Sun City West, Hazel discovered that some people were not installing washers and driers and were using their laundry rooms for dens or studios. She decided to open a Laundromat.

"I had never been in a Laundromat," she admits, "but I thought it was a service that was needed here." Without conducting any market research, she signed a lease on some commercial space. She found out too late that fewer people than she thought had actually converted their laundry rooms. The amount of laundry the business takes in barely covers the overhead, Hazel says. She would like to sell out and start some other enterprise, but she sees no prospect of selling an unprofitable venture. Suds City West Laundromat has two years to go on its three-year lease. "We're working for the landlord," says Hazel.

Mike Parker says that retirees and prospective retirees who think they have a product or service that could mushroom into a business should test it out on friends and do plenty of market research to see if consumers are really receptive to the intended product or service. He also suggests they glean advice from other older entrepreneurs and from people of whatever age who already are in a business like the one they are considering.

And would-be entrepreneurs should be certain they are willing to give up their freedom for a business commitment, he cautions. Like Ugly Duckling and Kids Korner, small businesses can grow unexpectedly into big enterprises.

Another caveat: A salary a business owner draws can impact on Social Security payments. Retirees between 62 and 65 who continue to work may earn up to $5,760 a year and still receive their full Social Security benefits. Retirees age 65 to 69 may earn up to $7,800 annually before their Social Security benefits are reduced. Once a retiree exceeds those earnings limits, benefits are cut $1 for every $2 earned. (In 1990 that will change to $1 for every $3.) After age 70, however, retirees may collect full benefits no matter how much they earn.

Dividends and salary from a business, as well as interest payments, can impact on the tax-exempt status of Social Security benefits. Since 1984 recipients with adjusted gross incomes over $25,000—$32,000 for married couples filing jointly—have had to pay income tax on as much as half of the amount of the Social Security benefits that carry them over those levels. (Fifty percent of their Social Security benefits are counted in figuring adjusted grosses in such cases.)

Jack Fenimore says older would-be entrepreneurs should carefully weigh all the factors before going into business. Once they have decided the positives outweigh negatives, he says, they should "never let anyone talk them into putting it off." He explains: "When you're our age, you don't have enough time to wait."

ACTIONS OF ALCOHOL & DRUGS
IN OLDER PEOPLE

PETER P. LAMY

Peter P. Lamy, Ph.D., Sc.D., is a professor and assistant dean, geriatrics, and director of the Center for the Study of Pharmacy and Therapeutics for the Elderly, School of Pharmacy, University of Maryland at Baltimore. He is also a professor of epidemiology and preventive medicine at the university's School of Medicine.

CHANGES WITH AGE

It is still extremely difficult to differentiate between primary age changes (normal physical changes with age), secondary age changes (those resulting from diseases in old age), and tertiary age changes (those associated with social, behavioral, or environmental changes with age) (Lamy, 1987). All of these changes, individually or combined, can and do alter an elderly individual's response to pharmacologically active agents, including alcohol. Of overriding concern are the loss of physiologic reserve and the increasing individual variation in the degree of loss with advancing age (Heckler, 1985). Loss of reserve capacity is directly related to inability to respond to stress or to recover as easily from stress-induced problems as at an earlier age. Significant symptoms can occur, especially in the most limited systems, such as the central nervous system and the cardiovascular system. These changes may also be responsible for the well-known "atypical" presentation of symptoms among the elderly (Rowe, 1984), explaining at least partially why elderly alcohol abusers often are not recognized.

With advancing age, major negative changes occur in the body's ability to absorb and dispose of drugs and alcohol. These changes may be heightened if the aging person has co-existing diseases that are being managed with drugs. General nutritional depletion and specific nutrient deficiencies, often encountered in the elderly, can also interfere with drug actions in the body (Lamy, 1984). Following are specific bodily changes that occur with aging that may heighten the elderly's risk of suffering adverse effects of alcohol and other drugs.

Body composition. With advancing age, the ratio of lean body weight to fatty tissue changes, with an increase in fat occurring even in the absence of overall weight changes. There is a reduction in intra- and extracellular fluids, reducing the volume available for the distribution of water-soluble drugs. In the presence of disease, there may also be a decline in plasma albumin (Lamy, 1987).

The kidneys. Primary age-related changes may alter kidney function substantially in many, but not all, elderly (Lamy, 1987). Renal function declines progressively with age, and renal blood and plasma flow also decrease. With advancing age, the ability to concentrate urine decreases, as does the maximum diluting ability. Furthermore, older people do not conserve sodium efficiently. Thus, both of the broad excretory functions of the kidney, to preserve the volume of body fluids and to maintain the proper composition of these fluids, are affected by normal aging. Secondary age changes associated with diseases occur with greater frequency in older persons, and many may cause end-organ damage, such as kidney impairment. Use of drugs to manage these diseases or problems of aging may further impair kidney function in certain instances.

The liver. Primary age changes may be responsible for decreased blood flow in the liver as well as reducing the liver's microsomal metabolism of drugs. Many drugs, in turn, also reduce the liver blood flow, thus further altering drug metabolism, while others may stimulate or reduce enzyme activity in the liver (Lamy, 1987).

Brain changes. With age, cellular brain mass and cerebral blood flow decrease, and the time needed for sensory conduction increases. It is also likely that the blood-brain barrier becomes increasingly permeable. These changes may result in decreased physical coordination, prolongation of reaction time, and impairment of shortterm memory, manifested by an increased number of falls and increased frequency of confusion. The brains of older people also appear to be more sensitive to the side effects of drugs and alcohol (Lamy, 1987).

Cardiovascular system changes. Aging is associated with structural changes in the heart and blood vessels, including major negative changes in electrical, mechanical, and biochemical properties. These functional declines are responsible for the high incidence of drug-induced orthostatic hypotension (low blood pressure), the risk being increased by the loss of blood volume because of salt or water depletion or both (Lamy, 1987).

Gastrointestinal system changes. Aging is associated with both structural and functional impairment in the stomach. For example, accelerated and sustained cell turnover and shortening of the period of maturity of differentiated cells are responsible for the stomach's reduced secretion of protective mucus. These changes, coupled with an increased intake of drugs active or toxic in the stomach, heighten the risk to older people of gastric injury due to drugs or other noxious substances (Lamy, 1987).

EFFECTS OF ALCOHOL ABUSE

Reasonably small and controlled alcohol intake may be of benefit to the elderly, as it may stimulate appetite, increase socialization, and may play a "protective" role against coronary artery disease. On the other hand, excessive or prolonged consumption of alcohol by older people can lead to physical, psychological, social, and other serious consequences (Schuckit, 1977). Virtually every organ system in the body is directly or indirectly and adversely affected by alcohol.

Alcohol can profoundly affect the structure and function of the central nervous system, particularly at the level of the neuronal membrane. For example, alcohol tolerance, physical dependence, and the alcohol withdrawal syndrome appear to be the result of changes within the neuronal membrane (NIAAA, 1987). Intellectual deterioration and dementia are common complications of chronic al-

cohol abuse. Mental functions most affected are abstract reasoning and shortterm memory. The system used to retrieve encoded and consolidated memory is disrupted by alcohol. Alcoholic patients show more signs of mental aging at every chronological age. Among elderly patients admitted to psychiatric hospitals with organic brain syndrome, those who abused alcohol were significantly younger than those who did not. Alcoholics with organic brain syndrome also have a higher mortality rate than nonalcoholics with this condition (Gaitz and Baer, 1971; Tamkin, 1983).

Alcohol alters motility, metabolism, blood circulation, and cellular structure of the gastrointestinal system. Alcohol causes gastric lesions (the elderly are more sensitive to this effect than younger people), especially when taken with other substances toxic to the stomach (vitamin C, potassium supplements, aspirin, nonsteroidal anti-inflammatory drugs, such as ibuprofen, and the like). In turn, alcohol enhances the effect of aspirin on bleeding time, even when the two are ingested 36 hours apart (Deykin et al., 1982). Alcohol abuse may also interfere with the absorption of some nutrients. Furthermore, in men drinking more than 1.25 ounces of alcohol per day, the percentage of calories per day derived from alcohol can exceed 20 percent of total caloric intake (Hillus and Massey, 1985). Although much discussion has centered on a possible link between breast cancer and alcohol intake, a recent study of a white population that was both ethnically and socioeconomically homogeneous showed no association (Graham, 1987; Lindegard, 1987).

Elderly people suffer from cardiovascular problems much more frequently than do younger persons, and alcohol often profoundly affects the cardiovascular system. Alcohol consumption is associated with hypertension and increased mortality from stroke (Kozararevic et al., 1980; Blackwelder et al., 1980). Patients with alcohol-related heart muscle disorders exhibit symptoms of rapid heartbeat or irregular rhythm, cardiac enlargement, pulmonary crackles (rales), peripheral swelling, distension of the jugular vein, and liver enlargement (Regan, 1982; Braunwald,

1984). Alcoholics also exhibit supraventricular as well as ventricular arrhythmias (irregular heartbeat) (Ettinger et al., 1978; Rich et al., 1985). Alcohol consumption may also be associated with coagulation disorders.

Alcohol abuse is also associated with an increased susceptibility to infectious disease and can have major adverse effects on the endocrine system. Malnourished or fasting drinkers whose glycogen stores are greatly depleted will experience hypoglycemia even in the absence of liver disease. Recurrent attacks of hypoglycemia, of course, can result in brain injury, and severe hypoglycemia can end fatally (Cohen, 1976). Men who drink as little as three drinks a day and women who drink as little as one and one-half drinks a day are at heightened risk of developing liver cirrhosis (NIAAA, 1987).

Drinking patterns vary among ethnic and racial groups and between the sexes, as do morbidity and mortality related to alcohol abuse. The incidence of alcohol-related medical problems, especially liver cirrhosis and cancer of the esophagus, is very high among blacks. In fact, the cirrhosis mortality rate for blacks is twice as high as that for whites, higher in males than in females. A high rate of mortality from cirrhosis exists also among Hispanic American males. Alcohol-related illness and injury rates among Native Americans are three times higher than in the general population, and liver cirrhosis is the fourth leading cause of death among this group.

Asian Americans, on the other hand, regardless of national origin, have very low levels of alcohol abuse and alcoholism. Abstention is very high among Asian Americans, especially Koreans, Chinese, and women of all Asian groups. There is considerable evidence that Asian populations have a very high prevalence of a condition that causes the body to be inefficient in removing acetaldehyde, a key chemical constituent of alcohol. Rapid accumulation of acetaldehyde, after only a few drinks, produces skin flushing, a rapid pulse, and other uncomfortable symptoms, deterring further drinking (NIAAA, 1987). While none of these patterns is specific to the elderly, it is assumed that all would apply generally to older members of these ethnic groups.

With advancing age, major negative changes occur in the body's ability to absorb and dispose of drugs and alcohol.

ALCOHOL-DRUG INTERACTION

Some time ago, the Food and Drug Administration stated that about 50 percent of all drugs that the elderly take can interact with alcohol, and this is true of the drugs the elderly take most frequently. Since the elderly take more drugs than any other segment of the U.S. population, alcohol-drug interactions are to be expected. Concurrent use of alcohol with drugs, even 10 or more hours apart, can significantly change a drug's action because of changes in the drug's toxic effects (in the stomach, for example) or changes in its absorption and disposition. Interactions, then, can occur by several mechanisms and on several levels.

Adverse effects due to alcohol-drug interactions can be particularly serious in the elderly because of the already existing changes in drug disposition and increased sensitivity to drugs (that is, increased brain sensitivity). This effect may be heightened by age- or disease-related changes in the various organ systems described above.

Pharmacokinetic interactions. Alcohol is rapidly absorbed from the stomach and small intestine (absorption rate is increased when alcohol is consumed with carbonated drinks) and converted in the liver to acetaldehyde by the enzyme alcohol dehydrogenase. Acetaldehyde is further metabolized to an acetate, which is incorporated into the citric acid cycle. Several drugs may inhibit the metabolism of alcohol at the level of alcohol dehydrogenase, causing cumulation of acetaldehyde in the liver. This, in turn, will result in flushing, rapid heartbeat, shortness of breath, vomiting, headache, and giddiness. The blood pressure may fall drastically (D'Arcy and Merkus, 1981).

Pharmacokinetically (related to the body's disposition of a drug), alcohol can increase or decrease a drug's absorption by changing its solubility, by altering the rate at which the stomach empties, or by causing an inflammatory response in the stomach that could alter the absorption profile of a drug. Compared to beer or wine, hard liquor is more likely to cause gastric irritation and inflammation of the gastric mucosa and may do so more quickly. In those who abuse alcohol, plasma albumin levels may be lowered. Thus, for drugs that are highly albumin-bound (the bound fraction is not active), there may be a larger free (active) fraction of the drug, and the intensity or duration of its action in the body may change.

Alcohol-induced alteration of drug metabolism varies with the amount ingested, the duration of ingestion, and the presence of alcohol at the time of drug ingestion (Mezey, 1981). Tolbutamide, warfarin, and phenytoin may be affected, possibly for as long as three weeks after discontinuation of alcohol. On the other hand, alcohol and some drugs compete for enzyme metabolism in the liver. Meprobamate, pentobarbital, and benzodiazepines (for example, Valium) exhibit increased bioavailability when used together with alcohol, possibly increasing their toxic effects.

Pharmacodynamic interactions. Pharmacodynamically (related to action of a drug on the body), alcohol may potentiate, or increase, the effects of many drugs, perhaps via changes in tolerance or through synergistic effects. Of particular concern in the elderly is the potentiation of central nervous system depressants—the psychotropics (antipsychotics, antidepressants, anti-anxiety agents [or anxiolytics], and sedatives/hypnotics). Among nursing home residents, antipsychotics rank seventh and eighth among the most frequently used drugs. Among older people living in the community, possibly as many as 50 percent receive antianxiety agents and between 10 and 20 percent may receive antidepressants. The use of sedatives/hypnotics among the frail elderly, who often complain about inability to sleep, is, unfortunately, high. This still-poorly-understood interaction may cause heightened confusion, memory loss, dizziness (increasing the risk of falls and fractures), urinary incontinence, and many other problems and may also result in fatalities. Overall, alcohol abuse may destabilize elderly patients who are taking anticoagulants, oral hypoglycemics, and antiseizure drugs. Finally, the hypotensive (blood pressure-lowering) action of antihypertensive agents may be enhanced by alcohol (D'Arcy and Merkus, 1981).

Other interaction concerns. In the general population, alcohol-drug interactions account for nearly 2,500 deaths and 47,000 admissions to emergency rooms annually (Food and Drug Administration, 1979). Comparable data specific to older persons who abuse alcohol are not available. However, it is reasonable to project that the problem is heightened in the elderly. In one study, 17.4 percent of the elderly, designated as "generally healthy," were using alcohol, prescription drugs, and nonprescription drugs simultaneously (Guttmann, 1978). Quite obviously, aside from the adverse effects already documented, alcohol abuse and alcohol-drug interactions can lead to increased errors in compliance and to increased noncompliance, a situation among the elderly that has been identified by the Food and Drug Administration as a major problem. This problem is aggravated among older people living alone, who are already known to make more medication errors than those with some social support structure or a family caregiver.

ALCOHOL WITHDRAWAL

The use of disulfiram (Antabuse) to prevent alcohol intake is not recommended for older persons. They may not be able to cope with the adverse effects that may occur with inadvertent or even deliberate alcohol intake while receiving disulfiram. While the treatment of alcohol withdrawal symptoms in the elderly is essentially the same as in younger people, a cautionary note should be added: elderly patients tolerate a mild degree of dehydration much better than overhydration, so caution should be exercised when parenteral fluids are used (Walker and Covington, 1984). Otherwise, treatment may involve the use of thiamine, folic acid, multivitamins,

Among older people living in the community, possibly as many as 50 percent receive antianxiety agents and between 10 and 20 percent may receive antidepressants.

magnesium sulfate, other electrolytes as necessary, diazepam (Valium), and, possibly, phenytoin.

CONCLUSION

Alcohol abuse, age- and disease-related changes, and drug-induced problems are more likely to converge in the elderly, making them more vulnerable than younger people to the combined effects of these conditions. The psychological and social consequences of alcohol abuse might include loss of a sense of reality, loss of correct self-judgment, a psychiatric syndrome including fear and depression, as well as conflicts in family relations (NIAAA, 1987). Older people in general may exhibit similar problems that are due to age- or disease-related changes. Similarly, progressive intellectual deterioration and deficiencies in attention, memory, and other cognitive functions have been attributed to many drugs, such as the psychotropics, certain diuretics, antiparkinson agents, and sedatives (Lamy, 1984). In addition, the elderly metabolize and excrete alcohol more slowly than do younger persons. The capacity of elders to drink safely is reduced, and their sensitivity to the adverse effects of alcohol is increased (Lamy, 1980). Among medical problems that the elderly may exhibit, cirrhosis of the liver, gastritis, peptic ulcer, heart muscle disorder, diseases of the nervous system, malnutrition, cerebrovascular disease, and mental status changes suggest an alcohol connec-

tion. It is, therefore, quite apparent that alcohol misuse and abuse present a clear danger to older people, particularly those with multiple diseases who are receiving multiple drugs, whether prescription or nonprescription medications.

REFERENCES

Blackwelder, W. C. et al., 1980. "Alcohol and Mortality: The Honolulu Heart Study." *American Journal of Medicine* 68(2):164–69.

Braunwald, E., 1984. *Heart Disease: A Textbook of Cardiovascular Medicine*. Philadelphia: W. B. Saunders Company.

Cohen, S., 1976. "A Review of Hypoglycemia and Alcoholism with or without Liver Disease." *Annals of the New York Academy of Science* 273:338–42.

D'Arcy, P. F. and Merkus, F. W. H. M., 1981. "Alcohol and Drug Interactions." *Pharmacy International* 2:273–80.

Deykin, D., Janson, P. and McMahon, L., 1982. "Ethanol Potentiation of Aspirin-induced Prolongation of Bleeding Time." *New England Journal of Medicine* 306(4):852–54.

Ettinger, P. O. et al., 1978. "Arrhythmias and the Holiday Heart: Alcohol-associated Cardiac Rhythm Disorders". *American Heart Journal* 95(5):555–62.

Food and Drug Administration, 1979. "Alcohol and Drug Interactions." *FDA Drug Bulletin* 9(2):10–12.

Gaitz, C. M. and Baer, P. E., 1971. "Characteristics of Elderly Patients with Alcoholism." *Archives of General Psychiatry* 24(4):372–78.

Graham, S., 1987. "Alcohol and Breast Cancer." *New England Journal of Medicine* 316(19):1211–13.

Guttmann, D., 1978. "Patterns of Legal Drug Use by Older Americans." *Addictive Diseases* 3(3):337–56.

Heckler, R. B., 1985. "The Physiology of Aging: Implications for Drug Therapy. In E. P. Hofer, ed., *Emergency Problems in the Elderly*. Oradell, N.J.: Medical Economics Books.

Hillus, V. N. and Massey, L. K., 1985. "Inter-

relationship of Moderate and High Alcohol Consumption and Diet and Health Status." *American Journal of Clinical Nutrition* 41(2):356–62.

Kozararevic, D. J. et al., 1980. "Frequency of Alcohol Consumption and Morbidity and Mortality. The Yugoslavia Cardiovascular Disease Study." *Lancet* 1(8169):613–16.

Lamy, P. P., 1980. *Prescribing for the Elderly*. Littleton, Mass.: PSG Publishing Co.

Lamy, P. P., 1984. "Modifying Drug Dosage in the Elderly." In T. R. Covington and J. I. Walker, eds., *Current Geriatric Therapy*. Philadelphia: W. B. Saunders Company.

Lamy, P. P., 1987. "Introduction to the Aging Process." In J. C. Delafuente and R. B. Stewart, eds., *Therapeutics in the Elderly*. Baltimore: Williams & Wilkins.

Lindegard, B., 1987. "Survival and Age at Diagnosis in Breast Cancer." *New England Journal of Medicine* 316(12):750–52.

Mezey, E., 1981. "Alcohol and Drug Interactions in Injury to the Digestive Tract." *Clinics of Gastroenterology* 10(2):485–95.

National Institute on Alcohol Abuse and Alcoholism, 1987. *Alcohol and Health*. Rockville, Md.: U.S. Department of Health and Human Services. DHHS Publ. No. (ADM) 87–1519.

Regan, T. J., 1982. "Alcohol: Is it a Risk Factor for Cardiovascular Disease?" *Baylor College Medical Cardiology Series* 5:6–26.

Rich, E. C., Siebold, C. and Campion, B., 1985. "Alcohol-related Acute Atrial Fibrillation." *Archives of Internal Medicine* 145(5):830–33.

Rowe, J. W., 1984. "Physiological Changes with Age and their Clinical Relevance." In R. N. Butler and A. G. Bearns, eds., *The Aging Process: Therapeutic Implications*. New York: Raven Press.

Schuckit, M. A., 1977. "Geriatric Alcoholism and Drug Abuse." *The Gerontologist* 17(2):168–74.

Tamkin, A. S., 1983. "Impairment of Cognitive Functioning in Alcoholics." *Military Medicine* 148(10):793–95.

Walker, J. I. and Covington, T. R., 1984. "Psychiatric Disorders." In T. R. Covington and J. I. Walker, eds., *Current Geriatric Therapy*. Philadelphia: W. B. Saunders Company.

In this first large-scale random sample survey of elder abuse and neglect, interviews were conducted with 2020 community-dwelling elderly persons in the Boston metropolitan area regarding their experience of physical violence, verbal aggression, and neglect. The prevalence rate of overall maltreatment was 32 elderly persons per 1000. Spouses were found to be the most likely abusers and roughly equal numbers of men and women were victims, although women suffered more serious abuse. Implications for public policy are discussed.
Key Words: Elder abuse, Families of the aged, Neglect.

The Prevalence of Elder Abuse: A Random Sample Survey

Karl Pillemer, PhD

Family Research Laboratory, University of New Hampshire, Durham, NH 03824.

David Finkelhor, PhD

Department of Sociology, University of New Hampshire.

The past decade has witnessed increasing research attention to the problem of elder abuse. With rare exceptions, researchers have relied on samples of cases that have come to the attention of a social agency or reporting authority (see Johnson et al., 1985, for a comprehensive review). It is widely recognized, however, that these are highly selective samples and that there is a large reservoir of unreported and undetected cases of elder abuse about which very little is known. Unreported cases may be similar to cases that are reported; however, they may be quite different. Most important, the question of the extent of elder abuse cannot be answered by studies of reported cases.

Indeed, one common refrain in virtually every report on elder abuse is the lack of firm findings on the prevalence of the problem and on risk factors for maltreatment. The writers of review articles (Hudson, 1986; Pedrick-Cornell & Gelles, 1982; Pillemer & Suitor, in press; Yin, 1985) have frequently cited the conceptual and methodological weaknesses of most of the existing studies. These problems included unclear definitions of elder abuse, reliance on professional reports rather than victim interviews, and failure to use rigorous research designs, such as random-sample surveys and case-comparison studies. Thus, it is not known from prior research how much elder abuse there is. Further, there is only a preliminary picture of who is most likely to be abused.

Two earlier attempts have been made to estimate the prevalence of elder abuse in the population at large. A statistic that has been very widely cited in the past, that 4% of the elderly are abused, was derived from a survey by Block and Sinnott (1979). Unfortunately, Block and Sinnott's statistic was generated in an unreliable survey of the elderly, and is not generalizable. These investigators attempted a random sample survey in the Washington, D.C. area, but the response rate was so low (16%) and the final sample size so small (73 persons) as to invalidate the findings. Moreover, the researchers appear to have asked about knowledge of abuse, rather than the actual experience.

A survey with a more sound scientific basis was conducted by Gioglio & Blakemore (1983), who questioned a random sample of 342 elders in the state of New Jersey. Only 5 of these respondents reported some form of maltreatment, yielding an estimate of 15 per 1000. Although this figure is lower than in the present study, it is based on a small sample and thus has a very large confidence interval (2–28 per 1000); therefore, the estimate is not very precise. Moreover, the New Jersey study used volunteer interviewers and somewhat vague measures of abuse.

The present study was conducted to more accurately assess the scope and nature of maltreatment of the elderly occurring in the community at large. It was the first large scale random sample survey of the problem, involving over 2000 elderly persons in the Boston, Massachusetts metropolitan area. The study revealed prevalence rates for various types of maltreatment and allowed for the identification of subgroups of the elderly population who appeared to be at greatest risk.

Methodology

Sample Design

The study was designed as a stratified random sample of all community-dwelling elderly persons

The study was a project of the Family Violence Research Program, University of New Hampshire, Durham, NH 03824. We are indebted to Daniel Malloy and James Grosch for assistance with computer programming; to members of the Family Violence Research Program Seminar, including Murray A. Straus and J. Jill Suitor, for helpful comments and suggestions; to Gerda Fillenbaum, Duke University, for assistance in developing the research instrument; to Donna Wilson for preparing the manuscript, and to Clare McMillan for editorial advice. We would also like to acknowledge Jack Fowler and his colleagues at the Center for Survey Research at the University of Massachusetts, Boston, who conducted the survey. The research was carried out with support from the National Institute on Aging (1 Rol AG043301).

(65 or older) in the Boston metropolitan area. Under Massachusetts law, each municipality in the state is required to conduct and publish an annual listing of the residents of every dwelling, which includes their birthdates. Potential respondents were randomly selected from persons on the lists who were 65 years of age or older.

A two-stage interview process was employed in this study. The screening stage consisted of an interview of approximately 30 minutes intended to identify whether the respondent was a victim of maltreatment. The interviews were conducted either by telephone or in person. Starting with the names selected from the city and town lists, an attempt was made to obtain a phone number for the respondent from the telephone directory assistance, contact him or her, make an appointment, and conduct the interview by telephone (an introductory letter had been sent out in advance). If a telephone number could not be obtained for the respondent, if the respondent had obvious difficulty using the telephone, or if the respondent preferred it for any reason, an interviewer was sent to the household to conduct the interview. Of the 3366 elderly households selected for the study from the city and town lists, 16% turned out to be ineligible (because of moves or mistakes on the lists). Of the 2813 eligible respondents, 72% could be interviewed directly or by proxy (see below), for a total of 2020 interviews.

The follow-up stage consisted of another 30 to 45 minute interview with individuals who were identified as abuse victims. Follow-up interviews were conducted by telephone or in person according to the mode of the initial interview and depending on the respondent's wishes. The follow-up interview contained detailed items regarding the context of abusive incidents and their consequences. Primarily reported in this article are the screen interview data, although some follow-up findings are also included.

The study was designed to oversample some groups of the elderly of particular interest to the project. From the literature, it is clear that aged persons who live with others are at higher risk for abuse compared to those living alone (O'Malley et al., 1979; Wolf et al., 1984; 1986) because the opportunities for abuse are greater. Moreover, researchers on elder abuse and family conflict have been especially interested in elderly persons living together with their children, even though they constitute no more than 10% of all the elderly. Therefore, elderly individuals living with others were oversampled, especially those living with persons of a younger generation. In the statistical analyses presented, weights were applied to compensate for the over-sampling.

Of course, not all elderly persons living in the community are capable of being interviewed. Individuals who are too physically or mentally impaired, unfortunately, may for these reasons be at particular risk of maltreatment. Thus, every effort was made to also obtain information on these persons. When interviewers contacting a household were informed that the designated respondent was incapable of being interviewed and were convinced that this was not simply a subterfuge to prevent direct contact with the respondent, they conducted interviews with a proxy. The proxy was the person in the household who was the primary caregiver to the designated elderly respondent.

It might seem fruitless to interview a family member about abuse that he or she may have perpetrated against the elderly person. Investigators (Finkelhor, 1984; Straus & Gelles, 1986) of a number of forms of family maltreatment, however, have found perpetrators surprisingly willing to admit to abuse. Similarly, in this study, the rates of reported maltreatment were actually higher in the proxy interviews than in the interviews with the elderly themselves. This does not necessarily mean that family members are generally more candid about maltreatment than the elderly themselves. The proxy interviews were conducted in situations where, because of the incapacitation of the elderly person, the risk of maltreatment was expected to be higher.

The final sample was quite similar demographically to the population of the greater Boston area. In all, 65% of the sample was female; 94% was white; 60% of the sample was between the ages of 65–74 and 40% over 75; 58% was Catholic, 30% protestant, 8% Jewish, and 4% other; 38% had family incomes that exceeded $15,000 per year and 62% had incomes below $15,000; and 40% lived alone, 37% with spouse only, 5% with a child only, 10% with spouse and someone else (usually a child), and 7% with others.

Definitions

To develop meaningful operational definitions, those employed in previous studies were reviewed, as well as those used by states in mandatory reporting and protective services legislation. No generally accepted definitions of elder abuse and neglect were found. Indeed, some writers have commented extensively on the disparities among definitions used in various research studies (Johnson, 1986) and in state laws (Salend et al., 1984). In this vein, a recent conference of 30 experts was unable to recommend a working definition of elder abuse and neglect (Family Research Laboratory, 1986).

To overcome this definitional disarray, those types of maltreatment on which there appeared to be consensus were identified. First, all discussions of elder abuse included physical violence; there is nearly universal agreement that physical assault against an elder constitutes abusive behavior.

Second, most of the research literature (although not all state laws) included a category of psychological, emotional, or mental abuse. These terms were generally very vaguely defined, and the types of abusive behavior varied greatly from study to study (for examples, see Johnson, 1986; Pillemer & Suitor, in press). Further, the category of psychological abuse has been widely criticized as including all types of family problems under the label abuse (Callahan, 1982; Crystal, 1986; Pedrick-Cornell & Gelles, 1982). The persistent, widespread concern, however, regarding this type of maltreatment mandated that a measure of psychological abuse be included.

Third, the category of neglect appeared in many studies and state laws, although it is also a controversial term. There is general agreement that the failure of a clearly designated caregiver to meet the needs of an elder constitutes neglect. This failure can result from the conscious intention of the caregiver (active neglect) or can occur unintentionally (passive neglect). Categories have also been created, however, to cover situations in which older persons' care needs are not being met due to the absence of a defined caregiver: so-called self-neglect or self-abuse. These categories have been criticized on the grounds that they do not represent a family maltreatment problem, but rather society's failure to meet the needs of the aged (Callahan, 1982; Crystal, 1986; Family Research Laboratory, 1986; Salend et al., 1984). Because of the focus on domestic maltreatment by relatives or acquaintances, it was decided to limit the definition of neglect to situations that involved a caretaker's intentional or unintentional failure to assist the elder.

Thus, three major areas of inquiry were identified: physical abuse, psychological abuse, and neglect. These categories were then operationalized in the following way.

Physical abuse meant at least one act of physical violence against the respondent since he or she had turned 65 years of age. It was operationalized using a modified form of the Conflict Tactics Scale (CTS), an instrument that has been used in many studies of family violence (Straus, 1979). The 10 items encompass a range of violent behaviors, from being pushed, grabbed or shoved to being assaulted with a knife or gun. Respondents were administered the CTS regarding their relationships with their spouse, one co-resident child (if present), and one other member of their social network with whom they reported significant conflict. If any of these persons had been violent towards the respondent at least once since he or she had turned 65, the respondent was placed in the physical abuse category.

Neglect was defined as the deprivation of some assistance that the elderly person needed for important activities of daily living. Neglect was operationalized using a section of the Older Americans Resources and Services (OARS) instrument concerned with activities of daily living (Duke University Center for the Study of Aging and Human Development, 1978), which was augmented to ascertain whether needed help was withheld. The 10 activities of daily living included meal preparation, housework, and shopping, as well as personal care activities such as dressing and toileting. If the neglect had occurred 10 or more times in the preceding year, or was termed somewhat or very serious by the respondent, he or she was placed in the neglect category.

Psychological abuse, for reasons given, was a particularly difficult concept to operationalize. The review of the literature indicated, however, that one of the major manifestations of psychological abuse appears to be repeated insults and threats. For this study, the scope of psychological abuse was restricted to such behaviors and was termed "chronic verbal aggression." This form of maltreatment was defined as the elderly person being insulted, sworn at, or threatened at least 10 or more times in the preceding year. These verbal aggression items were administered as part of the CTS.

In summary, this study was focused on the three categories on which there appeared greatest consensus. Based on the review of state programs, it seemed clear that most states would consider persons in any of these categories as eligible for some form of initial intervention. Further, the three categories and their measurement appeared consistent with prior research on family violence and elder abuse and neglect.

It is important, however, to note certain limitations of the study definitions. First, material abuse, such as the theft or misuse of an elder's money or other assets, is not included. Although such abuse is a serious problem, it has already been addressed relatively thoroughly in the literature on criminal victimization of the elderly (Yin, 1985). Second, self-neglect or self-abuse is not addressed in the study. As noted, there is no consensus on the definition of these categories and debate even exists over whether they constitute abuse at all. Further, a goal of the study was to compare rates of elder abuse with child and spouse abuse, for which no category of self-inflicted abuse or neglect exists. Finally, it is possible that elderly persons could be neglected in ways other than those covered by the OARS instrument.

No claim is made here that the concept of elder abuse and neglect should be defined for purposes of social policy in the same way as for this study. In any study, difficult decisions must be made regarding restrictions on the phenomena under consideration. Future studies are in fact needed to address other problems, such as self-neglect.

Prevalence Findings

As shown in Table 1, the survey revealed 63 elderly persons (55 via direct interviews and 8 via proxy respondents) who had been maltreated according to one of the three study criteria. For the sample, this translated into a rate of 32 maltreated elderly per 1000. Given the sample size, this yields a 95% confidence interval of 25 to 39 maltreated elderly per 1000 (that is, the true figure has a 95% chance of being in this range). With an elderly population in the Boston

Table 1. Rates of Elder Abuse (weighted)

Type of abuse	Rate/1000	95% Confidence Interval	# in Boston SMSA
All types	32	25–39	8,646–13,487
Physical violence	20	14–26	4,841– 8,991
Chronic verbal aggression	11	7–15	2,420– 5,187
Neglect	4	1– 7	346– 2,421

SMSA estimated at 345,827 for 1985, this results in an estimate of between 8,646 and 13,487 abused and neglected elderly persons in the Boston area. If a survey of the entire United States were to find a rate similar to the one in Boston, it would indicate between 701,000 and 1,093,560 abused elders in the nation. Rates were also calculated for each type of maltreatment. In all, 40 elderly persons had experienced physical violence (20 per 1000), 26 verbal aggression (11 per 1000), and 7 neglect (4 per 1000).

Physical violence emerged as the most widespread form of maltreatment uncovered in the survey. The severity of violent incidents varied somewhat: 45% of the victims of physical violence reported having something thrown at them; 63% had been pushed, grabbed or shoved, 42% had been slapped, and 10% had been hit with a fist, bitten, or kicked. Thus, although the physical abuse varied in intensity, it is clear that the study uncovered some cases similar to those reported to adult protective services agencies.

Considering all three forms of maltreatment, the respondents also indicated the identities of those who had maltreated them. As shown in Table 2, nearly three-fifths of the perpetrators were spouses (23 wives and 14 husbands). In 10 cases the perpetrators were sons; in 5, daughters; and in 11 cases, other persons (grandchildren, siblings, boarders) were the perpetrators.

Characteristics of Victims

The data were examined to determine whether any particular groups of the elderly were at higher risk for maltreatment. Interestingly, the rates of abuse and neglect were no higher for minority than for white elderly, no higher for older (over 75) than for younger (65–74) elderly, and not significantly different for those of any religious, economic or educational background. Some groups of the elderly were at higher or lower risk, however. As shown in Table 3, elderly persons living alone, as predicted, had much lower rates of abuse, about one-fourth that of those living with others. Consistent with this finding, the widowed, divorced, and never married were less likely to be abused. Among persons living with others, those living with a spouse and at least one other person seemed particularly vulnerable to maltreatment. Another factor associated with risk for overall maltreatment was health status. Those in poor health were 3 to 4 times as likely to be abused. In addition, males were more likely to be abused than females.

Physical violence and neglect were somewhat distinct in terms of the characteristics that best predicted risk. Living situation and gender seemed most associated with risk for physical violence, whereas neglected elderly persons tended to be in poor health and to report that they did not have close contacts on whom they could rely for help in time of difficulty.

In certain respects, the portrait of the abused elderly presented by this study confirmed the picture painted by earlier investigations using reported cases as their source. Abused elders are more likely to be

Table 2. Perpetrator — Victim Relationship (Including Proxy Respondents, unweighted data)

	All types[a]	Physical violence	Chronic verbal aggression	Neglect
Husband to wife	14 (22%)	7 (17%)	7 (27%)	2 (29%)
Wife to husband	23 (36%)	17 (43%)	7 (27%)	—
Son to mother	5 (8%)	4 (10%)	2 (8%)	—
Son to father	5 (8%)	3 (7%)	3 (11%)	—
Daughter to mother	4 (6%)	1 (3%)	2 (8%)	2 (29%)
Daughter to father	1 (2%)	1 (3%)	—	—
Other	11 (18%)	7 (17%)	5 (19%)	3 (42%)
Total	63	40	26	7

[a]The total number of cases in specific categories exceeds the All Types category, because more than one type of abuse was sometimes present.

Table 3. Rates (Per Thousand) of Elder Abuse by Characteristics of Victim

	All types	Physical violence	Verbal aggression	neglect
Male	51*	37*	21	1
Female	23*	13*	9	5
Married	49*	32	19	4
Widowed	22*	16	9	3
Divorced	28*	25	18	9
Never married	7*	25	—	—
Live alone	15**	7*	6	5
Spouse only	41**	33*	19	2
Child only	44**	25*	18	4
Spouse & child	67**	42*	23	11
Other	16**	16*	—	—
Health				
excellent	17*	12	5	—
good	31*	24	13	—
fair	36*	18	12	8***
poor	77*	47	30	22***
No helper	35	—	9	26**
Helper	33	23	14	2**

* = .01
** = .001
*** = .0001

living with someone else (O'Malley et al., 1979; Wolf et al., 1984; 1986), and are more likely to be those who are in poor health (Lau & Kosberg, 1979; Steinmetz & Amsden, 1983; Wolf et al., 1986). Neglected elders are most likely to have no one to turn to for support (Fulmer & Ashley, 1986; Quinn & Tomita, 1986; Rathbone-McCuan & Hashimi, 1980).

In a number of ways, however, the findings from the current study are at odds with earlier efforts. Neither economic circumstances nor age were related to the risk of abuse. In previous studies (Hudson, 1986; Johnson et al., 1985), elder abuse victims seemed to come disproportionately from the older and disadvantaged segments of the population. The current findings suggested that some of this disproportion stemmed not from a greater risk for abuse but from the greater visibility of the very old and disadvantaged to potential reporters of abuse. There are, however, two more striking differences between the current study and many earlier reports on elder abuse: The findings of high rates of spouse abuse and of men as equally likely victims. These two issues are discussed in turn.

Elder Abuse as Spouse Abuse.

The predominant image of elder abuse, derived from certain earlier studies and reinforced by the popular media, is that abuse is primarily committed against elders by their children. The stereotype is of a mentally and physically dependent elder who moves in with and becomes a difficult burden to a resentful daughter or son; the latter, in response to frustration, lashes out or withholds certain necessities of life. Elder abuse has been discussed (Steinmetz & Amsden, 1983) in the context of "generational inversion": children who were once cared for now having to care for their parents. Here it was found, however, that abuse primarily was committed not by children, but by spouses. Of the perpetrators, 58% were spouses, compared to 24% who were children.

This comparison, however, does exaggerate the difference. The underlying dynamic is that an elder is most likely to be abused by the person with whom he or she lives. Many more elders live with their spouses than with their children. That is why so many more elders are abused by spouses. Statistics from the study illustrated this point. Among elders who lived with just their spouses, the rate of abuse was 41 per 1000. Among those who lived with just their children the rate was 44 per 1000. So actually spouses do not seem inherently more violent toward their partners than children toward their parents. But because spouses are more likely to be present in an elderly person's household, their opportunities for abusive behavior appear to be greater. If more elderly persons lived with their children, there would probably be more child-to-elder violence.

Nonetheless, the findings about perpetrators in this study are very important. They suggest that a fundamental reformulation of the problem of elder maltreatment is necessary. In the past, elder abuse was described primarily in analogy with child abuse. The present study suggests that elder abuse has much more in common with spouse abuse than child abuse.

In light of the data just presented, it is interesting that spouse abuse among the elderly has not drawn more public attention. Other studies have, in fact, reported substantial proportions of spousal elder abuse, although such findings have largely been ignored in public discussion of the problem. For example, in Hageboeck and Brandt's (1981) study, 32.5% of the abusers were spouses. In Wolf et al. (1984), 23% were spouses. In her analysis of a large sample of reported cases, Giordano (1982) found that in the case of physical abuse, abusers were most likely to be a spouse. But despite such findings, the spouse abuse part of the problem of elder abuse has generally not received serious attention.

The reason for this situation can perhaps best be explained in terms of the dynamics of social problem formulation (Spector & Kitsuse, 1977). Elder abuse has been the most recent and most neglected form of family violence to vie for public attention. Those who have sought to gain this attention have strived to cast this problem in its most compelling light. The image of one elderly person hitting or neglecting another does not convey the same pathos as an elderly person being abused by an adult child. As commentators from the battered wives movement have pointed out (R.E. Dobash & R.P. Dobash, 1981), among all forms of family violence, there has historically been a strong tendency to hold the victims of spouse abuse responsible for their victimization.

Another reason that spousal abuse among the elderly may seem less compelling is that many people may assume that it is less severe and damaging than abuse by an adult child against an elderly parent. There is no evidence, however, from the current study that this is the case. There were no statistically significant differences between spouse perpetrators and child perpetrators in the level of violence they inflicted, in the number of injuries they caused or in the degree of upset they engendered in their victims. Abuse by spouses and abuse by children is equally serious. If spouse abuse among the elderly has been a neglected problem, it is probably not due to the less serious nature of this abuse, but instead to the more ambiguous moral imagery that this problem conures up.

Abused Men

There is a second finding from the current study that runs counter to most studies based on reported cases. Almost all previous investigators have found that most elder abuse victims are women. By contrast, in the current study, roughly equal numbers of abused men and women (52% to 48%) were found; further, the risk of abuse for elderly men is double that of elderly women (51 per 1000 versus 23 per 1000). (The differential in risk is much higher than the differential in absolute numbers because there are fewer men than women in the elderly population.) Thus men seem more vulnerable to elder abuse, a particularly puzzling finding, because males are considered much less likely than females to be the victims of serious intimate violence (Finkelhor, 1983).

There are two explanations for this finding. First, elderly men have a higher rate of abuse in part because they are more likely to be living with someone else. Because males typically predecease their wives, a high proportion of elderly women are widows. Moreover, if men become widowed or divorced, they are much more likely than their female counterparts to remarry. Only 17% of the men lived alone compared to 42% of the women, and 68% of men were married compared to 28% of women. As discussed earlier, abuse is almost three times more common for those living with someone than for those living alone (as illustrated in Table 3) because the opportunities are so much greater. Because men are more likely to be living with someone, they are also more likely to be abused.

An alternative explanation is that elderly men, who are typically older than their wives, may be frail and therefore vulnerable to abuse. The male and female victims in the sample were compared, however, on health and functional status; no statistically significant differences were found. Abused men were also compared to non-abused men and no significant differences were found.

The fact that men tend to live with others may explain in part why the rate of abuse of men is high compared to that of women. It does not, however, explain why elder abuse victims whose cases are officially reported seem to be predominantly female. A second finding from the follow-up interviews conducted for the study provided an explanation for this phenomenon: Abuse against elderly men appears less serious than abuse against elderly women.

Of the 16 physically abused men in the sample for whom there are follow-up data, only 1 (6%) said he suffered injuries. By contrast, of the 14 female victims for whom follow-up data are available, 8 (57%) suffered injuries. A similar difference emerged on questions about emotional upset. When asked how upset they were by the violence, all but one of the 13 women for whom there are follow-up data on this item responded "very upset." In contrast, less than half (7) of 15 abused men reported such a high level of emotional upset. As another indication of emotional distress, 11 (58%) of the abused women reported that the abusive incidents had caused them to have trouble eating, compared to 4 (17%) of the men. The abused women have thus suffered more physical and psychological consequences from the violence than the men.

This may explain the difference between the current study and most studies based on reported cases. Women appeared to be more seriously abused than men. It seems likely that the more serious and upsetting forms of abuse are reported to protective agencies, which, in turn, become the source for statistics on elder abuse.

Implications for Policy and Practice

Prevalence figures by themselves tell only a part of the story. They only take on policy implications in the light of some political, social or ethical context. In fact, a prevalence rate of 32 abused elderly per 1000 population may not seem very high in comparison with other problems the elderly experience. For example, 132 elderly persons per 1000 elderly have incomes below the poverty level (Ward, 1984), and 60 per 1000 elderly have Alzheimer's disease or related disorders (Heckler, 1985). Further, rates of elder abuse seem lower than those for other forms of maltreatment. For example, rates of physical assault by parents against children have been estimated as high as 110 per 1000 (Straus & Gelles, 1986). It is encouraging to know that the majority of elderly persons appear to live relatively free from some of the most unpleasant types of maltreatment perpetrated by intimates. But does this mean that elder abuse is not the serious public policy issue some people have been urging?

It seems clear that elder abuse does warrant serious policy attention. Even prevalence rates that appear small by some standards can translate into impressive numbers of individuals in the population at large: potentially 701,000 to 1,093,560 maltreated elderly in the U.S. as estimated earlier. Further, on a deeper level, the argument for serious attention to elder abuse stems not so much from the size of the problem (although its size is certainly substantial enough) as from ethical principles that are widely shared in American society. Elderly citizens, like others, are entitled to live in environments where they are safe and respected. Simply because they are living with family does not guarantee, as might have once been thought, that these conditions prevail. Moreover, unlike some other problems of aging, prevention and treatment modalities are available (Wolf et al., 1984). The importance of the principle, the magnitude of the suffering, and the existence of solutions make the argument for concerted social action very compelling.

Further, the present survey indicated that substantial underreporting of elder abuse exists. Massachusetts is a state with one of the most active programs in the nation for identifying elder abuse. In addition, the categories of maltreatment used in Massachusetts are similar to those used in this study: physical abuse, psychological abuse, and neglect (self-neglect is not included under Massachusetts law). Between July 1, 1985 and June 30, 1986, Massachusetts authorities opened 1401 cases of elder abuse statewide. This translates to an incidence rate of about 1.8 per 1000.

It was possible to calculate an incidence rate for the Boston study because respondents were asked about maltreatment in the past year. The rate for maltreatment in the previous year was 26 per 1000. The comparison here suggested that in Massachusetts, approximately 1 case of elder abuse in 14 comes to public attention. This seems plausible for other states as well, given that elder abuse is a sensitive and embarrassing problem for which people tend not to seek help. Thus, in spite of mandatory reporting laws (Faulkner, 1981) existing intervention programs may be treating only a fraction of potential victims.

Beyond the prevalence rates from the present study, at least one finding is of substantial importance for practitioners because it contrasts with accepted beliefs about elder abuse. This study suggests that the largest proportion of elder abuse is, in fact, spouse abuse. The elderly are more likely to be abused by spouses than by others and this abuse, especially for elderly women, is as serious as any kind of elder abuse that has been identified. Full recognition of this problem demands a revision of the public's understanding about elder abuse and a re-orientation of the way in which the problem is handled. These are among the changes that should be considered.

1) Service providers to the elderly need to be

educated about the problem of spouse abuse. If their image of elder abuse is limited to the current stereotype of elderly persons mistreated by their children, they will not be likely to properly identify situations where the aged are being abused by spouses.

2) The elderly themselves need to be educated about spouse abuse. Many of the elderly grew up in a generation when spouse abuse was a great deal more tolerated and when information on the subject was not available. Elderly victims may be vulnerable to spouse abuse because they believe it to be acceptable. They need to be encouraged not to accept it, but rather to see it as a serious problem. Education can reduce the feelings of embarrassment and shame at being a victim and thereby make it easier to take action to stop the abuse.

3) Services need to be provided that are tailored to the problem of spouse abuse among the elderly. Nursing homes, which are used as a solution to elder abuse in a substantial number of cases, are often not truly appropriate because they are designed for persons much less capable of taking care of themselves. Battered women's shelters may be better solutions, but many of them are also not readily suited to the needs of the older woman. Further, the presence of young women and children may intimidate older women from seeking assistance. It may be more appropriate to establish safe apartments in congregate housing units where abused elders can take refuge. Moreover, the kinds of self-help groups that have been very effective for younger abused wives should be tried with groups of abused elderly to see if they can help the elderly stop the abuse, escape from it or get other kinds of assistance (cf., Finkelhor & Pillemer, in press; Pillemer, 1985). Consideration of the problem of spouse abuse among the elderly can undoubtedly lead to a great many other policy and service innovations, as well.

Conclusion

Elder abuse is one of the last types of family maltreatment to come to public attention. As with other family problems, it is difficult to study because of its sensitivity. Clear ideas about the prevalence and nature of elder abuse have been hard to obtain. Misconceptions have flourished in the absence of solid evidence.

The current study clearly establishes that elder abuse can be the subject of general population surveys. Undetected abuse can be detected. Samples can be obtained that are free from some of the biases of clinical samples and reported cases. It is hoped that this effort will open the door to other investigations and that many of the remaining troubling questions about this disturbing problem will soon yield to greater insight.

References

Block, M., & Sinnott, J. (1979). *The Battered Elder Syndrome*. College Park, MD: Center on Aging, unpublished manuscript.
Callahan, J. J. (1982). Elder abuse programming: Will it help the elderly? *Urban Social Change Review, 15*, 15–19.
Crystal, S. (1986). Social policy and elderly abuse. In K. Pillemer & R. Wolf (Eds.), *Elder abuse: Conflict in the family*. Dover, MA: Auburn House.
Dobash, R. E., & Dobash, R. P. (1981). *Violence against wives*. New York: Free Press.
Duke University Center for the Study of Aging and Human Development. (1978). *Multidimensional functional assessment: The OARS methodology*. Durham, NC: Duke University, unpublished manuscript.
Family Research Laboratory. (1986). *Elder abuse and neglect: Recommendations from the research conference on elder abuse and neglect*. Durham, NH: University of New Hampshire, unpublished manuscript.
Faulkner, L. (1981). Mandating the reporting of suspected cases of elder abuse: An inappropriate, ineffective, and ageist response to the abuse of older adults. *Family Law Quarterly, 16*, 69–91.
Finkelhor, D. (1983). Common features of family abuse. In D. Finkelhor, R. Gelles, G. Hotaling, & M. Straus (Eds.), *The dark side of families: Current family violence research*. Beverly Hills, CA: Sage.
Finkelhor, D. (1984). *Child sexual abuse: New theory and research*. New York: Free Press.
Finkelhor, D., & Pillemer, K. (In press). Elder abuse: Its relationship to other forms of family violence. In G. Hotaling, D. Finkelhor, R. Gelles, & M. Straus (Eds.), *New directions in family violence*. Beverly Hills, CA: Sage.
Fulmer, T., & Ashley, J. (1986). Neglect: What part of abuse? *Pride Institute Journal of Long Term Home Health Care, 5*, 18–24.
Gioglio, G., & Blakemore, P. (1983). *Elder abuse in New Jersey: The knowledge and experience of abuse among older New Jerseyans*. Trenton, NJ: New Jersey Division on Aging, unpublished manuscript.
Giordano, N. H. (1982). *Individual and family correlates of elder abuse*. Unpublished doctoral dissertation, University of Georgia.
Hageboeck, H., & Brandt, K. (1981). *Characteristics of elderly abuse*. Iowa City: University of Iowa Gerontology Center, unpublished manuscript.
Heckler, M. (1985). The fight against Alzheimer's Disease. *American Psychologist, 40*, 1240–1244.
Hudson, M. (1986). Elder mistreatment: Current research. In K. Pillemer & R. Wolf (Eds.), *Elder abuse: Conflict in the family*. Dover, MA: Auburn House.
Johnson, T. (1986). Critical issues in the definition of elder mistreatment. In K. Pillemer & R. Wolf (Eds.), *Elder abuse: Conflict in the family*. Dover, MA: Auburn House.
Johnson, T., O'Brien, J., & Hudson, M. (1985). *Elder neglect and abuse: An annotated bibliography*. New York: Greenwood Press.
Lau, E., & Kosberg, J. (1979). Abuse of the elderly by informal care providers. *Aging*, September–October, 10–15.
O'Malley, H., Segars, H., Perez, R., Mitchell, V., & Knuepfel, G. (1979). *Elder abuse in Massachusetts: A survey of professionals and paraprofessionals*. Boston, MA: Legal Research and Services for the Elderly, unpublished manuscript.
Pedrick-Cornell, C., & Gelles, R. (1982). Elderly abuse: The status of current knowledge. *Family Relations, 31*, 457–465.
Pillemer, K. (1985). The dangers of dependency: New findings on domestic violence against the elderly. *Social Problems, 33*, 146–158.
Pillemer, K., & Suitor, J. J. (In press). Elder abuse. In V. Van Hasselt, R. L. Morrison, A. S. Bellack, & M. Hersen (Eds.), *Handbook of family violence*.
Quinn, M., & Tomita, S. (1986). *Elder abuse and neglect: Causes, diagnosis, and intervention strategies*. New York: Springer.
Rathbone-McCuan, E., & Hashimi, J. (1982). *Isolated elders: Health and social intervention*. Rockville, MD: Aspen Systems Corporation.
Salend, E., Kane, R. A., Satz, M., & Pynoos, J. (1984). Elder abuse reporting: Limitations of statutes. *Gerontologist, 24*, 61–69.
Spector, M., & Kitsuse, J. I. (1977). *Constructing social problems*. Reading, MA: Cummings.
Steinmetz, S., & Amsden, D. J. (1983). Dependent elders, family stress and abuse. In T. H. Brubaker (Ed.), *Family relationships in later life*. Beverly Hills, CA: Sage.
Straus, M. A. (1979). Measuring intra-family conflict and violence: The conflict tactics (CT) scales. *Journal of Marriage and the Family, 41*, 75–88.
Straus, M. A., & Gelles, R. J. (1986). Social change and change in family violence from 1975 to 1985 as revealed in two national surveys. *Journal of Marriage and the Family, 48*, 465–479.
Ward, R. A. (1984). *The aging experience*. New York: Harper and Row.
Wolf, R., Godkin, M., & Pillemer, K. (1984). *Elder abuse and neglect: Report from three model projects*. Worcester, MA: University of Massachusetts Medical Center.
Wolf, R., Godkin, M., & Pillemer, K. (1986). Maltreatment of the elderly: A comparative analysis. *Pride Institute Journal of Long Term Home Health Care, 5*, 10–17.
Yin, P. (1985). *Victimization and the aged*. Springfield, IL: Charles C Thomas.

AGING: CAN IT BE SLOWED?

LEARNING WHY WE GROW OLD MAY HELP SCIENCE DELAY THE RAVAGES OF TIME

"Why do we grow old, get sick, and die?" asks Noel K. Johnson. "We should live forever." Johnson is taking his best shot at it. When he turned 70, he had heart trouble, arthritis, and gout. He drank too much, was 50 pounds overweight. He was in such bad shape that his son suggested he enter a convalescent home. Today, at 88, he's a trim 138 pounds and claims his earlier afflictions have disappeared. He spends three hours a day running, jumping on a trampoline, lifting weights, and going one-on-one with a punching bag. Last year he ran his sixth New York Marathon (7 hours, 41 minutes), then embarked on a tour of Southeast Asia to promote his book, *A Dud at 70. A Stud at 80.*

Nearly everyone wants to lead an active and healthy life in old age. That's why drugs and nostrums that promise to restore youthfulness have always been big business. In the U.S., where the population is aging rapidly, business is booming as never before. "There's so much concern with aging that quackery is now a real growth industry," says Edward L. Schneider, director of the Andrus Gerontology Center at the University of Southern California (USC).

A NEW WRINKLE. The quackery, however, can't obscure the fact that real scientific progress is being made. For the first time, drugs are coming to market with solid research indicating they really do reverse some of the minor ravages of age. On Jan. 21 a standing-room-only crowd saw Ortho Pharmaceutical Corp. unveil scientific research that showed its 17-year-old acne drug Retin-A can make some wrinkles and age spots disappear from sun-damaged skin. The Food & Drug Administration is expected soon to approve the use of Upjohn Co.'s Rogaine, developed to control hypertension, as an ointment that can promote hair growth on some balding pates.

These largely serendipitous discoveries are the vanguard of a new generation of drugs that promise to lessen—and perhaps one day prevent—some of the cosmetic and physical afflictions of old age. "This is a new era for anti-aging products," declares John P. Bennett, president of Senetek, a British company that is experimenting with a drug that may rejuvenate skin cells.

Meanwhile, a rapidly growing research effort is beginning to unravel some of aging's most intractable puzzles. "Research has exploded in the past five years," says Vincent J. Cristofalo, director of the University of Pennsylvania's Center for the Study of Aging. Using the new techniques of molecular biology and aided by such advanced medical technologies as magnetic resonance imaging, scientists are probing the myriad changes in the body that add up to aging.

Just a few years ago, researchers studying aging commanded about as much respect as 19th century snake-oil peddlers. But since 1975, when Congress founded the National Institute of Aging, research funding has jumped from $15.8 million to $195 million.

TIME BOMB. There's a good reason for the increased spending. Walk through any nursing home and it's obvious that, for most people, growing old is not nearly as satisfying as it is for Noel Johnson. Since the turn of the century, the average life expectancy in the U.S. has risen from about 50 years to 75. Experts predict that changes in lifestyles and advances in medicine could push that figure to 85 by the year 2050. But living longer does not mean living better. For every four years of life that are gained, estimates Jacob A. Brody, dean of the School of Public Health at the University of Illinois, only one is productive. The rest are compromised by the scourges of old age: arthritis, hypertension, hearing loss, and heart problems.

With the baby boomers heading for

Golden Pond, increased longevity is a medical time bomb. By the year 2050, nearly 22% of the U.S. population will be 65 or older. And the elderly already account for 40% of the nation's health care bill. But if scientists can decipher the aging process, "then we can intervene to prevent or retard the multiple disorders associated with it," says George M. Martin, professor of pathology at the University of Washington.

Does that mean humans may one day live forever? Don't count on it. Most scientists now believe the maximum lifespan is about 120 years—no matter what we do. "The aging process is built in, we have obsolescence," says Robin Holliday, head of genetics at Britain's National Institute for Medical Research.

But just finding ways to stave off the infirmities of age is a tall order. The long downhill slide of life begins to accelerate at about age 30. It involves hundreds of thousands of minute changes in the body's cells. Many of them may be either triggered by genes or caused by errors in the genetic coding that controls functioning of the cells and membranes that form the brain, skin, bones, and other organs. Lifestyle, too, plays a role.

Many of those changes are visible—wrinkling skin, graying hair, and sagging muscles. But much is not—like the millions of brain cells that die and the immune system's weakened ability to stave off disease. Nor do the changes occur at the same rate in each person.

DIET RESTRICTION. So far, the search for clues has generated no fewer than 11 theories of aging, replete with dead ends, inconclusive evidence—and controversy. For now, the hottest clues point to the genes, the internal machinery of cells, the body's system of chemical messengers, and the immune system.

Some of the most compelling leads are coming from a colony of aged laboratory rats being studied by Edward J. Masoro, a

Reprinted from February 8, 1988, pp. 58-64, issue of *Business Week* by special permission, copyright © 1988 by McGraw-Hill, Inc.

THE WAR ON AGING

No two people age alike. Genetics may rule many of the changes, but habits of lifestyle such as smoking make a difference. Sooner or later, though, time takes its toll. But new drugs and treatments already are beginning to make the Golden Years more livable.

SELF–DEFENSE
Defenses against disease decline to 20% of peak strength in old age. Immune system boosters being tested for cancer may help restore aging defense systems.

THE BRAIN DRAIN
By 60, millions of nerve cells are dead; memory begins to fail. Memory drugs are in the lab. But mental stimulation also keeps older people functioning well.

SAVING YOUR SKIN
Skin shows wear in the 20s; by 50 it can be wrinkled, blotchy, and coarse. New drugs that can erase some of the damage caused by sunlight are nearing the market.

MISSING MUSCLE
Between the ages of 30 and 70, the average person loses 30% to 40% of the body's muscle mass. Exercise can retard these changes by as much as 20 years.

REWINDING THE TICKER
The heart's pumping efficiency drops 30% between 30 and 70; lung capacity is cut in half. Diet and exercise can slow these declines by at least 10 years.

BRITTLE BONES
By age 40, men and women begin to lose bone because of a decreased ability to absorb calcium. Weight-bearing exercises can cut the loss.

physiologist at the University of Texas at San Antonio. These rodent Methuselahs are alert, active, and healthy, with the shiny white coats of adolescent rats. By cutting the caloric—but not the nutritional—intake of the rats to 60% of what they would normally eat, Masoro has extended their average lifespan by 50%, compared with rats on a normal diet.

He and others working on so-called diet restriction, first explored in the 1930s, believe the changes in diet somehow retard many of the physiological changes that occur with age. Masoro hopes to find out just what makes the rats live longer—and, consequently, what makes normal rats get old—by carefully measuring changes in key hormones, disease, and metabolism.

Already, researchers have a pretty good idea of some of the processes likely to be involved. Not the least is the body's disease-fighting immune system. Scientists have already observed that the thymus, the master gland that controls the production of white blood cells, is one of the first organs in the body to reach old age. It shrinks away until it's almost invisible by age 50. So the body's ability to recognize foreign invaders deteriorates, and it becomes more likely to develop diseases caused by the malfunctions in the immune system itself, such as rheumatoid arthritis.

Help may be on the way from the camp of cancer research, however. Biotechnology made it possible to isolate substances produced in the body that control the immune system and to produce them in large quantities. Most testing of immune boosters, such as interleukin 2, so far has been on cancer patients and people whose immune systems are being destroyed by AIDS. But some researchers, including Dr. Jordan U. Gutterman, a leading oncologist at the University of Texas, think small doses of these substances may be just what the doctor ordered for the aged.

One biotechnology company, Alpha 1 Biomedicals Inc. in Washington, is already testing the idea. It is giving a combination of immune system boosters and flu vaccine to elderly patients. Because their immune systems are weak, only 25% of the elderly who are given vaccine alone build an immunity. But when it is combined with thymosin, a thymus hormone, the number jumps to 65%.

SHRIVELING NEURONS. Studies of other glands are also turning up intriguing leads. A fall-off of the production of pituitary growth hormone contributes to the loss of muscle tissue and skin wrinkling. DHEA, a steroid pumped out by the adrenal gland, also declines with age. But in rodents, DHEA injections can inhibit various cancers and delay the onset of diabetes. This approach could lead to preventive treatments for the elderly.

What about memory? Scientists have discovered that glucocorticoids, stress hormones produced by the adrenal gland, can touch off what Caleb E. Finch, professor of the neurobiology of aging at USC, describes as "a vicious cycle of stress-induced aging" that can hasten memory impairment.

Recently, Robert M. Sapolsky, a neuroscientist at Stanford University, found out why. He exposed rats to high levels of chemicals that mimic these stress hormones and found that the neurons in their brains shriveled or died faster than normal. Under stress—and during aging—the hormones build up and block the neurons' ability to absorb nutrients.

Avoiding stress can help, but drugs may also intervene in the process. Beta blockers, for example, which are used to treat hypertension, work by blocking the cellular receptors that respond to adrenal hormones. Scientists recently identified a group of chemicals, dubbed nerve-growth factors, that revitalize damaged neurons and trigger new nerve connections that compensate for damaged cells. Give the factors to rats and they can recall maze patterns that they had forgotten.

Hormones are not the only natural substances that can wreak havoc in the body. Look at free radicals. These molecules are created as the cells perform their daily work, and they contain a highly reactive form of oxygen. Studies show that free radicals can damage blood vessels and the heart. They are also implicated in cancer, arthritis, and glaucoma.

The body has its own defenses against these renegade oxygen atoms. Some 15 anti-oxidants such as vitamin E, beta-carotene, sodium oxide dismutase (SOD), and glutathione course through the cells. Popping anti-oxidants is a popular anti-aging remedy, even though evidence that they work is sparse. But studies in rodents do show that beta-carotene can help prevent lung cancer, and the National Cancer Institute is conducting a study to see if it can prevent cancer in humans. Meanwhile, DDI Pharmaceuticals Inc. and others are testing SOD as a way to prevent tissue damage after heart attacks and strokes.

FADED GENES. What scientists would really like to know, however, is why those organs and other cells in the body deteriorate at an apparently programmed rate. Even skin cells, when removed from the body, will divide about 50 times and then simply stop and die. "How does the cell know it's old?" asks the University of Pennsylvania's Christofalo. "If they learn to time their life history by some set of mechanisms—that will be a key to aging," he says. Cristofalo and James R. Smith, professor of cellular genetics at Baylor College of Medicine, have found evidence of proteins that turn cell division on and off.

All the indications point to genetics. Each species lives out its existence to a different limit suggesting that genes are the master agents of lifespan. Now, with the tools to identify and clone genes and even insert them in mice to see how they behave, "we will identify the genes for longevity in mammals, including humans," says Thomas E. Johnson, professor of molecular genetics at the University of California at Irvine.

That may take a decade or more. Scientists don't expect to find just one gene that "turns on" aging. Instead, they believe there are a number of "gerontogenes" that directly or indirectly affect the changes of aging. Martin at the University of Washington estimates that as many as 7,000 of the 100,000 genes in humans could play a role.

There is little question, though, that such gerontogenes exist. Early evidence comes from a lowly worm called C. elegans that has only 10,000 genes. Last year, Johnson hit the jackpot when he identified a gene he's christened AGE-1. When he removes this gene, the worms live some 70% longer—about 5 weeks. The rest of the development is normal, except that those worms without the gene produce 25% fewer offspring than their cousins, indicating that the very genes that encourage reproduction may lower the rate of survival later on in life.

Researchers have also identified one complex of genes that seems to influence life expectancy. Called the MHC locus, it controls the machinery that causes organ transplants to be rejected and seems to play a role in the body's ability to repair damaged genes. Scientists have found that some long-living mice have a certain combination of these genes. Last year, a similar genetic pattern was identified in a group of centenarians on Okinawa.

SPARE PARTS. Taking a very different approach to the problems of aging, one company believes it can grow new organs to replace those that wear out. Headed by Eugene Bell, a 69-year-old retired biology professor from the Massachusetts Institute of Technology, Organogenesis Inc. has fabricated skin and blood vessels. Experiments indicate that bones, the pancreas, and thyroid glands could be fashioned as well. "We are creating new life," says Bell.

The secret is taking advantage of the way specialized cells are programmed to behave in the body. Graduate biology students at MIT studying cell growth were amazed when skin cells in a solution spon-

'How does the cell know when it's old?' If there is some mechanism, 'that will be a key to aging'

WANNA BE A METHUSELAH? STEP RIGHT UP

Want to live forever? You can get plenty of help. Exercise and special diets. Megadoses of vitamins, minerals, and enzymes. Bee pollen. Glandular extracts. Michael Jackson spends time in a pressurized chamber filled with oxygen. Actor George Hamilton lauds animal cell injections. Skeptical? Then you can have your body frozen until scientists come up with better treatments.

From simple common sense to pseudoscience and, some say, outright quackery, turning back the clock is big business. One congressional study puts the annual amount at $3 billion. Take Bill Faloon. He's the vice-president of Life Extension Foundation, a Hollywood (Fla.) group promoting anti-aging products and research—and he practices what he preaches. He pops 100 vitamin, mineral, and enzyme pills each day and doesn't smoke. He wears a fireproof crash helmet on airplanes. If it crashes, he says, his undamaged head can be "cryonically suspended," or frozen, with the hope that a fresh body can be cloned from it.

HARD TO SWALLOW. Megadosing on vitamins, minerals, and enzymes is becoming one of the most popular anti-aging regimens. Authors Durk Pearson and Sandy Shaw made such supplements a household item with their best-selling book *Life Extension.* The virtue of consuming some 25 supplements is a lot for some critics to swallow. "Once you start to take vitamins in large doses, they are no longer vitamins—they are drugs," says Dr. John Rennar, member of the National Council Against Health Fraud and an outspoken critic of such regimens.

The controversy doesn't bother many life extensionists. "We're human guinea pigs," says Dr. Bruce Thorkild-

sen, 33, a New York doctor who follows some treatments recommended in *Life Extension,* including the controversial use of Hydergine, a prescription drug used to treat Alzheimer's disease. *Life Extension* promotes it as a way to slow the aging of the brain.

Thousands of others flock to anti-aging spas in the U. S. and Europe for "revitalization" therapies, even though there is very little evidence that they make any difference. Even Pope Pius XII has trekked to the Romanian spa of Anna Aslan, who injects her patients with a drug she calls Gerovital. What is it? The common anesthetic, novocaine. Research in the U. S. has shown only that it acts as a mild antidepressant.

Randall Podals, 40, a real estate agent and interior designer from Honolulu, paid $7,700 for a week at La Prairie in Montreux, Switzerland. The clinic offers injections of animal tissue extracts that it says will boost immune systems—though it refuses to release evidence to back up the claim. But to Podals, "when it comes to my health, nothing matters—not money or time."

Regulators take a more jaundiced view of those who hawk longevity. Last year the Food & Drug Administration launched an investigation of the seven-year-old Life Extension Foundation; that led to the seizure of a warehouse full of vitamins, creams, and shampoos that the company promoted as anti-aging. Just as Faloon resumed sales of the vitamins, without the offending claims, controversy erupted again. This time the Riverside (Calif.) coroner's office wants some answers from Saul Kent, the foundation's founder and president. Kent had the head of his 83-year-old mother frozen by Alcor Life Extension Foundation, a cryonics company. Kent insists she

died of natural causes. The coroner wants to be sure.

CHILLY DOG. The idea of freezing bodies—or more frequently these days, just the head—in the belief that they can eventually be brought back to life, has been controversial for years. Every so often it slips back into the headlines. Last year, Paul Segall, director of biological research for Trans-Time, which performs suspensions for the American Cryonics Society, won himself a storm of publicity. He revived a beagle—named Miles, from the thawed-out character in Woody Allen's movie *Sleeper*—after draining the dog's blood, replacing it with a substitute, and dropping the body temperature to 37F. For 15 minutes, Miles had no circulation, pulse, or breath—by all accounts a dead dog.

But the feat didn't do much to improve the prospects of those frozen solid in liquid nitrogen. "It was an experiment in hypothermia," says Arthur W. Rowe, director of the Red Cross Cryobiology Laboratory in New York. "To give the false sense of hope that someone can be frozen and reanimated is wrong. It's like trying to reconstitute a cow out of hamburger."

Maybe that's why cryonics has never caught on. So far the American Cryonics Society—one of three such groups in the U. S.—has frozen only two whole bodies, two heads, and one brain. "It's a long-shot gamble," admits Irving Rand, 48, a New York insurance representative and the founder of Cryonics Coordinators of America. But, he adds, "when you consider the alternative, there is no alternative." Not unless you adopt the "mind over matter" approach of the Eternal Flame Foundation in Scottsdale, Ariz. That group says that believing in immortality is tantamount to achieving it.

By Gail DeGeorge in Miami

taneously formed themselves into living skin. They had simply created the right environment for the cells. In 1985, Bell's lab was spun off from the university as Organogenesis, with his former students serving as researchers.

The company's "living skin equivalent" will soon be tested on burn patients at Western Pennsylvania Hospital in Pittsburgh. The "living blood vessel equivalent" is being tested in animals. Supplied with nutrients, both blood vessels and skin can sit on a shelf for up to a year. For these two products alone, Bell predicts multibillion-dollar markets.

PLANNED OBSOLESCENCE. And then there

are those Methuselah rats. "Who knows? It may turn out that we're eating ourselves to death," says Ronald W. Hart, director of the National Center for Toxicological Research. At least one researcher is convinced that's the case, and he's not waiting for any studies.

Roy L. Walford lives in a Venice Beach (Calif.) warehouse decorated with an improbable mix of erotic art and a 3-D Jesus. From this sanctum, he promotes his '120-year diet" of 1,500 calories—half the average American's intake—with such staples as tofu and whole-wheat spaghetti. But 63-year old Walford is hardly another New Age crackpot. He is a respected gerontolo-

gist at the University of California at Los Angeles who formulated a theory for the role of the immune system in aging. Walford isn't interested simply in living longer but in retaining vitality in old age. "I'm talking about people being chronologically older and functionally younger," he says.

Even if dietary restriction doesn't live up to its promise, both Walford and Johnson may be onto something else: Use it or lose it. "A lot of what we commonly call aging comes from disuse and atrophy," says Everett L. Smith, director of the biogerontology lab at the University of Wisconsin.

Indeed, a properly tailored program of aerobic exercise, such as brisk walking, can postpone such physical changes as muscle deterioration, bone loss, and shrinkage of lung capacity "by as much as 20 years," says Roy J. Shephard, director of the School of Physical & Health Education at the University of Toronto. The same holds true for the brain. Psychologists have repeatedly shown that healthy, mentally active elderly people do not suffer the debilitating slowdowns of the less active.

Although the clocks keep ticking along, scientists are convinced they can be adjusted. New drugs and treatments that will come out of the nascent aging-research effort promise to make the Golden Years a better time. "I'd like to see everyone living to a maximum lifespan, then drop dead with full mental and physical capabilities,"

says Leonard Hayflick, professor of anatomy at the University of California, San Francisco. For most people, that would be close enough to the Fountain of Youth.

By Emily T. Smith in New York with Kevin Kelly in Los Angeles, Corie Brown in Boston, and bureau reports

DELIVERING WHAT MAKEUP ONLY PROMISES

Coming soon: Drugs that can truly keep you looking young

Saks Fifth Avenue's cosmetics counters were abuzz with shoppers. Carefully coiffed matrons sniffed, sprayed, and primped next to chirping teens in stone-washed jeans. A display for Christian Dior's Capture, promoting "complex liposomes" that are an "anti-aging complex for the face," drew one shopper's attention.

"What are liposomes?" she asked. The clerk didn't bat a mascara-laden lash: "Liposomes are found naturally in your skin. They help you better rejuvenate new cells." Another clerk chimed in when the customer still looked puzzled: "They penetrate the skin and repair free-radical damage caused by oxygen electrons. This has full FDA approval."

'ROCKET SCIENTISTS.' Such indecipherable, $65-per-ounce "explanations" bombard cosmetics shoppers constantly. But those deftly vague descriptions of mysterious-sounding substances are often plain wrong. Liposomes, for example, are synthetic spheres of fat that may be used to release drugs inside the body. They don't penetrate the skin, and there is no evidence that they repair anything. "It's gotten to where they're acting like rocket scientists when they're selling cream in a jar," says cosmetics industry consultant Allan Mottus.

To obtain those facial creams, lotions, and potions, Americans pony up $1.5 billion each year. But what if they actually could reverse some of the ravages of age? It's not an empty question, for science seems at the threshold of a new business: 'cosmeceuticals,' legitimate drugs that truly keep you looking young. Unlike the plethora of scientific-sounding cosmetics now on the market, these are backed by solid research.

Take Retin-A. The publicity about the powers of Ortho Pharmaceutical Corp.'s compound may seem like just another pretty promise. But a team led by University of Michigan researcher John J. Voorhees just published the results of a clinical study showing that the prescription acne remedy may be the first compound to repair skin damaged by sunlight. The company has been besieged by cosmetics makers eager to add the key ingredient, retinoic acid, to their products. "Everybody is going absolutely crazy over this," says Georgette Klinger, a Czech-born cosmetics maker and salon operator.

So far, however, only a few such products are even close to market (table). The closest is Upjohn Co.'s Rogaine, the first bona fide chemical to stimulate hair growth in people with classic "male-pattern baldness." As a cream for those with thinning hair, it could rack up more than $100 million in sales in 1988, assuming it wins approval. Chantal Pharmaceutical Corp. is also testing an acne drug, called Cyoctol, that also may induce hair growth and repair wrinkles. And Senetek in London is about to start tests of a mysterious drug that it says makes old skin cells look young.

Basic discoveries into the nature of aging promise more products in the future. Included: a category of "growth factors" and other rare skin chemicals that can now be produced in quantity by biotechnology, as well as several hundred related "retinoids" with other skin-repairing properties.

QUITE AN EYEFUL. Most cosmetics companies say they are stepping up their research and development, but so far none is conducting clinical tests of any substance with pharmacologic properties. Dermatologists believe collagen, liposomes, and other fancy-sounding substances may someday play a role in anti-

SEARCHING FOR 'COSMECEUTICALS'

UPJOHN Its Rogaine, an antihypertensive, can stimulate some hair growth in patients with "male-pattern baldness." FDA approval is expected in 1988.

ORTHO PHARMACEUTICAL Its Retin-A, a form of retinoic acid now marketed as an acne treatment, can reverse the wrinkles caused by sunlight. Early tests combining it with Rogaine indicate it also enhances the hair-growing effect of that drug. Approval for use against photo-aging is expected by 1991.

HOFFMANN–LA ROCHE It sells Accutane, a potent oral retinoid acne remedy, and the company recently launched clinical trials on another retinoid as a treatment for skin. Approval could take several years.

SENETEK It plans to begin tests with humans this summer of an undisclosed compound that makes old skin cells appear young in laboratory experiments. The drug could reach the market within three years.

CHANTAL PHARMACEUTICAL It is conducting clinical tests on Cyoctol, an anti-acne treatment that also induces hair growth. The product could be approved in 1989 for acne treatment, later for baldness.

CHIRON It has an agreement with a Belgian unit of Petrofina to investigate the non-pharmaceutical properties of superoxide dismutase (SOD), an enzyme that may have anti-aging properties. Development is in the very early stages.

DATA: BW

aging products. But in current formulations they are either so scarce as to be irrelevant or used in ways that produce no effect.

A case in point is hyaluronic acid, a chemical found in rooster combs and newborns' umbilical cords. It retains moisture and has lubricating powers. It's used in ophthalmic surgery to replace the fluids that fill the eye. But James W. Bracke, president of Minneapolis-based LifeCore Biomedical, which supplies the substance to Revlon and Mary Kay Cosmetics, says his company analyzed the night cream of a third cosmetics maker that touted hyaluronic acid as its key ingredient. "We could barely find any," says Bracke.

Similarly, collagen, which is the building block of skin and other tissues, is being studied for a number of conditions related to aging, including degenerative jaw problems and osteoporosis. But in skin creams from Ultima II, La Prairie, and others, it probably does nothing more than moisturize the skin. The molecule is so large "you'd need a sledgehammer to actually get it to permeate the skin," says Howard D. Palefsky, president of Collagen Corp., a company that pioneered development of collagen-based products. "It creates a film that traps moisture—but so do Vaseline and Crisco," he says.

OUT OF BOUNDS. Some cosmetics makers have run afoul of the Food & Drug Administration for making unsubstantiated claims. The agency, which does not "approve" cosmetics but does investigate claims of their safety and effectiveness, typically has given these products a low priority. But when heart-transplant pioneer Christiaan Barnard began promoting a compound called Glycel amid widespread skepticism, the FDA began an investigation of anti-aging claims. It eventually sent letters to 23 cosmetic makers warning that their claims were exceeding its definition of cosmetics and wandering into the realm of drugs.

The posture at Estée Lauder Inc.'s Clinique division is not unusual. Her flawless hands finished with cantaloupe-tinted fingernails, Senior Vice-President Iris Model dabs samples of the company's product on the wrists of guests with the loving care of an antiques restorer. But when the conversation turns to the chemicals in the potions she plies, Model says: "Do we incorporate scientific findings? Yes, of course. But when it comes to claims, Clinique has always taken the position that it's the consumer who decides."

From drug companies, such an answer would be unthinkable. They must spell out the contents, side effects, and contraindications for their products in such excruciating detail that package inserts for their drugs read like invitations to avoid the product. Yet in the end, it may be the drug companies that deliver the miracles cosmetics makers promise.

By Joan O'C. Hamilton in New York and San Francisco

ALBERT KLIGMAN
MAY BE YOUR SKIN'S BEST FRIEND

Frowning, Albert M. Kligman peers closely at his visitor's face. "Your skin is terrible," he declares. A carefree youth spent in the sun has left its mark. Underneath the surface, he warns, is damage that will show up in a decade or two.

Most visitors get an instant skin analysis from the University of Pennsylvania dermatologist. Kligman considers the cosmetic condition of the skin to be an important medical issue. "The wrinkle," he says, "is a serious lesion."

Dubbed "the pope of dermatology" by French cosmetics makers, Kligman has devoted most of his 40-year career to serious research on skin. Now the youth-conscious have good reason to be thankful for his work—Kligman developed Retin-A, the Ortho Pharmaceutical Corp. acne drug that is recognized as the first compound capable of reversing the signs of aging caused by sun damage.

The drug's active ingredients, one of a group of vitamin A derivatives known as retinoids, were synthesized in the 1930s and 1940s. But in 1969, Kligman showed that one of them, tretinoin, could combat acne. Kligman was also one of the first to study the aging effects of the sun on skin. He coined the term photo-aging to describe the leathery, wrinkled appearance of sun-damaged skin.

When women reported that using Retin-A made their skin look and feel younger, Kligman did the initial studies to check its effect. Today he is one of its biggest boosters. "Try Retin-A while you're still young and the damage is light," he urges the visitor. He also has a patent pending on another retinoid, a pill to treat stubborn skin conditions such as the enlarged oil glands and mottled, flaking skin that plague older people. The oral medication is being developed by Daltex Medical Sciences Inc.

'MASSAGE DAMAGE.' Kligman is courted by cosmetics companies for his advice and endorsements. But he's hardly a fan of conventional makeup.

"Women who use the most cosmetics have the worst skin," he says. He's particularly vocal about the products that claim they can make wrinkles disappear. He has tested some of these compounds and found that they produce a low-grade inflammation that causes the skin to fill up with fluid and puff out. That erases wrinkles but leads to problems in the long run: "After 15 years the skin will show massive damage," he says.

The doctor's prescription for a youthful skin is simple—and inexpensive: Stay out of the sun whenever you can. If you can't, don't leave the house without a potent sunscreen. "The sun beats the bejesus out of skin," says Kligman, who believes that as much as 70% of what we think is aging is actually sun damage. Does he follow his own advice? Find him out on the beach of his weekend house on the New Jersey Shore, and he'll be wearing a hat for sure.

By Emily T. Smith in Philadelphia

Retirement: American Dream or Dilemma?

Since 1900 the number of persons in America aged 65 and over has been increasing steadily, but a decreasing proportion of that age group remains in the work force. In 1900 nearly two-thirds of those over 65 worked. Frank Sammarlino (1979) reports that by 1947 this figure had declined to 47.8 percent. By 1975, only 21.7 percent of men 65 and older were still in the work force. The long-range trend indicates that fewer and fewer persons are being employed beyond age 65. Some people choose to retire at this age; for others retirement is mandatory. A recent change in the law, however, allows individuals to work to age 70 before retiring.

Strieb and Schneider (1971) observe that for retirement to become an institutionalized social pattern in any society, certain conditions must be present. A large group of people must live long enough to retire; the economy must be productive enough to support people who are not in the work force; and there must be pensions or insurance programs to support retirees.

Retirement is a rite of passage. People can consider it either the culmination of the American Dream, or a serious problem. Those who have ample incomes, interesting things to do, and friends to associate with often find the freedom of time and choice that retirement offers very rewarding. For others, however, retirement brings difficulties and personal losses. Often, these individuals find their incomes decreased, and they miss the status, privilege, and power associated with holding a position in the occupational hierarchy. They may feel socially isolated if they don't find new activities to replace their previous work-related ones. Additionally, they must sometimes cope with the death of a spouse and/or with their own failing health.

The articles in this section provide a clearer picture of the factors in the retirement decision as well as the reasons some choose to return to work after retiring.

"Productive Aging and the Future of Retirement" considers how the current pattern of retirement developed, the factors that determine today's early retirement patterns, and whether a flexible retirement plan could be introduced to enable more older persons to be productive. People who have retired often find that they feel better physically and mentally if they reenter the work force. In "The 'Unretired'—Seniors Are Returning to Work," this trend is examined. When a person does elect to retire, a number of options are available—one being a life-care community. These communities can, however, fail. "Life-Care Contracts for the Elderly: A Risky Retirement?" discusses the dynamics of these communities.

Looking Ahead: Challenge Questions

If given the choice of retiring or continuing to work, some people would choose to continue working. How would you explain the decision not to retire?

Why do you believe many older persons decide to retire early? What factors cause this decision?

In your opinion, what are the major advantages of retirement? What are its major disadvantages?

From an economic point of view, should people be encouraged to retire earlier, or later?

Productive Aging and the Future of Retirement

Malcolm H. Morrison

Malcolm H. Morrison is a professional lecturer in aging and public policy at George Washington University in Washington, D.C. He is an internationally recognized authority in employment and retirement policies and formerly served as an adviser to the secretary and under secretary of labor on retirement issues. Morrison is the author of numerous publications on aging, work, and retirement, including Economics of Aging: The Future of Retirement *(Van Nostrand Reinhold, 1982). The opinions and conclusions expressed are solely those of the author and should not be attributed to any organization.*

What will be the productive economic potential of older persons in the future aging society? Can the aging hope to make meaningful and significant contributions to both economic and social productivity as we approach and enter the twenty-first century? What are the forces that will affect this potential and what are the key choices that society must make to achieve a productive aging society?

These concerns, along with growing interest in employment alternatives by some older persons, are leading some to challenge the traditional meaning of "retirement" as a complete cessation from work and to suggest that retirement may become an inappropriate description of future societal patterns; that is, in the future the meaning of retirement will change or a different social definition of aging will be needed.

After many years of effort and many social policy decisions, we have clearly developed an extremely beneficial set of choices for older persons which allow most to limit or entirely refrain from work if they choose to do so. As it turns out, some of our policies may have caused the pendulum to swing too far away from productivity in favor of leisure life-styles for the aging. However, a reversal of the pendulum in the opposite direction is not necessarily desirable either, and clearly would not be a popular policy for most older people today.

THUS, IN CONSIDERING the future productive roles of older people, it is important to clarify views of work and retirement based on both today's actual circumstances, which of course are influenced by past policies, and tomorrow's possible trends which can be influenced by future policies.

A frequent misconception is to consider the decisions that older people make regarding retirement as "point-in-time" choices that are made based on immediate circumstances near the time of retirement. In reality, retirement decisions are influenced by *life-cycle circumstances* of people, including concerns about health, economic status, personal priorities, and public and private sector policies that have, over time, conditioned their understanding of the choices actually available for them. If these factors change, then the timing and content of retirement and employment decisions may change as well. In general, the overall economy and the incentives of public and private pension plans will continue to significantly influence the choices of older people both today and in the future.

Thus, to understand what may occur in the years ahead that might encourage economic productivity by older persons, it is necessary to consider how the current pattern of retirement developed, the factors that influence and determine today's early retirement patterns, and whether any flexibility in retirement could be introduced in the future that would encourage and enable more older persons to be productive?

THE CHANGING MEANINGS OF 'RETIREMENT'

In today's society, "retirement" clearly has multiple meanings and it is no longer a safe assumption that someone who either says he is retired or is classified as retired, does not work. Yet, since less than 3 percent of the entire work force of the United States are aged 65 and above and those 55-64 represent only 11 percent of American workers, there is a clear connection between retirement and a nonemployed status.

At the initiation of the Social Security Program in 1935, age 65 was considered "normal" retirement age, and as retirement became more and more institutionalized over time, most workers came to accept and expect retirement as an important portion of their lifetime. It was clearly recognized at the beginning of the Social Security program that the goal of

From *The World & I*, December 1988, pp. 525-531. *The World & I*, a publication of The Washington Times Corporation, copyright © 1988.

American retirement policy was to provide a period of leisure (or rest) after the conclusion of working life. While it took some time to make this goal a realistic possibility for many Americans, its achievement, notably in the last 25 years, certainly is considered a major accomplishment of United States' policy for the aging.

Therefore, the major pattern since the passage of Social Security in 1935 has been decreasing employment of the aging and, in fact, an acceleration of this trend in the last 20 years, particularly because of the earlier availability of pension income. Both federal and private sector policies influence the timing of retirement decisions, and today, the key provisions of these policies allow workers to receive pension benefits at early ages—and when benefits are offered, most older persons accept them readily. On the other hand, few government or private sector policies provide incentives for older persons to either remain at work after pension benefits become available or return to work after receiving benefits.

There are some recent developments that could slightly alter the current relatively rigid retirement programs. Probably the most important of these changes is the fact that nearly 25 percent of all people who begin receiving Social Security benefits now continue to work for short periods of time—usually one to three years. This indicates that acceptance of pension benefits need not mean complete withdrawal from the labor force. In addition, it now appears that the decline in the number of younger people entering the work force between now and the early part of the next century (the "baby-bust" generation) will produce some shortages of workers and that it may be possible to draw older workers back into the work force to meet such labor demands.

Older worker employment service programs, notably *Operation ABLE* (Ability Based on Long Experience) and *SCORE* (Service Corps of Retired Executives), now located in many major metropolitan areas of the United States, have been increasingly successful in placing older workers into jobs. (A federally supported project, the Senior Community Service Employment Program also has success-

fully assisted significant numbers of lower-income older persons to secure productive employment.) In fact, in many areas where these programs operate, the demand for workers now exceeds the supply of older persons willing to be employed. (However, most of the jobs being offered are relatively low-paying service positions.)

Recently, these private older-worker employment programs have reported that many more older job seekers with substantial education and experience are seeking postretirement jobs, but that employers either do not have these jobs or do not offer vacant high level positions to these job seekers. This is one aspect of a general problem in the United States—too-limited development of flexible work schedules for older workers. With a few notable

In today's society, "retirement" clearly has multiple meanings.

exceptions, employers have not modified their employment policies in ways that would be attractive to older workers who usually are interested in part-time employment on flexible schedules and where earnings remain below the Social Security earnings test level. A small number of employers have experimented very successfully with specialized policies for older workers and have been able to rehire or newly hire significant numbers of experienced and productive employees. Despite significant efforts to publicize these programs, they have not been widely replicated. This is understandable since many organizations have been reducing their staffs through offering early retirement and most recognize that today's pension policies are not designed to encourage employment after retirement. Unless a particularly serious labor shortage exists or develops, it is not very likely that business organizations will choose to focus on policies to attract older workers. This does not mean that firms are opposed to older employees per se, but

rather that they do not believe that these workers represent a significant labor supply pool or that older workers can be easily motivated to return to employment.

UNDER THESE CIRCUMSTANCES, does "retirement" have only one meaning—complete cessation of economic productivity? Until recently, the unequivocal answer to this question was yes. But now, with more people continuing employment after receiving pension benefits and the number of specialized older-worker employment programs growing, the definition of retirement is beginning to change toward "pension recipient"—which does not automatically imply that a person in this status has no connection with the work force. This more neutral term is a more realistic definition of today's circumstances, where pensions are available after varying lengths of employment and are sometimes provided to persons as early as age 40. What we are beginning to observe therefore are changes in the way aging itself is both defined and viewed by society.

Pensions have historically been related to age because typically, to receive a pension, a person must work for many years and thus becomes "older." And it has been assumed (and is still accepted) that pension receipt and retirement—meaning complete cessation of work—are synonymous. But in aging societies such as those of Western Europe, Japan, and the United States, where life expectancy continues to increase, the meaning of retirement can change or its definition can become more flexible so that being retired (or receiving a pension) no longer means that a person is not economically productive or, more important, is not *expected* to be productive. The fact that despite enjoying their retirement, between one-third and one-half of today's retirees report that they would prefer to work (usually part-time) clearly indicates that in their view, retirement is not necessarily a period where work should not be performed. If more opportunities were actually available, no doubt more older people would work.

The key issues are:

● Will today's early retirement policies continue, and if they do, will future older workers leave the labor force entirely and permanently once pensions are available?

● Will different retirement policies be adopted in the future that will provide effective incentives for persons to work at older ages; that is, will flexible policies be implemented to increase labor force participation by older workers?

In the near term then, long before the major growth of the aging population begins in 2010, the youth population will be declining, the middle-aged population increasing, and the older population growing slowly. From a demographic perspective, these circumstances could be conducive for encouraging more economic productivity by older workers over the next 20 years, assuming that employment growth and demand are maintained. But to achieve this goal of productive aging, both public and private policies will have to be modified to encourage older people to either continue to work longer before accepting pensions or, more likely, to return to work after retiring.

ACHIEVING PRODUCTIVITY —WHOSE RESPONSIBILITY?

If retirement and employment patterns are to change in the years ahead, this will only occur if government pension policies, employer pension and personnel policies, and the attitudes of older persons also change to provide and support more choices for older persons to remain productive. The trends of an aging but increasingly educated work force and growing costs for supporting a larger retired population will characterize the future in both the short and long term. Yet even when these forces are combined with increasing length of life and continued job opportunities in the economy, we cannot realistically predict growth of economic productivity for the aging population. The key reason these trends will not bring about more productivity is that even taken together, they will not produce major changes in retirement behavior unless public and private policies, as well as the expectations and behavior of older persons themselves, are modified.

What then are the appropriate roles and responsibilities for the government, private employers, and older persons themselves relating to changing future retirement patterns?

First, it is clear that public retirement policy, especially as defined through the Social Security program, will have to change if work at older ages is to be encouraged. Such changes need not fundamentally alter income benefit levels provided to retirees or endanger benefits for persons facing disabling health conditions. Changes such as removing the earnings test penalty, providing more significant "bonus" benefit adjustments for deferred retirement, and delaying full retirement benefits until somewhat later ages, all deserve consideration as possible policy choices to encourage longer labor force participation and/or return to employment by older workers.

Second, employer policies also will have to change in order to assure more employment for older workers in the

Acceptance of pension benefits need not mean complete withdrawal from the labor force.

future. In fact, these changes may be more important than modification in public pension policies in order to encourage later life work for persons eligible to receive private pension benefits. This is the case since the current policy of early provision of private pensions (sometimes with supplements until the time of eligibility for Social Security benefits) strongly encourages early acceptance of pensions and leaving the regular work force long before Social Security eligibility begins.

It is unlikely in the near term that employer pension plans will be changed to provide benefits at *later* ages; however, other approaches, including bonuses for deferral of pension receipt and increases in pensions based on return to work, are certainly feasible —assuming that employers want to retain or rehire older workers. In addition, employers desiring to retain or hire these workers will need to adopt several personnel policy changes including flexible scheduling and part-time work choices, elimination of requirements limiting hours that can be worked in a year (this may also require

changes in federal law governing private pension plans), continuation of basic employee benefits for older employees, and possible readjustment of pensions, to account for earnings of older workers.

THESE CHANGES MAY not in fact be very hard to implement, as has been demonstrated in part by such companies as Travelers Insurance, Grumman Aerospace, and Lockheed Corporation. Some of these types of changes in fact can benefit other groups of employees, such as women with young children, students, younger entry-level workers, and part-time professionals. Therefore, employers may be able to change personnel policies in ways that will influence multiple groups of employees *including older workers* rather than developing specific older-worker policies and programs. In any event, in order to create conditions more suitable for the aging, employers will need to change both benefit and personnel policies.

And third, assuming public *and* private sector policy changes, there must also be changes in behavior of those older persons receiving Social Security retirement benefits and private pension payments. This means that older people must also shift their view of "retirement" or develop a new concept of "pension recipient" that does not imply complete cessation of productive work. Even though job opportunities may exist with appropriate incentives for older workers and older persons may have the training and experience for such jobs, unless they are interested in working, their employment patterns will not change significantly.

Because our society will experience unprecedented growth in the number of older persons over the next 40 years, it is certainly plausible to assume that the aging of the population represents a special historical situation. And thus far, with a population that is gradually aging, we have developed policies that permit the virtual elimination of employment at older ages while being unable to assure economic sufficiency for older persons. This does not mean of course that other forms of productivity are not available to older people, including volunteer work, care-giving, family support, education, and so forth. However, the emphasis of our current policies is to encourage people to leave employment and not to provide incentives to assist them to return to work.

With increased population aging, the costs of support for the "retired" will become very large and will be magnified further by decreasing mortality rates influenced by better health practices earlier in life and by improved medical technology. While much higher levels of care may be needed for people at the oldest ages, many of those who are younger—for example persons under age 75—will be able to continue active life-styles and will not be precluded in any major way from productive activity, including working.

AGING AND WORK IN THE TWENTY-FIRST CENTURY

Even with today's emphasis on early retirmenet, we do know that older people still have opportunities to be productive. Some are engaged in part- or full-time work; many assist with providing care and support for spouses or other relatives and friends; others volunteer their time in health services, education, and social services. At the same time, millions of Americans of all ages pursue leisure activities of all kinds with pleasure and satisfaction. The retired of course have more time (but not always the resources) to pursue leisure activities. This does not necessarily mean that retirees prefer

to spend most of their time in these activities—most report that this is not their preference. But at present there is so little opportunity or incentive for productive employment that leisure activities are often chosen by older people by default.

The overall evidence indicates that baby boomers who will continue to work will be those who will be in good health, have major interest in working or a high need for additional income, and have skills suited to available jobs. If current retirement policies persist through the time when baby boomers will be receiving pension benefits, then it is unlikely that substantial increases in employment of older ages will occur. But, if a combination of changes in government and employer policies could be gradually introduced, it is possible that baby boomers might increase their labor force participation. The changes that would be most significant in bringing about a new employment and retirement continuum include providing full retirement benefits at later ages; providing pension bonuses for delayed retirement, and creating more flexible employment arrangements coordinated with employee benefit arrangements that protect pension and health benefits, while also encouraging employment. These incentives might be effective for baby boomers, who will clearly be interested in great-

er flexibility during an extended period of older age. There remains a major question about whether retirement policies will change in these directions. And it is unlikely that anything more than informed speculation is possible about the policies and behavior of peo-

> # Employer policies will have to change in order to assure more employment for older workers in the future.

ple who will retire 30-40 years in the future.

It is probably more important to focus on gradual policy changes that could be introduced between now and the early years of the next century which could create more incentives for older persons to remain at work or return to work after receiving pension benefits. If we are to begin to assure a productive older age, these changes are a social imperative.

The "unretired" – seniors are returning to work, and loving it

Magaly Olivero

Magaly Olivero is a freelance writer who lives in New Haven.

Retire at age 65? More people are saying, "No way!"

Violet Lerch considers herself a solid, hard-working person, who tries hard to succeed at everything she does. There's one work-related area, though, in which Lerch readily admits she came up short.

"I flunked retirement," she says.

Lerch retired as an executive secretary at The Travelers Corporation at age 65, only to return to the company as a part-time employee six months later. "Some people might think I'm a little crazy. They don't quite understand it," Lerch says of her decision to return to the workplace. "But it's a lifestyle I've developed. I feel better when I'm working. I don't have the attitude to be a retired person."

She is not alone. Hundreds of retired individuals return to the workforce each year, saying part-time employment keeps them in better physical, mental and financial shape than full retirement.

Many people spend years dreaming of retiring, only to find they miss the hustle and bustle of work more than they ever expected. Others never wanted to leave, but were forced out by mandatory retirement rules.

Older, healthier, and abler Labor experts say the trend of older people returning to the workplace is a result of the aging of the country's population. According to the National Alliance of Business in Washington, D.C., the portion of the population over age 65 is expected to nearly double by the year 2020.

"People are living longer and staying healthier," says Kevin Mahoney, a spokesman for the Connecticut Conference of Municipalities, which employees retirees. He adds, "We are going to find that more older people are ready, willing and able to work to some degree. Some find the best way to relax is to keep working. It gives them a focus and helps them remain happy."

Natalie Radding, director of Employment Services for Sage Services Inc., which helps find employment for people aged 65 and older, says that many people look forward to retirement and have no thoughts of ever returning to work. Then, it changes.

"They troop in here, sometimes after a few weeks or after a few years," Radding says. "They find that a little leisure time is fine, but that too much of it is deadly. They miss their friends and the daily activities of getting up, dressed, and out of the house," she says.

Radding notes that many studies have shown people's emotional and physical health are maintained and even enhanced when they work. "So much of our self-esteem depends on the paycheck, and the type of work we do," she says. "It can be a significant loss to suddenly find yourself without a job to go to after so many years.

"Oldies" are goodies And how do employers feel about retaining workers who have retired from full-time jobs?

Quite well, actually. They perceive older employees as:
■ More motivated and better trained than temporary workers often provided by outside agencies
■ Out fewer days because of illness
■ Less likely to be late for work than younger employees
■ Less likely to have accidents on the job
■ Requiring less supervision, because of their years of experience

Employees in the (job) bank The Travelers Corporation recognized the value of older employees nearly a decade ago. According to Alice Simon of Travelers, the company decided to create a retiree job bank in 1980. Retirees are recruited regularly at "Un-Retirement Parties" hosted by the company.

Open to all retirees – not just those who retired from The Travelers – the job bank offers flexible, part-time temporary work to about 750 retired people. Equally important, the company gets experienced, dependable workers, says Simon. The Travelers abolished mandatory retirement and altered its pension plan, to allow retirees to work up to 960 hours per year, without jeopardizing their retirement benefits.

According to Dr. John Merritt, chief of geriatric medicine at the Hospital of Saint Raphael, Congress is considering ways to encourage retired workers to re-enter the workforce. One way would be to increase the amount of money workers can earn

From *St. Raphael's Better Health,* November/December 1989, pp. 31-37. *St. Raphael's Better Health,* Institute for Better Health, 1384 Chapel Street, New Haven, CT 06511.

without reducing their Social Security benefits.

A survey of 1,400 retirees by The Travelers showed that many retired people were concerned about their economic security and were unsatisfied with their decision to retire. Many said they returned to work to meet living expenses, to pay for extras, and to feel productive.

Lerch works up to three days a week as a receptionist at The Travelers dental clinic in Downtown Hartford. She originally planned to spend her retirement painting and caring for her house.

"I figured I would stay home and clean out all the cupboards and closets," she says. "I did one or two of those things and felt that was enough of that. When you've been working for so long, you develop shortcuts for housekeeping. You can't fill your day keeping the house clean."

She also tried painting, but admits "that didn't do it. It wasn't getting me out of the house and being with people. I missed getting dressed up and meeting friends for lunch. I was getting pretty depressed."

Depression is common in newly retired people, Dr. Merritt notes. "Suddenly, there is no more daily work routine, no interaction with coworkers," he says. "Even though most people dream of a more leisurely life following years of hard work, the reality is that they find themselves with too much time on their hands. Worse, they might not feel needed, and that only increases their depression and lowers their self-esteem."

Lerch's boredom convinced her to sign up with The Travelers' retiree job bank. It's a decision she hasn't regretted.

"I love the time I am at home, because it's just enough. I have plenty of time to take care of my house, paint, and see my friends. When it's time to go back to work, I am happy. I feel physically and mentally better when I'm working," she says.

Lerch adds she feels less pressured returning to work as a retiree. "I always like to do the best job I can. But I don't worry about my next review. I feel very independent. Being back at work is wonderful."

Retirement at 65 is a "crime"

That's the feeling of Richard D. Jenkins, age 72. "The biggest crime in the United States is to suggest to people that they should retire when they reach 65," Jenkins says. After more than 25 years in the banking business, he works part-time for the Connecticut Conference of Mu-

nicipalities (CCM) in Downtown New Haven, selling ad space for CCM's bimonthly publication, Connecticut Town and City.

"Some people should retire at 55 years of age, while some at 65 or 70 are still going strong," Jenkins says. It's a shame to have all this good talent go to waste."

Jenkins, who lives in Woodbridge, retired as vice president of Connecticut National Bank about six years ago. "It felt great to know I didn't have to look in my appointment book and be somewhere at 9:30 a.m., or 10a.m., or whenever," he says. During his tenure as a loan officer for the bank, Jenkins traveled extensively.

Retirement's novelty soon wore off, however, and boredom set in. "I watched the boob tube, but that was really demoralizing. I felt like an absolute moron watching that thing," he says. "I knew I needed to do something more significant, more earthly, more involved. It didn't seem right to stay home after years of getting up and having both a destination and responsibilities each day."

Now, Jenkins heads for work almost every day. In addition to selling ad space, he also sells booths to businesses that want to take part in the agency's annual convention.

Jenkins began at CCM by working a few hours a day, two or three days a week. He soon became more committed to his new job. "I'm so busy now, and I like it so much, I usually come in four days a week for a few hours. I hate to see Friday afternoon come, because it means I don't have to come on on Saturday and Sunday," he says.

Jenkins also is convinced his return to work has kept him healthy and alert. "I feel 1000 percent better when I'm working," he says. "My advice to anyone who has retired but who is physically able is to get out and get themselves a job. There's nothing like it."

Maloney calls Jenkins a "real asset. Not because of – or in spite of – his age, but because he makes a significant contribution to the success of this organization."

Ensuring domestic tranquility

There's another side to a retiree's return to work. Jenkins' wife, Elizabeth, was happy to see her husband return to the workplace. And, he agrees. "Having a man underfoot is not the nicest thing in the world," he says. "That doesn't mean I don't love her, or that she doesn't love me. But it's good to have some breathing room between us."

Active at 95, and going for 100

Retirement? The thought never occurred to William Zimmermann, who at age 95 works as a part-time bookkeeper at the Fair Haven Parents Ministry, a social service agency in New Haven.

"I don't see any reason to retire," he says adamantly. "I like working, and I like staying active. What's more, I like mixing with people and working with numbers. The New Haven resident adds, "I think working is what keeps me so alert. I don't have time to worry about myself."

Zimmermann – who at 95 says he "feels no different than when I was 70" – came to New Haven 60 years ago, as an accountant with the old Koppers Coke Company. He retired at age 68, after 45 years of service. At his retirement, he was three years beyond the company's mandatory retirement age.

"I wasn't anxious to retire, but they said I had to go," he says.

Just several months later, Zimmermann was working at Yale University's Sterling Library. He put in ten years there, but again, at age 78, he was forced to retire. Again, he was three years beyond the mandatory retirement age. "I was supposed to be out of there at 75, but I hung on for another three years," he says.

Zimmermann held bookkeeping jobs at an automobile dealership and at the Quinnipiack Club, before moving to his current post at the Fair Haven Parents Ministry. Four days a week, Zimmermann boards a city bus and heads for work. If the weather is nice, he sometimes walks.

"I love going to work and being around people. It's nice to get out" he says.

Zimmermann credits his longevity, in part, to the fact that he works and stays active. "My son, Frank, kids me because he retired three years ago and I'm still working," he says. "I don't intend to stop working for some time."

"Retirement" is a matter of degree

For William Wiedersheim, a former fundraiser with the Yale Development Office, retirement provided the perfect opportunity to enroll at the Southern Connecticut State University (SCSU) School of Library Science and Instructional Technology. He also worked as a volunteer at the New Haven Colony Historical Society.

"I always liked books and libraries. I thought getting a degree in library science would be an interesting thing to do,"

550 years among 'em, and they're still on the job

"How many card games can you play? How many times can you clean the house? You have to feel needed. It really keeps you going."

That is the philosophy of Mildred ("Molly") Levine, R.N., who at 76 years of age is still putting in a full day at Saint Regis Health Center, Inc., an affiliate of the Hospital of Saint Raphael. For Levine, retirement is a word that is not in her vocabulary. And, it never will be.

Levine is the oldest of the eight Saint Regis employees who are 65 years of age or older. She also is pretty typical of their attitude about staying active and on the job.

Levine's senior coworkers are: Muriel P. Brown, R.N.; Linda Giorgi, a recreation therapist; Nancy Mikosky, a nurse's aide; Leanna Moore, also a nurse's aide; George Redding, housekeeping supervisor; Ann Ryan, R.N., and Eileen Sweeney, senior housekeeper.

Brown, Mikosky and Sweeney are 65; Moore is 67; Redding is 68; Ryan is 69; and Giorgi is 75.

Sweeney also typifies the positive attitude shared by her coworkers. She says, "I have to be around people. I like to be with others. it keeps me feeling like a person, and someone who's doing her share."

Sweeney and the other "unretired" employees at Saint Regis say they will work as long as they can.

"I'll go forever," Sweeney says, smiling, but with firmness.

Two of the employees have children who also work for Saint Regis. Nancy Mikosky has two daughters at the center. One, Lucille, works in the Dietary Department; the other, Nancy Haddon, is a medical records clerk. And in an unusual twist, Linda Giorgi reports to her daughter, Carolyn Perrelli, who is head of recreation for Saint Regis.

Kim Czepiga, R.N., executive director at Saint Regis, calls her senior employees "top-notch." She adds, "You don't find more reliable, enthusiastic employees around here. Some even voluntarily work double shifts on occasion, to cover for employees who are sick or on vacation."

Czepiga also notes that everyone at Saint Regis, residents and staff alike, respects the abilities of the senior staff members. "Their strong work ethic is an example for all of us," she says.

A couple of Saint Regis employees returned to work after their spouses died. They say working does much more than fill in time; it gives them a great deal of satisfaction and makes them feel they are making a positive contribution to the lives of others.

At least two members, though, never retired at all. They just kept going, after reaching their 65th birthday. "Why stop?" Pat Brown asked. puzzled. "These people [the residents at the center] need our help."

—Jim Malerba

says Wiedersheim, who was a part-time librarian for CCM, and is now actively seeking new challenges. As an older student at SCSU, Wiedersheim notes he was in an unusual situation. "Some professors never thought I'd make it, and some of the students could have been my grandchildren," he says with a chuckle. "But, they all tolerated me, and I enjoyed it. I was the first senior citizen to get this degree," he says.

Wiedersheim, who did not divulge his age, returned to work at the Yale Psychiatric Institute as a fundraiser. He helped raise money for Yale's new children's hospital. Once the campaign was over, he left. "They gave me a luncheon, and I bowed out," he says.

After a short break, including traveling with his wife, Liz, Wiedersheim decided it was time to put his new college degree to good use. That's when he went to work for CCM.

His reasons for working are simple. "I get bored if I stay at home. I like to work, and I get out of my wife's hair if I get out of the house. Working gives me motivation and keeps me going."

Like his fellow "unretireds," Bill Wiedersheim wouldn't have it any other way.

Resources

Want facts about returning to the workplace after retirement? Information is available from the American Association of Retired Persons. Send a stamped, self-addressed envelope to: AARP, 1909 K Street, NW, Washington, DC 20049

Life-Care Contracts for the Elderly:

A RISKY RETIREMENT?

It is tempting for the elderly to pay the large life-care community entrance fee and make predictable monthly payments for shelter and health care, but is it really "risk-free" retirement? More than 10% of all facilities have gone bankrupt or have experienced extreme financial difficulties.

Anne Harvey

Ms. Harvey is the director of the program and field services division of the American Association of Retired Persons, Washington, D.C.

FOR more than 100,000 older Americans, the "life-care" or "continuing care" concept has proved irresistible. Under the traditional concept of life-care, in exchange for a one-time payment or entrance fee, $15,000 to more than $200,000, and fixed monthly fees, $250 to $1,300, these consumers receive all basic necessities for the rest of their lives, including meals, private apartments with housekeeping, and complete medical, including nursing home, care. Many of the more than 400 existing life-care communities also offer a variety of amenities including heated swimming pools, health clubs, craft classes, transportation and planned activities.

With census projections of a 40% increase in the number of people age 65 and older during the next 20 years, a rapid expansion of the life-care industry is expected—1,500 to 2,000 life-care communities by the 1990's and the industry will become a $10,000,000,000 business. Desirable facilities already maintain waiting lists that have been compiled for several years.

There are many attractive aspects of the life-care concept, among them the promise of financial and psychological security, combined with the continuous provision of shelter, health care, and other services. Since the prospect of entering an unfamiliar nursing home is depressing to many older persons, most life-care communities maintain a long-term nursing care facility on the premises for residents only. Life-care enables older persons to make only one housing and health-care-related decision for the rest of their lives without burdening children or society. Older consumers frequently consider life-care contracts as insurance policies against the potentially high cost of aging, including exorbitant expenses for long-term nursing care. Several states recognize the insurance aspect of life-care by regulating these facilities through their state departments of insurance.

The traditional life-care community providing both shelter and health care, is becoming less common. With the entrance of private, for-profit, corporations, "life-care" can have many meanings. Many of the newer communities offer only rental agreements with no large entrance fee requirement. Other facilities sell their units as coops or condominiums, where residents actually own their apartments, thereby having an equity interest in the facility.

The most dramatic changes are taking place in the delivery of health care, as developers shift an increasing share of the costs and risks to consumers. Some contracts cover all health-care costs, but most cover only a certain number of days per year, per illness, or per lifetime. Some facilities require applicants to carry supplemental health insurance in addition to Medicare Part A. Others require residents to pay as they go, making health-care costs unpredictable and undermining the financial security traditionally associated with the life-care community.

Instead of building a nursing home facility on their premises, newer developments may establish a cooperative relationship with an existing, nearby facility or offer nothing beyond home health care. Some facilities have medical personnel on duty 24 hours a day, during normal business hours, or several hours a week. Other communities make no provision for medical personnel. Despite these variations in the types of shelter and availability of health care, each development advertises itself as a life-care community. Senior consumers must carefully examine life-care contracts before signing them. Since there are so many variations, the best thing a consumer can do is to consider all the material issues in each contract. Open-ended or ambiguous language provide little financial or emotional solace to residents in life-care communities when they learn that they must pay for important health-care services.

Inherent problems

Threats of insolvency. It is tempting to cash in the equity in one's home, pay the large life-care community entrance fee, and then make predictable monthly payments for shelter and health-care, but is it really "risk-free" retirement? Although it is often presented this way by developers to prospective residents, there are many unpredictable and ever-changing variables involved in the success of a life-care community. Although the industry has good, sound communities, managers are still learning from their mistakes. More than 10% of all facilities have gone bankrupt or have experienced extreme financial difficulties. If a life-care community becomes bankrupt, its residents have no equity in their units, and since they usually have sold their former homes to pay the entry fee, they may be left with only their household goods. The only way to keep a community solvent may be to raise monthly fees to levels that are unaffordable for many community residents, or to reduce or eliminate promised services. In one instance, the fee was increased by 40%, forcing some residents to move.

Billboards and promotional materials for the Cloisters of DeLand (Florida), a community currently in receivership, offered "Life-Care . . . Assured" to residents. Yet, one year later, construction was shut down by the developers—an architect and a construction company with no experience in life-care—and 100 residents are now living on a building site, collecting rent to pay for utilities, security, and other required services. The developers have stopped putting any capital into the project. The promised on-site health-care facilty is just a blueprint and will probably never be built. Lawsuits and liens totaling more than $4,200,000 have been filed against the Cloisters, and consumers have sought refunds whose total exceeds

$1,500,000. Currently, the state of Florida is seeking a buyer. If that fails, the only options are liquidation or bankruptcy.

Potential risks. Other consumers have been victimized by fraudulent developers who eventually spent time behind bars for securities fraud, but neither fraudulent developers nor gross mismanagement have been the major causes of life-care insolvency. Until state regulation improves and new methods to guarantee a project's long-term solvency are developed, consumers should be alerted to the types of risks that can turn even a well-managed and completely honest operation into a nightmare:

● Construction costs may be underestimated.

● Medical costs or inflation may skyrocket, raising operating costs and requiring additional monthly fees. Yet, the financial life of the community may be in greater jeopardy if the contract does not allow for adequate fee increases.

● The units may be under-occupied because they have been under-marketed or are undesirable. With vacant units, the facility may not be able to remain financially solvent.

● The current increase in Americans' longevity reduces the frequency of capital "infusions" from entry fees. At the same time, longtime residents will require greater and more costly medical services. In addition, medical costs have been rising faster than inflation and Medicare has been paying a decreasing percentage of the total bill.

Insuring financial security. There is no life-care "formula for success," but there are steps which consumers can take to protect their investments. To properly investigate a life-care community, a consumer should seek the assistance of professional financial advisors who will be able to review the most recent audit conducted by an independent and reputable CPA; developmental budgets, which show construction and start-up costs and specify funding sources and amounts; monies placed in escrow and the time of release of escrow money; any actual studies which project occupancy rates and costs over time; the contract and other documents, to determine if residents maintain any control over the management and finances of the community; whether residents are given a lien on the property to secure the obligation for continued care—potentially important in a bankruptcy proceeding; whether state law requires or the developer has voluntarily placed an established amount—usually one year's operating expenses—in a "reserve fund" to insure solvency in the event of financial emergencies; the annual report and prospectus; and the over-all solvency of the developers—do they have the capacity or experi-

ence to construct and/or manage a life-care community? Some of this information may not be available and, because many professional advisors are unfamiliar with life-care communities, they may not be able to offer specific advice on whether the decision to enroll in a particular community is a wise one.

Other areas of concern

Screen out con artists and double-check claims of religious affiliations and bank involvement. Most life-care providers are non-profit organizations, but this is no guarantee against fraud. Private, for-profit management companies usually run communities for their non-profit owners, and many swindlers claim to run non-profit organizations. In fact, some of the latger life-care scam operators have been cloaked in clerical garb!

In 1981, the Rev. Jimmy Ballard was convicted of securities fraud by the Attorney General of Alabama in connection with the sale of worthless bonds to develop life-care communities. Many of the bonds were unwittingly sold to churchgoers by clergymen. Ballard used the proceeds to purchase himself a yacht and a airplane. When a state court terminated Ballard's association with the project, his successor was another minister, Dr. Kenneth Berg. Unbeknowst to all, Berg was already a defendant in several civil suits involving life-care communities he had managed through his firm, Christian Services International. The plaintiffs in these cases were retirees who had paid Berg hundreds of thousands of dollars for life-care services at facilities that were never constructed. Berg, too, was later convicted of securities fraud. He is currently on parole and has paid back part of the money.

If a life-care provider claims to be sponsored by a religious or other organization, consumers should determine the nature and degree of affiliation. Does the organization monitor the operation of the facility? Are members of the organization on the facility's board of directors? What legal or financial responsibilities does the organization have to the facility?

Another misrepresentation is when a developer exploits the name of the bank providing the project's financing, by implying the bank would not lend money if the project was not completely secure. A fraudulent developer may even imply that the bank is guaranteeing the project's solvency. A commercial lender protects only its interest with a first mortgage on all the community's land and buildings, and does not share the same risks as the community member who has no lien on his or her apartment and no other property rights. Consumers should be advised to be wary of a project advertising a large "reserve fund" which in fact only protects the mortgage bank's interest. Reserves are only helpful to consumers when they protect them against unforeseen costs.

Be wary of "future sites." Signing a life-care contract is a monumental decision involving s much capital that it should not be based on hasty impressions or conversations with salespeople. Make sure the contract specifically states when the consumer's residential unit and other promised facilities will be available for actual occupancy and use. A community in Kansas among other things, maintenance and nursing care. The developer died mid-project, leaving the nursing facility unbuilt and living units deteriorating.

Examine fee structures. The monthly service fee will increase over time, and consumers should try to determine if their future income level will match the expected increases. A history of past rate increases may help predict future increases. Other questions consumers should ask include: Are fee increases tied to external factors such as the consumer price index, utility rates, or Social Security increases? Or, are they set according to management's discretion? Does the life-care contract provide for the arbitration of rate increases? To increase revenue, some communities require additional charges for items previously included in the monthly fee. A brochure may picture swimming pools, golf courses, and health spas, but it may also underplay the extra charges for use of these facilities. A responsible provider will specify clearly in the contract exactly what is and what is not included in the monthly fee.

Determine what happens if the resident can no longer pay, wants to leave, has to move to a nursing facility, or changes marital status. What happens if, after taking occupancy, a resident can no longer afford to make the monthly payments? Recent court cases, and an IRS ruling, suggest that a "home for the aged" can only qualify for a tax-exempt status if it has some form of assistance for residents who encounter financial difficulties. Many contracts expressly state they will not evict a resident for inability to pay if the tenant can justify a fee reduction and the reduction will not impair the facility's ability to operate.

The life-care provider should agree to refund almost all of the entry fee if the contract is terminated before occupancy. Some providers' refund rates are based on whether termination of the contract was made by the community or the resident. Other providers have no refund provisions at all. Some contracts that require entrance fees of $150,000 or more provide for a refund of as high as 90% after the death of the resident, with the money going to the estate of the deceased.

The decision to place an elderly person in a nursing home can be difficult and painful. However, under some contacts, this decision is made exclusively by man-agement. If no Medicare funds are involved, the resident's family and physician may not even be consulted. Before they sign, residents should review their contracts to determine who has authority to make this important decision.

Other questions to ask include: If illness necessitates a transfer of indefinite length to a nursing facility, how long will the resident be permitted to retain his/her apartment before it is re-rented? If the apartment is re-rented, what arrangments will be made for storage of the resident's property, or to provide another apartment if he/she is able to return? If a resident is widowed, must he/she transfer to a smaller unit? Is the monthly fee affected by remarriage?

Ask about community rules, regulations, and governing structure. The decision to join a life-care community is essentially an agreement to abide by established rules governing almost all facets of a resident's life. In addition to the contract, prospective residents should acquire a copy of the resident's handbook, which contains important information on community life, available from sales agents or the community's management. While the contract is legally binding, the handbook may not be. Concerns about an issue absent in the contract but present in the handbook should always be voiced to the community's manager. If the issue is important, the resident should ask that it be incorporated into the formal contract.

Consumers should be advised to review contract clauses dealing with resident participation in community management. Does the resident council have access to the community's books and management plans? Is it independently funded to hire an accountant, attorney, or other professional advisor? What voice do residents have in determining policies that affect fee increases, recreational scheduling, or other operating procedures? Is there a resident on the board, or an association which represents community members and handles complaints? Is there a residents' council which can continue to monitor and help shape the operation of the community?

Bankruptcy. Careful research and continual oversight are the best protection against poor management and bankruptcy. However, if a development does seek relief from its creditors in court, there are several steps residents can take to protect their interests and investments. Residents can file a "proof-of-claim" for their damages in bankruptcy court and they could also hire an attorney to represent their interests. For example, the attorney could investigate whether the consumers are eligible for a special $900 "priority" consumer claim under the bankruptcy code, whether they have the right to any escrow deposits, and whether they can pursue the individual developers—as well as the bank-rupt company—for damages for unfair or deceptive acts. However, since most consumer claims are unsecured in cases like these (there is no collateral for the debts owed to consumers), the residents may not recover much money in bankruptcy court.

Regulating the life-care industry. The growing market of better-educated and more affluent older persons is directly responsible for the rapid expansion of the life-care industry. As the median age of Americans increases, so should interest in the life-care concept. Until now, the life-care industry has been the domain of non-profit organizations, but the private sector has recently recognized the profit potential of these developments. With the growth of life-care has come an increased need for industry regulation, which most states lack. However, the state of Maryland does supervise the industry through its department on aging and requires state approval of all contracts before they are offered to the public. Fifteen other states (Arizona, California, Colorado, Connecticut, Florida, Illinois, Indiana, Kansas, Michigan, Minnesota, Missouri, New Mexico, New York, Oregon, and Pennsylvania) have statutes which range from disclosure requirements to state regulation through insurance commissions, public health agencies, social service agencies, or others. The remaining 34 states have no industry regulation. Consumers should find out which agencies, if any, regulate the life-care industry in their states and what consumer protection is available.

Also missing is an industry-wide or governmental clearinghouse to monitor if life-care communities are fulfilling their contractual obligations and to assess communities' financial health. Most life-care developers are not required to perform an actuarial review, giving a more realistic assessment of future costs based on accurate projections on the lifespans and health needs of residents.

In its ideal form, a life-care community can provide its members with a strong sense of psychological and financial security, as well as the support services they need to maintain an independent and comfortable lifestyle. Several hundred communities have achieved these objectives, but the industry is still in its infancy, and many "kinks" are still being ironed out. In addition, the life-care business, by its very nature, is based on the management of unpredictable factors and the guesswork can never be eliminated completely.

Of course, a well-managed operation should be able to withstand financial ups and downs. Nonetheless, prospective life-care applicants should understand that no retirement community is entirely risk-free. The safest investments are those made with providers who can demonstrate that they have taken all available measures to minimize risks.

PARTICIPATION IN A DUAL ECONOMY AND ADJUSTMENT TO RETIREMENT

Toni M. Calasanti

Virginia Polytechnic Institute and State University

ABSTRACT

Past studies of adjustment to retirement have generally accepted social structure as a given, and have instead focused upon individual level variables. Based upon criticisms of the white-collar/blue-collar depiction of the work world, an alternative model of the economic system is introduced in an attempt to interject variability in the area of social structure. Utilizing a national sample of men derived from the National Opinion Research Center (1972-1977 inclusive), this dual economic model is employed to assess the effects of sectoral placement of workers on subsequent retirement satisfaction. Findings from multiple regression analysis suggest that such placement renders two qualitatively different groups of retirees, one which is primarily concerned with health, and one for which financial adequacy is more important for retirement adjustment. Overall, it was concluded that structural components must be included in research on the retirement process. In addition, the variability among the different scales used to indicate adjustment to retirement suggest that these may have to be altered to adequately reflect the process of adjustment for each of the groups of retirees. These changes must be based on the structural aspects of the economic order which mandate very different work experiences.

Retirement research has increased over the last three decades. One central question has been whether removal of the work force causes a major disruption in an individual's life, or merely calls forth preferences and habits established over a lifetime. Earlier findings indicated that retirement does precipitate a crisis in many lives. The original work of Friedman and Havighurst, for example, maintained that the loss of the work role had a negative effect on the totality of the retiree's life [1]. More recent evidence, however, points to a continuity of established patterns after withdrawal from the labor force [2].

Explanations of retirement adjustment usually contrast the personal attributes of successful and unsuccessful individuals. Health, perceived financial adequacy, occupational prestige, educational attainment, and marital status have each been identified as important factors in the successful adjustment process [3-10]. Despite these recent inroads, our understanding of the factors determining retirement adjustment is far from complete. Dowd discusses a major underlying problem, which is that the American economy is divided into two sectors, one of which has high wages and pension systems and one which does not [11]. Retirees from the first group live fairly well, while those from the second group "face certain impoverishment."

Researchers in the area of retirement adjustment have usually separated laborers into blue-collar and white-collar camps. This economic model, however, has recently been critically reexamined because of its failure to account for contemporary trends. These trends include:

a. the persistence of poverty;
b. the fact that, while educational gaps have narrowed, income discrepancies remain the same;
c. continued discrimination against minorities in employment and income; and
d. the inability of the white-collar/blue-collar framework to explain unemployment trends [12].

The validity of the white-collar, blue-collar depiction has also been challenged on the basis of empirical discrepancies. For example, there are presently more variations *within* groups defined in this way than there are *between* them, leading some economists to conclude that the distinction has lost much of its usefulness. Gordon notes several trends, including the divergence in income among workers performing the same task [13]. This is especially true among middle-range occupations of both white-collar and blue-collar groups, where "the range of income within occupations seems to be growing fairly rapidly" [13, p. 198].

Another challenge to the explanatory value of the white-collar/blue-collar differentiation is the observation that there is no longer a clear difference between white-collar and blue-collar jobs. Various occupations

From *International Journal of Aging and Human Development*, Vol. 26, No. 1, 1988, pp. 13-27. Copyright © 1988 by Baywood Publishing Co., Inc. Reprinted by permission of the author and Baywood Publishing Co., Inc.

within the white-collar group are taking on characteristics formerly thought to be the exclusive property of blue-collar laborers; for example, white-collar workers have less and less authority. "Routinization" of work (highly structured routines; an overall rationalization of the process) previously occurred predominantly in the domain of blue-collar laborers. Increasingly, however, white-collar workers encounter precisely the same kind of routinized working conditions as their blue-collar counterparts [13]. Furthermore, machines are being introduced into ever-growing numbers of white-collar occupations, so that white-collar duties now include more "manual" labor [14]. Lower-level white-collar workers now fulfill the duties of traditional technicians [15].

THE DUAL ECONOMIC PERSPECTIVE

It appears that a different approach is necessary to account for the present structure of the working world. The present state of capitalism in the United States is illustrated by the *dual economic model*, by which American businesses are divided into two categories: core firms and peripheral firms. (For further elucidation of the historical events leading to this dichotomy, see [16-18].)

Core firms are monopolistic, and are larger than peripheral firms in all respects: the make more money, employ more people, and have the greatest amount of total assets. Core firms produce many and varied products, so that these firms are never totally dependent upon the sales of one product, or even the vicissitudes of the national economy. The technology used by these firms is very complex, and employee training is costly. Core enterprises therefore wish to maintain a stable workforce. For these reasons, employees within such establishments have relatively greater power, command higher wages, and have the ability to unionize [19]. Civil servants and law enforcement officials are also considered core workers, because they enjoy job stability, good pensions, and union representation. The modicum of financial security offered to core firm workers and retirees allows them to turn their attention to other components of life satisfaction.

Peripheral firms comprise the competitive sector of the economy. These establishments are essentially small, dependent upon one product, and subject to the mood and vascillations of the national economy. Assets are often minimal, and it is possible to concentrate only on short-run production. Unlike core firms, management in peripheral enterprises is often the responsibility of a single individual. The technology employed by peripheral firms is not as complex as that used by the core; thus, these firms are more labor intensive [19, 20].

Overall, peripheral firms have organizational characteristics associated with powerless occupational groups. According to Bibb and Form, workers in such enterprises have low social cohesion [20, p. 978]. Workers in this sector have less power to organize, because firms have not invested as much in them and do not require a stable workforce. Peripheral workers have fewer avenues to prevent and protest sudden unemployment and low wages, and to lobby for benefits.

Empirical applications of the dual economic perspective began to appear in the mid-seventies. This model has been particularly effective in the area of earnings determination [20-24]. The results of studies using this model indicate that core workers make more money and are accorded higher prestige than their peripheral counterparts [21] and that core workers are likely to be white and male [22]. Dual economic research using the 1976 Current Population Survey found that basic sectoral difference in earnings remain "regardless of controls for race and gender, of whether or not income is adjusted for labor force participation, of whether effects are estimated in dollar returns or rates of return, and of whether low earners are included or excluded" [23, p. 718].

Of greater interest to the present agenda is another study of earnings determination which not only points to the discovery of disparate reward, accruing to sectors, but adds: "Theories of dual economy suggest that . . . sectoral differences have important implications for the . . . *experiences faced by individual workers*" [24, p. 707; italics mine]. Of the utilization of the dual economic model, Beck and his colleagues say [23, p. 113]:

> . . . we do not argue . . . that the industrial economy is divisible only into two mutually exclusive sectors. Rather, it is our position that the dual economic approach represents a convenient, albeit simplified, starting point for research into the effects of economic segmentation on labor market outcomes. Thus, rather than representing a theoretical destination, the ideal-type sectors in a dual economy theory represent a conceptual point of departure.

In the present discussion, the contention that sectoral differences influence the experiences of individual workers is a point of departure for the effort to ascertain the effect of the dualistic structure of the work world upon adjustment to retirement. Differences in satisfaction expressed by retired workers may be more a consequence of their sectoral placement than a result of their rank in the neoclassical status hierarchy. The main impetus for this study was the belief that the location of workers in either the core or the periphery will influence subsequent adjustment to retirement.

THE DUAL ECONOMY AND ADJUSTMENT TO RETIREMENT

The intent of the present study is to place into a dual-economic framework the individual attributes which are identified by status attainment research and are thought to be important to retirement adaptation. The differential impact of these variables is assessed by economic sector. The premise is not that micro-level factors are unimportant, but rather that these variables interact with the structure to differentially affect workers in their respective spheres. The broad hypothesis governing the study can now be stated as follows:

> The power of individual level variables in accounting for adjustment to retirement will vary by economic sector of (previous) employment.

This does not mean that micro-level factors are expected to account for more total variation explained in one sector than in another (although this may indeed be the case). Rather, it is felt that the relative explanatory importance of each factor will vary between core and peripheral retirees, creating distinct patterns of adjustment. Although it is difficult to anticipate the precise form that these differences will take, it was hypothesized that, in keeping with the tenets of the dual economic model,

> Peripheral workers will demonstrate a primary concern with financial matters, while core workers will place greater emphasis upon other components of life satisfaction.

These differences are based upon the aforementioned financial characteristics of the two sectors, which it is felt, will have a strong influence upon laborers who subsequently depart their respective spheres.

METHODS

Samples
The data base used was taken from the General Social Survey conducted by the National Opinion Research Center (NORC) over a six-year span, 1972-1977, inclusive. Respondents to the yearly survey were chosen from within the United States, and were non-institutionalized, English-speaking, and aged eighteen and over. Research conducted during the first three years of this survey utilized block quota sampling techniques, while the surveys taken in 1975 and 1976 employed one-half full probability and one-half block quota methods. The final year, 1977, used a full probability design. Respondents for the present study included only the male retirees represented by the NORC data, so as to facilitate analysis and to prevent any confounding factors that might be attributed to sex. The total N will vary, depending upon the test being run.

Independent Variables
Occupational prestige—already provided by the NORC data, which utilized the index developed by Hodge, Siegel, and Rossi [25].
Education—highest grade completed.

Health—excellent to poor.
Marital status—married, never married, divorced, separated, widowed.
Perceived financial adequacy—"pretty well satisfied" to "not satisfied at all." All independent variables were self-reported.

Dependent Variables: Adjustment to Retirement
In the past, evaluation of successful adaption has taken two general forms: subjective measures of personal happiness or morale, or objective (though often self-reported) calculations of the frequency and extent of social participation [9]. Although each technique has its problems, the latter is far more open to the interpretation of the researcher. Therefore, the present study attempted to assess adjustment to retirement by allowing the respondents to evaluate various dimensions of their lives.

Three different sets of dependent variables were used to test the main hypothesis in order to attain the broadest possible picture of retirement adjustment. An overall score for live satisfaction was generated in response to the following questions:

> How much satisfaction do you get from:
> a. non-working activities—hobbies and so on;
> b. your family life;
> c. your friendships;
> d. your health and physical condition.

Scores for each item range from 1 (high) to 7 (low). Overall tallies span a scale of 4 (extremely satisfied) to 24 (very dissatisfied). Although the final dimension might be redundant, the earlier measurement of health, which will be used as an independent variable in this analysis, does not tap the subjective aspect of the respondents' condition. Although there will obviously be a relationship between these two factors (one's rating of health, and one's feelings about it), scores should not be any higher in one economic sector than another. Since health is of major importance with increasing age, it is imperative to measure the respondent's evaluation of it.

In addition, measures other than life satisfaction were used to further examine satisfaction with retirement. As provided by NORC, these include a global question of all-around happiness, as well as a scale geared to assessing anomie (sense of estrangement).

Variations in the Economic Model
Division of enterprises into core (monopolistic) and peripheral (competitive) categories is methodologically complex. Not only is the total enumeration of firms a difficult task, but establishing ownership is often problematic. For this reason, dual economists tend to identify core and peripheral enterprises by their level of monopolization. It should be noted that this is not only for convenience, but has sound theoretical and empirical backing as well.

An "industry" refers to a specific commodity or group of related commodities. "Firm" denotes the organization of an industry [19, p. 3]. Economists speak of "key" industries, a term which reflects the importance of these industries to the economy. Almost all key industries are dominated by large firms [19, p. 73]. It is this empirical revelation which allows scholars to approximate the existence of monopolies by zeroing in on "key" industries.

The present study uses the scheme created by Tolbert, Horan, and Beck [21]. Their sectoral assignment of industries is shown in Appendix A. Individual respondents were placed in core or peripheral work spheres based on this scheme. Since mobility between sectors is rare [26], the industries into which the retiree placed himself is felt to adequately represent the one in which the majority of his work experience occurred.

ANALYSIS

Labor Characteristics in a Dual Economy
To establish the validity of this, the structural framework of the present research, a preliminary analysis of the data was undertaken. Two questions were asked:

1. does union membership vary by sector?; and
2. does racial and sexual makeup vary by sector?

To test these questions, cross-tabulations on the total NORC data (men and women) were computed. The results indicated that members of the core sector were more likely to be unionized. Both females and blacks were over-represented in the periphery; the frequencies within this sector were 63 percent and 60 percent, respectively. Overall, it is felt that there is sufficient support for the dual economic framework.

Retirement Adjustment in a Dual Economy
Research has identified many personal characteristics that influence adjustment to retirement. Good health [3,4,27,28], satisfaction with the adequacy of one's finances [6-8], higher occupational and educational levels [3,4,10], and the presence of a spouse [3-5] correlate with successfully completing the transition from workforce to retirement. In order to measure the ways in which these individual level variables differentially affect adjustment to retirement within the two economic sectors, multiple regression, with a stepwise technique, was utilized. Since there is no theoretical basis for ordering the independent variables, a stepwise design allows each variable to enter the respective equation in proportion to its importance in explaining the variance. At each intermediate step, F-scores were computed to test the significance of the most recent variable.

Once the pattern for each sector was determined, a Spearman's rho statistic was computed. This test looks at the ranking of the variables for each equation in order to ascertain if the differences truly represent variations, and not chance. Accordingly, a score of 1 represents perfect agreement between populations, while a -1 reflects perfect disagreement. A zero indicates no relationship between the two groups. For this computation, all variables entered into each equation were used, regardless of their overall significance.

Tables 1 through 3 present only those variables which proved significant for each equation. Although there is some variation in the ordering of variables for the two populations, health generally plays a more significant role for core retirees, while satisfaction with finances has a greater impact on former peripheral employees. Admittedly, health enters the equation first for both sectors in Table 1; this is not surprising given the fact that satisfaction with one's health was one component of the overall dependent measure. (It might be argued, on statistical grounds, that inclusion of the health variable has inflated the amount of variance explained. However, for the theoretical reasons described above, this factor was deemed important to the overall index of life satisfaction, and was therefore included.)

The question of structural differences in the patterning of independent variables for each sector was addressed through the calculation of a rho statistic for the equations for each dependent variable. The results provide mixed support for the main hypothesis. For life satisfaction, rho was found to equal -.321; this number falls between no agreement and perfect disagreement, suggesting that the two populations are indeed different. Similarly, the rho statistic for anomie yielded a figure of .286, indicating little association. The dependent variable happiness was an exception; here, rho equaled .535, a midway point between perfect agreement and no association between the two groups. The most that can be said of this particular case is that the evidence put forth is inconclusive.

Table 1. Life Satisfaction[a]

	Cum. r^2	r^2 Change	B	Beta
Core				
Health	.255	--	2.449	.501
Married	.315	.06	-2.644	-.244
Total	.322			
N = 377				
Periphery				
Health	.231	--	2.083	.419
Divorced/ Separated	.301	.07	3.396	.182
Satfin	.329	.028	1.077	.168
Married	.345	.016	-1.539	-.144
Total	.367			
N = 213				

[a]Given that certain questions used to compose the dependent variables were only asked in specific years, overall Ns for each sector will vary between life satisfaction, anomie, and happiness.

The dynamics of retirement need to be considered in a subjective light. Life satisfaction, happiness, and a sense of purpose must be viewed as they relate to the retired person.

Table 2. Happiness

	Cum. r²	r² Change	B	Beta
Core				
Health	.099	--	.207	.294
Married	.140	.041	−.305	−.197
Satfin	.151	.011	.097	.109
Total	.155			
N = 453				
Periphery				
Married	.118	--	−.503	−.324
Satfin	.178	.06	.209	.217
Health	.187	.009	.072	.100
Total	.196			
N = 247				

Table 3. Anomie

	Cum. r²	r² Change	B	Beta
Core				
Education	.222	--	.220	.322
Prestige	.257	.035	.345	.190
Health	.274	.017	−.310	−.120
Satfin	.286	.012	−.382	−.114
Total	.290			
N = 196				
Periphery				
Satfin	.149	--	−1.150	−.349
Prestige	.202	.053	.393	.234
Total	.230			
N = 115				

DISCUSSION

A dual economic model was utilized to examine patterns of retirement adjustment. It was found that the structural placement of a worker in a core or peripheral job prior to retirement shapes the patterning of individual level variables, especially in those cases where adjustment to retirement is measured by more than one dimension. The regression runs and rho statistics calculated for both life satisfaction and anomie indicate that the two populations—core and peripheral—display more differences than similarities; although the rho statistic for happiness does not support this contention, it does not refute it, either.

Different variables appear to be especially important for each of the two populations: health is important to the core, and satisfaction with finances is important to the periphery. The reason for this difference is that retirement income inequalities are built into the economic structure. As late as 1981, 75 percent to 90 percent of workers in peripheral firms with under 500 employees were not covered by pension plans. Reasons for this lack of coverage include the expense of managing such plans, bankruptcy of firms, federal tax regulations which favor core industries, and the unstable work histories mandated by peripheral work [27]. Thus, the concerns of peripheral retirees reflect the monetary struggles they have experienced throughout their lives. On the other hand, greater benefits within the core guarantee that retirees from this sector can expect to maintain or rise above a basic threshold of income; they can therefore concern themselves with other components of life satisfaction, such as health.

Education is of importance only in the equation for anomie, and only for the core sector. The pattern for this sector indicates that high education contributes to less estrangement. Again, it appears that a relative freedom from financial worry allows other dimensions of one's life to dominate one's concerns.

While it is not the present intent to attribute concern with health as being "caused" by core placement, the relationship identified does correspond with past re-

search. For example, Lowenthal found that males facing imminent retirement were mostly worried about physical well-being: "Their objective . . . was survival in good health, in a context of 'no more hassles' " [28, pp. 9-10]. Further, these men "were not as anxious about their financial security. . . ." The sample for this research, however, although drawn from both "white- and blue-collar ranks," were described as men "firmly entrenched in the probable security of civil service and related bureaucracies (indeed most of them selected such work primarily because of its security). . . ." Regardless of traditional categorizations, these men were thus all core employees, working in occupations which provided stability.

CONCLUSION

It is felt that the present study demonstrates the need to include structural considerations into studies of adjustment to retirement. Individual attributes may be important, but they occur within a structural framework. This study also suggests that different measures for adaptation to retirement must be more closely examined, as each of the three measures utilized in this research rendered different patterns for each of the populations. Although health is primarily important to the core, and satisfaction with finances appears to be more relevant to the periphery, some inconsistencies remain. Education, for example, is the best predictor of anomie for core members, while it is insignificant for life satisfaction and happiness. Thus, to predict adjustment, disparate sets of factors may have to be employed based not only on the respective groups, but on various measures as well. This variability will have to be taken into account in further designs and analyses.

Further investigation is needed into the reasons that health seems to be of greater explanatory value for core retirees, while financial adequacy is of more importance to those in the periphery. It might also be found that, given the far greater numbers of women in the periphery, structural analyses that incorporate both

5. RETIREMENT

sexes might discover that gender differences may be at least partly due to sector. The effects of the independent variables, such as marital status, may also differ between men and women within and across sectors. Although the outcome of future investigations in this area cannot be predicted, the results of this study suggest that if the issue of economic structure is ignored, gerontologists will be ineffective at the level of intervention, no matter how sound their intent.

APPENDIX A
Sectoral Assignment of Industries

CORE
  Mining:
    Metal mining
    Coal Mining
    Crude petroleum and natural gas
    Nonmetallic mining and quarrying
  Construction:
    General building contractors
    General contractors, except building
    Special trade contractors
    Not specified construction
  Manufacturing—Durable Goods:
    Stone, clay, and glass products
    Primary metal
    Fabricated metal products
    Machinery, except electrical
    Electrical machinery, equipment
    Motor vehicles and equipment
    Other transportation equipment
    Professional, photographic, watches
    Ordinance
  Manufacturing—Nondurable Goods:
    Food and kindred products
    Tobacco manufacturers
    Textile—yarn, thread, fabric mills
    Paper and allied products
    Printing, publishing
    Chemicals and allied products
    Petroleum and coal products
    Rubber products
    Footwear, except rubber
  Transportation, Communications, and Other Public Utilities:
    Railroads and railway express
    Trucking service
    Warehousing and storage
    Water transportation
    Air transportation
    Pipelines, except natural gas
    Communications
    Electric, gas, and steam power
  Wholesale Trade:
    Drugs, chemical and allied products
    Food and related products
    Electrical goods
    Machinery, equipment, and supplies
    Metals and minerals, n.e.c.
    Alcoholic beverages
  Finance, Insurance, and Real Estate:
    Banking
    Credit agencies
    Security brokerage and investment
    Insurance
  Professional and Related Services:
    Offices of physicians, dentists, practitioners, and health services
    Legal services
    Engineering and architectural firms
    Accounting and auditing services
    Miscellaneous professional services
  Public Administration

PERIPHERY
  Agriculture, Forestry, Fisheries:
    Agricultural production
    Agricultural services
  Manufacturing—Durable Goods:
    Lumber and wood products
    Furniture and fixtures
    Miscellaneous manufacturing
  Manufacturing—Non-durable Goods:
    Textile—knitting mills
    Textile—floor covering
    Textile—miscellaneous products
    Apparel and other related products
    Miscellaneous plastic products
    Tanned, curried, and finished leather
    Leather products, except footwear
  Transportation, Communications, and Other Public Utilities:
    Street railways and bus lines
    Taxicab service
    Services related to transportation
    Water, sanitary, and other utilities
  Wholesale Trade:
    Motor vehicles and equipment
    Drug goods and apparel
    Farm products—raw materials
    Hardware, plumbing, heating supplies
    Not specified electrical, hardware
    Petroleum products
    Scrap and waste materials
    Paper and its products
    Lumber and construction materials
    Wholesalers, not specified, n.e.c.
  Retail Trade:
    Lumber, building materials, hardware
    Department, general merchandise stores
    Food stores
    Motor vehicles, gasoline, accessories
    Apparel and shoe stores
    Furniture and household appliances

Eating and drinking places
Other retail trade
Finance, Insurance, and Real Estate:
Real Estate
Business and Repair Services:
Advertising
Automobile repair
Other business services
Personal Services:
Hotels and motels
Other personal services
Entertainment and Recreation Services
Professional and Related Services:
Hospitals, convalescent institutions
Educational services
Museums and other nonprofit firms

REFERENCES

1. E. A. Friedmann and R. J. Havighurst, *The Meaning of Work and Retirement*, University of Chicago Press, Chicago, IL, 1954.
2. R. C. Atchley, Retirement and Leisure Participation: Continuity or Crisis?, *The Gerontologist*, 11:1, pp. 13–17, 1971.
3. J. Hendricks and C. D. Hendricks, *Aging in Mass Society*, 3rd Edition, Little, Brown and Company, Boston, MA, 1986.
4. L. K. George and G. L. Maddox, Subjective Adaptation to Loss of the Work Role: A Longitudinal Study, in *Dimensions of Aging*, J. Hendricks and C. D. Hendricks (eds.), Winthrop Publishers, Cambridge, MA, pp. 331–338, 1981.
5. R. Larson, Thirty Years of Research on the Subjective Well-Being of Older Americans, *Journal of Gerontology*, 33:1, pp. 109–125, 1978.
6. H. L. Sheppard, Work and Retirement, in *Handbook of Aging and the Social Sciences*, R. Binstock and E. Shanas (eds.), Van Nostrand Reinhold Co., New York, NY, pp. 286–309, 1976.
7. R. E. Barfield and J. N. Morgan, Trends in Satisfaction with Retirement, *The Gerontologist*, 18:1, pp. 19–23, 1978.
8. R. C. Atchley, Adjustment to Loss of Job at Retirement, *International Journal of Aging and Human Development*, 6:1, pp. 17–28, 1975.
9. E. A. Friedmann and H. Orbach, Adjustment to Retirement, in *The Foundations of Psychology*, S. Arieti (ed.), Basic Books, New York, NY, pp. 609–645, 1974.
10. V. L. Bengtson, Occupational Differences in Retirement: Patterns of Role Activity and Life-Outlook Among Chicago Teachers and Steel Workers, in *Adjustment to Retirement*, 3rd Edition, R. J. Havighurst, *et al.* (eds.), Van Gorcum & Co., Netherlands, pp. 53–70, 1969.
11. J. J. Dowd, *Stratification Among the Aged*, Brooks Cole Publishing Co., Monterey, CA, 1980.
12. G. G. Cain, The Challenge of Segmented Labor Market Theories to Orthodox Theory, *Journal of Economic Literature*, 14, pp. 1215–1257, 1976.
13. D. M. Gordon, From Steam Whistles to Coffee Breaks, *Dissent*, pp. 197–210, Winter 1972.
14. H. Braverman, *Labor and Monopoly Capital*, Monthly Review Press, New York, NY, 1975.
15. J. H. Goldthorpe, D. Lockwood, F. Bechhofer, and J. Platt, *The Affluent Worker in the Class Structure*, Cambridge University Press, Cambridge, MA, 1969.
16. P. A. Baran and P. M. Sweezy, *Monopoly Capital*, Monthly Review Press, New York, NY, 1966.
17. R. C. Edwards, M. Reich, and D. M. Gordon (eds.), *Labor Market Segmentation*, D.C. Heath and Co., Lexington, MA, 1975.
18. R. C. Edwards, *Contested Terrain: The Transformation of the Workplace in the Twentieth Century*, Basic Books, New York, NY, 1979.
19. R. T. Averitt, *The Dual Economy*, W. W. Norton and Co., New York, NY, 1968.
20. R. Bibb and W. H. Form, The Effects of Industrial, Occupational and Sex Stratification on Wages in Blue-Collar Markets, *Social Forces*, 55:4, pp. 974–986, 1977.
21. C. Tolbert, P. M. Horan, and E. M. Beck, The Structure of Economic Segregation: A Dual Economy Approach, *American Journal of Sociology*, 85:5, pp. 1095–1116, 1980.
22. E. M. Beck, P. M. Horan, and C. M. Tolbert, Industrial Segmentation and Labor Market Discrimination, *Social Problems*, 28:2, pp. 113–130, 1980.
23. _____, Social Stratification in Industrial Society: Further Evidence for a Structural Alternative, *American Sociological Review*, 45:4, pp. 712–718, 1980.
24. _____, Stratification in a Dual Economy: A Sectoral Model of Earnings Determination, *American Sociological Review*, 43:5, pp. 704–720, 1978.
25. J. A. Davis and T. W. Smith, *General Social Surveys, 1972–1982: Cumulative Codebook*, National Opinion Research Center, University of Chicago, Chicago, IL, 1980.
26. M. Carnoy and R. Rumberger, Segmented Labor Markets: Some Empirical Forays, discussion paper presented to the National Institute of Education, Department of Health, Education, and Welfare, September 1975.
27. J. Hendricks and C. E. McAllister, An Alternative Perspective on Retirement: A Dual Economic Approach, *Ageing and Society*, 3:3, pp. 279–296, 1983.
28. M. Lowenthal, Psychological Variation Across the Adult Life Course: Frontiers for Research and Policy, *The Gerontologist*, 15:1, part one, pp. 6–12, 1975.

The Experience of Dying

Modern science has allowed individuals to have some control over the conception of their children, and has provided people with the ability to prolong life. But life and death still defy scientific explanation or reason. The world can be divided into two categories: sacred and secular. The sacred (that which is embodied in the religion of a culture) is used to explain all the forces of nature and the environment that can neither be understood nor controlled. On the other hand, the secular (defined as "of or relating to the world") is used to explain all the aspects of the world that *can* be understood or controlled. Through scientific invention, more and more of the natural world can be controlled. It is still highly doubtful, however, that science will ever be able to provide an acceptable explanation of the meaning of death. In this domain, religion may always prevail.

Death is universally feared. Sometimes it is more bearable for those who believe in a life after death. Here, religion offers a solution. In the words of anthropologist Bronislaw Malinowski (1884-1942):

> Religion steps in, selecting the positive creed, the comforting view, the culturally valuable belief in immortality, in the spirit of the body, and in the continuance of life after death. (Bronislaw Malinowski, *Magic, Science and Religion and Other Essays*, Glencoe, Illinois: Free Press, 1948)

The fear of death leads people to develop defense mechanisms in order to insulate themselves psychologically from its reality. Individuals know that some day everyone must die, death's inevitability. The individual knows that someday he or she must die, but this event is thought to be likely to occur in the far distant future. The individual does not think of himself or herself as dying tomorrow or the next day, but years from now. In this way people are able to control their anxiety about death.

Losing a close friend or relative brings people dangerously close to the reality of death. Individuals come face to face with the fact that there is always an end to life. Latent fears surface. During times of mourning, people grieve not only for the dead, but for themselves, and for the finiteness of life.

The readings in this section address bereavement, grief, the arguments for and against euthanasia, and adjustments to the stages of dying. In "The Many Faces of Grief" the author examines the conditions under which people die, and relates this to the grief experienced by their loved ones. The right to die or to have one's life sustained by medical technology is discussed in "Health Technology vs. Death: Should We Prolong the Inevitable?" Euthanasia, or the assisting of a person to a painless death, has long been a topic of controversy for the medical profession. In "Euthanasia: The Time Is Now" the author argues for assisting a person to a painless death if there is constant pain and no hope of survival. In the following article, "In Defense of the Humane and Dignified Death Act," the author presents a case for letting nature take its course and allowing the patient to die naturally. The stages dying people pass through—anger, denial, bargaining, depression, and acceptance—were originally defined by Kübler-Ross. The author of "A Theoretical Reassessment of the Applicability of Kübler-Ross's Stages of Dying" suggests that these stages do not necessarily explain the reactions to impending death that elderly persons experience.

Looking Ahead: Challenge Questions

Is the fear of dying really universal? Do all people share it equally?

What are the techniques by which people alleviate their anxieties about dying?

Should dying patients be told the truth about their impending deaths, or should this information be withheld?

Are the elderly more afraid of death than the young?

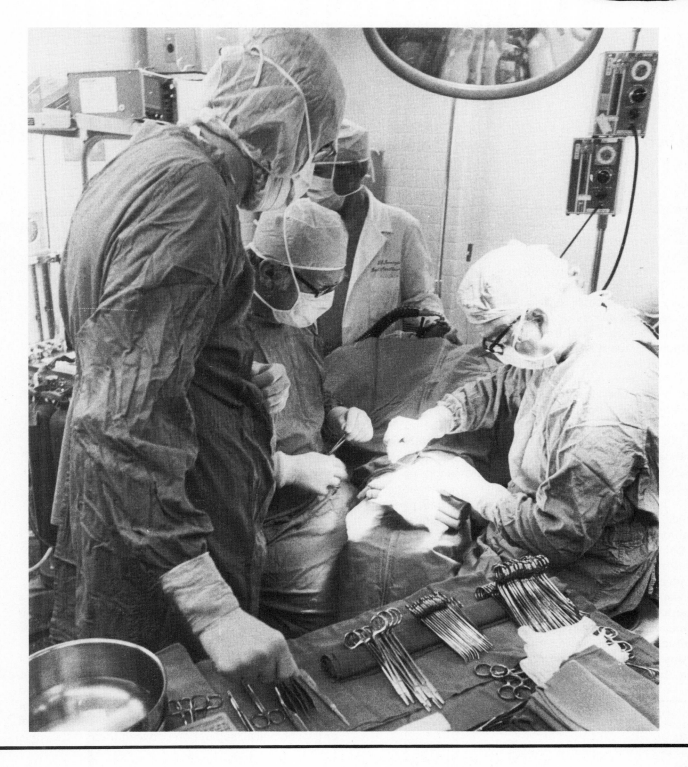

THE MANY FACES OF GRIEF

Robert Fulton

University of Minnesota, Minneapolis

The purpose of this paper, within the brief space available, is to discuss some aspects of loss and grief that have been of interest to me and I hope will prove to be of interest to the reader as well.

I will comment on three different, but related, topics. First I will discuss briefly the sociologic conditions under which people die today. Second I will offer several observations about our contemporary understanding of grief, and third I will conclude by saying something about the concept of anticipatory grief and its significance for us, especially in connection with a relatively new concept that I want to introduce here—the "Stockholm Syndrome."

People involved in the care of the terminally ill represent that segment of the population, the professional caregiver and/or volunteer, who, with both skill and concern, moniter to those among us who are most likely to die—the elderly. The phenomenon of the dying elderly affects not only health care professionals here in Florida, but is also an important challenge to other retirement-related states such as Arizona and California.

Let me begin not at the beginning, but at the end, by presenting you the obituary of a man I will call John Anderson, that recently appeared in a Minneapolis newspaper. I think you will find the profile of this man's life—and his death—as outlined in the obituary, familiar to you. You will also recognize how this brief obituary tends to sum up much about American society as it relates to the death of our citizens. As you read the obituary, note what it implicitly says about family life and social change. Note also what is says about social mobility and human mortality. As you do so, you will begin to see the patterns of social life that I wish to discuss merge. The obituary:

> John Anderson, age 75, passed away suddenly on Easter Sunday in a Fort Lauderdale nursing home after a long illness. He is survived by his wife, Mary, who lives in Vero Beach, Florida. He is also survived by four sons: John, of Grand Rapids, Minnesota; Fredrick, of Albert Lea, Minnesota; Harry, of Columbus, Ohio, and Daniel, of Mt. Vernon, Illinois, as well as their wives and eight grandchildren, Mary, Audrey, Sally, Melissa, Ann Katherine, Lauren, Elizabeth and Joanne. Also by a brother, James, who resides in St. Paul, Minnesota, and a sister, Francis, of Newton, Massachusetts. Mr. Anderson began his career in the electronics industry in the early 1920s and was founder and president of that corporation until his retirement in the late 1960s. Memorial services will be held on Thursday at the Lyndale Avenue Congregational Church in Minneapolis. There will be no reviewal or visitation. A private interment in Greenwood Park Cemetery in Fort Lauderdale is planned. Desired memorials may be given to the University of Minnesota Hospital Foundation in Minnesota, or to the donor's choice. Services are under the arrangements of the Harper Funeral Home, Fort Lauderdale.

Mr. Anderson's obituary tells us many things in a brief paragraph. It tells us first who is dying in contemporary America—the elderly. It tells us where—the sunbelt. It tells us under what circumstances—in a nursing home. Mr. Anderson in all probability died of cancer, a heart attack, or a stroke after a long illness. He was a resident of a nursing home for a long period of time. His wife resided in another city at the time of his death. There was at least some physical, if not social or psychological, separation between them at the time.

This paper is an adapted version of the 1985 Arthur G. Peterson Lecture presented at the University of Florida, Gainesville, February 27, 1985.

He also died away from his four sons, his brother, sister, and eight grandchildren. Mobility in American society has long been observed by social scientists. Migrations of people have characterized our country since its inception. According to demographers, one out of every five families move yearly in the United States. What is important for us to consider regarding Mr. Anderson and the thousands, indeed tens of thousands, like him is his age and the fact that he represents a new phenomenon in American social life. This new social fact of life is the large scale migration of elderly persons from their place of birth or long-term residence in the snowbound North to the sunbelt South. The young, of course, are also very mobile in our society—they always have been. We have only to think of the mass movement of young families to California after the Second World War, white and black alike, or the politically inspired wanderings of young people to San Francisco and Seattle at the time of the Vietnam War. Even Mr. Anderson's four sons have been mobile. Indeed, except for his brother James in St. Paul, no one stayed at home—everybody moved.

Mr. Anderson left Minneapolis in the 1960s. He had been absent from Minnesota 20 years before his death and separated from his friends and business associates, as well as from his children and grandchildren, presumably all that time. We are not told in the obituary what happened to his body—whether it was donated to a hospital or cremated, or where the body or ashes were interred. But we are told that there was no reviewal or visitation. There was a memorial service in Minneapolis, but many who attended probably had not laid eyes on Mr. Anderson in 20 years.

We are witness to what Mr. Anderson's life and death bear testimony to—a very remarkable change in American society. That is to say, not just how and where people live, but how and under what circumstances they die.

The elderly in America have a monopoly on death. By this I mean more than 70 percent of those persons who will die this year will be over 65 years of age. Up until the turn of the century, children had a monopoly on death. Of all deaths in 1900, 53 percent were those of children under 15 years of age. At that time less than 17 percent of the deaths were of persons over 65. They made up about 4 percent of the population. Now children under 15 represent about one-third of the population, just as they did at the turn of the century, yet they contribute less than 5 percent of the deaths.

If we relate these few demographic facts to our previous observations regarding the mobility of elderly persons and their increasing penchant for living in the sunbelt areas of the country, we can begin to see the basic outlines of the issues that confront us. The issues multiply, however, and they take different directions: some are personal and private, others relate to more social or public matters.

At the personal level, medical knowledge and technologies allow elderly persons to live longer, healthier lives, and also serve to prolong their dying. From a sociological perspective, Mr. Anderson's enhanced living conditions in Florida mean a decided loss for the Minneapolis community. On retiring 20 years ago at age 54 and leaving the community of his birth, Mr. Anderson took his talents, creativity, leadership, and all those qualities that made him a wealthy, successful business person. Those qualities were lost to the Minneapolis community which could have benefited from his participation in any number of civic activities: his church, the schools, the park board, the local government, to say nothing of the charities and philanthropies on behalf of the arts and sciences. Fort Lauderdale's gain was Minneapolis' loss.

Mr. Anderson's departure from Minneapolis is represented many times over in hundreds of cities and towns yearly throughout the northern states. The long term sociological and psychological consequences of such mobility can only be speculated upon at this time, but they are deserving of our greater attention and study.

Let us turn to some of the psychological implications associated with these sociolgical developments. More specifically, what does Mr. Anderson's death mean to his survivors? What will their reactions be, given the circumstances as we know them? What can we expect? Our understanding of grief and its symptomatology we primarily know from Lindemann's remarkable work with the survivors of the Cocoanut Grove Fire in Boston, in 1942. The symptomatology he described is familiar to all caregivers. From his research he concluded that when a person suffers the sudden unexpected loss of a loved one, profound psychological, physiological, and behavioral reactions can be expected: shock, confusion, crying, vomiting, soiling oneself, searching for the lost person, and in extreme cases, attempts to injure oneself as a result of overwhelming feelings of guilt or shame. These and other psychological reactions and behaviors are indelibly impressed upon us as being expected responses as a result of the publication of a great number of books and articles on grief that have relied on Lindemann's classic study, *The Symtomatology and Management of Acute Grief.*

I am sure that most of us, caregivers, are secure in our understanding of the loss response. We are confident that sooner or later we are going to observe the grief response in the survivors of those for whom we care. What we have to appreciate, however, is the fact that what we share is one particular experience with loss—albeit as extraordinary as it was tragic. The symptomatology of grief so painstakingly described by Lindemann is based on observations and interviews with the survivors of the Cocoanut Grove fire. The fire occurred a year after the Japanese attack on Pearl

Harbor, when over 2,200 persons lost their lives. It is important to remember that there were no studies of the survivors of Pearl Harbor. At that time no one attempted to study the grief reactions of the parents or spouses or other relatives of those who dies in that holocaust. Therefore, the Cocoanut Grove tragedy holds a meaning for us because it involved a very special group men and women in the United States in 1941. They were primarily college students celebrating homecoming and Thanksgiving weekend. For the most part they were the sons and daughters of the well-to-do. Ask yourselves what class of young men generally were enlisted in the Army or Navy before the War. What the Cocoanut Grove fire did, among other things, was bring the war home to the continental United States, to the East Coast, to Boston, to Massachussets General Hospital, and to Harvard. Before the advent of television the Fire made the distant trauma of Pearl Harbor an immediate living reality. The fire was a flash experience, similar to the Kennedy assassination and had the same impact on many of us old enough to remember it. It is indelibly imprinted on our minds. If I asked where were we on the day of President Kennedy's assassination, what were we doing, whom were we with, etc., most of us would be able to recount that day and those events without hesitation. That day is fixed in our minds. The same, I think, applies to our understanding of Lindemann's account of the grief reactions he observed. That is, there was a psychosocial impactment, an instantaneous freezing of time and emotion in one dramatic moment in our country's history. I would argue that much of what we think and believe about grief today comes from that one profound experience.

Lindemann was, however, a psychoanalytically-oriented psychiatrist. His observations were informed by Freudian perceptions of human bonding and social relationships and, like Freud, argued that grief was a time-bounded experience. That is, he believed that after a period of two years or so one would essentially be over one's grief as a result of decathexis—the giving up of the attachment to the deceased—that one would experience. He proposed that the work of mourning was basically the process of divesting oneself of the feelings and experiences associated with the intimate relationship one had had with the deceased. Implicit in this idea is the assumption that the shorter the relationship, the fewer the experiences, the less unraveling that has to be done, the quicker the work of mourning is accomplished. These ideas are basic to much of our present day thinking and research.

For instance, they are reflected in our research on widows, our attitudes toward bereavement, and implicit in the medical practice of separating a mother from her stillborn child. Let me comment on this last point. As we know from experience, a woman who has had a miscarriage or a stillbirth can, and more often than not does, experience grief. This is very hard to explain psychoanalytically. The woman has had no relationship with the unborn child, yet she grieves. Another example: the elderly woman whose husband has been dead a quarter of a century. How is it possible that she should have what we call an anniversary reaction? According to psychoanalytic theory, the grief experience should have exhausted itself over this period of time. The work of mourning should have been completed, yet she too, grieves. We do not have the space to go into a discussion of all the theoretical issues that are involved here. Nevertheless, we need to appreciate the fact that the concept of grief that we all generally accept is based upon a model we have embraced since the 1940s and that has been intrinsic to the literature since Freud.

What does the model say about our position as caregivers? It says, in effect, that we will not experience grief in the context of our ministrations, since we are not related to the patient. Think of what we do institutionally to signify who is entitled to wear the badge of griever. People who are designated as grievers are placed behind a screen or in the "family section" of a church or funeral home. They are the bereaved. All others are members of an audience and are spectators. They are participants at a ceremony, but are not perceived a grievers.

Going back to Mr. Anderson's sons who are now presumably in their 40s or 50s. The possibility is that they had not seen their father for some time. Some of them, of course, might have been in contact with him, others might not have seen him at all. They are now fathers in their own right. Their father's death occurred after many years of physical separation—a separation that could have been emotional as well as physical. Many of us caregivers have had the experience of a relative, coming into the hospital or nursing home, who has not had anything to do with his/her elderly parent for years and who has inquired about the parent's body or parent's effects in such an impersonal or business-like way that we are left with the impression that that person is experiencing no grief whatsoever. What this person may be experiencing (or may have already experienced), is anticipatory grief.

The concept of anticipatory grief is an attempt to understand the experience of grief other than that particular syndrome which can follow a death. Lindemann's description of grief is based on a postdeath reaction. Moreover, he describes a reaction to death that is both sudden and unexpected. It is the reaction of a mother who runs out of the house after hearing the screech of tires to discover her son beneath the wheels of a car. It is the reaction of a father who has just learned that his son has drowned. It is the reaction of a wife who comes home to discover that her husband has accidentally killed himself or committed suicide. Such sudden, unexpected, and unwanted death precipitates the kinds of grief reactions that Lindemann described; there seems to be little question about that. But these reactions are certainly not the same and rarely, if ever, will be observed in adult sons and daughters who have been anticipating the death of an elderly parent for five or ten years or more. Here were are considering a different kind of death and a different set of reactions than what Lindemann described four decades ago. I will refer to a study that was conducted at the Center for Death Education and Research at the University of Minnesota. The study involved almost 600 persons: widowed husbands and wives, parents who had lost children, and surviving adult children whose average age was 48 years. The findings with respect to the unexpected death of a spouse or child were in keeping with what Lindemann reported, basically. However, the reactions of adult children to their parents' deaths were very different. They did not respond in the way we would expect, nor did they do the things we would expect, if they had experienced grief in the manner described by Lindemann. In contrast to the surviving spouses or parents of our study, the adult children replied to our questions in both a controlled and rational way. For example, in response to his mother's death a son wrote: "Mother had been active in her church and respected in her community. She is now relieved of the pain of her cancer and is now with the Lord." Another son responded: "Everyone has to die. Dad was ready to go; he has lived out his round of life." Somewhat more dramatically a son stated: "My father lived and my father died, and his body for me now is just a piece of meat. I don't wish to be described as bereaved. I am not bereaved or grieved."

What confronts us here with respect to survivor's reactions to loss are entirely different responses to death than what Lindemann observed. Here I would content the anticipation of the death has allowed for the discharge of feelings prior to the death and has obviated behaviors that one would normally expect.

The respondents were studied in several different ways. We administered questionnaires and conducted home interviews. Different tests and measures were employed in an attempt to plumb the respondents' most intimate thoughts and feelings. The interviews sometimes lasted as long as three or four hours. In general, what I can report is that the surviving spouse or parent reported a symptomatology of grief that we are familiar with: that is, anxiety, anger, a sense of fear and guilt, and behaviors such as crying, insomnia, drinking and smoking more, increased distrust of people, and quarrels with relatives. Specific anger toward somebody such as a physician or funeral director was often indicated. These respondents also reported withdrawal from and avoidance of, other people. And so on. Adult children, on the other hand, showed essentially no change in their attitudes or behaviors. For the most part they reported no guilt, no anger, no change in affect, no disturbance in life pattern. There was not even a desire to change one's place of residence. One of the items of behavior we found particularly common to widows was the compelling impulse to move after the death of the husband. Interestingly, one of the things that people often do when the death of a mate occurs is move away. It is a pattern that has been observed in over 70 countries. For many of our adult children, however, the parents had already done the moving.

Permit me to describe the events surrounding my own father's death. My father had his first heart attack when he was only 52 years of age. He subsequently had more. At age 65 he contracted prostate cancer. At the time of his first heart attack, my four brothers and I came from various parts of the United States and Canada to be with our mother at his bedside. With successive heart attacks, however, telegrams or phone calls substituted for our presence. We were with out mother when our father had his first cancer operation, but not when he had his second or his third. My father died at the age of 81. Over the course of the 29 years of his dying, plans were made and remade with respect to where our mother should live, what to do with the house, what kind of funeral service should be held, where he should be buried, who the pallbearers should be, and so on. His death became a part of our family's conversation. We were forewarned of our father's death and, if I am correct in my observations, the behavior that my other family members and I evidenced at the time of his death was in keeping with the anticipatory grief that we had experienced over those intervening years.

One small incident can demonstrate my point. Our mother, my four brothers, and I were in a limousine on the way to the cemetery, immediately behind the hearse. We came to an intersection just as the light turned red. The police escort had gone through the intersection, but for some reason the hearse stopped. Our limousine did likewise. But as it would happen, we were stopped in front of our father's favorite bar. It was just 10 feet away. My mother immediately commented, "They'd better hurry up, or we'll never get this over with." One moment more and my father was going to be out of the hearse and into that bar, where he had spent the previous 29 years of his life administering his own medicine as only he knew how best to do. My mother was not an unfeeling woman. She loved my father, but the long experience of his dying, and the anticipation of his death, brought her to a state of mind different from what we would normally expect.

Another story refers to a young physician who died of cancer. He had originally experimented on himself at a medical school, ingesting radioactive fats as part of his work toward a Ph.D. dissertation on carcinogenic substances. As he was about to graduate 2½ years later, he became ill, and his cancer was subsequently diagnosed. A university medical team persuaded him to film his dying for educational purposes. They subsequently videotaped a series of interviews with him, his wife, and a psychiatrist colleague.

Over the four to five month period that the interviews were conducted, his wife's appearance changed dramatically. Initially she wore her long hair severely pulled back, dark horn-rimmed glasses, long skirts, and "sensible" shoes. By the end of the interviews she had become "vogue-like" in appearance—just the opposite of the image she had first presented to the viewer. Neither she nor the psychiatrist acknowledged this change, nor were they conscious of talking about her husband in the *past tense*. They never realized or acknowledged the mental shift that they had both experienced.

I would argue that the phenomenon of "anticipatory grief" played a very important part in the change in the wife's physical appearance, as well as in her emotional transformation. One is left to imagine how she thought of herself, or what others who knew her thought of her appearance or behavior at the time of her husband's dying—to say nothing of what he thought.

Patients also anticipate their own deaths. They are often aware of the emotional currents in an environment in which everyone is waiting for something to happen. As we stretch out the lives of dying patients we increase the likelihood of such things as I have described happening. It would appear that much of what we do, both institutionally and personally, contributes to the possibility of anticipatory grief being a part of the life of the dying elderly.

That is only half the story. The other half has to do with you, the professional caregiver, and your involvement in the lives of your dying patients. Many of you share the opinion that you are not personally involved in any way. You believe you are just practicing your professions and doing your jobs.

Research has shown that professional caregivers frequently experience grief at the loss of a patient and in many other ways react like bereaved survivors. If the traditional kinship network falters or if family members disengage from their dying relative, attending nurses and other caregivers find themselves participating in the social and emotional support of patients under their care. Such involvement, albeit at times inadvertent, brings with it a new responsibility, since it involves new emotional risks. As Dr. Mary Vachon found in her research, the stress level of critical care nurses is often as high as the stress levels of the patients for whom they care, while nurses' stress levels have been reported registering even higher than the stress levels of recent widows. Other studies have shown that in some instances health care personnel

became caught up in the patient's life. Emotional bonds were established and the health care team members found that they were the grievers when the patient died. The phenomenon of "anticipatory grief" helps turn professional caregivers into grievers, or what I have termed elsewhere "surrogate grievers."

With what result? I believe the phenomenon gives rise to the potential for role discrepancy and role reversal on the part of the caregiver and the survivor. The caregiver grieves but is not bereaved, while the bereft survivor may be beyond experiencing his or her grief. Thus, the role of the "surrogate griever" not only has the capacity for complicating the dying process, but also has the potential for casting the muted responses or misunderstood reactions of the immediate survivor into a bad light. For example, I remember an incident at Wayne State University some years ago when a group of physicians and nurses met to discuss the issue of staff "burn-out." A nurse jumped up and said with great emotion, "If family survivors can't behave more fittingly following a death, they should stay away from the hospital and from the funeral!" I would like to emphasize once again that by the time the patient dies, the staff will experience the loss more deeply than they could possibly anticipate, while a spouse or adult child, not understanding his or her lack of affect, will attempt to act out the role of host or hostess.

I do not think, however, that role reversal in and of itself adequately explains the behavior Dr. Vachon and others have observed with respect to the stress of grief of professional caregivers. We need to consider another phenomenon: the Stockholm Syndrome which refers to two bank clerks in Stockholm and their bizarre experience. I hope that the presentation of this syndrome as well as two other examples will cast new light on our subject and permit you to appreciate just how personally involved you can become in the lives of dying patients.

The Stockholm Syndrome gets its name from an incident that occurred some years ago in Stockholm. Two men, attempting to rob a bank, ended up by holding two women clerks hostage for some days in the bank's vault. Once captured, the men were found guilty of kidnapping and attempted bank robbery and were sentenced to prison. Upon their release from prison, one of the kidnappers married one of the hostages.

The distinguished psychiatrist, Robert J. Lifton, first introduced this concept some years ago at the Patty Hearst trial. As an expert witness appearing on her behalf, he proposed that she had come to identify with the Symbianese Liberation Army, due to the trauma of her kidnapping and intensity of the life-threatening experience she had undergone. I believe we need to recognize the important parallel between the victim-victimizer relationship Lifton described and the patient-caregiver bond that is sometimes established in the terminal care setting.

Some years ago in Wisconsin the son of one of its wealthiest families was kidnapped and held for ransom. He was confined to a bedroom, bound, fed irregularly, and sometimes physically abused. However, one of the kidnappers treated him with kindness, loosened his bonds on occasion, and provided him with additional portions of food. The child was eventually released and the kidnappers were subsequently apprehended. They were given long prison sentences. Upon his release many years later, the kidnapper who befriended th boy contacted his former victim. His victim was now an executive in the family's business. The kidnapper asked him for a job. His victim did better than that. He not only gave his former kidnapper a job, he made him his chauffeur and personal valet. The kidnapper remained with his former victim in that capacity for the rest of his life.

What we are observing in these several accounts is a remarkable psychological phenomenon. It occurs in extreme life and death situations where the victim identifies with the victimizer. The result is a profound emotional bonding.

I recently talked to a professor of medicine from St. Luke's College, Tokyo, who was a passenger on a Japanese airliner when it was hijacked by Japanese and North Korean terroists. Two of the seven terrorists were medical students known to him. The passengers were threatened with guns and hand grenades and the pilot was instructed to fly the pane to North Korea. The plane landed, not in North Korea as instructed, but rather in Seoul, South Korea. The authorities had hastily erected signs with North Korean slogans, in the hope that the terrorists would believe that they had arrived safely in Pyongyang. Unfortunately the ploy was discovered by the terrorists before they had allowed the passengers to disembark. For three days the passengers were prisoners on the plane while the terrorists negotiated with the South Korean authorities. Finally an agreement was reached and the passengers were released. They entered the airline terminal where the authorities and medical personnel were waiting with strechers, food, and drink. But, to everyone's surprise the passengers avoided them and instead rushed to the windows to assure themselves that the terrorists would be allowed to leave in the hijacked plane. When the plane finally left the ground

the passengers bust into applause. Dr. Hinohara, my colleague, told me that during the three days he and the other passengers were confined on the airplane, the terrorists taught them to sing the Communist Internationale, engaged the passengers in heated debate over the hijacking and other causes and concerns. That is the Stockholm Syndrome with an oriental flavor. You must realize that the phenomenon, whether experienced in the East or West, has direct and immediate implications for you as caregivers. The emotional involvement that you have with some patients in the intense life and death situation in which you occasionally find yourselves is probably much greater than you suspect. This is particularly true, given the socioemotional relationship that you may have established with a particular patient and the institutional environment in which you work. In such a situation you, the caregiver, can identify with the patient and experience grief at the time of his or her death.

I believe "burn-out" comes from such a structured situation and not from emotional weakness or from being too motherly or not characterologically strong enough to bear the conditions of caring for the terminally ill. The English hospice physician, Dr. Richard Lamerton, berated 700 American nurses at a meeting in Phoenix some years ago. He told the nurses who were expressing their distress, "If you can't stand the heat, get out of the kitchen." He was putting the blame for "burn-out" directly on the shoulders of the caregivers themselves. I think he, was, and is, wrong.

Institutionally you are caught up in a situation in which more and more elderly persons look to you for care. At the same time they are slowly divesting themselves of their familial or other relationships. You, in turn, come into the situation ready to open yourselves to them by virtue of your training. That is, you approach the patient holistically—in terms of his or her medical, social, spiritual, or psychological needs—as a person as well as a patient. On occasion you may establish a profound emotional bond with a particular patient and you may be devastated when that that patient dies.

The time may not be too far distant when signs are posted over the entrance to terminal care wards that read, "The Surgeon General of the United States has determined that the care of the terminally ill may be detrimental to your health."

Received November 15, 1986

Health Technology vs. Death: Should We Prolong the Inevitable?

"There has been a significant increase in the U.S. during the past decade of those who believe a person has the right to die, rather than linger on when no hope for health improvement is in sight."

William E. Phipps

Dr. Phipps is professor of religion and philosophy, Davis & Elkins College, Elkins, W. Va.

"THERE is a time to be born and a time to die; / A time to plant and a time to uproot. . . . '' Those words of an ancient Israelite poet have articulated the feelings of many people throughout history that there is an appropriate, as well as an inappropriate, time for dying. Death is appreciated when it comes at the time we would choose if we knew what the options were.

Until this century, untimely death nearly always meant premature death. In the course of history, many humans have not survived long enough to reproduce. The highest death rate was in the first few years of infancy. We are still aware of premature dying when we read of vehicular fatalities, because the percentage of the young who are killed in those accidents is much higher than the old. Humans continue to be outraged on receiving prognoses that they, or their friends, probably will die before or during the prime of life.

Untimely death now also refers to another kind of tragedy. Deaths are now increasingly likely to be *postmature*, to coin a word. Seventy percent of deaths in the U.S. are among persons over 65 years old. This fact is both a cause for celebration and for concern. Millions continue to function vivaciously long after they would have died in an earlier era. Yet, there are others whose human functioning has deteriorated irreversibly, even though they are officially alive. Consider the following two examples of postmature death.

A patient in an advanced stage of cancer had his stomach removed. It then was found that the malignancy had spread further. The patient, a retired physician, fully understood his condition. His pain was constant, despite the continual administration of drugs. While in the hospital, another operation was performed to remove a clot from a lung. The patient then asked members of the hospital staff to allow him to die peacefully should another crisis arise. To make sure everyone understood his feelings, he wrote a note to that effect and had it placed in his case file. However, two weeks later, he had a heart attack and was resuscitated. The hospital team rushed to revive him four more times that same day. A battery of machines was used feverishly to sustain his life. His frequent heart stoppages damaged his mind, so he no longer could respond in a human way. The patient lingered on for three more weeks, kept "alive" by intravenous feeding and blood transfusions. Violent vomiting and convulsions displayed his intense suffering. At last, the hospital technicians were unable to revive him, despite an aggressive effort, when his heart stopped again.

Or, consider the case of a 75-year-old man who had arthritis in his joints and emphysema in his lungs. After he collapsed one day, a rescue squad activated his heart by an injection of adrenaline. However, most of his brain cells had been destroyed from oxygen deprivation even before the squad "saved his life." The comatose body was placed on a hospital respirator. Once it was connected, the law did not permit disconnecting it until the patient's electroencephalogram recorded a completely "flat" reading. The attending physician told the family that, despite some brain stem activity, there was little possibility of their father regaining any pulmonary or mental functioning. She pointed out that most patients in a similar condition die within a few days, but that some continue to live for years. "Your father is another Karen Ann Quinlan," she commented, "except that she was a young woman when she collapsed, and your father is an old man." He lived for another month attached to a respirator. His daughter described the situation in this way: "My handsome, energetic father, a man who always took great pride in his appearance, lay on a hospital bed paralyzed from the neck down. There were tubes running in and tubes running out. His nostrils were taped back and open. . . . For the elderly who are totally incapacitated, there comes a time to call it quits. . . . There was nothing uglier than the fashion in which my decent father was forced to die."

Thousands lie in American hospitals in a comatose condition. For many of these, it can be diagnosed reliably that their loss of consciousness is permanent. Their worn-out bodies may be ventilated artificially when no real hope of human life remains. Other comatose patients may be in essentially the same condition, except that the involuntary portion of their brains are functioning enough to facilitate natural breathing.

Why are postmature deaths becoming more common? Medical, economic, and theological factors need to be considered to answer this question adequately.

Resuscitation techniques continually are being refined and used to revive patients who will have many productive years ahead. Careless use of such procedures results, as we have seen, in making it impossible to die at the proper time. Electric shock treatment, for example, is sometimes like jump-starting a worn-out engine, enabling it to quiver and sputter on a little further. Some physicians feel guilty of patient neglect or have anxiety over malpractice suits if they do not try out every way of continuing some form of life. Robert Fraser's paraphrase of a famous psalm conveys what can happen when ultimate value is placed on medical technology: "Medical science is my shepherd; I shall not want. . . . It leadeth me beside the marvels of technology. . . . It maintains me in a persistent vegetative state for its namesake. Yea, though I walk through the valley of the shadow of death, I shall find no end to life. . . . Thy respirator and heart machine, they sustain me. Thou preparest intravenous feeding for me in the presence of irreversible disability. . . . Surely coma and unconsciousness shall follow me all the days of my continued breathing; and I will dwell in the intensive-care unit forever."

Postmature death is also prominent in the the American culture because of massive public and private health care funding. Hospitals are tempted to continue treating hopeless patients in their beds because they know that thousands of dollars daily can be billed to the government, to private insurance companies, and/or to affluent pa-

tients. Although monetary motivation would not likely be admitted, the ability to pay causes physicians to prolong respiration and metabolism beyond the point at which it has meaning. Nations which do not have the wealth to spend billions of dollars on cardiopulmonary devices are confronted less with the postmature death syndrome.

Theological considerations also impact postmature death. Religious people long have affirmed that only God has the right to terminate life. Some of them further believe that a definite number of years and days are assigned to individuals by God, so it would be wrong to make decisions which would shorten the maximum number of days in a person's life. By the same logic, however, widely approved measures for extending life also can be viewed as "playing God." Scientific medicine and hygiene greatly have prolonged life beyond the average span of earlier centuries, and who would claim that such developments are wrong? It may be unwise to think of God as directly in the death business, dictating a time and place. In contrast to fate, can it not be presumed that God works through the human and the scientific? Decision-making by humans on length of life can be viewed as one way by which the divine intervenes in human life.

Curtailing postmature death

There are several ways of curtailing postmature death. Mercy killing is an effective, but an illegal and generally detested, means. During 1985, there was a great deal of national publicity pertaining to 73-year-old Emily Gilbert, who was killed

by her husband because he could not bear to see her suffer from a combination of Alzheimer's disease and an agonizing bone illness. Roswell Gilbert's action brought him a murder conviction and imprisonment in Florida.

Suicide is another generally unaccepted solution to postmature death. Eighty-year-old Elizabeth Van Dusen described the syndrome in this way: "There are many helpless old people who without modern medical care would have died, and we feel God would have allowed them to die when their time had come. Nowadays it is difficult to die." These words were part of the suicide pact statement she wrote before she and her husband swallowed overdoses of sleeping pills. Elizabeth and Pitney Van Dusen were unwilling to tolerate any longer her debilitating illness and his total incapacitation by a stroke five years earlier. Pitney vomited up the pills and did not die until weeks later.

In contrast to these two types of active euthanasia, there are some generally approved ways of allowing persons to die. Persons who are mentally competent have the right to refuse medication, even though they recognize that such action will hasten death. In 1976, 71-year-old Abe Perlmutter was stricken with the incurable "Lou Gehrig's disease." After his chest muscles deteriorated, he was unable to breathe naturally. Having decided that life was no longer worth living, he became the first person in the U.S. to win a suit to have a respirator removed. A Florida court ruled that Perlmutter could exercise his constitutional right of privacy and could not be required to inflict "never-ending

Recently there has been an increase in those who believe that a person has a right to die. The alternative of using technology to prolong life unnecessarily has become unacceptable.

physical torture on his body until the inevitable—but artificially-suspended—moment of death.'' Shortly after Perlmutter disconnected the tube pumping oxygen to his lungs, he expired from natural causes.

When Pope John Paul II addressed himself to problems raised by medical technology, he must have had in mind cases similar to those of Abe Perlmutter. His "Declaration on Euthanasia'' states: "When inevitable death is imminent in spite of the means used, it is permitted in conscience to take the decision to refuse forms of treatment that would only secure a precarious and burdensome prolongation of life.'' Included in the 1980 declaration is this clarification: "Such refusal is not the equivalent of suicide; on the contrary, it should be considered as an acceptance of the human condition, or a wish to avoid the application of a medical procedure disproportionate to the results . . . or a desire not to impose excessive expense on the family or the community.''

Terminal patients sometimes lack the competence for making a decision on whether life continues to be worth living. Even if they are conscious and are able to communicate rationally, they lack the energy to take the initiative to see that their will is respected. In anticipation of such situations, the "Living Will" has been developed to enable persons to write down while thinking clearly what they would like to have done if their physicians foresee no hope of recovery. The key paragraph of the document states: "If at such a time the situation should arise in which there is no reasonable expectation of my recovery from extreme physical or mental disability, I direct that I be allowed to die and not be kept alive by medications, artificial means or 'heroic measures.' I do, however, ask that medication be mercifully administered to me to alleviate suffering even though this may shorten my remaining life.'' Many states have approved right-to-die legislation which adds societal sanction to expressions of individual conviction in the Living Will or in similar declarations. Physicians generally support such declarations, which millions have now signed, because they enable them to know more fully terminal patients' wishes as to extent of extraordinary treatment. Also, having in hand patients' statements pertaining to terminal situations reduces doctors' malpractice fears when they turn off life-prolonging machines after judging the chances of recovery to be nil. The newsletter of Concern for Dying occasionally tells of cases where the Living Will, which that organization distributes, has assisted in curbing postmature death. It has served to lessen the ordeal that many patients and their families undergo in situations of irreversible deterioration.

Awareness now is growing that death can be a friend to the elderly. There has been a significant increase in the U.S. during the past decade of those who believe a person has the right to die, rather than linger on when no hope for health improvement is in sight. Separate recent Gallup and Harris polls indicated that four out of five Americans favor withholding life-support systems from competent or incompetent terminally ill patients, if that is what they want or would want. Although most people assume that death is generally a bad thing, exposure to terminal patients often brings understanding of specific situations where it is futile to prolong respiration. If the conscious mind can no longer function, the body should be released from its trauma by passively allowing it to die in some dignity.

Euthanasia: The Time Is Now

Gerald A. Larue

Gerald Larue is President Emeritus of the National Hemlock Society, and is Emeritus Professor of Religion and Adjunct Professor of Gerontology at the University of Southern California.

The phone rings. The caller is a professor in Canada. Her mother is in the hospital, in extreme pain and slowly dying of cancer. Medications cause grogginess or put her to sleep, but even in her drugged state she experiences pain. She begs her daughter to help her die, to relieve the suffering, to take away the pain. Even as the daughter talks with me from the hospital room the mother is moaning in her sleep. I ask what the prognosis is. There is no cure. The pain will continue and become more severe as the cancer continues to invade vital organs. It is estimated that there will be two or three weeks of suffering before the exhausted, cancer-ridden woman will die. What can the daughter do?

I note the details, record phone numbers—the daughter's home, the hospital room. I have no magic prescription. I tell the daughter to talk to the doctor and then call me back.

Two days pass. I am haunted by the call, by the pain in the professor's voice, by feelings of my own helplessness. I dial the hospital room. The daughter answers. "Oh, I am so glad you phoned. I have just given my mother the lethal injection." I am stunned. What happened? "I did what you told me. I talked to the doctor. Today he came down the hall and put a syringe in my hand and told me he never wanted to talk to me again about this matter." I ask what is happening now. "My mother and I said goodbye. I gave her the injection. She is sleeping now and seems to be without pain. She has that wonderful little smile that I love. It is the first time I've seen it in weeks."

We meet a year later when she is in Los Angeles. What are her feelings now? "I feel wonderful. My mother's death was peaceful. The suffering stopped. We said how much we loved each other. She thanked me for what I was about to do. I gave her the injection and shortly afterward she died. I feel that I acted in love." But is there any guilt? "None at all. I feel proud of what I did. I stopped her agony. She wanted to die and I fulfilled her wishes. There is no guilt."

I have heard stories like this over and over again. Never have there been any feelings of guilt or of betrayal of trust or of having unnecessarily killed someone. In each instance, the act of assisting death has been described as a final statement of love.

I *have* encountered guilt in those whose loved one died in agony, begging for death, and the friend or relative or lover did nothing to end the suffering. A rugged, elderly Norwegian said, "He was my best friend. He asked me to help him. He died in agony and I did nothing to help him die. I have carried that burden ever since." A man in Arizona, in pained reminiscence, said, "She cried and moaned in the morning, she cried and moaned at noon and during the night. She begged me to help her die. She died crying and moaning. I can hear her cries still. I feel that I failed my wife when she needed me most."

The phone rings. The call is from an East Coast man I met at a humanist conference nearly twenty years ago. He has AIDS and before the disease wastes his body and strength to the point where he becomes helpless and unable to act, he wants to stockpile medication and die by his own hand. I cannot recommend medication. I refer him to the book *Let Me Die Before I Wake,* by Derek Humphry.[1] He asks about euthanasia in Holland and I tell him of the magnificent work of Pieter Admiraal, but warn him that Dr. Admiraal helps only his own patients. I probably will not hear from him again.

His call reminds me of a young man who had had throat cancer. It was in remission when he talked to my Death and Dying class at the University of Southern California. Then, some eight months later, he phoned. He wanted to say goodbye. His voice was weak and hoarse. The cancer had returned and there was no cure. He owned a small, isolated cabin. He was inviting his closest friends (I was not one) to visit with him, one or two at a time, to make their farewells. He died a short time later by his own hand. He was in control of his own death. He determined the moment and the mode of his death. He was in charge. He had time to make closure with those who mattered most to him and even with some, like me, who were more distant friends. He died with dignity.

There are others who did not die with dignity. Max Ferber, who wrote the moving piece, "I Cried, but Not for Irma,"[2] told my class that he watched his wife die in a hospital with tubes attached to almost every orifice of her body. She was comatose because of her medications. As he looked at this woman whom he loved and to whom he had been married

Reprinted from *Free Inquiry,* Winter 1988/89, pp. 4-6, by permission.

for nearly fifty years, he felt anger at the indignity of her death. He wept, not because she was dead, but because of the manner of her dying. She was receiving the best medical treatment, but her case was hopeless and the treatment simply prolonged her dying.

Max's anger drove him to actively support the California Natural Death Act, which gives individuals the right to deny "heroic treatment" by signing a living will. This document enables healthy persons to make known their wishes that heroic measures not be taken to prolong their lives should they become incompetent during a terminal illness.

I recall the young man I met at a Right to Die Conference at Oxford. He was a quadraplegic, confined to a motorized wheelchair that he maneuvered with amazing skill. He hated his life. It had no quality. He wanted to die, but nobody would help him. He once attempted to steer his chair over a cliff, but someone intervened. After I returned to America, I read about his death. He had purchased a considerable quantity of gasoline and spread it throughout the small cottage he owned. He then managed to ignite it and was cremated alive. What a horrible way to die! How much more dignified and merciful his death would have been if a compassionate medical friend had been able to provide a lethal injection.

Notions about the sanctity of life have meaning and significance only when we are healthy and life is under our control. The sanctity concept is reinforced by religious dogma and social abhorrence of killing except in extenuating circumstances, such as during wartime or in self-defense. To violate such generally accepted norms is to come under judgment from religion, from society, and most of all from the law. We are told that "God gives life and only God should take life." In nontheological language this means that "nature produces life, nature terminates." Life and death are natural facets of existence on planet earth. When this naturalistic concept is theologized, the caring dimensions of our common humanity are set aside. We are informed that it is legally right and just, and theologically and sociologically proper, to prolong the life of a terminally ill person who is in intractable pain. The doors of mercy and compassion are closed and legalistic thinking is in charge.

To challenge these beliefs is not to sanction suicide or murder. It is clear that the depression and despair that prompts normally healthy individuals to suicide can be dealt with psychologically; likewise, killing another for a selfish reason such as anger cannot be justified. But euthanasia is something quite different and must be separated from suicide and murder in the eyes of society.

The wonderful progress of modern medical science has given us longer lives, medications to fight disease and control illness, and engineering that can cleanse kidneys, maintain heart and lung functions, and so on. Our trained medical practitioners are committed to sustaining life through the fullest use of such technology, but there are times when this commitment can become a burden to the patient, to the family, to the hospital, and to modest bank accounts. When the illness is terminal and the patient is in intractable pain and has expressed the wish to die with dignity, the time has come when the medical doctor should be allowed to respond to the request for death. This act is not murder, it is voluntary euthanasia—providing a good death, a dignified death. Similarly, when such a patient is able to end his life without assistance, the result should not be classified as suicide.

The word euthanasia means a good death, a beneficial death, a dignified death. It signifies the termination of life when the quality of life as defined by the patient has degenerated to the point of meaninglessness, when the illness has reached a stage beyond the help of any physician or medicine, when the pain has become unremitting and the palliatives are inadequate and ineffective. At that point the afflicted person should have a choice: to continue to live in

In each instance, the act of assisting death has been described as a final statement of love. I have encountered guilt [only] in those whose loved one died in agony, begging for death, and the friend or relative or lover did nothing to end the suffering.

pain or to die and end the suffering. Because many terminally ill persons have been reduced to helplessness by their disease, they need aid in dying. The time has come when the aid-in-dying should be as readily available as a palliative when the patient requests it.

A properly signed and witnessed living will justifies legally, morally and, in most instances, theologically, the removal of life-support equipment when a life that would otherwise end is being sustained artificially by machines. This form of euthanasia, popularly known as "passive" euthanasia, is widely practiced throughout the world. Nevertheless, there have been cases, like that of Karen Ann Quinlan, when the heart continued to beat and the lungs continued to function after the machinery was removed. In such cases, if the patient has made the proper request, a lethal injection should be legally available, lending moral and perhaps theological support.

Of course, some physicians may refuse to participate in euthanasia, and some hospitals may refuse the right to practice euthanasia. The objections rest on religious, moral, and ethical interpretations, and decisions based on them deserve respect. The patient and his family can find physicians and hospitals willing to cooperate. Indeed, the wise patient and family will check with both the physician and the hospital to be sure that the patient's wishes will be honored.

On the other hand, there is good evidence that some doctors currently do give assistance in dying. There are those who, like Dr. Meyers in Scotland, Dr. Admiraal in Holland, and Dr. Christiaan Bernard, formerly of South Africa, have made no secret of their participation in acts of active euthanasia. In addition, polls taken in France, California, and Australia have demonstrated that physicians are willing to admit to the practice of voluntary active euthanasia, as long as their identities are not revealed.[3]

In public, medical doctors generally maintain that they are opposed to euthanasia. Off the record, however, some will admit that on numerous occasions they have administered huge overdoses of morphine to terminally ill patients for "pain control," knowing full well that the dosage is lethal and the patient will die. They protect themselves from potential lawsuits or murder charges by using vague medical language to justify their actions; they do not practice euthanasia, they practice pain control. But in so doing they often bring about the patient's death.

> **Notions about the sanctity of life have meaning and significance only when we are healthy and life is under our control. [But] the doors of mercy and compassion are closed when legalistic thinking is in charge.**

At present, though most religious organizations oppose voluntary active euthanasia, they support "passive" euthanasia[4] based on the belief that by removing life-sustaining machines, the physicians are not actively doing anything to bring on death, but are merely removing an impediment to natural death. This argument is obviously specious, for in the act of removing the machinery, death is engendered. There is fundamentally no difference between so-called passive euthanasia and active euthanasia where lethal medication causes death.

Humanist groups and Unitarian Universalists openly support active euthanasia. When I have talked with clergy belonging to denominations that oppose euthanasia, I have encountered some church leaders who are well acquainted with the indignities and agony of terminal disease. They have witnessed death without dignity among their parishioners and in their own families. But until their denomination takes a stand, they will maintain silence about their private beliefs.

The time has come to release medical personnel and hospitals from the fear of legal prosecution for practicing euthanasia with patients who are terminally ill and who truly wish to die. It is possible to provide protective legislation against abuse. It is important that families and caring nonmedical persons be relieved of the burden of employing secretive ways to assist those they love who suffer terminal illness to die with dignity.

One might argue against the young man in England who died in his self-made holocaust, but, horrible as his death was, he was in charge, he made the decision. It was not a good death, but there was nobody to help him to achieve that end. Of course, not all quadriplegics want to die. I have met many who, despite their limitations, are living wonderfully fulfilling, happy, and constructive lives. One world-class gymnast suffered a fall that left him quadraplegic. He controls his motorized chair by blowing into small tubes mounted near his face. He is now a sportscaster and a consultant to a firm that designs equipment for the handicapped. He exudes enthusiasm about life and has no desire to die.

But we are not all the same. I believe that if I were to become helplessly bedbound, limited in action and in the ability to perform for myself, I would want to have the right to choose for myself whether to continue to live. And should I, in my helpless state, decide not to live, I should like to have a caring physician administer a poison that would permit me to die quietly and with dignity. I should not like to have a nonmedical friend provide the lethal medication; there are just too many instances of bungled help. Furthermore, should I be terminally ill and in intractable pain, and should my continuing existence be a matter of only a few weeks, I should like to be able to bid farewell to those I love. To know that I am in control of my death would provide peace of mind even in the midst of pain. To be able to tell those who matter most to me how much I love them, to clear up any misunderstandings, to decide about the distribution of small possessions (my will takes care of other matters) would place me in control of my being and my life right up to the last moment.

Not everyone would choose euthanasia. There are those who would prefer to fight for life in the midst of pain up to their last breath. This is their right. But we should all have the power to choose. The time has come for the legalization of voluntary medical euthanasia for the terminally ill.

Doctors Polled on Life Support

Nearly eighty percent of American physicians favor withdrawing life-support systems from "hopelessly ill" or irreversibly comatose patients if the patients or their families request it, according to a survey conducted by the American Medical Association.

The physicians were selected at random from the association's files of active doctors, including members and nonmembers and physicians of various ages and both sexes.

The doctors were asked: "Would you favor or oppose withdrawing life support systems, including food and water, from hopelessly ill or irreversibly comatose patients if they or their families request it?" Fifty-eight percent answered "favor strongly," twenty percent answered "favor," five percent answered "oppose," ten percent answered "oppose strongly," and seven percent answered "unsure." Sixty-seven percent of the doctors said they had been directly involved in such cases.

Fifty-four percent said they were uncertain of the legal risks and responsibilities, while forty-three percent said they were certain. Ninety percent said doctors should initiate discussions with patients or families, while 7 percent said they should not.

Notes

1. Derek Humphry, *Let Me Die Before I Wake,* Los Angeles: Hemlock/Grove, 1986.

2. Max Ferber, "I Cried, but not for Irma," *Readers Digest,* April 1976.

3. *November 1987 Survey of California Physicians Regarding Voluntary Euthanasia for the Terminally Ill,* Los Angeles: The National Hemlock Society, 1988. See also Helga Kuhse and Peter Singer, "Doctors' Practices and Attitudes Regarding Voluntary Euthanasia," *The Medical Journal of Australia,* Vol. 148, 1988, pp. 623-627; and "5 French Doctors Aided in Deaths of Ill," *International Herald Tribune,* September 30, 1984.

4. Larue, Gerald A., *Euthanasia and Religion,* Los Angeles: Hemlock, 1985.

In Defense of the Humane and Dignified Death Act

Robert L. Risley

Robert L. Risley is an attorney and a partner in the law corporation of Risley and White in Los Angeles. He is president of Americans Against Human Suffering.

Americans Against Human Suffering (AAHS), a nonprofit corporation, was established in 1986 for the purpose of changing state laws to permit physician aid-in-dying for the terminally ill. The organization has developed the Humane and Dignified Death Act Initiative, which it hopes to qualify in the 1990 general elections in California, Oregon, Florida, and Washington.

The proposed act permits an adult the right to request and receive a physician's aid in dying under carefully defined circumstances. It enlarges upon the California Natural Death Act and the Durable Power of Attorney for Health Care Decisions Act. Under these statutes, an adult can declare that he does not wish to be kept alive artificially by life-support systems, and can provide in advance for the appointment of an attorney-in-fact or proxy decision-maker who can determine when life supports should be withheld or withdrawn if the patient becomes incompetent.

In addition to combining the two older laws and establishing the patient's right to a physician's aid, the initiative also protects and immunizes physicians and health-care workers from liability for carrying out a patient's wishes. To take advantage of this law, a competent adult must sign a Humane and Dignified Death Act Directive in the presence of two disinterested witnesses.

Before signing the directive, the patient must inform his family and indicate that he has considered their opinion, though the patient still retains the right of final decision as long as he is competent. The directive is good for seven years, but can be extended if the seven-year period ends while the patient is incompetent.

Several conditions must be met before a physician may legally comply with a patient's directive. First, the HDDA directive must have been properly signed by a competent adult and properly witnessed. Second, it may not have been revoked. Third, the action must be taken within the seven-year period allowed. Fourth, two licensed physicians must certify to a reasonable medical certainty that the patient is terminal and that death is likely to occur within six months. Fifth, if the patient becomes incompetent after that certification, and the final decision is made by his agent, the decision must be reviewed by a three-person ethics committee.

The initiative protects physicians and other health-care workers acting under a physician's instructions from civil, criminal, and administrative liability. It requires hospitals and other health-care providers to keep records and to confidentially report certain information to the state health department. It also provides a means of limiting physicians' fees for professional activities related to complying with patients' directives.

The law specifically forbids aid-in-dying to any patient solely because he is a burden to anyone else. It does not change the law that makes aiding, abetting, advising, or counseling suicide a crime. It does not permit aid-in-dying to be performed by loved ones, friends, or strangers, and does not apply to children or to pregnant women. Indeed, it does not affect anyone who has not voluntarily and intentionally completed and signed a properly witnessed directive according to the law.

Following are twelve objections to the Humane and Dignified Death Act. The first nine are objections to the basic concept of physician aid-in-dying and voluntary active euthanasia, and the last three are specific technical objections to the law as written.

1. The law would be abused.

The principal objection to a law permitting physician aid-

Reprinted from *Free Inquiry,* Winter 1988/89, pp. 11-15, by permission.

in-dying is that it may be abused; that is, a patient's life may be ended without his consent, for malicious—not merciful—reasons.

The abuse of any law is always a possibility, and the HDDA is no different. However, law enforcement and the criminal-justice system exist so that we may identify, apprehend, and punish those who break the law. The HDDA has built-in protection from abuse: Only licensed physicians are permitted to give aid-in-dying to the terminally ill patient who requests it. Merciful euthanasia performed by friends or loved ones will remain illegal. Society in general—particularly the weak and the elderly, who are most vulnerable—is protected because licensed physicians are not likely to abuse the law, as they work under numerous constraints. Physicians are supervised by state licensing authorities and practice under a well-recognized code of ethics. Also, they are partially controlled by peer pressure from colleagues, by hospital staff and administration guidelines, by the desire to protect their reputations, and by conscience and the law in general. Moreover, a physician's economic interests generally run counter to his desire to fulfill aid-in-dying. It is axiomatic that since most physicians get paid for treating patients, the longer the patient lives, the longer the treatments will continue, and the longer the physician will get paid. If purely mercenary considerations were involved, the physician would wish to keep the patient alive as long as possible. The physician would comply with a patient's directive to withhold or withdraw life-support measures or to give aid-in-dying out of compassion for the patient, as many physicians do today quietly and illegally at great risk to themselves. Under the HDDA, physicians could legally assist dying patients who request help with the training, skill, and license that laymen do not possess. In complying with patients' requests out of compassion, the physicians must conform strictly to the terms of the proposed act.

Ordinarily, the physician has no reason to abuse the system. However, for those who may be tempted to do so, the initiative provides an additional constraint: a limitation of fees that may be charged for complying with any part of the directive.

Moreover, permitting physicians to actively help patients to die upon request may be safer for society as a whole than is the present practice of passive euthanasia. Active euthanasia requires that the physician confront the act head-on because it is such an open deed. The morality of the act must be faced squarely since no one who is asked to help another to die will be indifferent to the request. Physicians in Holland who have helped patients to die on request say that it is always a very emotional act, whereas passive euthanasia allows the physician a certain lack of responsibility. When life-support systems are removed, the physician claims that he is simply letting nature take its course, or that it is now "in God's hands" and not his responsibility. The physician who decides to provide the help knows precisely what he is doing. He is not simply pulling a plug, walking from the room, and handing the responsibility to nature or God. He is deciding to help a fellow human being to ease out of this life, knowing full well the measure of his responsibility.

Some opponents say that irresponsible physicians will be able to sweep away their mistakes and dispose of incriminating evidence if physician aid-in-dying is legally permitted for the terminally ill.

Our response to this is simple. Regrettably, mistakes are made by everyone—including doctors. We see evidence of this in the numerous medical malpractice suits being brought to court throughout the country. But we find no evidence of physician abuse of living-will statutes, where physicians routinely remove life-support systems on the patient's prior written request. The living-will statutes contain specific constraints that guard against physician abuse—the Humane and Dignified Death Act contains similar constraints. Physicians have the opportunity to hide their mistakes under present law, but none of the opponents of HDDA claim that that is happening. Moreover, the medical profession is well aware of the risks presently associated with the removal of life-support systems. In any case, if misconduct is suspected, it must be investigated and those found guilty must be prosecuted by the appropriate authorities.

In one celebrated case in California, two doctors who removed life-support systems were charged with murder. They were exonerated by the appellate court, which found that the physicians were simply following the patient's previously expressed wishes and his family's instructions.

If a doctor ends a life on his own initiative or at his own discretion, without having been requested by the patient to do so, he has committed murder. But physicians do not simply murder their patients.

Some opponents claim that affirmatively ending life is an abuse of nature. But if active euthanasia is an abuse of nature because it involves our determining the time that death will occur, then we are also abusing nature in a similar way when we engage in passive euthanasia. In both cases, we choose death in preference to prolonging life—either by administering a lethal substance or by discontinuing life-sustaining treatment. Why is it an abuse of nature to determine the time of our own death when nature has given us autonomy, the ability to choose? Is it not precisely this ability that gives us special value and dignity as human beings? Is that not equally a part of human nature?

2. Diagnoses and prognoses may be erroneous.

Critics point out that physicians are fallible human beings like the rest of us, and may be mistaken in their diagnoses or prognoses. They say that sometimes doctors tell patients they only have a few months to live and the patients continue living for years.

The Humane and Dignified Death Act anticipates this problem and requires a second opinion. The initiative specifically requires that *two* licensed physicians agree that the patient is terminal; even then, the statute recognizes that two physicians may be mistaken as well.

In practice, physicians know end-stage disease when it exists. They know, for instance, that when a cancer is coursing through the body with massive metastatic processes at work, it is only a matter of days, weeks, or months. Physicians also know when treatment options have been exhausted. They should, and most do, inform patients and their families when this occurs. If there is any question about their opinion they inform their patient of that as well. Moreover, they should inform their patient of any new "medical breakthrough" that may yet save his life. Armed with this information, the patient can decide whether to continue to endure the pain and indignity a while longer, or request assistance in dying at the time and place of his own choosing and in the manner he sees fit.

Specifically in relation to the HDDA, many claim that a physician's prognosis is always imprecise and that it is impossible for any physician to determine with any degree of precision whether a person will die within six months. But the directive specifically states:

> I recognize that a physician's judgment is not always certain, and that medical science continues to make progress in extending life, but in spite of these facts, I nevertheless wish aid-in-dying rather than letting my terminal condition take its natural course.

3. The right to die will become a duty to die.

Opponents claim that if we are given the legal right to decide the time, place, and manner of our own death, many people will be psychologically pressured by family, friends, the government, health-care providers, social workers, or other terminally ill patients to exercise that right against their will.

However, the will to live is enormously strong, too strong to give way to the suggestions of others. The dying person may lovingly consider his survivors' well-being. But it is more likely that the pain, indignities, and loss of control resulting from the dying process will be the motivation for requesting help in dying. Self-interest will prevail, though it may involve great loving concern. Psychologically, it is not likely that a third person's malevolent suggestion will motivate the patient to make the request.

The right to die becoming a duty to die is a concern only in the abstract. If a greedy relative wants his dying loved one out of the way sooner, he will have to convince a treating physician that the dying person's life should be ended for reasons not involving the terminal illness but for other, malicious reasons. The principal check on this kind of abuse is obviously the presence of a doctor.

If pressure is applied to patients to end their lives, those persons pressuring their dying relative, friend, or ward should be prosecuted for aiding, abetting, and advocating a suicide, which is now a crime in every state in the union. Encouraging a suicide will remain a crime after the Humane and Dignified Death Act is passed.

4. The patient/physician relationship will be weakened.

Opponents claim that if physicians are given the right to end their patients' lives when the patients request it, patients will lose trust in their doctors. Some critics have even suggested that people in rest homes will be afraid to drink their tea for fear that it is poisoned.

This claim is farfetched, but deserves attention. We must be vigilant and careful of the interests of the weakest and most susceptible members of society. We must give them the love and treatment they deserve. We must constantly guard against any abuses of their rights as human beings.

A doctor who could gently relieve the suffering of his dying patient but refuses to do so because it is illegal does not generate confidence in either the patient or his family. Honesty and the knowledge that the physician will relieve the patient of the horrible suffering associated with a terminal illness when requested will in fact strengthen the patient/physician relationship and create greater confidence in the physician.

Today, despite the fact that abetting a suicide is a felony, compassionate and caring doctors, at risk to themselves, surreptitiously help their patients with end-stage disease to die. They do this in the name of pain control. However, they are well advised not to discuss this with other health-care professionals or with their patients, as several recent prosecutions have demonstrated. Aside from the risks involved for compassionate physicians, the real question becomes one of patient autonomy: "Whose life is it, anyway?" The answer is clear.

Simply saving life and prolonging it for years is an improper goal of medicine. The question for medicine today should be whether the patient is better off after the treatment than before. We traditionally value length of life, but we must now learn to focus on the *quality* of life instead; and the true goal of medicine should be to improve the quality of life. Patients understand this better than doctors; seldom are they obsessed with surviving at all costs, and they often become less concerned with it as their illnesses become more severe. Most American doctors feel compelled to treat those they can neither save nor comfort. It seems paradoxical that in a nation where doctors may through abortion end what could be a productive life, they are charged with murder for ending a life where hope no longer exists.

5. Physicians should not be executioners.

Our more strident opponents say that doctors should not kill their patients. They should not be executioners. Get someone else to do this dirty job, they say.

The merciful ending of suffering at life's end upon a patient's request is not killing. Killing implies ending the life of someone who does not want to die. The man on the gallows, in the electric chair, or in the gas chamber usually wants to live; the person who ends the condemned criminal's life is an executioner. But abiding by a terminally ill patient's own request for release from the agonies of the final days of the natural dying process simply is not killing in the ordinary sense of the word. It is an act of mercy. The disease or the trauma is the killer, not the gracious human being who helps the patient out of his final agony. To suggest that this humane act of a physician makes him an executioner is to misuse terms.

Physicians have the knowledge necessary to help us the way we sometimes want and need help at life's end. The merciful application of their knowledge upon request is appropriate, as physicians are often with us at life's end anyway: Eighty percent of Americans today die in some kind of health-care facility under a doctor's control and management. Physicians are licensed and have access to the needed drugs. Therefore, because of the doctor's knowledge, license, and proximity and because merciful release on request is not killing, physicians are the appropriate helping agents.

6. A new law is unnecessary.

Opponents claim that it is possible to control the pain associated with terminal illness in ninety-five percent of the cases; all that is needed is to teach doctors not to worry about making addicts of dying people. If physicians would only learn to administer enough morphine or other narcotics, patients would never suffer.

On the contrary, in many cases the pain of terminal illness cannot be controlled. Even if it were true that pain could be lessened for ninety-five percent of the patients, the other five percent deserve consideration.

Furthermore, many of those patients who are not in a great deal of pain nonetheless do not wish to live the final days, weeks, or months of their lives in a zombielike stupor with nearly no cognition remaining and little control over most aspects of their lives. They may not be able to control bodily and/or mental functions, perceptions, and responses. Those terminal persons who are not in great pain and agony should have the right to make their own decisions about their own lives. They should not be compelled to be dependent on others for every menial function; for most people it is important to retain personal dignity and self-control. They should have the freedom to choose when death is imminent and treatment options have been exhausted.

7. Physicians who administer aid-in-dying will violate the Hippocratic oath.

The full text of the Hippocratic oath reads:

> I swear by Apollo the physician, by Aesculapius, Hygeia, and Panacea, and I take to witness all the gods, all the goddesses, to keep according to my ability and my judgment the following oath:
> To consider dear to me as my parents him who taught me this art; to live in common with him and if necessary to share my goods with him; to look upon his children as my own brothers, to teach them this art if they so desire without fee or written promise; to impart to my sons and the sons of the master who taught me and the disciples who have enrolled themselves and have agreed to the rules of the profession, but to these alone, the precepts and the instruction. I will prescribe regimen for the good of my patients according

> to my ability and my judgment and never do harm to anyone. To please no one will I prescribe a deadly drug, nor give advice which may cause his death. Nor will I give a woman a pessary to procure abortion. But I will preserve the purity of my life and my art. I will not cut for stone, even for patients in whom the disease is manifest; I will leave this operation to be performed by practitioners. In every house where I come I will enter only for the good of my patients, keeping myself far from all intentional ill-doing and all seduction, and especially from the pleasures of love with women or with men, be they free or slaves. All that may come to my knowledge in the exercise of my profession or outside of my profession or in daily commerce with men, which ought not to be spread abroad, I will keep secret and will never reveal. If I keep this oath faithfully, may I enjoy my life and practice my art, respected by all men and in all times; but if I swerve from it or violate it, may the reverse be my lot.

Few, if any, physicians today believe in the Greek gods, much less swear by them. To many Catholic, Protestant, and Jewish physicians, taking such an oath would be anathema. Many doctors have never taken the oath; it is not routinely administered by medical schools or by state licensing authorities. It is recited at some graduation ceremonies and is studied by medical students only as a part of medical history and tradition.

Nevertheless, the oath has served as a reminder to those who practice the healing arts of their high obligation to patients and their corresponding duty to sublimate their own good and passion for the concern of patients. The essential provision of the oath is: "I will prescribe regimen for the good of my patients according to my ability and my judgment and will never do harm to anyone."

The oath has not remained inviolate and sacrosanct throughout the years. One of its prescriptions provides: "Nor will I give a woman a pessary to procure abortion"; yet most physicians in this country now agree with freedom of choice for pregnant women. The medical profession has not blindly followed the dictates of the oath, but applied common sense and modern understanding in a way that sometimes violates the oath's literal terms.

If Hippocrates were alive today and could see the extent of medical technology, the pumps, tubes, syringes, dialysis machines, respirators, and endless numbers of drugs that exist, controlling nearly every life function, he would probably word his oath differently. The oath is more than two thousand years old, and following its terms literally surely is not required, particularly when many physicians do not actually swear to it in the manner prescribed.

8. Legalizing physician aid-in-dying is the first step on a slippery slope.

Critics suggest that once society accepts physician aid-in-dying for the terminally ill, there is no rational way to limit voluntary active euthanasia and prevent its abuse; once voluntary euthanasia is legalized, it will lead to involuntary euthanasia and society will seek to kill those of its members who are a burden to others.

But the slope is not slippery, because the distinction is clear. It is a matter of rightfully ending one's own life with a physician's assistance, as opposed to wrongfully ending someone else's life for whatever reason. The laws in our society make the distinctions every day. Men and women of ordinary conscience make them every day as well. There is no slippery slope; it is but a step in the right direction.

9. We may become like Nazi Germany if we adopt the Humane and Dignified Death Act.

It has been suggested that we run the risk of becoming a violent and uncaring nation if we adopt the Humane and Dignified Death Act. Opponents claim that euthanasia was permitted in Nazi Germany and escalated into mass genocide.

Answering this criticism is hardly necessary because it is apparent that America is not Nazi Germany and Americans are not Nazis. This is not to say that we should be complacent or that we should allow our government to violate basic human rights. If a government, a family member, or a health-care provider arbitrarily decides that someone must die, it is murder, and the perpetrator must be prosecuted.

Under the Humane and Dignified Death Act, the decision is an individual action made by an autonomous person about his own life and no one else's. Freedom to choose the time and place of your own death is a part of the inalienable right of self-determination.

10. The Humane and Dignified Death Act is not limited to persons in intractable pain.

The criticism is unjustified that the initiative is not restricted to persons in intractable pain and arguably should be. Most dying people wish to end their lives because of the indignities of the dying process and because of their loss of control; not because of intractable pain. Terminally ill people who are unable to control any of their bodily functions, who cannot move their limbs, are unable to talk, and are totally dependent upon others for every element of their existence should have the same rights as those who are in intractable pain. Their self-determination is of overriding importance.

11. The law is not limited to cases where all treatment options have been exhausted.

This objection is based on doubletalk. The Humane and Dignity Death Act is limited to people suffering from a terminal condition, which is defined as "an incurable condition which would, in the opinion of two certifying physicians exercising reasonable medical judgment, produce death" within six months, "when the application of life-sustaining procedures would serve only to postpone the moment of death of the patient."

If the condition is incurable, surely there can be no treatment option available, and conversely, if there were treatment options, surely the condition would be curable. Moreover, the law requires that two physicians declare the patient to be terminal before he can legally receive aid in dying.

However, the HDDA does not contemplate precise prognosis; it requires only that the physician determine with reasonable medical judgment that death will occur within a six-month period. This is certainly well within most physicians' prognostic abilities. Indeed, most physicians agree that they can determine when death is imminent within a time span much narrower than that delineated in the HDDA. Moreover, the possibility that a physician may make a mistake must be assumed by the patient.

12. Surrogate decision-making is inappropriate.

Some criticize the Humane and Dignified Death Act's durable-power-of-attorney-for-health-care provision, which permits the patient to designate an attorney-in-fact or surrogate decision-maker to act in his stead. These critics assert that the provision is too risky because the dying person might change his mind while incompetent or might have changed his mind while competent but failed to notify anyone of that change. They maintain that the request for aid in dying should be limited only to those persons who can have a face-to-face conversation with their physician.

Thousands of people would be excluded from the operation of the act if the surrogate decision-maker concept were eliminated from its provisions.

Alzheimer's victims and others who become incompetent after signing a directive would not have their wishes carried out, since the condition for its activation—that is, concurrence of two licensed physicians that the patient is terminal—would not occur until after the patient had become incompetent. At that time, a face-to-face patient/physician conversation would be neither meaningful nor legally binding. Since cases of Alzheimer's disease are increasing throughout the country at an enormous rate, the provision for a surrogate decision-maker seems appropriate. Moreover, the statute provides for revocation by several means and there is the added safeguard of review by an ethics committee when a decision is made by an attorney-in-fact.

Summary

Although Americans Against Human Suffering continues to receive formal opposition from the California Medical Association, California medicine is a house divided on this issue. In the May 1988 issue of *Physician,* published by the Los Angeles County Medical Association, a survey of members indicated that forty percent of the physician respondents favored the initiative, and forty-two percent favor active euthanasia. This survey is supported by the National Hemlock Society's California Physician's survey made in November 1987, which indicated that nearly two-thirds of the physician respondents believed the law should be changed to allow doctors to take active steps to bring about a patient's death under some circumstances. Fifty-one percent of those surveyed indicated they would practice active voluntary euthanasia if it were legal. On May 8, 1988, the *Los Angeles Times* reported on a survey conducted by the San Francisco Medical Society of its members: Of the 750 physicians who participated, seventy percent supported making voluntary euthanasia legally

available to patients. Forty-five percent said they would carry out the request for euthanasia from patients.

Though the Catholic church and a few Protestant denominations, as well as the Jewish hierarchy, are officially opposed to legislation such as the HDDA, the Unitarian church and the Humanist Society support the initiative. Furthermore, surveys indicate that as much as two-thirds of the American public, including those who identify themselves as religious, favor active voluntary euthanasia.

Though it still has a long way to go, AAHS has come a long way in the fight for the right of self-determination for the terminally ill. Achievement of this goal is inevitable.

A Theoretical Reassessment of the Applicability of Kübler-Ross's Stages of Dying

Joan Retsinas
Brown University

This paper analyzes the applicability of Kübler-Ross's stages of dying (denial, anger, bargaining, depression, acceptance) to the dying experiences of elderly patients, who present the most commonly encountered cases of death for family physicians.

As of 1980, 58 percent of medical schools included a course on death and dying[1] and the standard curriculum generally focuses on Kübler-Ross's stages.[2] Indeed, the stages are so ingrained into the consciousness of most medical students that they can recite them, from denial to anger to bargaining to depression to acceptance. Psychologists regard Kübler-Ross's stages critically, recognizing that they are not necessarily a valid description of the process of dying; but physicians have accepted them as almost axiomatic. Although physicians recognize that all people may not pass neatly from stage to stage, but may vacillate back and forth, or may bypass a stage or stages, the stages remain the central reference point in medical discussions of dying.

Although not empirically tested, Kübler-Ross's benchmark work influences the majority of researchers, who, like Kübler-Ross, focus on untimely death. Kübler-Ross's theory sprang from her work with 200 cancer patients. Largely middle-aged, they confronted a capricious fate that sentenced them to leave families and careers before they had finished developing the relationships and doing the tasks that they had planned. Similarly, many of the current studies focus on middle-aged people who must reconcile their expectations of a normal lifespan against the reality of a shortened one. Such deaths are unexpected, bitter interruptions to individuals' life plans, and, to the extent that those patients confront the same capriciousness that Kübler-Ross's patients confronted, they probably do experience some mixture of bargaining, anger, denial, depression, and acceptance.

As for physicians' training in treating the dying patient, again the literature has generally focused on helping physicians "bear the news"[3] to people who very likely will be surprised by the news—in short, to people who will die untimely deaths, often from a specific disease such as cancer.

The purpose of this essay is not to question the validity of the model of untimely death as a learning tool for physicians. Kübler-Ross's stages have passed into the popular lexicon of death in part because intuitively the stages make sense to middle-aged readers who recognize themselves in the study subjects. Since physicians, furthermore, are charged with announcing the futility of medicine and, concurrently, their patients' impending death, physicians need to

The author gratefully acknowledges the insights offered by Thomas Scaramella, M.D., Department of Family Medicine.

From *Death Studies*, Vol. 12, 1988, pp. 207-216. Copyright © 1988, Hemisphere Publishing Corporation. Reprinted by permission.

understand the psychological orientations and reactions of those patients. The purpose is to suggest that such a model is not generally applicable. For the vast majority of people who die, not in middle age, but in senescence, the expected-stage model is inapplicable. Over 20 percent of people aged 65 or more die in nursing homes;[4] over 20 percent of people aged 85 or older live in nursing homes. Statistically, more people are living longer than ever before in this country; but they are living with an array of chronic, debilitative, degenerative diseases that has made aging itself into a kind of dying. And since family physicians care for these dying patients, family medicine must put forth a new model, one more attuned to the reality of death for the majority of their patients. For the individual patient, dying is not simply a physical cessation of life, but a sociological experience. The norms, values, and customs of the larger society mediate and make sense of the dying experience; so that any understanding of death must encompass that larger sociological perspective.

Toward a Model of Death in Elderly Patients

A heuristic model of dying for the elderly must encompass several factors. First, unlike the middle-aged cancer patients in Kübler-Ross's study, very old people see themselves in relation to a "reference group" that is also confronting senescence and, with senescence, an impending death. Middle-aged people will be leaving behind friends; people in nursing homes may have no friends yet living, or if they do, those friends may themselves be in nursing homes. When two gerontologists, Tobin and Lieberman,[5] sought to assess the well-being of people in nursing homes against the well-being of residents' friends in the community, they could not marshall a sufficient sample of community-based friends to complete the study. The majority of nursing home residents are widowed, some twice. The joke about the elderly woman who checks the obituary columns every morning to see whether she is there has some credence. Very old people, especially people living in nursing homes, see their counterparts dying steadily; indeed, the isolation and loneliness of the person who has outlived all the people whom he or she loved and was loved by is grim. However biologically intact, that person has experienced what Sudnow[6] called a "social death." As Simone de Beauvoir[7] suggested, death for the aged is less feared because life may no longer hold interest.

Second, although researchers discuss a "dying trajectory" marked by the initial news of the terminal illness and the actual death, elderly people have no such clearly marked trajectory. A middle-aged person may well have one defined illness that will be the ultimate cause of death—usually, cancer—yet the list of illnesses of an octogenarian is generally longer. In-deed, the list lengthens even as the person grows older. Blindness, deafness, strokes, diabetes, arthritis—the incidence of each increases with age. Elderly people are used to the "sick role" and are used to making accommodations in their lifestyles so that they remain active. The jogger becomes a walker; the woman foregoes needlepoint for crocheting; the couple moves to a barrier-free housing development; naps become routine. The failure of the body does not begin with the discovery of an encroaching disease, one foreign to the body, to be battled by the immune system, but comes instead as an almost inevitable gradual diminution of vitality. The trajectory begins with middle age itself. Although an autopsy may pinpoint one "cause of death," the elderly person coping with insulin, a pacemaker, memory loss, and a pharmacopeia of medications has confronted the frailty of his or her body.

The fact that middle-aged people do not recognize this ineluctable trajectory toward death reflects not only an exaltation of youthfulness in our society, but a masking of aging. Jeremey Taylor,[8] chaplain to Charles I of England, noted the obvious signs our body gives us that it is failing:

> Baldness is but a dressing to our funerals, the proper ornament of mourning and of a person entered very far into the regions and possession of death: and we have many more of the same signification: grey hairs, rotten teeth, dim eyes, trembling joints, short breath, stiff limbs, wrinkled skin, short memory, decayed appetite.

Today we still have those signs; yet we have learned to mask them not only from others, but also from ourselves. Wigs, hair dyes, dental caps, contact lenses, pacemakers, facelifts, hip replacements—all help us to compensate for, yet not truly forestall, the aging of our bodies.

The obvious retort is that the equation of aging as dying marks a needlessly gloomy stance, that many old people live healthy, vibrant lives until a specific disease signals the beginning of their trajectory. Unfortunately, however, we may have overestimated the numbers of healthy vibrant elderly people, perhaps because we ourselves want to envision a disease-free senescence. Certainly our historical images of forceful elderly people suggest a vitality untroubled by diseases; yet, as the historian David Fischer notes, those images may be myths. Taking opium to relieve gout, Benjamin Franklin wrote, "For my own personal ease I should have died years ago, but though those years have been spent in excruciating pain, I am pleased that I have lived them."[9] Franklin forcefully states his pleasure in life, as well as the pain. If we overlook the long trajectory from middle age to death, we do not necessarily negate it. Like Franklin, very old people may relish their days; but they are unlikely to escape the signals of bodily deterioration.

Third, aging itself involves a series of role definitions. As stated, illness forces a redefinition of role, especially if medical intervention cannot enable the individual to overcome the illness. Patients who used to dance or garden or climb mountains before illness are legion. Society, however, also forces a redefinition of role upon the individual. For many people, forced retirement signals their obsolescence insomuch as society has pronounced them no longer productive. Retired people can and do contribute meaningfully to society; but in a capitalist society that values productivity, this nonwage labor is construed as less meaningful. Rosow,[10] a sociologist, calls retirement in the United States a "normless" state where people confront society's nonexpectations for them. Even a woman accustomed to social roles as wife and homemaker may feel redundant if she no longer has people to cook for, to clean for, to preside over. Housing exemplifies this shifting of functions, as the couple moves from a house, where they filled caregiver roles for dependent children and/or dependent parents, to an apartment, often in an elderly housing complex, where they have no caregiving responsibilities and few caretaking ones (an apartment is touted as a place "easier to take care of"), finally to a child's home or an institutional one if they themselves require caregiver attention. A theory of "social disengagement" suggests that people withdraw from social life as they age, corresponding to declining health.[11] Although elderly people may not withdraw to the extent suggested by the theory, and that withdrawal may itself be spurred by social forces more than illness, the reality remains that the social world of the individual changes with age; and those changes are often harsh, unwelcome, and recognized as undesirable.

In contrast, the middle-aged person has experienced no such wrenching role redefinitions. She or he generally is fully occupied, either in an employed position in the work force or with a full load of domestic family responsibilities. The person can easily define his place in the social structure: parent, lawyer, artist, pianist, gardener. The news of a terminal illness will force the patient to confront the loss of his or her social niche, the negation of a social identity. In short, cancer may make the middle-aged patient stop practicing law, while the octogenarian has usually left his or her legal practice long before, in response to an array of social and personal forces.

Indeed, a major worry for dying middle-aged patients focuses on the people whose lives will be affected—not just emotionally, but concretely—by the impending death. To some extent healthy non-aged people serve as hubs of domestic and career wheels. The breadwinner, the nurturing parent, the caregiving child, the executive, the physician, the organist—all have people who depend upon their continued vitality. Socially, illness marks the inability of that hub individual to perform all the tasks expected of him or her. Death will leave a social vacuum, and survivors will need to regroup to compensate.

Fourth, while death of a middle-aged person is untimely, death of a very old person may truly be timely. Humans are not spared the cycle of birth-growth-death of all other living beings. To cite Ecclesiastes, "to everything there is a season . . . a time to live, a time to die." If bodily deterioration marks a person's "time," then perhaps very old people psychologically recognize, not their impending death, but, rather, the timeliness of that death. Studies have suggested that fear of death declines with age.[12] Ironically, the medicalization of death may mark a societal denial of death,[13-15] and physicians may be less willing to accept death than patients. Often physicians shy away from conversations with dying patients, preferring to shift the subject to pain management or to treatment of specific symptoms. A physician may even define a patient's mention of being "ready for death" as a mark of defeatism, or a mark of depression[16]—an expected depression, in light of Kübler-Ross's stages. Instead, the readiness to die may mark an honest acceptance of participation in nature's cycle. Medical technology, improved sanitation, and better nutrition have lengthened life expectancy: people born today are more likely to live to old age than their grandparents; yet the life span itself has not changed.

Elderly Death: A Trajectory of Acceptance

Death is not the same as dying. Most people fear the disability and dependency inherent in dying, but do not truly fear death;[17, 18] and, for elderly people, aging itself forces them the losses associated with dying. One psychologist[19] has enumerated 10 fears of dying. A very old person, especially one who has lived in a nursing home, has confronted the first eight fears. She or he is lonely as friends have gone to nursing homes or themselves died; has mourned loved ones; has grown dependent on others for daily care; has experienced sorrow, disability, pain; and, if she or he has entered a nursing home, has experienced some loss of identity in the transition to "resident" status. Finally, the patient who has lost lucidity may have begun to regress.

If death marks an end to life, it also marks an end to the process of dying; and elderly patients' acceptance of death may grow stronger as they await an end to pain, to sorrow, to social isolation, to dependency, to days devoid of meaningful or creative activity. The very process of dying may condition the individual to accept death.

Summary

Kübler-Ross's cancer patients greeted news of their impending death with denial; elderly people who suffer from painful, chronic, debilitating illnesses are not likely to deny the deterioration of their bodies. Similarly, a middle-aged cancer patient can justifiably react with anger: if he or she has lived a decent life, why must he or she now desert the people who love and depend upon him or her? Why must he or she die before having parented children, climbed a mountain, travelled to exotic lands, fallen in love—in short, experienced the joys as well as the pain inherent in living? The question Why me? haunts the patient. The three fates purportedly snipping lifelines are not just, and the middle-aged patient may understandably rail against that injustice. The very old person, especially the person in pain, is not so likely to be angry. Indeed, he or she is more likely to react angrily to the isolation, the loss of control, and the dependence that may have characterized old age. As for bargaining, the middle-aged person may well bargain with God for more time. The elderly person recognizes that more time will not necessarily offer joy, tranquility, a chance to rebuild troubled relationships, an opportunity to accomplish one more pressing task. Especially in a nursing home, the elderly person lives in a kind of timeless routine dominated by staff ministrations on/for his or her body ("bed and body work").[20] Admittedly, very old people, like younger people, may suffer from what seems depression; but, on closer analysis, that withdrawn state may not mark depression as much as a natural "regression." Ironically, acceptance, the stage that many middle-aged patients never reach, is not so elusive for the elderly patient.

For the elderly person, death is an event not unexpected. Perhaps middle-aged patients confronted with an unexpected announcement of a terminal illness react with anger, denial, bargaining, depression, and acceptance—although social scientists have questioned the validity of that schema.[21] For elderly people, however, those stages are not salient. Social and psychological theory suggest that the elderly may be more cognizant of what Shakespeare dubbed a "necessary end" than their medical caregivers. Allen Kellehear,[22] a social scientist, links theories of patient denial to the influence of medical personnel, who construe death as a disease to be conquered.

> Behavior related to the aversion of death and then the subsequent interpretation of this behavior in relation to their patients may be related to medical behavior and medical attitudes to death. In psychiatric terms, the long-standing view of the dying as denying may in fact be a projection of denial by medical people. In sociological terms, the medical myth may not be in accordance with patient reality.

Physicians are trained to treat disease, to help patients overcome disability. In an era when people died of infectious diseases, that training forestalled death. In an era when people live well into old age and die from chronic, debilitating diseases, the physician no longer is forestalling death, but with elaborate technology simply prolonging the process of dying. Kübler-Ross's stages suggest a frightened, confused angry person, involved with family, career, and friends, suffering from a specific "killer" disease that medicine has not yet cured. The elderly person does not fit that model, and the physician should not expect that patient to experience a series of stages that include anger, denial, bargaining, and depression.

NOTES

1. Dickinson, G. E. (1981). Death education in United States medical schools 1975–1980. *Journal of Medical Education, 56,* 111–114.
2. Kübler-Ross, E. (1969). *On death and dying.* New York: Macmillan.
3. Radovsky, S. Bearing the news. *New England Journal of Medicine, 313,* 586–588.
4. Ingram, D. K., & Barry, J. R. (1977). National statistics on deaths in nursing homes: Interpretation and implications. *The Gerontologist, 17,* 303–308.
5. Tobin, S., & Lieberman, M. (1976). *The last home of the aged.* San Francisco: Jossey-Bass.
6. Sudnow, D. (1967). *Passing on: The social organization of death.* Englewood Cliffs, NJ: Prentice-Hall.
7. de Beauvoir, S. (1972). *The coming of age.* (P. O'Brian, Trans.). New York: Putnam.
8. Taylor, J. (1615). *Holy dying* (1819 ed.). London, pp. 4–5. Cited in R. Kastenbaum (1977), *Death, society and human experience* (p. 155). St. Louis, MO: C. V. Mosby.
9. Fischer, D. (1977). *Growing old in America: The Bland-Lee lectures delivered at Clark University.* New York: Oxford University Press, p. 67.
10. Rosow, I. (1967). *Social integration of the aged.* New York: Free Press.
11. Cumming, E., & Henry, W. E. (1961). *Growing old: The process of disengagement.* New York: Basic Books.
12. Smith, D. K., Nehemkis, A. M., & Charter, R. A. (1983–1984). Fear of death, death attitudes and religious conviction in the terminally ill. *International Journal of Psychiatry in Medicine, 13,* 221–232.
13. Aries, P. (1975). The reversal of death: Changes in attitudes toward death in western societies. In D. E. Stanndard (Ed.), *Death in America.* Philadelphia: University of Pennsylvania Press.
14. Becker, E. (1973). *The denial of death.* New York: Collier-Macmillan.
15. Illich, I. (1976). *Limits to medicine.* New York: Penguin.
16. Maguire, P. (1985). Barriers to psychological care of the dying. *British Medical Journal, 291,* 1711–1713.
17. Feifel, H. (1959). Attitudes to death in some normal and mentally ill populations. In H. Feifel (Ed.), *The meaning of death* (pp. 114–129). New York: McGraw-Hill.
18. Matthews, S. (1976). Old women and identity maintenance: Outwitting the grim reaper. In L. H. Lofland (Ed.), *Toward a sociology of death and dying* (pp. 105–114). Beverly Hills, CA: Sage.
19. Rando, T. A. (1984). *Grief, dying and death: Clinical interventions for caregivers.* Champaign, IL: Research Press.
20. Gubrium, J. (1975). *Living and dying at Murray Manor.* New York: St. Martin's.
21. Kastenbaum, R. J. (1977). *Death, society and human experience.* St. Louis, MO: C. V. Mosby, pp. 210–213.
22. Kellehear, A. (1984). Are we a death-denying society? A sociological review. *Social Science and Medicine, 18,* 713–723.

Received May 28, 1987

Living Environments in Later Life

Unit 4 noted that old age is often a period of shrinking life space. This concept is crucial to an understanding of the living environments of older Americans. When older people retire, they may find that they travel less frequently and over shorter distances, because they no longer work, and most neighborhoods have stores, gas stations, and churches in close proximity. As the retirement years roll by, older people may feel less in control of their environments due to a decline in their hearing and vision, as well as other health problems. As the aging process continues, the elderly are likely to restrict their mobility to the areas where they feel most secure. This usually means an increasing amount of time spent at home. It has been estimated that individuals 65 and over spend 80 to 90 percent of their lives in their home environments. Of all other age groups, only small children are as house- and neighborhood-bound.

The house, neighborhood, and community environments are, therefore, more crucial to the elderly than to any other adult age group. The interaction with others that they experience within their homes and neighborhoods can be either stimulating or foreboding, pleasant or threatening. Across the country, older Americans find themselves living in a variety of circumstances, ranging from desirable to undesirable.

Approximately 70 percent of the elderly live in a family setting, usually a husband-wife household; 20 percent live alone or with non-relatives; and the rest live in institutions such as nursing homes. Although only about 5 percent of the elderly will live in nursing homes at any one time, a total of 25 percent of persons 65 and over will spend some time in a nursing home. The longer one lives, the more likely he or she is eventually to live in a total care institution. Since most older Americans would prefer to live independently in their own homes for as long as possible, their relocation—to other houses, apartments, or nursing homes—is often accompanied by considerable trauma and unrest. The fact that the aged are less mobile and more neighborhood-bound than any other adult age group makes their living environment crucial to their sense of well-being.

Articles in this section focus on some of the alternatives available to the aged: institutionalization, the provision of adequate health care, and the dynamics of family care. In "Options for Aging" the author examines the care alternatives that need to be considered for the elderly. Adequate health care for the elderly, minorities, and the poor is not good. In "Access to Health Care in a Black Urban Elderly Population" the author examines the success or failure of the public health policies for these groups. Traditionally the family was the main support for elderly relatives, but the family's capacity to provide care has been eroded by economic pressures. In "Aging, Generational Continuity, and Filial Support" the author emphasizes that public policy in the United States must recognize the limitations of the family as the sole caregiver for older persons. The following article, "Family Caregivers: America's Primary Long-Term Care Resource," argues the point that home care by the family will necessarily increase because it is less costly than hospital or nursing home care.

Looking Ahead: Challenge Questions

As medical technology increases the life expectancy of the average American, will it be more or less common for people to spend some of their later years living in a nursing home? What are some positive and negative aspects of nursing home life?

As both the number and the percentage of older Americans in the population increase, will neighborhoods become more age-segregated?

What new kinds of living arrangements will become more usual for older Americans in the future?

Is relocating sick or feeble older persons a threat to their health and survival?

Options for Aging

Andrea Boroff Eagan

Andrea Boroff Eagan is president of the National Writers Union and a free-lance writer specializing in health and medicine.

*When the elderly are
our own parents, the question
of care strikes close to home*

ILLUSTRATIONS: DAVID JOHNSON

I N MY FAMILY," a friend of mine comments, "no one talks about what we'll do when my folks get too old to take care of themselves." My friend thinks his family is unusual in the lengths they go to avoid this nasty subject. The fact, however, is that the family who faces up to the inevitable future before a crisis forces the issue is the one that's truly unusual.

Belonging to a generation that for the most part reproduced late, many of us fear being financially responsible for aging parents and young children at the same time. Women who have just resumed careers, men in midlife crises, families with adolescent children who are having problems—none feel ready to assume responsibility for the old. Because of the increasing restrictions on Medicare payments, old people are being discharged from the hospital long before they can care for themselves and care at home is rarely covered. Eventually, most of us will be forced to cope with such grim realities, ready or not.

In my family, we never used to talk about these things either. For years the general, if unspoken, assumption on my husband's side seemed to be that my father-in-law was the frailer

of his parents and the likelier to have the first serious problem. And so the shock was doubled when it was my mother-in-law who had a disabling stroke one night. Modern medicine pulled her through, to an extent. The rest of us learned a lot, and fast, about the limitations of modern medicine and, worse, about the limitations in services and coverage of services for the elderly in this country.

If we think about our parents' insurance, we probably comfort ourselves with the existence of Medicare. Medicare covered my mother-in-law's stay in the hospital and in a rehabilitation hospital after that. A few weeks in a nursing home were also covered, but only because she was there for a limited time for convalescence. She hated the nursing home and didn't want to stay anyway. So, she came home. For a few months a speech therapist and a physical therapist visited regularly, and a homemaker came for a few hours a day to help out. But soon Medicare was used up.

Today my mother-in-law is still at home. She is in a wheelchair. She needs help to dress herself, to bathe, to

go to the bathroom. Her speech is frequently garbled; she often can't remember the word she wants. My father-in-law, once considered the less strong of the two is now eighty-seven and cares for her almost entirely alone. A homemaker–health aide comes in four hours a day, five days a week. She bathes my mother-in-law, helps her dress. She does some cooking and cleaning. She is paid from their own funds. Once relatively comfortable financially, they are no longer so: the home aide costs more than $10,000 a year. Over five years, that can put quite a dent in your savings.

Nonetheless, my in-laws are extremely fortunate. They can afford some help; my father-in-law is still able to drive in daylight, so he can shop and run errands while the health aide is there; he hasn't gotten sick himself. So, again, we avoid thinking about the situation too much and hope, in violation of all reason, that nothing will change.

Something *will* change, of course, and the change will likely be for the worse. My father-in-law might become too weak to continue

caring for his wife twenty hours a day. Or he could become seriously ill or disabled. Any of these eventualities leaves us—his two sons and me—with a crisis for which we need to be prepared.

The widespread belief that the old in our country are abandoned by their children is, happy to say, a myth. The truth is that families generally remain close: Studies compiled by the National Institute on Aging show that 80 percent of the elderly see a close family member every week. While 75 percent of those over 65 are in independent living situations, another 18 percent live with their adult children; only 5 percent are in nursing homes. But of those over 85 (the fastest-growing group within the population), 23 percent are in nursing homes. Families expend tremendous effort to keep their older relatives out of nursing homes. The old don't want to end their lives there; their children don't want to face the guilt of "putting Mama in a home." A recent survey of the Travelers Companies, a Connecticut-based insurance company, found that 28 percent of the sampled employees aged thirty or over were taking care of elderly relatives, spending an average of more than ten (and sometimes up to eighty) hours a week providing companionship, transportation, household help, and financial management.

This article first appeared in the April 1986 issue of *New Age Journal*, pp. 54-59.

On Their Own but Not Alone

THE NUMBER and quality of services for the elderly varies widely from one locality to another, with the greatest problems existing usually in sparsely populated rural areas. Still, for those who think the alternatives for aging parents are moving in with their children or going to a nursing home, the services available to the elderly who want to maintain their independence can come as a real surprise.

● **Community services.** In most areas agencies on the aging (there are more than 650 of these nationwide, established under the Older Americans Act) can provide at least a list of services available locally. Religious agencies and community-service societies in some places will arrange and coordinate services for families who live too far away or for some other reason can't take on the tasks themselves. Local senior centers have lists of available agencies, group activities, and services.

Most people, as they age, want to remain in their homes, and some communities provide a great variety of services to enable the aging to do just that. A health aide can help a frail or partly disabled person with housework, bathing or dressing, cooking, and shopping. Depending on the particular community, there may be escort services so that someone can go shopping after her eyesight has become too limited to permit her to drive safely; check-in services that call older people daily and visit them immediately if they don't answer the phone; meals-on-wheels and friendly visitors for the housebound. Some communities offer Lifeline services —a button that a person in the house can push to

Our parents' old age is a difficult subject to contemplate. Psychologically, their aging involves their mortality and our own, our own aging and the role reversal that may accompany our having to assume some measure of responsibility for them. Financially and socially, our society does not provide well for the comfort and dignity of the old. But knowledge and planning—planning that takes into account everyone and everything involved—makes the inevitable easier to face. For example, now that my family has had some time to think about my in-laws, we know we could provide extended home care for my mother-in-law should my father-in-law have to be hospitalized. Without planning, families are likely to be rushed into putting an older parent into a nursing home when illness or senility sets in without considering what she wants or what is available.

summon help in an emergency.

All this costs, however. Home health aides are hired through private or voluntary agencies. Their fees range from $4–$10 per hour, depending on what they do and where you live. Thus, a medium-priced aide, twenty hours a week, could cost as much as $8,000 per year. This cost is usually *not* covered by Medicare or insurance, except possibly for a short time after discharge from a hospital. Other services may be available on a sliding scale; a few communities provide some services free.

• **Geriatric-care managers.** A growing specialty is that of geriatric-care managers (GMCs). Increasingly, these are private individuals, usually but not always social workers, who arrange and coordinate services. Their initial home evaluation (which may be all you want) usually costs about $150 and tells you what your parent needs, what is available, and what it will cost. Their fees can run as high as $400–$500 per month, which does not include the cost of services they arrange.

Some GCMs offer to oversee a client's financial affairs or be appointed conservators of the elderly person's estate. Just as you would want to know a lawyer well before entrusting her with your mother's or father's finances, you should investigate a GCM's credentials carefully—especially since this specialty at this point is unlicensed and unregulated.

Other questions about GCMs have to do with confidentiality: Can the older person's privacy and confidentiality be assured when someone else is paying the GCM? Who has the power to make decisions? Suppose your mother hates the housekeeper who's been hired or becomes severely depressed the moment she enters the

nursing home chosen for her? How do you determine the GCM's competence, reliability, compassion? Some adult children who can afford them feel GCMs give them more control than they would have over a voluntary agency, and they certainly offer reassurance to distant children who want to ensure that a parent is properly cared for. The reality is probably as variable as the individuals involved, and until this specialty comes under some form of regulation (which GCMs themselves are urging), the buyer can only beware.

• **Respite care.** In the Traveler Companies study, 30 percent of those who were caring for their relatives had not had a vacation from their caregiving duties for more than a year. In some communities respite care is available, though it is not covered by Medicare. When no other family member can come in to take responsibility for the older person and let the regular caregiver have a week's vacation, or even an occasional night out, a local agency will provide someone to come and take over. A few nursing homes have a number of beds set aside for short-term admissions, as

well, but they are not covered by Medicare.

Options for living

BETWEEN a private home and a nursing home, there is a wide range of living arrangements for the older person.

• **Retirement communities,** of course, are concentrated in warmer climates, but there are many in the North as well. More to the point, for the family thinking about their parents' future, are facilities in which the residents are independent, but have access to emergency and nursing care, should they become necessary.

Most retirement communities offer private housing in houses or apartments with common grounds, recreational facilities, and sometimes housekeeping services. The housing unit is usually purchased, and a monthly fee covers other services. A retirement community is intended for the healthy, though some have extensive volunteer programs offering partial home care, transportation, and other services to those who can no longer be completely independent.

• **Life-care facilities** also

generally require those moving in to be in good health. An entrance fee (which can be as high as $100,000) and a monthly maintenance fee are charged. Meals and housekeeping services are usually provided. If the resident becomes ill, medical and nursing care are provided, and some life-care facilities have built-in nursing homes. Some offer unlimited nursing care to residents; others set a limit. A contract, which you should read carefully and probably have reviewed by an attorney, is signed before moving in.

• **House sharing** in some areas is arranged by local agencies. A private house, which may be too big for the older person living alone, is shared with someone else—another elderly person, a student, or a single mother with a child. Needless to say, the success of these arrangements varies with the personalities and flexibility of those involved.

• **Group homes** are basically communes for the old. They are usually sponsored by voluntary or religious agencies, who provide various services—including shopping and cooking, laundry and financial management—to the residents. Residents pay the sponsoring agency. Each resident has a private bedroom and shares the rest of the house. The National Shared Housing Resource Center helps sponsor local match-up and group-residence programs and provides information for a small fee about existing shared-housing options across the nation.

• **Low-cost, government-subsidized housing** for the elderly is available in some communities. Apartments are usually built with the needs of the elderly in mind, with wide doorways and ramps and often good security systems. No services are provided, as a rule, but Meals on Wheels and other local agencies often pay special attention to these housing clusters.

• **Foster care** for the elderly, in which a family shops, cooks, and cares for an elderly person with the help of government subsidies, is not widely available. It can provide a family atmosphere for the person who needs supervision, but who is, in the main, capable of taking care of himself.

When Your Parent Moves in with You

HAVING AN older parent in your home is never without stress, says Mirca Liberti, cofounder of a Pennsylvania-based organization called Children of Aging Parents (CAPS), who has counseled many three-generation families. A study conducted at the University of Michigan School of Nursing found the caregiving child was depressed and angry much more often than the parent. In the Travelers Corporation study, "80 percent of the caregivers said that caring for the elderly had interfered with other family responsibilities and with their social and emotional needs."

A nationwide network of support groups has grown up in the past few years, providing a crucial service for families who are responsible for elderly relatives. These groups provide emotional support in a nonjudgmental setting, as well as information on available services in particular communities. A list of these groups is available through Children of Aging Parents (see "Resources"). Support groups and family therapists can also help resolve old conflicts that seem, inevitably, to arise when families are aging and to help the adult child torn between

---

A Model—but the Only One of Its Kind

In Columbus. Ohio, a unique program rehabilitates people (of all ages) who are being discharged from the hospital and who would ordinarily be sent to nursing homes. William Conway, medical director of the Center for Independent Living, believes that *half* of those people sent to nursing homes can be rehabilitated sufficiently to be able to go back to their community. He points out that the effects of illness, medication, isolation, fear, and depression likely to afflict the older person who is hospitalized can cause them to appear severely disoriented and incapable of caring for themselves. Candidates for the center undergo a careful evaluation before admission to determine that they really can be rehabilitated.

The center has a model store, bank, driving simulator, kitchen, and specially equipped bathroom where patients are retrained for independent life. Patients practice shopping and cooking, housekeeping and entertaining, driving, caring for themselves, and reading or writing if necessary. They also learn to use computers, which they may use for banking and shopping, as well as for communication, and to manage equipment such as lift chairs and walkers.

As a rehabilitation facility, the center's services are generally covered under Medicare. But the center is, unfortunately, the only one in the country. Until it is replicated elsewhere, some patients will continue to travel to Columbus from around the United States to restore their chance for independent living, and many, many more will be institutionalized unnecessarily.

—A.B.E.

---

responsibility to an older parent and his or her own spouse and children.

Take Sarah P., for instance. Her parents were killed in an accident a few years ago. Sarah's maternal grandmother had been living with them, and Sarah felt that she had no choice but to invite her grandmother, then eighty-six, to live with her, her husband, and infant daughter. "I'd always been very fond of my grandmother, and I was at home anyway," Sarah says, "so I didn't think it would make that much difference." For a while, things were fine.

When her daughter was almost three, Sarah had another baby. At first, Sarah's grandmother was still active enough to help with the housework and to babysit occasionally. Three years later, after a couple of mild

strokes, she was less able and less alert and much more demanding, Sarah says. "She wanted to eat at a particular time, and she got very fussy about *what* she ate. She complained all the time about the noise."

Through the local office on the aging Sarah found her way to a support group, which gave her a place to vent her increasingly hostile feelings. "All the affection I had for Nana was going fast," she says. "I kept wishing the last stroke had killed her, so I wouldn't have to deal with her problems anymore." But Sarah couldn't face putting Nana in a nursing home.

Through the social worker who ran the group Sarah found another solution. Since Sarah's grandmother is still fairly able bodied, she is eligible for a local adult day-care center. There,

she has company, lunch, and recreational and occupational activities. She is picked up at the house in the morning, returned there around dinnertime. The full cost is about $20 a day, but since she has only a small Social Security check, the fee is lower. Sarah, no longer afraid of what might happen to her grandmother if she were alone in the house, got a part-time job.

Nana's a lot happier," Sarah reports. She's made some friends, and she has a life of her own. We've been able to put off putting her in a nursing home, and I'm not so resentful, because she's not here so much of the time. I still go to my group, and I know they'll support me if the time comes when she does have to be institutionalized."

When a Nursing Home Becomes a Necessity

Even the best nursing home can look pretty grim. And homes look just as bad, if not worse, to mentally competent older people who must contemplate ending their lives there.

To ease the situation, social workers stress the importance of encouraging the elderly to make their own decisions, within the bounds of what is possible. You should be aware that there are many different levels of nursing-home care, which will determine prices and insurance coverage. Some homes offer total medical care, including rehabilitation facilities, for those who require twenty-four-hour treatment by nurses; these facilities must meet strict criteria set forth by Medicare. Other homes offer various ratios of RNs and LPNs, with intermediate levels of care for people who need some physical attention but can also care for themselves some of the time; these may be covered by Medicaid or private insurance (but not by Medicare). The minimal level of care are rest homes, which are for people who can mostly care for themselves, but may need supervision with taking their medication; these may have no nurses, only aides, and are usually not covered. A few homes offer all levels of care, so that as residents become older and less able to care for themselves, they can change status without being moved.

Your first view of a nursing home will probably be a shock. Many residents are ill or disabled; many appear severely depressed and disoriented; some are obviously overmedicated; others are incontinent; nearly all are very old. It often takes time and visits to more than one facility to see beyond your first discouraging impressions.

Among the things to look for: the general atmosphere and cleanliness; the attitude of staff toward the patients and visitors; openness of administrators to your questions and concerns; comfort and privacy of living quarters; quality of food; availability of medical care and nursing and emergency services; recreational and social programs; residents' participation in programs and input into administration (ask how they like it there); and up-to-date licenses.

Many nursing homes are understaffed, and the staff may be unqualified for the work that they are doing. In a recent study Congressman Claude Pepper's staff found that many nursing-home employees earn less than workers at McDonald's. Another factor in the nursing-home picture is the Reagan administration's establishment of diagnosis-related groups (DRGs) for Medicare reimbursement. A DRG determines exactly how long

Resources

Agencies
Area Agency for the Aging will be listed in your local telephone book under the city- or county-government section. It may appear under "Aging," "Services for the Elderly," etc. Keep looking.

Center for Independent Living, 1450 Hawthorne Ave., Suite 1502, Columbus, OH 43203; (614) 252-1061.

Children of Aging Parents, 2761 Trenton Rd., Levittown, PA 19056; (215) 547-1070.

National Shared Housing Resource Center, 6344 Greene St., Philadelphia, PA 19144; (215) 848-1220.

National Support Center for Families of the Aging, P.O. Box 245, Swarthmore, PA 19081; (215) 544-5933 (newsletter $10 per year, plus other materials).

Publications
You and Your Aging Parent by Barbara Silverstone and Helen K. Hyman, Pantheon, 1981, $8.95. Excellent guide to all aspects: physical and emotional health, care, planning, options. Includes information directories and referral services, home-health-care agencies, family-service societies nationwide and checklists for those investigating nursing homes.

Our Aging Parents edited by Colette Browne and Roberta Onzuka-Anderson, University of Hawaii Press. A guide to elderly care, focusing on illness and rehabilitation.

Supportive Living Arrangements for Older Citizens: A Guide by Anneta S. Kraus, R.N., Geriatric Planning Services, 36 E. Baltimore Pike, Media, PA 19063. $3.50, plus $.75 for shipping.

Political Action Groups
Gray Panthers, 311 South Juniper St., Philadelphia, PA 19107; (215) 545-6555.

American Association of Retired Persons, 1909 K St., NW, Washington, DC 20049; (202) 872-4700.

National Association of Retired Federal Employees, 1533 New Hampshire Ave., NW, Washington, DC 20036; (202) 234-0832.

National Council of Senior Citizens, 925 15th St., NW, Washington, DC 20005; (202) 347-8800.

Medicare will reimburse a hospital for a patient with a particular condition: about two weeks for a broken hip, for example. Then the patient is discharged. When the patient isn't able to take care of herself, a limited amount of home care may be paid for by Medicare, if the doctor orders it. Otherwise, care must be paid for privately, or a family caregiver must be found. (Some social workers seem to assume that any female relative within a hundred-mile radius should be able to drop everything to care for the recently discharged Uncle Louie.) If that fails, the person may be placed in a nursing home. "People who are sicker are being dumped into nursing homes," comments one of Pepper's staff, "just because of the DRGs." She points out, however, that the end of Medicare reimbursement needn't mean the absolute end of the hospital stay for those willing to fight. There is an appeal process available, though its existence is usually kept secret from patients and their families.

Ann Becker's father, Henry, lives with her in Georgia. He is quite frail and depressed. His wife, suffering from heart disease, is in a nursing home about fifteen miles away. Henry and his wife had their own home, which they had worked hard for. They had about $15,000 in savings, Social Security, and a tiny pension. When Ann's mother had a heart attack, she was in the hospital for almost three weeks. While another few weeks in a convalescent home might have restored her to sufficient health so that she could have gone home, Medicare would not cover convalescent care in her case. Since she had an "able-bodied" spouse, she was released from the hospital. Henry simply couldn't cope with his still-sick wife.

"We thought Medicare would cover a nursing home," Ann says, "because she was *sick*. Then we found out that, no matter how sick she was, she wasn't covered. I started running around, looking for someplace that wasn't too awful, running back and forth to my dad's house to help him, calling the social worker twenty times a day to see if there were any beds available in the one or two places that didn't stink. We finally got her a bed. Her roommate raves most of the night, half the people in the place are nodding out. She cries a lot. And this is a good place. Dad paid for about the first six months with his savings. Then he sold the house and moved in with us. Then he paid the nursing home everything he made on the house. That took care of another year. Now he's an old man who worked hard all his life, and his wife's on welfare, and he hasn't got a thing but a little bit they let you keep for a burial. Even if Mom by some miracle got well, he couldn't bring her home, because he hasn't got any home left to bring her to."

The lack of reimbursement for home care and for long-term care, even for those who cannot get along without it, is probably the greatest scandal of the health-care system in this country. For the very poor, there is government help through Medicaid. For the very wealthy, good care can be bought. But nursing homes can cost as much as $35,000-$50,000 per year, so that even those with reasonable savings can be bankrupted by a nursing-home stay of more than a few months. For the enormous middle class—which in this case includes everyone between destitute and rich—there is nothing at all.

Medicaid won't pay until a patient's personal assets are practically gone. For example, if one spouse must be in a nursing home, some states require that the other sell their house to pay for the care. Some couples divorce to protect themselves from impoverishment. The divorce must usually be final at least six months before the now-single person applies for Medicaid.

In some states, an older person may transfer his assets to someone else, to protect them from being "spent down," should he later need long-term care. But these transfers (which are not legal in all states) must usually take place at least two years before the person becomes eligible for Medicaid. In a few states you and your siblings can be held responsible for your parent's nursing-home bills—another Reagan-administration budget-cutting measure—but those regulations are being litigated everywhere they exist.

When a parent is hospitalized, another family member should head directly for the discharge planning office, the social worker, or the patient advocate. Hospitals seem to be trying to keep DRGs a secret, but the fact is that as soon as a diagnosis is made, they know exactly when your relative will be discharged. If your doctor is friendly, and there is some flexibility in the possible diagnosis, ask him to make the one that will give your relative the maximum possible stay. If there will be no one available (or willing) to help care for the person at home after discharge from the hospital, make that absolutely clear to the social worker from the beginning.

But the problem of the aging, the problem that transcends the particular situation of any individual family, is one that requires governmental support. The responsibility lies with the middle generation to begin to demand programs that enhance the lives of the elderly who remain in their communities, that provide decent living situations for those who are still healthy but unable to live alone and that provide insurance coverage for long-term as well as acute care. We have allowed the older generation, through their own organizations like the Gray Panthers and the American Association of Retired Persons, to carry the burden of demanding change for too long. To the responsibilities we bear for our parents and our children, we must now add a responsibility for our own future.

A community survey ($n = 396$) revealed that adequate financial coverage for health care for low-income black elderly has been prevented by out-of-pocket medical expenses. Although health care facilities were regularly available, the lack of regular physicians' services at the health care location was a major cause of dissatisfaction. Discussed are policy implications for improving the affordability and acceptability of health services for this population.
Key Words: Health status, Access, Minority aged

Access to Health Care in a Black Urban Elderly Population

Marcia K. Petchers, PhD

Associate Dean, School of Applied Social Sciences, Case Western Reserve University, 2035 Abington Road, Cleveland, OH 44106.

Sharon E. Milligan, PhD

Assistant Professor, School of Applied Social Sciences, Case Western Reserve University.

Providing access to a minimum level of health care for traditionally disadvantaged groups continues to be an important public policy concern. National studies of access have shown that although progress has been made and some of the inequities in access have disappeared as a result of federal financing and delivery initiatives, the elderly, the minorities, and the poor, in particular, are in the greatest need of health care and are still underserved (Aday & Andersen, 1984; Aday et al., 1980; U.S. Department of Health and Human Services, 1985).

Although aggregate national data are useful for monitoring the impact of health policy, these data often mask the specific problems encountered in especially underserved or high-risk populations because specific underserved subpopulations may experience a unique constellation of problems in different localities. Thus, the impact and appropriateness of health policy and service delivery arrangements may be more realistically portrayed through local data. In-depth community studies of subgroups selected for the characteristics that place them at risk can generate a greater understanding of the elements or combinations of elements that facilitate or inhibit service access.

In the 1970s, two community surveys of the underserved in New York shed light on access problems of the inner-city elderly (Auerbach, 1977 et al.; Cantor & Mayer, 1976). Shown by these local studies was the disparity between the enactment and implementation of public health policy for obtaining medical care. In turn, this report contributed to the continual need for monitoring of public policy by determining whether the patterns found 10 years ago in an eastern inner-city area paralleled those of a mid-western inner-city area that also had an abundance of medical facilities. As with the studies by Cantor and Mayer (1976) and Auerbach et al. (1977), the primary goal was to examine access to medical care in a traditionally underserved population group. By studying a geographic area with ample health services, it was possible to determine if other dimensions of access are barriers to utilization.

Efforts to increase health care access of the poor in inner-city neighborhoods have included increasing the availability of services and the removal of some financial barriers. Access is not initiated by the mere physical presence of resources or health care facilities; rather access is a complex, multifaceted phenomenon (Wan, 1982). Four major dimensions generally comprise the concept of access: availability, affordability, accessibility, and acceptability.

Several investigators (Brown, 1976; Morrison, 1983; Wright et al., 1979) have sought to learn if the availability of health facilities made a difference in access to members of ethnic minorities. Bullough (1974) reported that when services were supplied, poor blacks revealed the highest level of use. Thus, the presence of medical services in a given area is, apparently, a crucial aspect of utilization and allocation of health services and can thus be viewed as a means of increasing opportunity and well-being and decreasing the inequality of conditions in disadvantaged areas (Hickey, 1979).

Both income and insurance coverage are critical factors in affording health services (Bice et al., 1972; Wan, 1977). Cantor and Mayer (1976) reported, however, that black and Hispanic aged are less likely than their white counterparts to receive the advantages of important entitlements. They reported that although 85% of black aged in their New York City sample were covered by Medicare, the cost of co-insurance and lack of clarity regarding eligibility and enrollment procedures still created problems, as did the issue of non-covered (i.e., out-of-pocket) medical expenses.

Transportation problems have frequently been cited as accessibility barriers to service utilization

This research was funded by The Cleveland Foundation. The authors wish to acknowledge Robert Staib and Anthony Thomas for their help with data analysis and Henry Ziegler, MD and William True for their assistance in survey implementation. We also wish to thank Ann Roy, PhD, for her valuable editorial assistance.

From The Gerontologist, Vol. 28, No. 2, April 1988, pp. 213-217. Copyright © 1988 by The Gerontological Society of America. Reprinted by permission.

(Dancy, 1977; Morrison, 1983). In a Texas study by Eve and Friedsam (1979), non-white aged were more likely to report difficulty in obtaining needed care because of transportation problems. Conversely, in her sample of New York elderly German (1975) found relative ease of accessibility, as did Auerbach et al. (1977).

Fragmentation and depersonalization have also been cited as major barriers to acceptability of formal health care services (Morrison, 1983). A number of service delivery elements, advertently or inadvertently, can create barriers to acceptability of services. Most common among them are long waiting time, inconvenient hours of service, a confusing atmosphere, and not seeing the same doctor twice (Cantor & Mayer, 1976). Other barriers include insensitivity of doctors and nurses and a lack of effective communication (Morrison, 1983). Structural limitations that create a dehumanizing climate are often compounded by fear of doctors and hospitals, fear of diagnosis and prognosis, and a lack of faith in the medical profession (Cheng, 1978; Dancy, 1977). Although there is agreement that acceptability of care greatly influences utilization, there is contradictory evidence regarding the acceptability of services to minority groups. Gylys and Gylys (1974) found that lower income blacks did not have negative attitudes toward medical institutions or the medical profession and, indeed, tended to place considerable trust in medical care and believed they would receive quality care.

Methodology

Sample

Surveyed were urban elderly residents aged 60 and over who lived in a 15-block area located in an inner-city, virtually all-black Cleveland neighborhood known as Fairfax. In the neighborhood, 98% of the residents were black and about one-third were 60 years and over. These 15 blocks were selected as representative of the population and of housing characteristics of the 68-block area. Because the focus was on a non-institutionalized sample, elderly persons residing in nursing homes and other long-term care facilities were not represented.

The household was the unit of analysis. Within each household, one individual was selected to be interviewed on behalf of the household. Following an introductory letter, respondents were contacted to arrange an appointment for a face-to-face interview. Because the respondents were identified in a previous survey, at least three attempts were made to locate and interview potential respondents. In all, 441 elderly persons were interviewed, with 396 completed interviews suitable for analysis. All interviews, which lasted about 30 minutes, were conducted by trained black interviewers.

Measures

Three classes of variables following the work of Aday et al. (1980) were measured in this study: pre-disposing, need, and enabling characteristics. Measures of predisposing characteristics were age, sex, marital status, household structure, employment status, and education. Need characteristics were measured by asking respondents about perceived health status, physical conditions, physical symptoms, Activities of Daily Living (ADL) scale, and the Instrumental Activities of Daily Living (IADL) scale. Self-report measures were used to probe the health status of the sample. Self-evaluation of health and functional capacity have been validated as useful proxy measures of clinical diagnosis (Auerbach et al., 1977; Cantor and Mayer, 1976; United States General Accounting Office [USGAO], 1975; Wolf et al., 1983). Four major enabling factors were measured. To assess service availability, inquiries were made into the respondents' sources of health care, regular use of health care sources, recency of service utilization, and use of preventive medicine. Affordability was measured by self-reported annual household income, the presence and type of health insurance coverage, and a direct question about whether respondents had trouble with medical expenses and whether the cost of medical care posed a burden. Accessibility of health care was determined by queries about the availability of transportation to health services, method(s) of transport, and a direct probe about whether transportation to health facilities created a problem. The final area was acceptability. This was measured by a Likert-type scale in which several aspects of health care delivery were asked about. Respondents were asked to rate their level of satisfaction on a 5-point scale ranging from very satisfied, slightly satisfied, uncertain, slightly dissatisfied, to very dissatisfied. The survey instrument drew largely from the Duke Multidimensional Functional Assessment Questionnaire, a structured interview tool designed and tested for use with older persons (Pfeiffer, 1975).

Characteristics of the Sample

Study respondents ranged in age from 60 to 96, with a median age of 76 years. The sex ratio for this sample was nearly 2 to 1, with females representing 65.7% and males 33.8%. The overwhelming majority of residents were retired (85.5%) and the average income for this group was $6,146 (in 1981 dollars). More than three-quarters of the sample (78.6%) claimed less than 12 years of education (i.e., did not complete high school). A comparison of the demographic characteristics of the sample to data on the elderly in the Fairfax area demonstrated that the sample was representative of elderly in the inner-city community.

Respondents were asked to rate their general health status, whether or not they suffered from 30 different illness conditions, and whether they were limited in their daily activities. Self-assessment of general health revealed that 5.6% of the respondents rated their health as excellent, 44.6% rated their health as good, 41.3% as fair, and 8.5% rated their health as poor. Similar results were found in studies by Cantor and Mayer (1976), Wolf et al. (1983) and the

USGAO (1975). This sample was thus split almost evenly between those who reported good to excellent health (50.2%) and those in fair to poor health (49.8%), which is a larger proportion of black elderly reporting fair-to-poor health than found in national data (30%) (United States Department of Health and Human Services, 1985).

In all, 1 in 3 (32%) reported no illness conditions at all, which is impressive for an elderly cohort. The number of illness conditions reported by the remainder of the group ranged from 1 to 9 with the average number of conditions reported just over 2 (mean = 2.3). For 60.1% of the sample, at least 1 condition was reported to limit activities, whereas 27.5% reported that at least 1 condition limited activities a great deal. In sum, approximately two-thirds (68%) declared some limitation due to at least one illness condition. This represents a larger proportion of black elderly than found in national data, which showed 57.5% of low income black elderly (65 and over) to have limitation of activity due to chronic illness (United States Department of Health and Human Services, 1985).

The most frequently cited conditions, as shown in Table 1, revealed extensive chronic illness. Fewer than 5% of the respondents indicated the presence of any of the other three conditions covered in the interview.

To augment the picture of health status, respondents were also asked as to whether they had any of 21 physical symptoms which usually require medical treatment. This was done to obtain information about physical complaints that might have been at the prediagnosis stage and did not constitute a disease entity per se. Symptoms of impaired health covered in the queries included pain, stiffness, weakness, headaches, coughing, indigestion, hearing or sight problems, backaches, and tiredness. For each symptom present, respondents were also asked if they had sought help for it. Well under half the sample (41.3%) claimed no symptoms at all over the past year. For the 58.7% reporting physical complaints, the range of symptoms noted was from 1 to 11. The median number of symptoms reported was one; the mean was just under two (1.93). Of those reporting symptoms, 38.8% identified from 1 to 3, whereas 19.9% cited as many as 4 to 11 of those listed.

As shown in Table 2, the most prevalent symptoms were, not surprisingly, those common to the aged. Note, as well, that in 4 out of 5 of these ailments, less than half of those suffering a given symptom reported seeking help. Eyesight difficulties seemed to require more attention, with over two-thirds of respondents seeking help. None of the other physical symptoms included in the investigation were reported by more than 10% of the sample.

Results

Availability

Sources of primary care for this sample were dispersed among 10 hospitals or health care centers. These included a teaching hospital clinic, the county health center and a not-for-profit hospital. Each of these medical centers are in proximity to the Fairfax area. Cantor and Mayer (1976) and Wan (1982) reported similar findings. Only 14.4% of the respondents reported any overnight stays in a hospital during the past year.

Most respondents reported a regular source of health care (89.4%). This figure is comparable to 1982 national percentages for the United States population as a whole (89.4%), but slightly lower than the recent national figure for those over 65 (93%) (Cantor & Mayer, 1976; German, 1975). Likewise, the preponderance of the sample (92.5%) reported having a medical visit within the past 2 years. The significance of this finding is the important relationship between having a regular source of medical care and the likelihood of using medical services when ill and for preventive health checkups. The utilization of preventive medicine, which has been linked to reduced morbidity and mortality rates, was also high in this sample. Of those who reported having complete physical exams within the past year, 63.5% had actually been examined.

Affordability

Results showed that a preponderance of the sample (90.2%) reported being enrolled in Medicare or Medicaid, whereas just under one-third of the group (31.8%) had private health insurance. The finding that 9.8% of this black elderly cohort were not covered by insurance closely paralleled that proportion of the United States population (9%) with no coverage in 1982 (Aday & Andersen, 1984). Although still in the same range, the present elderly black Cleveland sample had a slightly lower non-coverage rate than that reported by Cantor and Mayer (1976) for their New York City elderly black cohort (15%) or Aday and Andersen (1984) for non-whites nationwide (12%). Thus, it seems that insurance coverage for this black, urban elderly sample helps to alleviate the burden of medical costs.

Table 1. Physical Conditions Reported in the Black Elder Sample

Condition	Total n	n	(%)
High blood pressure	341	157	(46.3)
Arthritis	350	146	(41.7)
Circulation problems	367	70	(19.1)
Heart trouble	372	60	(16.1)
Diabetes	376	38	(10.1)

Table 2. The Five Most Common Physical Symptoms and Help-Seeking in the Black Elderly Sample

Symptom	Total n	With symptom n	With symptom (%)	Seeking help n	Seeking help (%)
Stiff joints and muscles	379	102	(24.9)	41	(40)
Shortness of breath	380	92	(24.2)	28	(30)
Pain in the joints	378	69	(18.3)	32	(46)
Trouble seeing	386	62	(16.1)	42	(68)
Frequent backache	378	59	(15.6)	26	(44)

Despite the large proportion of the sample with medical insurance, the data revealed that such coverage did not relieve the psychological distress associated with the high cost of medical care. Half of this low-income sample (50.7%) reported trouble with medical expenses; about one-third (34.6%) felt that medical fees were too high; and almost 1 in 3 (28.8%) reported that their medical insurance did not pay for all of their medical expenses. Generally, as Cantor and Mayer (1976) and Aday and Andersen (1984) found, lack of money is the chief reason for failing to seek medical assistance.

Accessibility

In this group of urban elderly, virtually no one indicated that transportation to health facilities posed a problem. In fact, a wide variety of transportation arrangements were cited, including being driven by someone, the use of public transportation, hospital vehicles, special community transit services for the elderly, taxis, and walking. This finding is consistent with that of German (1975) although it contrasts with the transportation problems reported by one-quarter of the Cantor and Mayer (1976) inner-city New York sample. In this case, it is likely that the large number of medical facilities located in and around the Fairfax area mitigates the transportation barrier.

Acceptability

A majority of respondents claimed to be very satisfied with medical services in general, with about one-third (31.3%) uncertain as to their level of satisfaction. Only 3.5% indicated a general lack of satisfaction with services. Also indicative of the perceived quality of medical services, 7 out of 10 respondents felt that they had been thoroughly checked during their last medical visit. Again, almost one-third were undecided (26.6%) and only a few (3%) disagreed. About 6 in 10 residents conveyed that their physicians had explained medications to them and, again, about one-third (31.4%) refrained from expressing an opinion and only 10.4% disagreed.

Several specific elements in the medical services received were cause for dissatisfaction. About one-third of respondents expressed some degree of dissatisfaction with each area of concern, as shown in Table 3. These data contrast with the findings of Gylys and Gylys (1974) which suggested that lower income blacks tended to place trust in medical care and generally believed that they would receive quality care.

Discussion and Implications

Affordability was a formidable barrier to medical care for the sample of poor, minority elderly. The elderly cohort had difficulty meeting medical expenses despite high enrollment rates in Medicare and Medicaid. This finding is actually not surprising in light of the fact that public insurance programs do not cover total health care expenses and have more

Table 3. Selected Satisfaction Items

Items	Total n	Dissatisfaction[a] n	(%)
The doctor did not spend enough time	371	144	(38.9)
The doctor did not advise on what to do	371	141	(38.0)
The wait was too long	371	137	(36.9)
The doctor did not sufficiently explain condition(s)	371	134	(36.2)
All questions had not been answered	373	131	(35.0)
Seldom see the same doctor	373	122	(32.7)

[a]Dissatisfaction consists of ratings of very and slightly dissatisfied.

favorable coverage rates for acute care. Consistent with these data, a substantial portion of the Auerbach et al. (1977) and Cantor & Mayer (1976) New York City samples reported some difficulty in meeting medical expenses.

Several interrelated explanations can be offered to explicate the affordability barrier that manifested itself in this low-income elderly cohort: Most (68%) suffer from at least one chronic illness, most receive health care in non-acute facilities (i.e., only 14% were hospitalized over the year), only a minority (less than one-third) reported having supplementary coverage, and a sizable percentage (39%) live alone. National data from Medicare showed that minority elderly persons, who tend to be poor, are less likely to purchase private health insurance (Cafferata, 1984). These results echo the concern expressed by Kovar (1986) that the burden of out-of-pocket expenses for medical care is significant.

For low income elderly, out-of-pocket charges are a significant burden because they consume a substantial portion of available income. Moreover, as Kovar (1986) pointed out, one-person elderly households spend an even larger proportion of their income on medical care. The problem of out-of-pocket charges as a deterrent to the use of services was identified by the federal government as early as 1971 (United States Department of Health, Education, and Welfare, 1971). Thus, affordability remains a barrier to health care for the minority elderly.

Public policy must take into account the impact of high health care expenditures for this subgroup of non-institutionalized elderly so that programs can be appropriately tailored to the needs of high-risk groups (Newacheck et al., 1980). In addition, the balance between covered and uncovered expenses should be analyzed, not only in terms of current dollar outlays, but also for its effects on prevention of disease and of institutionalization. Finally, policy formulations which promote, rather than discourage less costly alternatives of treating chronic illnesses in non-acute, out-patient facilities should be advocated.

Most respondents reported having a particular health facility or hospital as a regular place of care. This pattern has been previously established in the literature for the poor, minorities, and urban dwellers (Aday & Andersen, 1984; Cantor & Mayer, 1976).

Whether this trend is a result of service availability in urban areas, the declining numbers of private physicians in the inner-city or personal preference, remains to be seen (Wan, 1982). Worthy of note, however, is the observation that the lack of a regular physician at the health service location was a major source of dissatisfaction, which suggested that there is a desire for seeing the same physician at the health facility even though these elders had not elected (or do not have available) a private physician.

The data revealed an interesting twist to the concept of care availability because for this subpopulation, regular health care facilities were available but regular physicians (within those facilities) were not. Thus, the notion of availability as a barrier to health care may be more profitably conceptualized as a two-part concept. These findings have potentially important implications because a regular source of care is associated with, and a significant predictor of, prevention, early detection, and management of health problems (Bice, 1972; Schach et al., 1976; Wan & Soifer, 1974).

Along these same lines, Wright et al. (1979) noted that the mechanism linking an individual to the health care system has important implications for level and rate of utilization. In common usage, regular source of care refers to either a particular physician or a place. Assuming, however, that continuity of care is a critical, if not the critical, ingredient in having a regular care source, it is possible that many of the beneficial consequences attributed to regular care might be mitigated in systems that do not offer continuity in terms of assigning physicians to patients. This finding of lack of continuity parallels that reported by Auerbach et al. (1977) for an area serviced by a New York Medical Center.

A possible by-product of this discontinuity is the finding of dissatisfaction with relationship and communication between doctor and patient. Rapport between doctor and patient also has a well-established impact on utilization patterns, prevention, and patient compliance with medical regimes, all of which are essential elements for full and appropriate medical care for this high-risk group (Wan, 1982). Investigation of alternative service delivery strategies that would enhance continuity of care in health facilities and hospital clinics is warranted. Concomitant attempts to minimize the long waiting times, which may entail better staff ratios or different staffing or queuing patterns, would also be advisable to increase the acceptability of health services to poor, minority aged.

In this study the mosaic quality and the complexity of access to medical care has been illustrated. It adds to the evidence on underserved populations and shows the gap between the goals of public health policy and implementation. Results shed light on why adequate across-the-board protection for poor, elderly citizens has not been realized through the public financing of insurance and health care.

References

Aday, L., & Andersen, R. (1984). The national profile of access to medical care: Where do we stand? *American Journal of Public Health, 74,* 1331–1339.

Aday, L., Andersen, R., & Fleming, G. (1980). *Health care in the United States: Equitable for whom?* (Beverly Hills, CA: Sage).

Auerbach, M., Gordon, D. W., Ullman, A., & Weisel, M. J. (1977). Health care in a selected urban elderly population. *The Gerontologist, 17,* 341–346.

Bice, T. W., Eichhorn, R., & Fox, P. (1972). Socio-economic status and use of physician services: A reconsideration. *Medical Care, 10,* 261–272.

Brown, P. A. (1976). Differential utilization of the health care delivery system by members of ethnic minorities. *Journal of Sociology and Social Welfare, 3,* 516–523.

Bullough, B. (1974). The source of ambulatory health services as it relates to preventive care. *Journal of Public Health, 64,* 582–590.

Cafferata, T. (1984). *Private health insurance coverage of the medicare population: Data preview 18* (DHHS Publication no. PHS 84-3362). Rockville, MD: National Center for Health Services Research.

Cantor, M., & Mayer, M. (1976). Health and the inner-city elderly. *The Gerontologist, 16,* 17–26.

Cheng, E. (1978). *The elder Chinese.* San Diego: Campanile Press.

Dancy, J., Jr. (1977). *The elderly: A guide for practitioners.* Ann Arbor, MI: The Institute of Gerontology, University of Michigan-Wayne State University.

Eve, S., & Friedsam, H. J. (1979). Ethnic differences in the use of health care among older Texans. *Journal of Minority Aging, 4,* 62–75.

German, P. S. (1975). Characteristics and health behavior of the aged population. *The Gerontologist, 15,* 327–332.

Gylys, J., & Gylys, B. (1974). Cultural influences and the medical behavior of low income groups. *Journal of the National Medical Association, 66,* 310–313.

Hickey, A. A. (1979). Inequality and service access: The utilization of medical services. *Journal of Social Service Review, 2,* 77–87.

Kovar, M. G. (1986). Expenditures for the medical care of elderly living in the community 1980. *The Milbank Quarterly, 64,* 100–132.

Morrison, B. J. (1983). Physical health and the minority aged. In R. L. McNeely & J. N. Colen (Eds.), *Aging in minority groups.* Beverly Hills, CA: Sage.

Newacheck, P. W., Butler, L. H., Harper, A. I., Dyan, A. B., Piontkowski, A. B., & Franks, P. E. (1980). Income and illness. *Medical Care, 18,* 1165–1179.

Pfeiffer, E. (Ed.). (1975). *Multidimensional functional assessment: The OARS methodology.* Durham, NC: Center for the Study of Aging and Human Development.

Schach, E., Kalimo, K., & Haythorne, D. (1976). Predisposing and enabling factors. In R. Kohn & K. White (Eds.), *Health Care: An International Study.* NY: International Collaborative Study of Medical Care Utilization, World Health Organization.

United States General Accounting Office (USGAO). (1975). Cleveland, OH: Detroit Regional Office.

United States Department of Health and Human Services. (1985). *Health status of minorities and low income groups.* Public Health Service, USDHHS, (HRSA) HRS-P-DV85-1. Washington, DC: United States Government Printing Office.

United States Department of Health, Education, and Welfare. (1971). *Toward a comprehensive health policy for the 1970s.* Washington, DC: United States Government Printing Office.

Wan, T. (1977). The differential use of health services: A minority perspective. *Urban Health, 16,* 47–49.

Wan, T. (1982). Use of health service by the elderly in low income communities. *Milbank Memorial Fund Quarterly, 60,* 82–107.

Wan, T., & Soifer, S. (1974). Determinants of physician utilization. *Journal of Health and Social Behavior, 15,* 100–108.

Wolf, J., Breslau, N., Ford, A., Ziegler, H., & Ward, A. (1983). Access of the black urban elderly to medical care. *Journal of National Medical Association, 75.* 41–46.

Wright, R., Creecy, R., & Berg, W. (1979). The black elderly and their use of health care services: A causal analysis. *Journal of Gerontological Social Work, 2,* 11–28.

Aging, Generational Continuity, and Filial Support

Abraham Monk

Abraham Monk is professor of gerontology and social work at Columbia University. He is the author or editor of four books and has contributed over ninety articles and publications on social gerontology, social policy, and social services. He is currently working on a second edition of his Handbook of Gerontological Services *(first edition 1985) and on two research projects: one on international perspectives in home care, and the other on families of Alzheimer's victims.*

Aging is one of the salient themes of our time. It is gaining our attention both by the increase in life expectancy—that is, by the fact that people are living longer—and by the increasing proportion of older people as part of the total population.

Life expectancy, which in 1900 was 46.4 years for white males and 49.0 for females, rose to 69.9 and 77.5 in 1980 for white men and women, respectively. It will continue inching up—to over 80 by the year 2000.

As we keep adding years to life we also augment the number of living generations in family lineages. From the triad of grandparents, parents, and children we now find that four- and even five-generation families with two "older" generations—a younger one in its 60s and its octogenarian parents, are no longer a rarity. This increased longevity, coupled with a decline in birth rates, is changing the age profile of American society. In the year 1900 the 65-and-older age group were only 4 percent of all Americans, the almost imperceptible tip of the population pyramid. Demographic projections indicate that this group will almost quadruple by the year 2000, reaching the 15-percent mark of the population, or one in every six Americans.

The demographic expansion of the aged is primarily occurring in technologically advanced societies. Some, like the United States, are experiencing relentless economic growth while contracting unprecedented fiscal deficits. There is a lingering fear that the addition of more living generations will compound these economic woes. Older nonworking persons require costly health and social service supports. When resources are stretched to the limit, policymakers end up with the dilemma of having to choose whether to attend to the needs of their frail and dependent elders or to create instead a better start in life for the young.

ACCUSATIONS THAT THE old siphon away the precious assets needed by younger, succeeding generations are voiced quite frequently. Henry Fairlie recently compiled a litany of such apocalyptic invectives. "Something is wrong," he writes in the *New Republic,* "with a society that is willing to drain itself to foster such an unproductive section of its population."[1] He finds it unjustifiable that the elderly's standard of living has improved faster than that of younger people, and he resents that they accumulate so many benefits—Medicare, Social Security, special tax privileges,

From *The World & I,* December 1988, pp. 549-561. *The World & I,* a publication of The Washington Times Corporation, copyright © 1988.

and so forth—without challenge. Fairlie also regards these benefits as too generous and cannot reconcile himself to the idea that the proportion of elderly living below the poverty line is lower than that of the children's cohort (14 versus 20 percent).

Instead of proposing an improvement in the condition of the young, though, Fairlie's solution is that the aged should sacrifice themselves for those who hold more promise of productivity. At times he seems to imply the need for a more expeditious "final solution." "If one needs a psychiatrist by the time one is 65," Fairlie concludes, "one should take the quick way out—make a swan dive from the high bridge to the tarmac, and go meet the Great Therapist in the Sky."

THE 'INTERGENERATIONAL INEQUITY' THESIS

Fairlie's arguments are not original. They are just some of the most recent statements of the "intergenerational inequity" thesis. This theory takes for granted that there is animosity and competition between the young and the old. It then proceeds to lament that due to the sheer weight of their voting power, the old mercilessly hoard benefits at the expense of the young. (Let us recall that although one out of every nine Americans is over 65, this group constitutes one out of every four voters; children do not vote, hence the alleged crushing influence of the "senior" lobby.) Furthermore, the cost of those benefits will be borne by the young of today and of future generations. The thesis inevitably ends with a good dose of scapegoating: The cost of programs for the elderly is responsible for the fiscal deficit and will end up bankrupting America.

Eric R. Kingson and coauthors Barbara Hirshorn and John Cornman address those arguments in their book *Ties That Bind: The Interdependence of Generations.*[2] As they point out, although some of the aged are well off, large segments are poor and must cope with high living and health-related costs. Furthermore, not all the benefits they receive, like Social Security, are transfers from one generation to the next. Much of the funding is derived from contributions made by the aged beneficiaries

> Generations are not entirely divorced from each other, and may actually seek bilateral alliances.

during their working years. True, Social Security also provides a minimum floor of income protection for those who receive low benefits, which prevents severe hardship and thus serves all population groups.

The contention that future generations are saddled with a huge fiscal burden also ignores the expected growth in the GNP, which is projected to nearly double by 2020, and even triple 30 years later. It also fails to take into consideration that significant portions of the aged will remain longer in the work force. With the postponement of mandatory retirement age and its actual abolition in some sectors of the economy, more older persons will be working well into their 60s and even to the mid-70s. To a large extent this will depend on such factors as prevailing unemployment and inflation rates, but there is a move toward delayed retirement or retirement substitution with more flexible work-leisure arrangements. Thus, the aged not only consume benefits, but also generate more wealth and resources with their work.

Finally, the argument that younger generations resent having to pay higher Social Security taxes to take care of the elderly is contradicted by every public opinion poll in the last decade. A national survey recently conducted by RL Associates of Princeton on behalf of the American Association of Retired Persons found that 86 percent of all registered voters favor a public program for long-term care for the dependent and frail elderly, and almost two-thirds, or 60 percent, do not mind paying higher taxes to finance such a program.[3]

THE GENERATIONAL DRIFT

It is not inconceivable that as living generations increase in number

they might drift apart, and even turn against each other in a bitter competition for services and opportunities.

While the human life cycle is permanent and resists the theories of history and social organization, the extent of segregation of different age groups varies from culture to culture. Tamara Hareven claims that socioeconomic changes in the United States in the past century have resulted in the more pronounced fragmentation of the life course into formalized stages, a more rigid transition from one state to the next, and a loss of common interests among age groups.[4] The end result has been a weakening of familial values and reverence for age, and conversely, an emphasis on individualism.

IT WAS ONLY 20 years ago that social scientists and the media began dealing with the differences that keep generations apart. Karl Manheimm's earlier claim that each generation is imbued with a distinct ideological consciousness and collective identity paved the way for the vision that the selfless morality of the young would cleanse and save the world from its impending doom.[5] Charles A. Reich later asserted in his *Greening of America* that our society is stratified in three self-contained generations, which he labeled as Consciousness I, II, and III.[6]

The first upholds the conservative tradition. It values self-reliance, frugality, ordinary virtues, and honesty. It sees America reflected in the orderliness and hard work of its small towns.

Consciousness II is more liberal and progressive. It represents commitment to both social responsibility and meritocracy. It believes in planning, regulation, the welfare state, and the subordination of personal freedoms to the requirements of the common good.

Consciousness III sees young people moving into a communitarian family of affections, devoid of all traces of competitiveness and selfish material ambition. It perceives genuine relations arising spontaneously, free of oppressive authority systems, without contractual constraints or standardized conformity. Young people should do what they want, when they want, and as they see fit, according to Reich. The power of this new consciousness, Reich announced,

is not the power of manipulating procedures, or the power of politics or street fighting but the power of new values and a new way of life. Consciousness III is capable of changing and of destroying the corporate state, without violence, without seizure of power. . . . The old political forms will simply be swept away in the flood.

Reich carried to the absurd the mysticism of a continuum of age cohorts, as ranging from oppression to liberation. His generations are engaged in an irreconcilable struggle, with the aged playing the "villains" role. The young, in turn, herald a messianic age of love and freedom.

There was nothing new in Reich's glorification of youth and concomitant vilification of old age. Yet intergenerational conflict is only an extreme outcome in Reich's analysis of the America of the sixties. Generations are still seen, as living apart from each other, as if living in separate worlds.

Richard Kalish, in a classic paper that actually preceded Reich's speculations, also alluded to three generations, similarly self-contained. "Today we are so alert to social class and ethnic differences in values," he wrote, "it seems strikingly naive to ignore that age cohort differences have the same impact."[7] For Kalish, however, generations are not entirely divorced from each other, and may actually seek bilateral alliances. This is particularly the case of the two "underdog" generations—the young and the old. Both find themselves stereotyped in ways that the middle-aged—the villains in his dramatization—rarely have to suffer. Both generations perform nonproductive roles. They are poor and dependent. They have little say in society's major decisions and are suspicious of the technocracies that rule the world. Kalish finally concluded that alienation is not the exclusive province of the young. "If youth is alienated, so is old age." The young feel estranged from a society that does not understand their aspirations. The old are uprooted, in turn, from a community that refuses to find dignified roles for them.

The emotional pathos of the generational polarization of the sixties gave way to the more realistic mood of the seventies and eighties. The pendulum swung, in many instances, to the opposite extreme, and generational differences were then summarily dismissed as wholly "irrelevant."

OVERCOMING THE 'GENERATIONAL GAP'

Studies of intergenerational relations conducted during the sixties and seventies yielded contradictory evidence as to the reality of the so-called generational gap. Some claimed to have found a nearly complete break or discontinuity between one generation and the next. Others noticed instead a surprising degree of similarity beneath the surface. In any event, they centered for the most part around the extent of identification

> A growing body of evidence points to extensive intergenerational supports and care-giving.

linking one generation to the other. Other researchers aimed to overcome the constraining reductionism of the "generation gap" studies and probed into specific cognitive styles, values patterns, relative affective distance, perceived competition, and support patterns across generational lines.

It is precisely the latter area —namely, the degree of services family members extend to their younger or older relatives—that has been the focus of more recent attention. A growing body of evidence points to extensive intergenerational supports and care-giving. Elaine Brody observes that "nowadays adult children provide more care and more difficult care to more parents over much longer periods of time, than they did in the good old days."[8] In 1980, almost half of the people in their late 50s and at least one in five of those in their early 60s in the United States had at least

one surviving parent and, as Ethel Shanas indicates, provides as much as 80 percent of the home health-care needs of their dependent older relatives. Based on data from the 1975 national survey of noninstitutionalized aged, Shanas concludes that the immediate family of the old person is the major source of support in times of illness.[9] Old people resort first to their families for assistance, then to their friends and neighbors, and only as a last resort to more formal community services. It is precisely this extensive family support that prevents more older persons from being confined to long-term nursing institutions.

THERE ARE AT present over 1.2 million people in nursing homes, 5 percent of all the aged. There are, however, between 1.6 and 2 million chronically dependent older persons who manage to stay in their homes thanks to the intensive or intermittent care they receive from relatives.

Families assist them with all their needs, including filling in the gaps and shortcomings of the service system. They contend with a bewildering maze of benefit and insurance regulations and they negotiate with pension funds, hospitals, and community services.

Yet no matter how extensive that support is, the "myth of family, or filial abandonment" continues to exist. Brody claims the myth may reflect the guilt of a youth-oriented society seeking to justify its lack of compliance with the etiquette of "filial behavior" that is, the deference and submissive respect to elders practiced in the past in more traditional cultures.[10] Brody lists multiple determinants that feed the myth and keep it alive. Professional social workers, nurses, physicians, and others who are frequently in touch with a biased sample of aged persons—that is, those older persons who are childless, separated, or even alienated from their offspring—often assume that this sampling actually reflects normative or established patterns of intergenerational relations.

THE STRESSES OF FAMILIAL SUPPORT

Geographical distance does not necessarily hamper filial responsibility.

In 1950 close to one-third of the aged lived with a child. This proportion has dwindled to less than 15 percent today, and even these instances are often determined by economic necessity, rather than a commitment to a multigenerational life-style.

Supportive relations, however, tend to transcend physical distance. The family of obligation, that is, based on duties prescribed by law, may no longer exist, but voluntary responses ingrained in moral values and affection continue to be strong. Middle-aged children assume, on the whole, a considerable share of the care-giving functions for their older dependent parents. Moreover, as Amy Horowitz found, the quality of previous affective relations between parents and children bears little consequence on those parental care tasks.[11] Children thus come to their parents' aid because their earlier sense of filial duty has not vanished; the myth that families abandon their elderly, as Brody alerts us, is therefore false and unfair to the middle generation.

Role strains emerge, however, when a family has to make a decision concerning to whom these middle-aged children owe their primary allegiance. Gordon Streib's research on retired fathers and their adult offspring suggests that when faced with the crucial dilemma of choosing between their own children and spouses, or their aging parents, the adult offspring will decide in favor of the former, that is, their own family of procreation, not their family of orientation.[12] In addition, as is often observed, the stated willingness to help aging parents is not always a valid indicator of the ability, actual readiness, or endurance necessary to provide such help on a continuous day-in, day-out basis.

Some middle-aged children simply cannot contend with what Kastenbaum and Aisenberg label the "bereavement overload" of their elderly —namely, the devastating sense of grief produced by repeated, multiple, and irreparable losses.[13]

There are many filial crises that bring the adult children to the attention of the counseling services. Some relate to caring for parents who are geographically distant. Others deal with parents who refuse treatment

Children come to their parents' aid because their earlier sense of filial duty has not vanished.

or chase away all homemaking and home health-care services secured by the family.

There are three stressful situations, however, that relatives of the frail aged experienced as perennial dilemmas. The first involves bringing a parent, usually widowed, into their household. No matter how respectful and loving their relationship may be, the mere relocation is bound to require substantial readjustment in the host couple's routines, life agendas, and timetables. It affects everybody's sense of privacy. The sheer physical exertion imposed by the home care function may also negatively impinge on the quality of emotional life and marital relations of the host couple.

The second revolves around the decision to place a severely incapacitated parent in a nursing home or home for the aged. This is one of the most guilt-inducing situations, and a time when adult siblings often blame each other for "not doing enough" for the parent. Those who have already acted as care-givers but cannot continue doing so may accuse other siblings of not doing their share. They simply overlook indications that the parent may have deteriorated to the point where he or she needs round-the-clock nursing care. Even in the absence of such recriminations, adult children may be so immobilized with grief and shame that they cannot provide the emotional reassurance their parent may be needing when being uprooted and relocated to an unfamiliar environment.

It makes matters worse when older persons point the finger and accuse their offspring of dumping them in an institution for the "senile." Parents often conceal or deny their handicaps and insist they are quite capable of living alone, or that they prefer to put up with all the hardships of solitary

living rather than being confined for life and giving up a home filled with memories. The coup de grace comes when the parent resorts to the ultimate manipulative argument: the threat that he or she will surely die if thrown into a nursing home.

The worst crisis occurs, however, when the middle-aged child has to contend with a mentally ill, acting-out, or even violent parent. The concurrent disorientation, loss of memory, confusion, incontinence, insomnia, and irrational behavior can cause both pain and total havoc in the life of the adult child. Some break down in desperation when they cannot locate home care services or a nursing home willing to take in a parent in such an uncontrollable condition.

THE MIDDLE-AGED CARE-GIVER

Neighbors, friends, and relatives may occasionally offer help, but that does not necessarily qualify them as care-givers. To meet this designation they would have to provide continuous help according to the 1982 Long Term Care Survey of the United States Department of Health and Human Services with at least two "activities of daily living" (ADL), such as dressing, feeding, bathing, toileting, and transferring from bed.

The research conducted on the subject since the 1960s reveals that principal care-givers of dependent elderly are usually middle-aged daughters who are mostly married. They also carry on major responsibilities toward their own offspring. Many of these women have entered the labor force and work full time, but find it increasingly difficult to reconcile the three roles: mother, daughter/ care-giver, and worker. It is a juggling act they cannot perform indefinitely without succumbing to stress and physical exhaustion.

In 1984 the Bureau of Labor Statistics reported that 69 percent of all women between the ages of 35 and 44 were employed. In the middle-aged group 45 to 54, some 62 percent were employed, and this figure dropped to 42 percent in the preretirement group 55 to 64.[14] Brody found that 28 percent of her sample of nonworking women had left their jobs because of an elderly parent's need for assist-

The myth that families abandon their elderly is false and unfair to the middle generation.

ance. A similar proportion of working women experienced conflicting demands and were seriously considering getting out of the labor force or working reduced hours.

THE CRITICAL DECISION—opting for work or care-giving—is complicated by the fact that most adult children do not live under the same roof with their ailing parents and must therefore cope with the homemaking and home management requirements of two separate households. Because nearly 70 percent of the very old cohort, those 75 and older, already experience multiple chronic conditions, there is virtually no end to the care-providing demands assumed by relatives. The burden is relentless and indefinite.

Moreover, it is by no means an episodic assignment performed on occasion or accommodated to better suit the care-givers' convenience. Care-givers must be on call literally at all times. They are no longer in control of their life schedules. The first thing they usually sacrifice are their own leisure interests and pursuits; then they give up their social life and a good portion of the time spent with their families. They ultimately end up neglecting their own health needs, to the detriment of their much-needed care-giving capacity.

Yet as Joseph Kuypers and Vern Bengston found in their studies, most families accept chronic conditions and impairment as a normative life transition.[15] As a result, even if families must make all pertinent adjustments, finally they do manage to continue a semblance of normal life. Of all care-giving families interviewed by Linda Noelker and S. Walter Poulshock, only 20 percent felt severely burdened by their care-giving. Over 60 percent denied experiencing any discomfort and apparent-

ly accepted the exigencies of the role and the resulting deprivations as a natural concomitant of family life.[16]

To what extent does public policy lighten the care-giving task? If judging by the effects of the recent Prospective Payment System incorporated into the Medicare legislation, families will end up carrying a heavier, not a lighter care-giving load.

FAMILY POLICY: THE DRGs EXPERIENCE

Congress recently instituted a new method of Medicare reimbursement to hospitals. A fixed Medicare payment for inpatient operating costs is established in advance of the provision of services. The rates are determined by classifying illnesses into 475 diagnosis-related groups, or DRGs.

Each of these DRGs has indicators determining the length of hospital stay (LOS) for each illness. Hospitals are consequently reimbursed only for that precise number of days. If a hospital can treat a patient for less than the DRG allowed payment ceiling, it pockets the difference. If the treatment requires instead a longer stay, the hospital must absorb the loss. As may be surmised, it is in the hospitals' interest to release Medicare patients within the DRGs' allotted time limits, or even earlier.

It was justifiably feared that with the DRGs, patients would be prematurely and inappropriately discharged from hospitals, adding to their families' burdens as care-givers. A study conducted by Health Economics Research found that patients are discharged from hospitals "sicker and quicker," and that patients fear retaliation, including being saddled with their entire medical bill, if they protest discharge. Moreover, they are altogether unaware of available mechanisms for appealing discharge decisions.[17] Moreover, findings showed that community care was inaccessible, unaffordable, or altogether nonexistent. A report submitted in 1985 to Sen. John Heinz of Pennsylvania by the U.S. General Accounting Office found that as a consequence of DRGs, home health agencies are increasing the frequency of visits per case, receiving more requests for multiple visits per week, and seeing a greater need for more

specialized services such as intravenous therapy and catheters. Discharges to home health agencies have also increased because some nursing homes opt for accepting no Medicaid-eligible patients once their Medicare benefits have been exhausted.[18] Researchers similarly found an increase in the demand for home health nursing visits after the DRGs were implemented.[19]

There is no doubt that the need and demand for professional home health care service is expanding because the elderly are living longer and experiencing debilitating, long-term illnesses. But if reimbursement for hospital costs is restricted, older patients are then forced into nursing homes or into receiving highly sophisticated and even round-the-clock nursing supports in their own homes. If the newly established DRGs' policy seeks to sanction the transfer of those nursing services from inpatient hospital services to formal professional and paraprofessional home care services, there would apparently be no losers: Medicare would probably save a portion of the high hospital costs and patients would continue receiving the required care.

The reality, however, turned out to be different: the DRGs were followed by equally stringent Medicare regulations that severely curb home care services. Many of the patients ended up in what Senator Heinz has termed "the no-care zone." Patients either receive an inadequate level of care because they do not qualify for Medicare's restrictive home coverage, or cannot locate the appropriate services in their communities, or for the most part, do not have the means to pay privately for such services. In the last resort, families are saddled with

Many women find it difficult to reconcile the three roles: mother, daughter/ care-giver, and worker.

the costs in time, money, and the actual provision of care. They are big losers in an unfair transfer of fiscal and service responsibilities. There are no incentives either in the form of tax exemptions or direct compensation for families to assume this added home health-care burden.

Some countries, like Norway and Sweden, have successfully experimented with cash payments to relatives for performing home-care tasks. This service strategy was introduced as a consequence of a severe shortage of home-care personnel in their full employment economies. Policymakers there soon perceived that these transitional and emergency measures had some intrinsic merits. Many family care-givers were forced to leave better-paying jobs and stayed home to care for their ailing elders. They were then paid less than it would cost the public coffers to hire professional home-care workers. Many relatives were willing to make such sacrifices rather than leave their aged relatives unattended. The payment for home care they receive is therefore only a partial, almost symbolic compensation for the economic losses they surely incur when giving up their jobs. The sacrifices in terms of their own family's needs and personal leisure or freedom remain economically incalculable.

COPING WITH CATASTROPHIC EXPENSES

One recent policy development that provides modest but promising economic relief to relatives is the Medicare Catastrophic Coverage Act of 1986. This act constitutes the largest single expansion of Medicare in its twenty-three years of existence. The provisions of the bill were to be phased over the next three years and will include unlimited hospital coverage beyond an annual deductible of about $600, and acute care in skilled nursing homes will be extended from 100 to 150 days a year. Medicaid will pick up the Medicare deductibles, premiums, and coinsurance for those with incomes of up to 85 percent of the federal poverty level, and spouses of Medicaid nursing home residents will be able to keep $786 in monthly income in 1989 and $12,000, or half of the couple's assets, whichever is

> Care-givers must be on call literally at all times. They are no longer in control of their own life schedules.

greater. The maximum out-of-pocket expenses for physician services will be $1,370 a year; home health services will be extended from a limit of 15 to 38 days a year and up to 80 hours of health aids to provide respite care for relatives attending to patients at home. Finally, Medicare will start paying 50 percent of outpatient prescription drug expenses exceeding $600 a year. This share will gradually increase until reaching 80 percent in 1993.

Substantial gaps remain, such as dental and hearing services, and physician charges that exceed the limit set by Medicare. The biggest gap relates to indefinite stays in nursing homes. This is the greatest source of catastrophic expense for older Americans. The new bill, however, offers substantial relief for spouses: Even if it does not cover long-term care, it helps the noninstitutionalized spouse of the nursing home resident to survive economically and avoid becoming totally destitute.

The unfinished policy agenda therefore includes provisions for some form of long-term care insurance and a more encompassing program for care in the home. Medicare, it must be borne in mind, pays less than 2 percent of all nursing home expenses, and more than half of the nursing home costs are still paid out of pocket by aged patients and their families. Only the poorest of the poor, those left without any assets, qualify for Medicaid coverage.

THE SHORTSIGHTEDNESS OF PUBLIC POLICY

Public policy remains predicated on the notion that families will not

only continue indefinitely in the care-giving role but will even assume greater responsibilities. An awareness of the family's resilience must, however, be tempered with a recognition of its limitations. Families provide the place where members of different generations help each other but they are not an omnipotent panacea that is available to everybody at all times.

The idealization of the family often rests on the fact that families already provide most of the home health-care services for older relatives. It is comforting indeed to know that families fill so many of the gaps and deficiencies of the service system, far beyond routine household chores. Some family members even take courses that will enable them to perform complete rehabilitative care, but one may wonder how much maintenance the average family can provide beyond socioemotional supports and essential chores? Isn't there an erosion with time of such a capacity? A study in western New York found, to this effect, that families' ability or willingness to continue home care services drops by 50 percent after the second hospitalization of a disabled elderly relative.[20] The average family is not insensitive or indifferent, but the extent of its capacity to provide care for an older relative should not be taken for granted indefinitely. Public policy rests on the naturalness of filial responsibility, but it has not fully awakened to the protracted and complex demands of care-giving. The theoretical debate about the "generation gap" and the degree of psychological identification or distance among generations notwithstanding, there has probably been no generation in history confronted with so many service exigencies to their senior relatives as the middle-aged and the "young" old of today—those between 45 and 70 years of age. They are truly meeting their obligations. Some do it begrudgingly but they do not abandon their frail aged. Because they all pay an inordinate price, public policy must move faster with the provision of fiscal relief and concurrent community-based services. This will insure that families remain as the most effective source of support for the increasing numbers of frail aged.

1. Henry Fairlie, "Talkin' 'bout My Generation." *The New Republic* (March 28, 1988): 19–22.

2. Eric R. Kingson, Barbara A. Hirshorn and John M. Cornman, *"Ties that Bind: The Interdependence of Generations."* (Washington, D.C.: Seven Locks Press; 1986): 3–9.

3. American Association of Retired Persons, "AARP Leads Drive to Put 'Care' Issue in '88 Race." *AARP News Bulletin,* 28 (10) (November 1988): 4.

4. Tamara K. Hareven, "The Last Stage: Historical Adulthood and Old Age." In Eric H. Erickson (Editor), *Adulthood.* (New York: W.W. Norton and Co., 1978).

5. Karl Manheim, "The Problem of Generations." In D. Kecskemi (Editor), *Essays on the Sociology of Knowledge.* (London: Routledge and Kegan Paul, 1952): 276–322.

6. Charles A. Reich, *"The Greening of America."* (New York: Random House, 1970.)

7. Richard Kalish, "The Young and the Old as Generation Gap Allies." *The Gerontologist,* 9 (1969): 83–89.

8. Elaine M. Brody, "Parent Care as a Normative Family Stress." *The Gerontologist,* 25 (1985): 19–29.

9. Ethel Shanas, "The Family as a Social Support System in Old Age." *The Gerontologist,* 19 (1979):169–174.

10. Elaine M. Brody, "Serving the Aged: Educational Needs as Viewed by Practice." *Social Work,* 15 (October 1970): 42.

11. Amy Horowitz, *"Adult Children as Caregivers to Elderly Parents: Correlates and Consequences."* Unpublished Doctoral Dissertation. Columbia University School of Social Work, New York, 1982.

12. Gordon F. Streib, "Intergenerational Relations: Perspectives of the Two-Generation Family on the Older Parent." *Journal of Marriage and the Family,* 27 (November 1965): 469–476.

13. Robert Kastenbaum and Robert Aisenberg, *"The Psychology of Death: Concise Edition.* (New York: Springer, 1976.)

14. United States Bureau of Labor Statistics, "Employment and Earnings" (Washington, D.C.: 1984): Table 3.

15. Joseph A. Kuypers and Vern L. Bengtson, "Toward Competence in the Older Family." In Timothy Brubaker (Editor), *Family Relationships in Later Life,* (Beverly Hills, Calif.: Sage, 1983): 211–223.

16. Linda S. Noelker and S. Walter Poulshock, "The Effect on Families of Caring for Impaired Elderly in Residence." *Final Report to the Administration on Aging.* (Cleveland, Ohio, The Benjamin Rose Institute, 1982.)

17. Margo L. Rosenback and Jerry Cromwell, "Physicians' Perceptions about the Short Run Impact of Medicare's Prospective Payment System: Final Report." *Health Economic Research,* (1985): 1–8.

18. U.S. General Accounting Office, "Information Requirements for Evaluating the Impacts of Medicare Prospective Payment on Post-Hospital Long Term Care Services: Preliminary Report" (Report to Senator John Heinz). (GAO/PEMD 85–8, February 21, 1985): 1–9.

19. Elayne Kornblatt, Mary E. Fisher and Donna J. MacMillan, "Impact of DRGs on Home Health Nursing." *Quality Review Bulletin, Journal of Quality Assurance* (October 1985): 290–294.

20. Gerald M. Eggert, Carl V. Granger, Robert Morris and Sylvia F. Pendleton, "Caring for the Patient with Long Term Disability." *Geriatrics,* 32 (10) (October 1977): 102–118.

FAMILY CAREGIVERS:
America's Primary Long-Term Care Resource

Lynn Osterkamp, Ph.D.

Lynn Osterkamp, a Research Associate in the Gerontology Center at the University of Kansas, is editor of Parent Care, *a national newsletter for professionals and families involved in caring for the elderly.*

"Aging is a family affair." "Caregivers need care too!" Such familiar slogans reflect the recent emphasis on the needs of American families caring for frail elderly relatives. Professional organizations, advocacy groups, and the popular media remind us that informal caregivers, primarily families, are providing most of the help needed by frail elderly persons, and that these caregivers themselves need help.

We know that in the past 20 years, the U.S.A.'s elderly population (age 65 and above) has grown twice as fast as the general population, and that the most rapidly growing age group is the "old-old" (over age 85). This oldest group numbers approximately 2 million and will increase to about 16 million by the mid-21st Century. While only about 5 percent of those aged 65 to 74 require help, by age 85, about 33 percent need personal assistance.

Families are our nation's primary resource for providing this help. Approximately 80 percent of the frail elderly in the community report that informal caregivers are their major source of assistance. In 1982 the National Long Term Care Survey found that approximately 2.2 million caregivers aged 14 or older were providing unpaid assistance to 1.6 million noninstitutionalized disabled elderly persons who had one or more limitations in activities of daily living. An estimated 6 million elderly Americans need some assistance from family or friends with activities ranging from personal care to household maintenance, shopping and transportation.

Even though providing care imposes extensive demands on families, home care is likely to continue to increase in the future for several reasons: families prefer it over institutional care, family caregiving costs less than hospital or nursing home care, and the number of patients now requiring extensive home care is increasing.

To help caregivers effectively, we need a picture of who they are, how they manage, what problems they face, and what types of assistance they need. Although there is considerable research describing caregivers, we find from the data that caregivers are not a homogeneous group who can be easily represented by some typical caregiver. As we consider caregivers' problems, it is important to keep in mind that this diverse population requires a broad range of assistance to meet its varying needs.

Who Are the Caregivers? What Care Do They Provide?

Surveys consistently find that the majority of caregivers (about 75 percent) are women and that their average age is between 55 and 60, with approximately one-third over age 65. The frail person's spouse is the most likely to become the caregiver; next likely are adult daughters, then daughters-in-law, sons and other relatives. Wives of severely impaired men provide the most informal care.

Caregivers described by research tend to be those who are caring for seriously impaired elderly persons, as, for example, the 6,400 elderly studied in the National Long Term Care Survey. That survey estimates that these 6,400 represent an actual 1.6 million frail elderly receiving care at home. Thus, when we use this research data to describe caregivers, we must realize that we are depicting primarily the estimated 2.2 million unpaid caregivers who care for these frail elderly. We cannot necessarily assume that we are also describing the larger population of family and friends who assist elderly people needing limited amounts of help with activities such as transportation, finances or home maintenance.

The frail elderly described in research are impaired on an average of two to three activities of daily living (such as bathing, feeding and toileting) and on an average of five instrumental activities of daily living (such as housework, meal preparation and shopping). The majority of their caregivers assist them with such tasks

From *Aging*, No. 358, 1988, pp. 2-5. Reprinted by permission.

seven days a week, averaging between four and five hours a day. About half of their caregivers have been providing care for less than four years, but about a fifth have been caregivers for five years or longer. Approximately three-fourths of the caregivers live with the care recipient.

Family caregivers increase the level of services they provide to match the older person's needs, and some, especially adult daughters, serve as a link between the elderly person and community services. In general, women give more overall help and more help with personal and household tasks, while men help more with home repairs, transportation, and financial management.

How Much Help Do Caregivers Get?

Most frail elderly people have one primary caregiver who assumes overall responsibility for their care. When the primary caregiver is an adult child, that child is most often a daughter who is geographically close to the parent. There is no evidence that oldest versus youngest or middle children are most likely to become caregivers or that the "most loved" child is chosen for the job.

Primary caregivers tend to take on most of the caregiving tasks themselves, often with little help from other family members or from community services. In general caregivers who do get help and support from family feel less burdened by the demands of caregiving. This does not necessarily imply, however, that family members can easily step in and relieve the primary caregiver's burden. In fact, professionals have repeatedly observed that the family dynamics surrounding caregiving are complex, and that not all primary caregivers are willing to ask for or even accept help.

Caregivers also use relatively few community services. Surveys show that only 10 to 20% of caregivers use paid helpers and that the frail elderly receive an average of five times as many hours per week of help from informal caregivers as they do from formal services. In general, families begin using formal services only when the older person's needs become too much for them to handle.

What Is the Impact of Caregiving on Caregivers?

Although the most frequently mentioned effects of caregiving on the caregiver are negative, some benefits are reported. Three quarters of caregivers say providing care makes them feel useful, and many anecdotal reports attest to caregivers' satisfaction in knowing that their older relative is receiving adequate care while remaining in the community. About one-fourth of caregivers report that the older person helps financially or with household chores.

The impact of caregiving on physical health has been investigated with confusing results. Reports of poor health are higher for women who are caregivers than for women of the same age who don't have this responsibility, but whether or not this difference is due to caregiving is unclear. Caregivers in some studies have reported rather large declines in their physical health over several years of caregiving; other studies have not found much decline.

Emotional strain and feelings of being burdened are the most often cited negative effects of caregiving, but again effects are by no means universal. Some caregivers report much more stress than do others, but interpretations are difficult because of the many different methods used to study caregiver stress. Caregivers don't necessarily agree on what constitutes "a great deal of strain," and may weigh such factors as obligation and family tradition when responding.

In general, it seems that the types of tasks caregivers must perform, the amount of assistance they get, and specific characteristics of caregivers, such as problem-solving style, are most related to the amount of strain the caregiver reports. Apparently, providing personal care is more burdensome than performing less intimate tasks. Several studies have found that women find care giving more stressful than men do, but the reason for such differences is not clear.

Caregivers who take a passive approach to problem-solving, using such strategies as avoidance, report more feelings of burden, as do those who feel little control over their situation or do not have confidence in their problem-solving abilities. Also, caregivers caring for elders who engage in

disruptive behavior such as yelling and swearing report more stress. However, the burden does not necessarily increase as the severity of an older person's cognitive impairment increases.

While caregivers' feelings of stress and burden are subjective states that are difficult to investigate, other negative effects of caregiving are more obvious. Between a quarter and a third of caregivers report that limitations on their social life and on relationships with family and friends pose a serious problem; about half report some problems in these areas.

Ten to twenty percent of caregivers report leaving their jobs to be full-time caregivers. Among employed caregivers, one-fifth to one-third say they have rearranged or restricted their working hours because of caregiving demands. Blue collar workers, who have the least flexibility, are most likely to take time off without pay to handle caregiving tasks, thus adding lost income to their problems.

Some caregivers have conflicting demands. About a quarter of adult child caregivers have dependent children competing for their time and attention. Forty to fifty percent of spousal caregivers have problems with their own health, assessing it as fair to poor.

What Is the Contribution Of Family Caregiving?

Decades of research have shown that feelings of family responsibility to the elderly are firmly rooted in our society. The idea that families today are abandoning their elderly has been repeatedly demonstrated to be false. In fact, family care is the most critical factor in preventing or delaying nursing home placement of the frail elderly.

Among elderly who do enter nursing homes, those who have family support enter at a higher level of impairment than do those without such support. Families tend to exhaust their own resources before turning to institutionalization. One study found that the majority of families in a sample who had placed relatives in nursing homes reported that their patient required 24-hour care or supervision before placement. On admission these patients had an average of four health problems per person, two other precipitating problems (such as frequent falls, confusion, incontinence), and more than 80 percent had been recently hospitalized. Nevertheless, families had been providing nearly total care before nursing home admission; only 19 percent of the elderly patients had been receiving any formal community-based services.

Several studies have shown that the level of family care does not decrease even when formal community-based servides are used. Increased use of formal services seems to serve primarily to improve the quality of life for caregivers and patients.

Obviously American families who care for frail elderly relatives are contributing immensely to society, both in terms of the quality of life for these elderly and in terms of the financial responsibility society would otherwise have to assume for such care. If families are to continue to carry this responsibility, however, they need more help.

What Do Caregivers Need?

This is a complex question since caregivers are a diverse group whose needs and resources vary, and since the effects of interventions designed to help them are difficult to evaluate.

Caregivers Need Education and Training. Surveys consistently show that caregivers want to know more about the diseases and conditions that afflict their elderly relatives. They want to know what to expect and how best to respond. They want to understand and know how to administer the drugs and treatments their relatives need. They want specific training in performing the increasingly complex medical procedures needed to care for their relatives when they are discharged from the hospital. They want to know what services are available to help their older relative and how to go about getting them. They want to learn how to cope with com-

plex health care reimbursement forms and regulations.

Caregivers Need Assistance. The types of assistance needed obviously vary with the caregiving situation and caregiver resources. We do not know why some caregivers use services while others do not or whether some services are more helpful than others. Research on the effects of providing such services as respite, adult day care, or case management is difficult to interpret since programs differ and varying measures of the impact of the services on caregivers have been used.

Although caregivers' anecdotal reports of the effects of new programs and services tend to be positive, specific consistent benefits generally have not shown up on measuring instruments. We need more carefully controlled research investigating the effects of specific interventions so that we can tailor programs to meet caregivers'

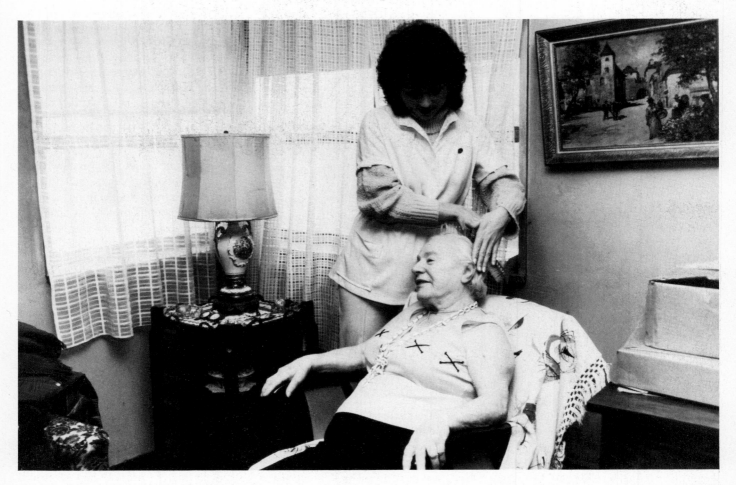

Care of the elderly can often be a long-term process. A majority of caregivers are middle-aged women, and adult daughters often find themselves with the responsibility of day-to-day support of their parents.

needs most effectively. We also need to find ways of assuring families that accepting help does not mean that they are giving up or failing in their caregiving role.

Caregivers Need Emotional Support. Caregivers who participate in support groups find comfort in being able to express their feelings in a supportive setting and in realizing that they are not alone in their emotional reactions. Again, the benefits of such groups are difficult to quantify, and research to date has yielded confusing results. Nevertheless, professionals and caregivers alike overwhelmingly report that caregivers need support in setting limits for themselves, in considering the effects of taking on or continuing caregiving responsibilities, and in making difficult decisions. Whether they can best find this support from friends and family, through a support group or in individual counseling may vary from case to case.

Caregivers Need Relief from Financial Strain. Fewer caregivers than we might expect actually report financial strain due to caregiving. Nevertheless, the costs of giving up or reducing employment, or straining one's physical and mental health to provide care for a long period may not be immediately apparent. We must carefully investigate what partnership between government and family will be most cost-effective in the long run.

Caregivers Need to Know We Care. Most of all caregivers need to know that they are not alone, that society supports them and is willing to share the burden. Families want to provide for their elderly, ideally as part of a coordinated societal approach to long term care.

Selected References
For Further Reading

Brody, Elaine M. Parent Care as Normative Family Stress. (1985) *The Gerontologist*, 25, 19-29.

Family Survival Project. (1986) *Employed Caregiver Study Research Summary.* 44 Page Street, Suite 600, San Francisco, CA 94102.

Stephens, Susan A. and Christianson, Jon. B. *Informal Care of the Elderly.* (1986) Lexington, MA: Lexington Books.

Stone, Robyn, Cafferata, Gail L., and Sangl, Judith. Caregivers of the Frail Elderly: A National Profile. (1987) *The Gerontologist*, 27, 616-626.

U.S. House of Representatives Select Committee on Aging. Subcommittee on Human Services. *Exploding the Myths: Caregiving in America.* (1987) Comm. Pub. No. 99-611. Washington D.C.: U.S. Government Printing Office.

Social Policies, Programs, and Services for Older Americans

It is a political reality that older Americans can obtain needed assistance from government programs only to the degree that they are perceived as politically powerful. Political involvement can include holding and expressing political opinions, voting in elections, participating in voluntary associations to help elect a candidate or party, and holding political office.

Research has indicated that older people are just as likely as any other age group to hold political opinions, are more likely than younger people to vote in an election, are about equally divided between Democrats and Republicans, and are more likely than young people to hold political office. Older people, however, have shown little inclination to vote as a bloc on issues affecting their welfare. Current activists, such as Maggie Kuhn and the leaders of the "Gray Panthers," have encouraged senior citizens to vote as a bloc, but so far they have not convinced them to do so.

Gerontologists have observed that a major factor contributing to the increased push for government services for the elderly has been the publicity on their plight generated by such groups as the National Council of Senior Citizens and the American Association of Retired Persons. The desire of adult children to shift the financial burden of aged parents from themselves onto the government has further contributed to the demand for services for the elderly. The resulting widespread support for such programs has practically guaranteed their passage in Congress.

Now, for the first time, groups are emerging which oppose increases in spending for services for older Americans. Requesting generational equity, some politically active groups argue that the federal government is spending so much on older Americans that it is depriving younger age groups of needed services.

The articles in this section address the current state of older Americans in the work force. Also considered are public opinion regarding older workers, public policy toward the elderly, and the roles of the older worker in the post-industrial society. There is presently a decrease in the number of young people in the general population, which has created a labor shortage for companies that traditionally rely on this age group. The article "A New Look at Companies That Hire Experience" addresses this phenomenon, and points out that some service industries are employing older workers, though not for critical high-paying positions. The following article, "Staying in the Work Force," takes this point further by suggesting that we need policies to encourage older workers to remain in the work force. As we approach the twenty-first century, the fastest-growing segment of the population will be women over the age of 85. In "Process, Politics, & Policy" the author emphasizes that provisions will have to be made for health and human services and for allocation of public benefits. These social service programs, many of which are already in place, will take an ever-increasing share of the tax dollar, while programs devoted to the other age groups will suffer. In "Generational Equity and the Future of Generational Politics" this growing problem is examined. As our post-industrial society matures and the need for a total work commitment is altered by technology, the quality of one's life will become of increasing importance. In "Roles for Aged Individuals in Post-Industrial Societies" the importance of such things as recreation, leisure, education, and avocational pursuits in the lives of our older citizens is discussed.

Looking Ahead: Challenge Questions

What new programs should the federal government institute in the next five years to assist older Americans?

What service programs for senior citizens could be more efficiently handled by state and local governments than by Washington? Give examples.

Do you think that the elderly are often abused in the name of protection? Explain why or why not.

Do you believe that the federal government is investing too much in social services for older Americans?

A New Look at Companies That Hire Experience

SONDRA K. MATCH

Sondra K. Match is a field representative for the Southeast Region of NCOA's Senior Community Employment Service Program. She has earned two master's degrees, from the Columbia University School of Social Work and from the University of Hawaii School of Public Health.

Smart companies are beginning to test the water in a pool of labor: the older worker. Is demographic expediency dictating this new development, or is American business finally beginning to recognize the unique talents older workers bring to increased productivity and customer satisfaction? Perhaps a bit of both.

But for those executives inventing new ways to tap the experience and energy of older workers, including those returning from the ranks of the retired, the rewards are substantial.

The statistical handwriting is on the wall.

According to the U.S. Department of Commerce.

■ Between 1985 and 1991, the number of 16- to 17-year-olds will decline 1.9 percent per year and the number of 18- to 19-year-olds will drop 1.6 percent annually.

■ At the same time, the older pop-ulation is increasing. The 55-74 population will grow to 11.1 million, a jump of 13 percent. The population 75 and over will escalate 4.7 million, a 45 percent rise.

Industries such as food service, retail stores, food stores, hotels, motels, and banks are beginning to compete for an ever-diminishing pool of young entry-level workers willing to accept a minimum wage. Already, service industries faced with acute labor shortages are turning to the other end of the spectrum: the mature worker.

Eventually, talents of experienced workers will be in demand for jobs that go far beyond entry level.

But it will take matchmaking and job adjustment: linking up the right job to the right worker, or even rewriting job descriptions to accommodate the employee.

That's certainly been the case at the Travelers Companies of Hartford, Connecticut. There, "unretirees" have been welcomed back to work in consumer assistance offices and elsewhere. The demand for their services has become so great that Travelers is actually hiring retirees from other companies in the Hartford area.

Travelers' personnel experts are also getting inquiries from their sister insurance companies on ways in which they can establish *their* retiree renewal programs.

Another well-known employee retention program is going on at Grumman Aerospace Company in Bethpage, New York. One reason for Grumman's diligence is that security clearances often cost the company as much as $100,000 each. It behooves management to find ways to retain experienced personnel.

Well-known as they are, Travelers and Grumman are only two examples of the ferment now going on in hiring and job reshaping to attract older workers. What follows is a gallery of others.

Walt Disney World Company: Of its 18,000 permanent employees in Orlando, Florida, 1,600 or 9 percent are over age 55. This giant corporation sponsors a booth at the local Senior Employment Fair and nominates employees for the Florida Older Worker Award held each year in Orlando. Older employees work throughout the company in food service, maintenance, offices and the numerous parks and attractions.

From *Perspectives on Aging*, September/October 1987, pp. 18-22. Copyright © 1987 by The National Council on the Aging.

Andy Frain Communications: This Chicago company is in the "crowd control" business, supplying personnel for sporting and political events and for passenger screening at airports. At the nearby O'Hare Airport, 25 percent of Frain's employees are over age 55. Of its 3,000 special events employees, 20 percent are older workers, most of whom earn an hourly wage of $3.50 to $4. A substantial number are full-time supervisory paid $250-350 weekly. Says personnel manager Matthew Vail, "Eighteen- to 25-year-olds are not as good in working with the public in security screening. We use older workers instead."

Kelly Services: This job agency for temporary employees has 700 branch offices in the United States and Canada. It is about to launch a North American-wide campaign to hire older workers. A mail campaign will be directed at organizations listing older persons as members, and recruitment speakers will be sent to likely sites. Kelly provides free training to upgrade skills. It will hire older persons in its four divisions: clerical, light industrial, marketing and technical support (lab technicians, draftpersons, computer programmers and operators). Temporaries at Kelly Services are paid vacation and holidays, cash bonuses and membership in a travel club. They can buy health insurance at reduced rates.

Good People: This is another employment agency for temporary workers. In the New York City area, it is attempting to attract older workers for business *and* industry. Good People's chairman Samuel Gave has issued a bulletin calling for workers to staff "Operation Seasoned Talent," described as "an all-out effort by Good People to supply temporary and permanent personnel from the region's growing pool of mature adults."

Gave refers to the "gold collar work force," which he describes as "productive, hardworking, punctual and dependable [individuals who] add a certain stability to the work place ... in these troubled times of mergers, acquisitions and reorganizations." He adds: "A few wrinkles and some gray heads in the work place are nothing but good signs, and we hope to see a lot more of them." Good People reports hiring 4,000 people annually, 20 percent of whom are 55-plus.

Builders Emporium: Headquartered in Irvine, California, this company proudly reports that 12 to 15 percent of its workforce of 5,200 people throughout the state are over 55. Says employment director Richard Taylor, "We hire these people because they come from a generation of do-it-yourselfers, like my father. Older workers are customer service-oriented. They were brought up to believe the customer comes first." Describing the opening of a store in a San Diego suburb, he adds: "We had 600 people standing in line to apply for jobs. At the head of the line was a 72-year-old man who had worked as a plumber for 40 years. You can believe we hired him on the spot."

Fliers to recruit older workers are posted in all Builder's Emporium stores. They are headlined, "Attention Senior Citizens—Let's talk." They conclude, "We're Interested in You." The company participates in Job Fairs sponsored by the National Council on the Aging. It honors Senior Achievers throughout the chain of stores and conducts "age issues in management" seminars for store managers.

(Two other home center merchandisers, the national **Wal-Mart** chain and **Hechinger** in the Washington, D.C., area, have an affinity for hiring older workers. Their managers find that many customers who lack do-it-yourself skills come to their stores for help. Whom do they choose to consult? The older male employee is the hands-down choice.)

The Bay Bank: Just outside Boston and the fourth largest bank in the state, this fast-growing firm lists 20 percent of its headquarters staff (367 out of 1,800) as 50-plus. Senior vice president Dick Turkfenjian is aggressive about hiring older people: "We have a bias for hiring qualified persons despite their age. And now I have the right climate for doing what I want to do." He hastens to add, "When the labor shortage eases—Boston currently reports unemployment figures of 2.3 percent—I hope they won't forget about hiring over-55-year-olds. The senior citizen organizations should stress the quality competence angle, which can add to a company's profitability."

(From Massachusetts to California, the banking industry is becoming a big employer of the older worker. At the **Great American First Savings Bank** in San Diego, one seventh of the employees are in their sixties and seventies. And in Florida, "A significant number of our 2,000 employees in 59 offices are over age 55," according to Dick Finnigan, senior vice president and personnel director of the **Sun Bank.**

Joseph Horn Department Store: It isn't only in labor shortage areas that more mature workers are in demand. Pittsburgh, Pennsylvania, has at least 8 percent unemployment, yet the Joseph Horn Department Store of that city reports that 32 percent of its hourly employees are over 50. Eileen Scott, benefits manager, says flatly: "We want assertive, aggressive people who want to wait on customers. We are not desperate. We hire older people by choice."

(Many other retailers apparently agree. **Grand Union,** a supermarket grocery chain with stores in 11 Eastern states and a starting wage of $5 an hour, has been recruiting at senior centers and state employment services for cashiers, carry-out clerks and other positions.)

The push to employ the older worker reported thus far mainly involves the lower paid hourly-wage work force. It is dictated somewhat by labor shortages in certain areas of the country, particularly those with a heavy concentration of service-occupation industries.

But what of the professional and managerial employees over age 55 who have retired voluntarily or involuntarily and who wish to return to the full-time work force? The situation at Korn-Ferry International, the world's largest executive search firm, is not promising. Older executives rarely land new jobs, says northeast managing partner David Smith, who has been flooded with résumés. He adds, "It's sad but there is really nothing I can do for these people."

Wesley Poriotis, chief executive officer of Wesley, Brown and Bartel—an executive-level "headhunting" firm that deals with persons earning $50,000 to $600,000 annually, would agree with Smith of Korn-Ferry: "Mergers and acquisitions have changed the landscape for corporate America, leaving senior executives with hats in hand. Over half of the executives who come to us are out of work and on short-term consulting assignments. There is activity among senior executives to begin small consulting firms for training, for executive search, and to evaluate companies for merger or divestiture. There is a tremendous amount of consulting involvement by older executives, but they get tired of that and want to go back to a company." Poriotis describes himself as a "job doctor" for those over age 46. He tries to help clients capitalize on their background. But, he admits, "hope for the employment of the professional executive is somewhat bleak."

A small but hopeful trend may be exemplified by the Association of Part-time Professionals in McLean, Virginia, which places part-time professionals and runs seminars on starting your own business.

Another positive development for older professionals seeking employment is an effort underway at the National Association of Temporary Services in Alexandria, Virginia. NATS, a trade association representing 6,000 temporary agencies, has a committee, chaired by Tedd Cobb of Denver, Colorado, to study the use of professionals seeking temporary work. "Temporaries are used mostly for clerical work, tele-marketing and light assembly," says Mr. Cobb. The NATS Committee will explore the placement of temporaries as finance managers, doctors, nurses and accountants.

Are older workers being encouraged to compete with 28-year-old yuppies by striving to earn six-figure incomes after starting their own businesses. Terms such as "older entrepreneur" and stories about older workers starting mini-businesses or micro-enterprises have been bandied about. Seminars for older entrepreneurs and tracts on how to start your own business are enjoying a vogue. One article describes the successful enterprise started in Tucson, Arizona, by Thomas Duck, now 72 years old. In 1977, Duck founded the Ugly Duckling Rent-a-Car System, Inc., which rents used cars at half the cost of what big name auto rentals charge for new cars. This particular Ugly Duckling has become a swan and is now the fifth largest auto rental firm in the United States, with more than 500 franchises.

Bernard Nash of the American Association of Retired Persons predicts that there is a potential for older workers in the purchase of franchise operations and that this trend may accelerate in the future.

Among older executives and professionals there are, of course, successful exceptions to the rule. Turkfenjian of Bay Bank has his own story about the hiring of older executives. Last year at age 55, upon retiring as executive vice president of the Sweetheart Plastics Corporation, he was called by the chairman of the board of the Bay Bank and asked to return to work full time as a senior vice president. Another noteworthy exception is the Warren Publishing Company, a fourth-generation family business founded 115 years ago in Boston, Massachusetts. Its newspaper is considered the "Bible" of the publishing industry. With fewer than 50 salaried workers, over half of Warren Publishing's work force is 55 or older. Employees serve in data entry, in production and in the mailing department, many on a flexible schedule of two to four days per week. The head of the mailing department is over 80 years old, as is an employee who works two days a week pasting up the newspaper.

Even in the academic world, where employees are exempted from the 1986 statute on the mandatory retirement, there are positive exceptions. The Hastings School of Law, a unit of the University of California in San Francisco with a faculty of 52, has 12 professors over age 65. Hiring older faculty is tradition that dates to World War II when younger professors left for the Armed Services. "These professors are valued and respected members of the faculty," according to Hillary Swendsen, personnel representative. Some of them came to Hastings because of the school's reputation for hiring those over 65. Two of the faculty are 86.

To sum up, this article must concede that although business's attitude toward the older worker is showing marked improvement, this change is mainly in the labor-short service industries and in areas of low unemployment throughout the country. So far, hourly part-time workers are the beneficiaries of this changing attitude. Opportunities for the salaried higher-paid employee lag far behind. The exception may be

New York City, where Victor Barocas and Claire O'Connor of Senior Employment Services report that job opportunities with growth potential for older workers exist in small- to medium-sized businesses. Says O'Connor in *Business and Health Magazine,* "Both family-owned businesses and new ventures rank high on the list of employers interested in hiring older workers."

Though a few interesting examples may bely this conclusion, in the main business and industry are only beginning to learn the value of hiring the older employee. In the future, perhaps labor demand driven by the shortage of younger workers, as well as the positive experience of service-sector industries, will influence more American businesses and industries to recognize an important human resource so far largely overlooked. □

SUGGESTED READING:

Blyskal, Marie. "Twenty Companies that Care." *Fifty Plus* 26 (2): 26-32.

"Food Service and the Older Worker." *National Restaurant Association,* *Current Issues Report* (a special in-house publication for members). Washington, D.C., 1984.

Managing a Changing Workforce. Washington, D.C.: American Association of Retired Persons, 1986.

Personnel Practices for an Aging Work Force: Private-sector Examples. An information paper prepared for use by the Special Committee on Aging, United States Senate. Washington, D.C., 1985.

Workers Over 50: Old Myths, New Realities. Prepared by Yankelovich, Skelly and White, Inc. for the American Association of Retired Persons. Washington D.C., 1985.

Staying in the Work Force

*An eminent authority takes questions and gives answers
on older workers, present and future.*

Philip M. Hauser is author or editor of 22 books and more than 500 articles. Dr. Hauser is a member of the National Academy of Sciences and a past president of several professional societies, including the American Sociological Association. He is Director Emeritus of the Population Research Center and Lucy Flower Professor Emeritus of Urban Sociology, both at the University of Chicago, and serves on the board of the Chicago Urban League.

Dr. Hauser, you expect a dramatic transformation in the relationship of older Americans to youth. What do you see in the future, as compared to the past?

Let's go back to 1900, when there were 11.8 persons 65 years of age and over for each 100 young persons under 15. By 1980, this relationship had changed so that there were 49.8 older persons for each 100 young. By the year 2000, trends indicate there would be 62.5 elders for each 100 young persons. Further projections indicate that persons 65 and over could actually outnumber youths under 15 before the year 2030. Such a change in population mix has important implications for social and economic policy and practices not only for the aged, but for the entire population.

Does this mean that older workers will be more in demand than they have been in the past?

It should, but we have to remember certain things about the history of older workers in the United States.

Older persons have become increasingly dependent on forces and institutions beyond the family and the immediate community, forces which were often beyond their control. In an unprecedented way, elders were confronted with problems of dwindling family and kinship relationships, maintaining adequate income flow, obtaining comprehensive medical care, effecting suitable living arrangements, and updating education and occupational skills. Perhaps the most difficult problem confronting elders was that of maintaining their places in the work force while they were still able and willing to continue to work. Provisions for compulsory retirement with inadequacies of public and private pensions, and the everpresent threat of inflation exacerbated the social and economic vulnerability of elders. Moreover, cyclical economic activity placed older workers especially at risk for unemployment and underemployment.

If the trend toward earlier and earlier retirement were moderated, would older workers' problems be eased considerably?

It should be noted that retirement is not the only means by which older workers leave the labor force. The decreased importance of the United States in the world economy, discriminatory practices in regard to older workers, work force reduction resulting from mergers, and plant relocations—including locations in foreign countries—have also been significant factors in the displacement of workers of all ages, including older workers. In addition, the adverse balance of trade in recent years has in effect resulted in the exportation of American jobs.

We'll get to your policy recommendations later, but first would you give more details on the numbers of older persons still in the work force?

For comparison, let's go back to 1900 again. Then, 63.1 percent of males 65 years and over were in the work force, and only 8.3 percent of the comparable females. By 1980, the proportion of older males still in the work force had diminished to 19 percent and by 1995, according to projections by the U.S. Bureau of Labor Statistics, will decline further to 13.3 percent. Older women in the work force remain at about the same level in 1980 as in 1900, namely 8.1 percent. It's projected to be 7 percent in 1995.

What changes are we seeing in the ratio of women to men in the work force?

At the turn of the century, 85.7 percent of males 14 and over were in the work force as contrasted with 20 percent of comparable females. By 1980, the proportion of males in the work force had declined to about three-fourths, whereas the proportion of women in the work force had increased to more than half. The increased entry of women into the work force had among its consequences the expulsion of older males. This resulted from the fact that given the inverse relationship between age and education, younger women often had more education and greater skills than older men and were better able to perform the newer types of jobs generated by economic and technological changes.

Are you suggesting that anyone above age 65 should expect to continue working for many more years?

I think we have to recognize the diversity that exists among the 28 million people we call older Americans. Persons 65 to 74 years of age who may be considered as the "young-old," constituted 73 percent of all persons 65 and over in 1900; they had diminished to 61 percent of all elders by 1980 and will drop further to 51 percent by the end of the century. In contrast, persons 75 to 84 years of age, who may be considered the "middle-old," made up 24 percent of all elders in 1900, had risen to 30 percent in 1980, and are projected to continue to rise to 35 percent by the century's end. Persons 85 years old and over, the "old-old," made up only 5 percent of all elders in 1900, but had increased to almost double this percentage, 9 percent by 1980, and are projected to increase further to 14 percent by the year 2000. Unless unanticipated change should occur in the health and work capacities of the "old-old," those 85 and over, it may be assumed that, in general, they would not be considered for labor force participation.

How should policy and practices be changed to help older workers adjust to new circumstances?

Up to this time, it is still a widely-accepted policy that older workers should retire from the work force. However, the tremendous increase in the proportion of older persons, together with the great decline in their labor force participation rate, combine to point up the need for new policies and practices in labor force participation of older persons. The census projections indicate that about a fourth of the American population would be 65 years of age and older by 2080. It would be especially important that older persons who wish to work, not only for income, but also to maintain a desired life style and quality, be enabled to do so. It would be wise first to focus on the "young-old," those 65 to 74 years old, as potential participants in the work force, and next to the "middle-old," those 75 to 84 years of age.

Will change come easily?

As a result of the nation's changed posture in the world economy, present efforts at the training, retraining, and placement of older persons in the work force are made more difficult by the types of structural changes under way, reducing smokestack jobs and increasing service occupations. Difficulties are also engendered by geographical shifts within the nation as industries continue to move to sunbelt areas and further technological developments continue to displace workers.

But we have to face the facts. If older workers do not contribute to current production but continue to have claims on current goods and services, tremendous economic burdens will be placed on younger workers. There is a need, therefore, for changes in policies and practices that would encourage and make possible the continued work activity of elders. Continued work force participation of the elderly, needless to say, will provide the nation not only increased economic output but will simultaneously provide older people with the opportunity to maintain their well-earned lifestyles and quality of life.

AGING FOR THE TWENTY-FIRST CENTURY

Process, Politics, & Policy

Fernando M. Torres-Gil

Fernando M. Torres-Gil, guest editor

The year 1988 will mark a transition in the processes, politics, and policies associated with aging and the elderly. That year will witness the election of a new president and reveal the political direction the nation will take into the twenty-first century. That year will also mark the passing of a generation of leaders who have shaped social policies since the New Deal. Those leadership changes signify a move from a politics of aging rooted in the outgrowth of the Depression, World War II, the cold war period, and the civil rights era to one of a generation that will age in the next century. That "baby boomer" cohort, and its leaders (who have yet to surface), will face a different set of processes, politics, and policies as they assume leadership on aging and social policies.

This article provides insights and raises issues about what policy and politics will mean for aging in the next 12 years and highlights the challenges that must be faced by the twenty-first century, when many of us will have the chance to practice and live what we have been preaching. Preparing for that period requires an understanding of where we have been relative to political developments in aging, what we now face in the existing system of services and benefits for older persons, and what changes may await the next generation of elders.

The United States is in the midst of a demographic revolution with few parallels. The statistical trends are well known. Fully 12 percent of people will live longer and have fewer children. There will be many more older people, with the largest number occurring after the year 2000. The fastest growing segment will be women over 85 years.

Those demographic facts have important implications for provision of health and human services to an older population and for allocation of public benefits and services. The demographic revolution also raises other issues about the role of government in the delivery of public services and benefits and the public's receptivity about paying for those services. Should government be primarily responsible, or should there be a decentralized role involving local governments, individuals, and other nongovernmental groups such as church, neighborhood, family? Who should pay for those benefits and services? And finally, aging, being a lifelong process, requires a fundamental reexamination of how we instruct and require the society to plan and prepare for their aging, particularly with predicted increases in life expectancy. The politics of aging must address those difficult issues, and the generations that age early in the next century must come to terms with a different set of circumstances and experiences than are now faced by older persons.

LOOKING BACK

The modern politics of aging has been with us since the 1930s. Advocacy by groups such as those in the Townsend and the McLain movements, passage of the Social Security Act, and a public recognition of the vulnerability older persons can face during economic crisis—all these factors created societal receptivity to the establishment of public benefits and services for a specific population that had age as a common characteristic. These factors also fostered the development of age-specific organizing and political activism. In short, age and aging became an accepted social and political movement during this period.

The development of gerontocracies and the importance of age for political and social standing is not new. What is new is the development of a politically potent older group in the midst of an aging society. Never before has society had to face a situation where the growth of political and social influence by older persons is coupled with the even greater growth of younger populations that can expect to live longer than the current generation of elderly.

Until this decade, the traditional response has been to assume that the federal government has a responsibility for devising public benefits and services for older persons. The public has accepted the notion that tax dollars and public financing are necessary for funding those services. An elaborate service-delivery system has been developed for one class, and age increasingly has been an accepted identifier for special treatment. Ideologically, despite the swing between conservative administrations that favor less government and liberal administrations that lean toward large, centralized federal authority, there has been little disagreement since the 1930s that the federal government should step in whenever a social need, crisis, or problem has arisen affecting the elderly.

That modern, traditional approach has met with significant accomplishments and overall success. The poverty rate for older persons has dropped. Older persons no longer have to face the specter of the poorhouse, as they did up through the Great Depression. They can rely, at the very least, on Supplemental Security Income, nutrition programs, and congregate senior centers. Medicare and Medicaid provide a basic level of healthcare. And the elderly have considerably greater participation in the democratic process (witness their high levels of voting and their organized interest groups). This participation gives elders, as a group, some control over the vagaries of political and economic life.

The politics of aging reflects the political influence of aged-based organizations and the growing influence of the elderly electorate—a group that no member of Congress would consciously alienate. But increasingly, aged-based groups no longer have a monopoly on aging issues. More organizations and institutions realize that they too have a stake in the decisions. Corporations, hospital and insurance associations, pension and retirement groups, small businesses, and others who previously had little knowledge and interest in aging are voicing opinions and positions on aging-related policies.

The politics of aging, however, is also about a change in public values and attitudes about aging. Younger and middle-aged people and families increasingly realize that aging is not just about being old but about growing old and living longer. The rise of longterm

From *Generations*, Journal of the American Society on Aging, Spring 1988, pp. 5-9. Copyright © 1988 by The American Society on Aging.

care as a political and policy priority signifies the newfound awareness by families and younger groups that political and policy actions toward the elderly can have a direct impact on their own lifestyle choices, economic status, and social relationships. So it can be said that the period from the 1930s up through the 1980s has been a long, gradual evolution in the awareness of the society about aging and living long.

The politics of aging has by all measures been a successful mix of political influence by older persons and their organized interest groups, public receptivity to the needs of the elderly, and creation of large-scale entitlement programs for older persons. And aging advocates and lobbyists should take great pride in what they have accomplished during the last five decades. The passing of Wilbur Cohen allows us to pay tribute not only to his tremendous contribution in shaping Medicare and Medicaid and serving as guardian of public responsibility to the needy, but also to honor the many men and women who have engaged in the battle to provide older persons a measure of dignity, freedom, and independence. And to that extent, the nation should pay homage and be grateful for the long distance we have traveled since the time of the Great Depression.

FACING A CROSSROAD

Nineteen eighty-eight marks a crossroad, however, in the transition from the politics of aging of this century to a twenty-first century aging society.

The 1980s have seen the election of a national administration committed to dismantling many public programs and entitlements and reducing the scope of the federal government. To some extent, the administration has been successful in reducing the overall growth of the federal bureaucracies and reducing benefits and services under existing programs for the poor, elderly, and middle class. This decade has also seen a public reassessment of the directions that the politics of aging has taken so far. No longer can older persons and aged-based groups expect automatic support for their proposals. For the first time, sacred public entitlement programs, particularly Social Security and Medicare, have been expected to put more responsibility on the elderly to shoulder the costs (by such means as raising entitlement age, taxing Social Security benefits, and increasing beneficiary costs in exchange for increased benefits). The rise of "generational equity" as a synonym for supposed conflict between the generations is symptomatic of increasing uneasiness about the scope and costs of public programs and political influence of older persons. Those tensions do not signify a decrease in public support and popularity for helping the needy elderly; polls and public opinion surveys consistently show high levels of support for Social Security, Medicare, and other benefits. What is indicated, however, is that individuals, their families, and taxpayers have been increasingly concerned about their own aging and the extent to which government would and could respond to a longer life span. They wonder whether the current system of public benefits and services should be modified to account for larger numbers of older persons living longer.

The decade of the 1990s presents an opportunity to reassess the directions of political developments and policy responses on behalf of the elderly and to develop appropriate political strategies. Demographically, we know that the growth of older persons will slow somewhat during the 1990s because of the relatively small number of babies born during the Great Depression of the 1930s. We also know that the post–World War II generation will reach its peak of economic productivity during the 1990s. We will have then a reprieve from dramatic demographic changes, an increase in economic resources, and, one hopes, a period of social and political stability. The 1990s will also be the last decade in which the nation will maintain a predominant racial and cultural homogeneity of Anglo-European descendants. The 1990s will probably also see a fundamental reexamination of the political processes by which political decisions are made; signs already abound that the constitutionally-developed system of checks and balances is not able to respond to modern exigencies, and there may be serious proposals to revamp the relationships between the legislative and executive branches. The 1990s then presents that one great moment of transition in which we can prepare for dramatic new developments in the next century—particularly the aging of the largest cohort of persons in the country and the increasing multiethnic and multiracial mix in the population.

THE TREND GENERATION

Much has been said and written about that very large group born between 1946 and 1964—the "baby boomers," who represent the largest age group. The baby boomers are, for better or worse, a trend generation that through its numbers establishes new trends as it moves through the life cycle.

The trend generation's relevance to aging goes much deeper than its influence on the popular culture. The trend generation has also created an anomaly now in vogue—generational politics. The 1984 and, thus far, the 1988 presidential elections have been replete with calls to arms for baby boomers and appeals to their supposed collective identity. Politicians have looked to them as a voting bloc with a common set of experiences (civil rights, Vietnam, Watergate) that would cause them to collectively support a politician who represented their generation's concerns. Generational politics has also led some to believe that differences between baby boomers and their parents and grand parents might lead to some form of generational conflict.

The extent to which the trend generation has a collective identity that can be mobilized into concerted political action is very uncertain. Castelli (1987) refers to the "myth of generational politics" in arguing that the trend generation does not have a collective identity (only a small percentage were actively engaged in protest activities), will not necessarily vote for someone their own age (a majority of this group voted for Ronald Reagan), and does not have an inherent distrust of their parents and grandparents. But, regardless of how we view the trend generation and its political interest, one thing remains certain: they will age and become, collectively, the largest group of older persons this nation will ever face. Sooner or later (probably later) members of that generation will recognize their mortality and develop a very deep interest in issues of older persons. And when that time comes, as it surely will, they will have a profound impact on the politics and policies of aging.

The trend generation is only now beginning to step onto the stage of political power and has yet to display any clear political directions or priorities or to identify its own leadership. It will be during the 1990s that the particular priorities and directions of the trend generation will begin to surface, and their leadership will begin to emerge. Their interests will intersect with the interests of those who are elderly at that time—people born between 1910 and 1926, who will be approaching their 70s and 80s, that period of time when their need for health and social services will be greatest. A third group, those born during the 1930s, will begin to obtain their share of public benefits and services at the moment when the solvencies and costs of many of those programs will come into question. And the trend generation will be exerting its political muscle. How to respond to and merge the competing interests of those generations will be the key challenge for policy makers and interest groups during the 1990s.

The future political profile of the trend generation as it ages requires much more understanding and analysis than this article can manage. But a close look at the questions and challenges that that generation presents is fundamental to understanding aging in the twenty-first century.

CHALLENGES FOR THE '90s

The 1990s will reveal a host of issues, problems, and challenges that will be particular to today's elderly and to those who follow. The four most central are outlined below.

1. A restructuring of the current system of benefits and eligibility. The current system of public benefits and services uses an extraordinary amount of public resources. Most of those benefits, particularly Social Security, have been earned by today's generations of elders. But in times of serious budget deficits and limited expansion of government, the large-scale entitlement programs become very visible to those who want to reduce government expenditures. Especially now that most older persons are reasonably healthy, well educated, and independent, serious consideration will be given to raising eligibility criteria and age. In addition, issues of targeting and means-testing benefits on criteria other than age will probably occur during the 1990s. Those criteria may center around need and functional ability rather than age. Serious examination of the organization and financing of services to the elderly will also occur.

2. Provision of health and longterm-care coverage. The aging of the generation born between 1910 and 1926 highlights the critical gaps in providing longterm care for a population that prefers to remain at home or in the community. Longterm care will be the domestic rallying point for 1988 and beyond. Not just because older persons desperately need longterm-care services, but because families with elders will realize that it is in their best interest to have those services available, and they may even be willing to pay for them, through public taxation. Also important is the increasing number of Americans without any healthcare coverage. If we adopt some form of comprehensive healthcare coverage for all Americans, regardless of age, it will help merge the political and social concerns of all generations.

3. Accepting a multiracial and multi-generational society. A major demographic change in the cultural and social profile of the nation will be its ethnic diversity coupled with its aging. By 2010, a large portion, perhaps a majority, of the U.S. population will be descendants of Hispanics, blacks, Asians and Pacific Islanders, and native Americans. That growing cultural diversity reflects two demographic realities: growing numbers of older persons will be members of minority groups, and young minority populations will be a critical part of the labor force. The life expectancies of minorities are increasing at a more rapid pace than those of the nonminority population, particularly Hispanics and Asians. And as they live longer, they will become a larger proportion of the elderly population. Issues of language and cultural difference, as well as racism and discrimination, will be even larger concerns early in the next century if they are not resolved in the 1990s. Perhaps more disturbing is the presence of growing minority groups who are relatively young. They will compose a large component of the labor force, and on them will lie the burden of maintaining productivity and economic prosperity. But if they remain a poorly trained and poorly educated group, faced with serious obstacles to full participation in American social and political institutions, then the next century will see the fearful results of neglecting their well-being. The 1990s will be the last opportunity for government, the private sector, the public, and the taxpayer to understand that it is in their best interest to launch a massive reinvestment in the human infrastructure (education, healthcare, job training) for those groups and to try even harder to mitigate all forms of racism, sexism, agism, and institutional discrimination.

It is in the increasing multiracial and multicultural makeup of the U.S. population that some disturbing trends could develop. The trend generation will be unusually potent as a political force. Their numbers and their history of political activism guarantee that they will have an inordinate impact on the electoral process. If their priorities concern their own particular desires and needs, we may find that as they age, and become an extraordinarily powerful senior lobby (much more so than today's elders), they may not pay attention to the concerns of a young population increasingly made up of poor minority young people. If that should occur, we may find real generational conflict centering around both age and race—a conflict that does not yet exist.

4. Preparing the population for the aging society. As stated earlier, the demographic revolution presents all institutions in the society—educational, political, economic, spiritual—with new realities. How do we prepare individuals, for example, to live up to 100 years and even longer, with most of that time in reasonable health?

Preparing the public for the aging of society also involves resocializing younger groups to look toward the long term and to plan for a 50-, 60-, and even 70-year career in the work force. It will involve educating children and young people (in primary and secondary grades) about aging and its effect on their lives. We will also see a redefinition of what it means to be old. And here the trend generation will probably make a positive contribution. If we no longer see 65 as old and view the 60s and even the 70s as active years, we can erase the stigmas attached to aging and be better prepared politically to make fundamental changes in the current system of public benefits and services for older persons.

STRATEGIES & LEADERSHIP

Those four challenges facing us in the 1990s will require certain types of political strategies and enlightened leadership.

Tremendous debates occur in any discussion about what government should do, can do, and must not do in responding to social and political needs. The 1980s have been, in a sense, a public experiment in decentralized government and free-market capitalism. What is becoming apparent during the last years of that decade is that the problems, challenges, and needs of the American population are so vast and complex that no one sector of society can be expected to fully respond. And it has become apparent that the attempts to rely on the marketplace and the private sector have created some critical imbalances in the distribution of material resources.

The 1980s have seen great disparity between rich and poor and increased poverty rates among certain segments of society. This growing imbalance in the distribution of material resources is a signal warning to government, the public, and the affluent. No nation—particularly one like the United States, with such high expectations for prosperity—can expect to maintain internal stability if it allows that gap to grow. More disturbing are the persistently high rates of poverty among children in households headed by unwed mothers and among Hispanics and blacks, minority elderly, and the homeless. The institutionalization of subcultures of poverty, particularly inner-city minorities, bodes ill for the social fabric.

The bleak picture facing minorities and the poor during a time of laissez-faire capitalism provides no comforts to the middle class. Notwithstanding stereotypes of baby boomers as "yuppies" (affluent, self-centered, living the good life), most baby boomers and much of the middle class can be characterized as the working middle class, identified by Greenberg (1986) as living from paycheck to paycheck, vulnerable to impoverishment and financial ruin by an economic dislocation, plant layoff, illness, or stock market fluctuation. And it is a population resentful of a political system they feel caters to the affluent and the poor. It is this very group, as Greenberg points out, that will determine the future of political parties and whose concerns must be integrated into any political strategies designed to respond to special interest groups.

Political strategies for the 1990s must take account of the middle class antipathy toward big government, special interest groups, the poor and minorities. Issues of daycare, longterm care, catastrophic illness, protection of pension and retirement benefits, and social supports that allow them to care for aging relatives without becoming financially drained will provide opportunities to obtain their support and receptivity toward aging policies.

Political strategies must also account for the "antigovernment" mood of the 1970s and 1980s. There are signs that the public is regaining an appreciation for strong federal leadership, particularly in the health and education areas. That receptivity must be cultivated, and any political administration will need to prove that tax dollars are spent wisely and compassionately.

Enlightened political leadership must be re-created—leadership that does not pit one group against the other, that does not perpetuate imbalances in material resources, and that does not look at the aging of the society as a phenomenon exclusive to the elderly. An aging society, with all its complexity and inherent contradictions, requires leaders with the moral vision and political courage to speak out for solutions, regardless of how potentially unpleasant or unpopular they may be. What we cannot afford are "cults of personality" and political celebrities who cater to our insecurities and political illusions and promise immediate palliatives. The "go it alone," "every man for himself" attitude will not suffice in the 1990s if the country is to redirect its resources toward regaining economic and social excellence.

We were fortunate during the last five decades to have men and women of moral and political vision—individuals who cared to develop social agendas for responding to social problems and who were willing to "labor in the vineyards" for decades, if that was what it took, to educate the public and bring about social reform. Robert Ball, Wilbur Cohen, Arthur Fleming, Maggie Kuhn, Tish Sommers, Claude Pepper, and Edward Roybal are but a few of those individuals who committed their careers to leadership. The success of the politics of aging during this century owes much to the political leaders cited above. The major question now becomes: Who will replace them? Those individuals are not yet known, but as they evolve and surface, one can only hope that they will emulate the vision and foresight of those who have preceded them.

Political strategies for the 1990s and enlightened leadership must come to terms with the prevailing politics of limitation, where we assume that we cannot help everyone and therefore, by default, leave people to fend for themselves. A politics of equity is required, wherein we attempt to respond to social problems and use government as the primary leader in devising solutions. How that will be done and when are uncertain, but the 1990s will provide an opportunity to redirect our energies and renew a social commitment to the entire society.

REFERENCES

Castelli, J., 1987. "Baby Boom Bang, Bust." *American Politics* (Nov.-Dec.): 32–35.
Greenberg, S., 1986. "Plain Speaking: Democrats State Their Minds." *Public Opinion* (Summer): 44–50.

ROLES FOR AGED INDIVIDUALS IN POST-INDUSTRIAL SOCIETIES

Harold G. Cox

Department of Sociology and Social Work
Indiana State University

ABSTRACT

Cowgill and Holmes in their book *Aging and Modernization* predicted an inverse relationship between industrialization and status accorded older persons. They argued that the more industrialized a country becomes the lower the status accorded older persons. A more careful examination of historical and anthropological work suggests that if we look at the status of the old over the course of history and make projections into the future an S curve is a more realistic pattern. The pattern projected would be one in which the old were accorded a low status in early nomadic tribes, a high status in settled agricultural communities, a low status in industrialized society and ultimately will receive a somewhat higher status in the post-industrial period.

Historically we find a wide variety of patterns of treatment of the aged in different societies. Fischer traced the statements of Herodotus which indicated that at one extreme were the Issedones who gilded the heads of their aged parents and offered sacrifices before them [1]. They seemed to worship their oldest tribal members. At the opposite extreme were the Bactria who disposed of their old folk by feeding them to dogs. Similarly, the Sardinians hurled their elders from a high cliff and shouted with laughter when they fell on the rocks. In traditional China the old men were granted a privileged position. In politics and in family the aged men occupied the top positions of power in a hierarchical society that lasted for thousands of years. This was a value of the prevalent Confucian ideology. Thus we can find diverse patterns of how the aged were treated in different societies and in different historical eras.

An attempt will be made in this article to trace the changing status of aged individuals in different historical periods and to make some educated guesses about what roles aged persons will occupy in post-industrial society.

CRITICAL VARIABLES DETERMINING THE STATUS OF THE AGED

There are a number of variables, often interrelated, which either separately or in combination seem to relate to the status accorded older persons in various cultures. These include: family form, religion, knowledge base of the culture, harshness of the environment, the means of production, and the speed of social changes.

In the consideration of cultural type and status of the aged person, the general rule has been that in the nonindustrial, settled, agricultural societies aged individuals exercise considerable power and are granted a high status. In industrial societies, on the other hand, aged individuals exercise relatively little power and are granted less status. Cowgill and Holmes, in their work on aging and modernization, found an inverse relationship between the degree of modernization and the status accorded old persons [2]. In other words, the more industrialized the system became, the lower the status of the older person. While this is generally the case, a closer look reveals differential treatment of the elders even in the traditional societies. Sheehan, in a study of forty-seven traditional societies, found three different patterns of treatment of aged individuals [3]. Approximately one-fifth of the traditional societies were geographically unstable, as semipermanent bands of people periodically relocating their villages or, in some cases, perpetually mobile. The lowest esteem for seniors was often found in these small and nomadic societies. They have the fewest material resources for seniors to accumulate, thereby gaining respect in the eyes of the youngest person; they are usually located in harsh environments which favor youth and vigor. Food is often in short supply and individual existence is precarious. Elderly individuals may have to be sacrificed to insure the survival of the entire group. Among

Reprinted from *International Journal of Aging and Human Development*, Vol. 30, No. 1, 1990, pp. 55-62. Copyright © 1990, Baywood Publishing Co., Inc.

the societies studied, a plurality were comprised of various forms of tribes which were basically permanently settled, inhabiting fairly large villages, and governed according to a belief in their common ancestry or kinship. Another group of the traditional societies was comprised of small peasant communities whose economic base centered around agriculture or animal husbandry. The most highly developed social organizations were the ones with large landed peasantries; there, the highest esteem was enjoyed by older persons.

It appears that once traditional societies become located in a permanent place with stated residence and property rights, the old began to exercise considerable power over the young by the ownership of the property and the ability to pass it on to their children. Fisher pointed out that [1, p. 6]:

> Nearly to our time, the story goes, western society remained nonliterate in its culture, agrarian in its economy, extended in its family structure, and rural in its residence. The old were few in number, but their authority was very great. Within the extended family the aged monopolized power: within our agrarian economy they controlled the land. A traditional culture surrounded them with an almost magical mystique of knowledge and authority.

Where property is the only means of production, by controlling property aged individuals are able to control younger generations. The future occupations and chances for success of the younger generation are tied to seeking the favor of their elders, who control all the resources. While one's parents are alive they are of critical importance because they provide employment and means of survival in the form of resources. After they die, the heirs inherit shares of their lands and control of these resources for themselves and their children. Therefore, in traditional societies that are permanently located, the individual is directly dependent upon his own senior generation for the acquisition of the means of production. The anticipated transfer of the property at the death of the parent provides the children with an incentive that encourages respect for their older family members. It is easy to see why the young defer to their elders and attempt to seek their special favor. Similarly, it is easy to understand how the old, by the development of stable institutions and the control of property, are able to maintain their power and privilege in the social system. This may also explain the higher value placed on the family in rural America where the transmission of land to the next generation may secure that generation a livelihood and a secure position in the social structure.

Thus, rather than Cowgill and Holmes's prediction of an inverse relationship between the degree of modernization and the status accorded old persons [2], we find a curvilinear one in which the old are accorded a low status in simple nomadic societies, a high status in settled agricultural communities, and a low status in modern industrial nations.

Sheehan equates what happens to older persons in the nomadic tribes to what happens to them in modern industrial societies [3]. Sheehan believes that with the development of modern technology, social and geographic mobility become goals and individual autonomy reemerges as a primary value. The young forfeit the security of the village or family to work in factories and offices. They attain financial and social separation from many traditional restraints. Lifestyles turn away from extended family ties. There is no special reason for younger family members to secure the favor of their parents and grandparents. The older family members lose their status, decision-making power, and the security they once had in earlier cultural settings. The result is that the old are considered much less valuable in modern contemporary states. In both the simple nomadic and modern industrial societies the old quickly become dependent on the young for their well-being and survival.

The form of the family is often related to the kind of culture and structural relations among institutions in a particular society. In traditional societies that are primarily agricultural in nature, the extended form of the family (most often comprised of mother, father, their sons and their wives and children) is the prevalent one. The extended family is most often patriarchical, which means that power and lineage are traced through the males of the family. The wife, upon marriage, moves in with the husband's family. When their children are old enough to marry, the parents arrange for their marriages; expect the wives of their sons to move into their household and their daughters to move into the households of their husbands. This family arrangement is one in which the oldest male member of the family exercises the greatest power, privilege, and authority. Individualism is discouraged. The individual is always subservient to the demands of the group. The concept of romantic love (strong, intense emotional attachment between members of the opposite sex) is nonexistent. The criterion for the success of the marriage is the amount of family disruption caused by the entrance of the new bride. If she gets along well with her in-laws and does not cause difficulty it is considered a good marriage. The son's happiness is secondary to the good of the group. The extended family works best in stable cultures which are primarily agriculturally based. This culture is one in which the older members exercise the greatest power and maintain the highest status.

Industrialization leads to the breakup of the extended family. One no longer depends upon land as the principle means of production. New jobs, careers, resources, and opportunities become available. Modern industry requires mobile labor which can be moved from place to place as needed. Extended family ties are broken in order to move the labor force where it is most needed; if not, the industrial system itself would break down. The nuclear family—husband, wife, children—is dominant. The influence of the father and mother over adult children is weakened. The size of the family declines as children become units of consumption rather than production and thereby become less desirable.

The difference between extended and nuclear families for the status of the aged persons can best be seen in Israel. Weihl observed that the older people among the migrants from the Orient are given a relatively high status in comparison to the relatively low status accorded older immigrants from the Western countries [4]. The migrants from the Orient evidence considerable commitment to the extended family concept in contrast with the commitment to nuclear family evidenced by migrants from the West.

The religions of the Far East have generally supported the extended family and higher status of elder members by the moral and ethical codes that they espouse. The Confucian concept is one in which the aged are to be given tender loving care. They are to be exempt from certain responsibilities when they reach old age. Pre-World War II families in China and Japan were ones in which children cared for their elders, and older family members exercised the most authority. This meant also that the elders were the most respected members of the family.

While Christianity clearly admonishes the individual to honor his father and mother, this religious principle has probably had less impact in the Western world than one might expect. The pressure of industrialization results in the educational functions being gradually removed from the family socialization process to formal training outside the home. The nature of wealth changes from land to tangible property. The emphasis shifts to productivity. The young are always seen as more productive and the old as less productive. Degradation generally occurs for the older, and supposedly slower, workers.

Another aspect of modern industrial society is the location of knowledge. In traditional agricultural societies, the old are the reservoirs of knowledge—of past problems and their solutions, of old customs and the appropriate religious rituals. In industrial societies, books, libraries, universities, and current research enterprises are a base for the generation and transmittal of knowledge. The freshly trained college student is often more valuable in the business and industrial world than the older and more experienced employee whose knowledge and expertise may have become obsolete. The inability to maintain control of critical knowledge in modern society has been another factor that has contributed to the general loss of status of older persons.

American society has a well-developed and sophisticated educational system which prepares young people to enter an occupation, but it is ill equipped to retrain older workers when new technologies require additional schooling.

The harshness of the environment in which the culture is found and the amount of physical labor required for survival are also factors that can reduce the usefulness and thereby the status of the older members of a culture.

Holmberg noted that among the Sirono of the Bolivian rain forest, it is the general belief that [5, pp. 224–225]:

> Actually the aged are quite a burden; they eat but are unable to hunt, fish or collect food; they sometimes hoard a young spouse, but are unable to beget children; they move at a snail's pace and hinder the mobility of the group. When a person becomes too ill or infirm to follow the fortunes of the band, he is abandoned to shift for himself.

Cowgill and Holmes noted that there is some difficulty in adjusting to reduced activity in old age when a society is so strongly dedicated to hard physical labor [2]. Kibbutz society in Israel is one example; there, older persons may arrive at an ambiguous status because of their inability to physically keep up with younger counterparts.

Related to the changing knowledge base in modern society is the speed with which social change occurs within the system. Cowgill and Holmes believe that rapid social change in modern societies tends to undermine the status of older persons [2]. Change renders many of the skills of older Americans obsolete. Not only can they no longer ply their trade, there is also no reason for them to teach it to others. In a rapidly changing society younger people are nearly always better educated and possess more knowledge of recent technology than their elders; thus, the latter lose their utility and the basis of their authority.

Referring to both the speed of social change in modern society and the location of the knowledge base in the system, Watson and Maxwell hypothesized that societies can be arranged along a continuum whose basis is the amount of useful information controlled by the aged individuals [6]. They believe the greater the elders are in control of critical information, the greater is their participation in community affairs. Their participation is, in turn, directly related to the degree of esteem in which they are held by other members of the community. Watson and Maxwell believe this control of information and consequent social participation declines with industrialization and its rapid sociocultural change [6, pp. 26–29].

Watson and Maxwell argued that one of the most fruitful models developed for the investigation of human societies has relied heavily on the information storage and exchange model and is described as systems theory [6]. Goffman has demonstrated that groups which share secret information will tend to be more integrated and unified than those which do not [7]. All stored information, according to Goffman, involves a stated arrangement of elements in the sense that they are a record of past events [7, p. 70].

In traditional societies, one of the main functions of old people is to remember legends, myths, ethical principles, and the appropriate relations that should be arranged with the supernatural, and they are frequently asked about these matters.

Elliott described this pattern among the Aleuts in northern Russia [8, pp. 170-171]:

> Before the advent of Russian priests, every village had one or two old men at least, who considered it their special business to educate the children, thereupon, in the morning or evening when all were home these aged teachers would seat themselves in the center of one of the largest village courts or oolagumuh; the young folks surrounded them and listened attentively to what they said.

Watson and Maxwell believe that the printing press was to end this kind of arrangement in the social system [6, p. 20]. In industrialized societies the information that is important is written down, printed, and sold in bookstores.

Some historians have argued that economically, politically, and socially older people are more conservative than younger people and tend to have a stabilizing effect on any social system. The young, being much more changeable in their view, offer adaptability and in some ways may increase the changes for survival in the social system.

One final factor which may in some way explain the declining status of aged individuals in modern industrial countries is the relative proportion of the entire population that they comprise. In most of the ancient and traditional societies they comprised less than 3 percent of the total population. It is easy to reserve a special status for a group of people that comprise a very small percent of the total. In modern society the old have come to comprise between 8 to 15 percent of the total population. Cox observed that it may become increasingly difficult to preserve privileged status for a group that comprises such a large percentage of a total population [9]. Cowgill's book, *Aging Around the World* indicates how rapidly the older age populations are now expanding in even the underdeveloped countries [10]. This is a phenomenon that neither the anthropologists nor the gerontologists had earlier anticipated.

ROLES FOR THE ELDERLY IN POST-INDUSTRIAL SOCIETY

While historically we find a curvilinear relationship with the old being accorded a low status in nomadic tribes, a high status in settled agricultural communities and a low status in modern industrial societies one wonders what roles and status older persons will be granted in post-industrial society. An educated guess would be that there will be a wider variety of roles to choose from and a slight upturn in the status of older persons in post-industrial society. Thus the pattern would be one of an S curve in which the status of the older adults improves following the low that was experienced by them during the industrial period.

Everett Hughes, Daniel Bell, and other social scientists have speculated on what life will be like in post-industrial society [11, 12]. The consensus of the social scientists seems to be that the post-industrial period will see a shift away from expansion in manufacturing and industry to the expansion of social services, entertainment, athletics, recreation and leisure enterprises. The basic argument of the scientists is that as the industrial development of a nation peaks and as an ever efficient manufacturing technology emerges, less of the population will be required to produce the nation's goods. This will make a surplus of manpower available which will ultimately be employed by the expanding service occupations, the entertainment industry, and industries catering to recreation and leisure activities. The post-industrial period will also bring reduced working hours, the advent of a four-day work week which will result in larger amounts of free time for the average citizen. For both the younger and the older members of the society this will mean greater opportunity for entertainment, athletic events, recreation, and leisure pursuits as well as opportunity for education and cultural enrichment. The Protestant ethic which admonished the person to be totally committed to the work role and view recreation and leisure roles as at best a waste of one's time and at worst as sinful will undoubtedly be altered. Recreation, leisure, education and a variety of other emerging roles will be seen as legitimate means of enriching the quality of one's life. They should do two things for the older members of society; first, it will provide a wide range of nonwork roles in which they may choose to participate; and second, these roles will be more highly valued and provide them with a higher status and more respected position in society.

Older persons upon retirement will be deciding whether or not to invest greater time and energy in family roles, recreation and leisure roles, volunteer roles, educational roles, political roles, or perhaps a second career. Post-industrial society will undoubtedly offer a wider range of roles for the elderly to choose whether they will or will not participate.

In all probability they will not have had this much freedom to choose among the different roles they wish to enter at any other time in their lives. Moreover, changing values in post-industrial society will include less emphasis on the importance of productivity and greater emphasis on the quality of life. Volunteer and leisure roles will be more highly valued, giving older persons who occupy them greater respect. In short it would seem that older persons will have a wide variety of roles to choose from in their retirement years and that these roles will bring them greater status than retirees have been accorded in the past.

REFERENCES

1. D. H. Fischer, *Growing Old in America*, Oxford University Press, New York, 1978.

2. D. O. Cowgill and L. D. Holmes, *Aging and Modernization*, Appleton Century Crofts, New York, 1972.

3. T. Sheehan, Senior Esteem as a Factor of Socioeconomic Complexity, *The Gerontologist*, 16:5, pp. 433–444, 1976.

4. H. Weihl, Aging in Israel, in *Aging in Contemporary Society*, E. Shanas (ed.), Sage Publications, Inc., Beverly Hills, California, pp. 107–117, 1970.

5. A. R. Holmberg, *Nomads of the Long Bow*, Natural History Press, Garden City, New York, pp. 224–225, 1969.

6. W. H. Watson and R. T. Maxwell, *Human Aging and Dying: A Study in Sociocultural Gerontology*, St. Martin's Press, New York, pp. 2–32, 1977.

7. E. Goffman, *The Presentation of Self in Everyday Life*, Doubleday, Garden City, New York, 1959.

8. H. W. Elliott, *Our Arctic Province: Alaska and the Sea Islands*, Scribner's, New York, pp. 170–171, 1887.

9. H. Cox, *Later Life: The Realities of Aging*, Prentice-Hall, Inc., Englewood Cliffs, New Jersey, 1988.

10. D. O. Cowgill, *Aging Around the World*, Wadsworth Publishing Company, Belmont, California, 1986.

11. E. Hughes, *Men and Their Work*, Free Press, New York, 1964.

12. D. Bell, *The Coming of Post Industrial Society*, Basic Books, New York, 1973.

GENERATIONAL EQUITY AND THE

Future of Generational Politics

PAUL S. HEWITT & NEIL HOWE

Paul S. Hewitt is the executive director and Neil Howe is the research director of Americans for Generational Equity, Washington, D.C.

Elizabeth Crews

Recent decades have seen a divergence between the interests of younger and older generations in U.S. aging policy, a fact increasingly publicized through the efforts of a small but influential "generational equity" movement. Some aging advocates, responding to sensational media accounts, have seen in this movement the seeds of a generational "conflict" and have peremptorily dismissed all its concerns. Yet the aging of America is forcing aging policy again into the forefront of national politics. As this debate unfolds, many in the aging field are straining to look past the myths surrounding generational equity to the essential logic that underlies its rising popularity.

Three principal concerns characterize the generational equity movement: The first is the magnitude of the coming upward shift in our society's age structure—and the enormous demands this shift will place on our future living standards. The second is society's failure to prepare our economy for the aging of America; instead of saving our resources and investing more in children, we are overconsuming and saddling our children with debt. The third is a political dilemma—how can a democratic society manage income transfers between generations in a way that is equitable to Americans who are young or unborn, those who cannot vote and whose interests are protected only by the sense of stewardship and the instinct for endowment shared by those of us who are older? Although today we are still not facing this dilemma, it is practically inevitable that we will confront it some time over the next 15 years.

THE AGING OF AMERICA

The aging of America is often interpreted as the maturing of that demographic bulge known as the "baby boom" (Americans born from 1946 through 1964). The birthrates that brought forth the baby boom were much higher than those that brought forth the generations just before and just after—on the older side, the small "silent generation" (those born roughly during the Depression, 1927 through 1945) and on the younger side by the small "postboom" generation (those born after 1964). Thus, as the baby boom ages, America ages with it. Since 1970, the median age of our population has already grown from 28 to 32, and 25 years from now it will probably pass 40.

Between the years 2010 and 2025—a period beginning just about when that 40-year median is reached—the baby boomers will reach their 60s and begin to retire. As a result, America will experience an unprecedented growth in the ratio of retirees to workers. Before 1935, there had never been fewer than ten working-age adults for every American over age 65; on the eve of World War II there were nine. Yet today there are only five, and in another 50 years there will only be barely more than two.

The implications for public resource-sharing are clear. Young workers today must pay well over 15 percent of their total salaries toward Social Security and Part A of Medicare. But 40 years from now, projections indicate that the share will be between 22 and 33 percent. Including the 75 percent taxpayer subsidy to fast-growing Part B of Medicare, that share will rise to 30 percent at a minimum. Under the Social Security Administration's "pessimistic" scenario, which some would say is most likely, the combined costs of these programs would total 50 percent of payroll (which is another way of saying that sooner or later changes in our benefit provisions are inevitable).

It would be tempting to imagine that demography has played a singularly cruel trick on the baby boom and that society's retirement problems will disappear once the baby boomers pass through the retirement system. Yet the baby boom's aging has merely served to mask a more fundamental aging trend that would certainly be occurring in any case. Fueling this trend are the following:

• *Improvements in mortality of elders.* Over the past two decades alone, American life expectancy at age 65 has risen from 14.5 to 16.5 years. Fifty years from now, it may rise as high as 23 years.

• *The persistence of very low fertility levels in the United States.* Just as longer lifespans mean relatively more elderly in the future, so fewer babies mean relatively fewer working-age adults in the future. (Since we currently devote so little public spending to children, moreover, it is unlikely that fewer children will compensate for the dependency cost of more elderly.)

• *The exploding interaction between chronological age and dependency.* As longevity increases, the number of "old old" grows at a far faster pace than the number of "young old." Between 1986 and 2040, for instance, the population age 65 to 74 will grow by about 85 percent, while the population age 80 and over will grow by 300 to 400 percent (and the population 90 and over will grow by an astounding 500 to 700 percent). These are the age groups most likely to live alone, most likely to need help with disabilities, and most likely by far to incur enormous acute care and nursing home expenses.

• *The ongoing trend toward earlier retirement.* The share of people

---

How can a democratic society manage income transfers between generations in a way that is equitable?

---

age 65–69 who are in the labor force, which stood at 40 percent as recently as 1950, has already fallen below 18 percent. Each new retiree, of course, means one less taxpayer and one more beneficiary.

One way to appreciate the combined magnitude of all these forces is simply to glance at the various future projections published by the Social Security Administration. Under no scenario will the population of the United States ever again—not even when the baby boom passes from the scene—be nearly as "youthful" as it is today. Nor will as little ever be expended for retirement benefits. Once the age composition of the U.S. population surpasses that of present-day Florida about 25 years from now, the "aging of America" will be more or less permanent. It is not a one-time blip that we can "tough out." Rather, it is an enduring reality to which our economic, political, and social institutions must adapt.

COLD DAWN AFTER REAGAN

Future demographic trends and current benefit laws guarantee an enormous growth in resource transfers to older generations over the next 50 years. The question we must confront is, How will younger Americans be able to afford this increase without a sizable decline in their future standard of living? In the past, our answer to such a question was simple: The way we afford any growth in our dependency burden is by generating even greater increases in goods and services produced per worker. By splitting our "productivity dividend" between workers and dependents, everyone could be a consumption winner. The consensus now emerging among economists, however, is that this traditional solution may no longer be feasible.

The main reason for this gloomy prognosis is that productivity growth in the United States is stagnating. The per-worker output growth we now generate annually (about 0.6 percent in the 1970s and 0.4 percent thus far in the 1980s) is only a small fraction of what it was during the earlier postwar era (2.9 percent in the 1950s and 1.9 percent in the 1960s). At the 1950s growth rate—just to illustrate the difference—real national income per worker doubles in only 25 years; at the 1980s growth rate, it doubles in 175 years.

But fading growth rates are by no means our only economic obstacle. It is also becoming apparent that almost none of the productivity growth we generate over the next decade can be translated into higher consumption. Instead, the additional product per worker must be dedicated to the reconstruction of our collapsing foreign and domestic investment balances—or, to put it more simply, it must all go into exports and into business plant and equipment. Allowing output to "catch up" with consumption is the inevitable sequel to eight years of demand-side extremism carried out under the name of supply-side economics.

Consider a few of the numbers. Putting an end to capital inflows from abroad will force us to substitute our own production for the $1,300 per fully-employed American that we are now borrowing each year from foreigners; restoring our anemic rate of net business investment here at home to what it was in the late 1970s (it is now at its lowest level since the Great Depression) will cost us another $700 per worker. Altogether, we thus have to find an extra $2,000 in unconsumed real output per worker. Twenty years ago, we could have managed this task with four or five years of fast economic growth and modest consumer belt-tightening. Yet, at our current productivity growth rate—with net output rising each year by less than $150 per worker—the arithmetic hardly justifies optimism even if we allow no growth at all in consumption per employed American for more than a decade.

It is more likely that we will see an absolute decline in our consumption living standards, perhaps by as much as $100 to $150 yearly per worker for many years to come. By comparison, during the 1970s—a decade now known to most of us as "hard times"—U.S. consumption per worker nonetheless rose by $200 per year in real terms. Neither the public nor our politicians are yet facing this prospect.

Clearly, we would like to believe that this is all just a "worst case" scenario. But it is not. It is optimistic—based, for instance, on the premise that we take immediate and decisive action to reduce our federal deficit, raise domestic investment, and expand sales of manufactured exports at a record pace for many years. The scenario is also based on the smooth and enthusiastic cooperation of our trading partners, no sharp rise in the price of our oil imports, no widespread default by third-world debtors, and no destabilizing global recession. A much worse scenario would assume, on the other hand, that one or more of these conditions would not hold. (One might imagine a very optimistic scenario based on new technological discoveries; our experience with Japanese competition, however, suggests that low-investment societies are the least capable of benefiting from them.)

For the long term, moreover, we cannot afford to reinvest only in the physical capital that we have let deteriorate in recent years—the infrastructure, factories, and innovation necessary for the prosperity of future generations. We must also reinvest in our children. For the first time in our history, an increasing proportion of American children are growing up in poverty, are graduating from high school less well educated than their parents, are not learning entry-level job skills, and are paying for exploding college tuition fees out of their own pocket.

The deteriorating abilities of our youngest citizens loom as perhaps the greatest threat to our aging society.

---

ing college tuition fees out of their own pocket.

The deteriorating abilities of our youngest citizens loom as perhaps the greatest threat to our aging society. Unless these trends are reversed, writes Mark S. Tucker, executive director of the Carnegie Forum on Education and the Economy, "the growing population of old people in our society can confidently look forward to closing years filled with poverty and social unrest, because a very large fraction of the work force, which is itself a declining proportion of the population as a whole, will be unable to support themselves, to say nothing of others" (1986).

THE 1990s

How did we get caught traveling down this avenue with no pleasant exit? One reason is that we became complacent. The very bright economic and demographic outlook we all shared back in the mid-1960s and early 1970s, when we first designed our most expensive intergenerational commitments, led us to believe that a future of swiftly growing living standards was practically assured. No one worried about a "birth dearth" or "competitiveness"; instead we talked about "zero population growth" and the "problem of affluence." The outlook emerging today, of course, is very different, and the direction it promises to impart to national policy over the next decade—particularly, aging policy—will be almost unrecognizable from that of our recent past.

The overriding concern of the 1990s will be the need to shift resources from consumption to savings, whatever the near-term discomfort. Public budgets will have to spend more on physical and human capital (such as infrastructure and education) while spending less overall and raising more revenue. Meanwhile, households will have to save a higher fraction of whatever is left, and firms (especially exporters) will have to invest more of their retained earnings. Simply put, the 1990s promise to be a decade of austerity—of dreams to be deferred, of debts to be repaid, and of children to be endowed. From a society of creative consumers, all of us who are able, at every age, will have to transform ourselves into a society of creative producers.

The outlook for aging policy in the 1990s will be determined not only by economics, but by the size and character of the generations involved. The expansion of old age benefits during the Johnson-Nixon era was undertaken under the political leadership of the "swing generation" (those born from 1900 through 1926). Because this group is large, it dominated the electorate at the time, and because it came of age during the New Deal and World War II, it has always been keenly interested in legislation and statecraft ("swing" leaders founded today's large elderly lobbies and have inhabited the White House since 1961). Younger Americans, moreover, have always felt that this group's many sacrifices, from the Great Depression and Iwo Jima to the Marshall Plan and polio vaccines, made the swing generation especially worthy of tribute.

Once again, the 1990s will find the situation quite altered. The older population will increasingly comprise "silent generation" (people born in the 1930s) cohorts. Their relative voting strength will be somewhat smaller; their political voice and self-identity are likely to be weak (they may *never* have a president); and unlike the swing generation elders, they are not likely to be seen by younger Americans as uniquely deserving. Many younger and middle-aged voters, in fact, will realize that a large share of the economically successful Silents will be retiring with houses, financial assets, and pension incomes that they themselves may have no hope of acquiring.

Meanwhile, the middle age bracket—the phase of life when people begin participating heavily in politics—will be increasingly dominated by the baby boom. In 1986, the age 40–64 bracket accounted for 42 percent of those who voted; but by 1998 (assuming constant rates of voter participation by age), it will account for 47 percent, and by 2010 it will account for 53 percent, a share never before equaled in our history and perhaps never again to be equaled.

How will this enormous group of middle-aged baby-boom voters perceive aging issues in the 1990s? Most likely, they will perceive them in intensely economic terms. Against a backdrop of national austerity, the baby-boom will have its eye on the bottom line. It will be watching Part A of Medicare spiral toward bankruptcy (which we already know will happen around the year 2000). It will be wondering how to control Part B (which is growing even faster than Part A). It will be puzzling over the approaching operating deficit in Social Security—and wondering how its children will be able to pay off the trillions of dollars worth of federal debt that will be accumulating in Social Security's trust funds. It will be fretting over the falling value of its retirement "nest egg," as home equity shrinks because of weak housing demand by the small and relatively poor postboom generation. And from the private sector, it will certainly be hearing about the financial woes of the Pension Benefit Guarantee Corporation.

The baby boomers' anxiety, of course, will be motivated by something more than altruism. Having reached maturity at a time of declining private-pension and retiree healthcare coverage, they will be profoundly worried about their own personal retirement security. By the 1990s, any policy option entailing public-sector deficits will appear out of the question, and steep hikes in payroll taxes on workers will seem equally impractical. Inevitably, the baby boomers will come to realize that part of our overall national savings agenda must include a drive to introduce economies into Social Security, Medicare, and other old-age entitlements. This move is certain to trigger a national debate over aging policy, principally among the baby boomers themselves.

Likely to emerge from this debate is a new and positive vision of aging in America. First, older citizens will be viewed increasingly as productive, vigorous members of mainstream society, rather than as dependent and frail. Age alone will be seen as an insufficient basis for exclusion either from endeavors of broad national sacrifice or from the benefits of social participation. Second, the extraordinary postwar trend toward early retirement for all Americans—in which (currently) a quarter of one's life is spent at ever-rising levels of subsidized income—will be viewed as an anachronism in an aging society.

The resulting policy and attitudinal shifts will almost certainly provoke resistance from the senior movement. For as policy comes to differentiate the able-bodied from the disabled, the "young old" from the "old old," and the affluent from the poor and near poor, today's monolithic political coalition of mature Americans will lose its unifying theme of "universality." But in spite of their misgivings, the elderly groups will pursue compromise in the face of the baby boomers' overwhelming expression of concern. The lobbies, quite simply, cannot afford to alienate large groups of future members.

In the end, as every political scientist knows, no lobby can encompass too large a public without the special benefits it seeks becoming unaffordable. As the aging of America renders almost half the population eligible to join the American Association of Retired Persons, this principle will become painfully obvious. At the same time, there will be more than enough disabled, frail, and poor older people to justify the existence of strong advocacy organizations. Spending that meets the needs of these subgroups will in fact be protected better by small and tightly focused lobbies than by organizations purporting to represent the diffuse interests of all mature citizens. Eventually, members of the subgroups will realize this and opt for the more efficient alternative.

GERONTOLOGISTS & EQUITY

The generational equity movement reminds us that the fate of the next century's elderly will be decided largely outside the field of aging. How we manage international trade, address the problems of poverty, illiteracy, and undereducation among the young, foster saving and investment, maintain the infrastructure, and reduce our deficits will ultimately determine what resources will be available to care for our aged, provide for our national defense, and carry out the other essential activities of government in the twenty-first century. This is what most arouses the ire of many aging advocates: the conclusion that aging policy must be sensitive—indeed, subordinate—to America's overriding priorities for the future.

Time will tell how controversial generational equity really is. We should not forget that the current institution of retirement has been with us for only a short time; thus, the possibility of further change should not surprise us. Today's rapidly growing population of affluent and healthy retirees cries out for a new vision of aging. The challenge for gerontology is to help shape this vision in a way that grasps the imagination of young and old alike. Indeed, to resist change will be to abdicate this leadership to others and to risk losing relevancy in the national policy debate that is soon to be upon us.

REFERENCE

Tucker, M. S., 1986. Testimony before the Joint Economic Committee of the U.S. Congress, Subcommittee on Economic Resources, Competitiveness, and Security Economics, July

Whatever happened to a dignified old age?

TALKIN' 'BOUT MY GENERATION

HENRY FAIRLIE

THIRTY PERCENT of the annual federal budget now goes to expenditures on people over the age of 65. Forty years from now, if the present array of programs and benefits is maintained, almost two-thirds of the budget will go to supporting and cosseting the old. Something is wrong with a society that is willing to drain itself to foster such an unproductive section of its population, one that does not even promise (as children do) one day to be productive.

It is always difficult to question the programs for the aging because of an understandable if increasingly misdirected sympathy for them. In addition to the widespread feeling that they have earned their reward here on earth (and need not wait until they get to heaven, as the old used to expect), there is our contemporary guilt about them—and our fear. Americans still do not accept aging, dying, and death from old age itself as part of living. Of course there are the needy, the infirm, the helpless, for whom society should care. But when the old people's lobbies rally their considerable resources for a ferocious fight to protect Medicare, or to oppose a cut in the cost-of-living adjustments (COLAs) to Social Security, they are not speaking only for the needy. They are arguing for the perpetuation of a massive entitlements system for anyone and everyone over 65.

Glance through the advertisements in *Modern Maturity*, the fat, glossy magazine published by the American Association of Retired Persons—one of America's most powerful lobbies. You can be tempted by the Florida country clubs: "RETIRE IN STYLE TO FORT MYERS, FLORIDA!! . . . the New Pine Lakes Country Club. Imagine . . . acres of lakes, 18-hole golf course, tennis, heated pool, a lakeside jacuzzi,

24-hour manned security, and an unbelievable clubhouse!" Not far away the Del Tura Country Club "features Florida's finest ($3.5 million) executive golf course and clubhouse complex." Or you can buy your own ranch on the Forbes Wagon Creek Ranch in the Sangre de Cristo mountains. If all this palls, you can take a Holland America Line Alaska Cruise, with "gourmet meals, sparkling entertainment, first-class service, swimming pools, tennis courts, casinos, and million-dollar art collections." But turn the pages and, perhaps most remarkable of all, the AARP's own Travel Service offers cruises or tours to Alaska, "North to the Future." From all of this, go back to the sheaf of question-and-answer sheets setting out the AARP's arguments for almost every proposed government expenditure on the old. Something jars.

The old people's lobbying groups have proliferated in recent years. The Leadership Council of Aging Organizations (surely they do not mean "aging organizations"; if they do, one could suggest some candidates) lists 29 such groups, starting, alphabetically, with the American Association for International Aging. They range from Catholic Golden Age to the scholarly sounding Gerontology Society of America, to the once slightly notorious Gray Panthers (senior citizen urban guerrillas), to the National Association of State Units on Aging, to the United Auto Workers/Retired Members. Anyone who knows the first thing about office rentals in Washington must be impressed by the addresses of some of these groups—not least on K Street, the capital's upscale strip for the suites of the powerful industrial and commercial lobbyists.

These groups are strong because no one, especially in election years—and it is always election year in Ameri-

Reprinted by permission of *The New Republic*, March 28, 1988, pp. 19-22. © 1988, The New Republic, Inc.

ca—dares to say a word that might offend the supposedly meek, ailing, frail, and deserving gray heads. The old have been set beside motherhood and apple pie. Yet meekness is hardly an attribute of the old in their new incarnation. And in some cases they don't even need one of the established lobbying groups to press their case before a credulous public. The notch babies, whom Timothy Noah rightly described in these pages as "spiteful, single-minded, and, to the uninitiated, deeply baffling—a parody of a special interest group" ("Notch Babies," December 1, 1986), reveal the lengths to which some of the elderly now feel entitled to go in claiming benefits that aren't rightly theirs. The notch babies are the unpleasantly angry bunch of people born between 1917 and 1921 who have convinced themselves that they are being cheated out of their rightful COLA benefits.

In fact, the AARP and most of the other groups have criticized the notch babies' claims. All the same, it is the general propaganda on behalf of the old, much of it "fired by greed, not fairness," as the *New York Times* said of the notch babies, that nurtures the clamoring and hysteria. It took only one letter to Dear Abby in 1983, and her endorsement of it (which she later partially retracted), to raise a storm on behalf of the notch babies that swept some members of Congress off their feet.

We should not let ourselves be peppered by the old people's organizations. Their hero, Representative Claude Pepper, is not an amiable soul caring for the downtrodden old. He is a shrewd, ambitious politician who, as the *Almanac for American Politics* puts it, was "floundering about, looking for a major cause." As a member and then chairman of the Select Committee on the Aging, he found one that provided a "good match of convictions and position," especially for a congressman who represents the 18th District of Florida (most of the city of Miami, all of Miami Beach, Bal Harbor, and Key Biscayne), where 30 percent of the adults are 65 and over. It can be said confidently that a substantial majority of those, as in the rest of Florida, do not need such extensive benefits or so many free services.

NOT SURPRISINGLY, over the past 30 years the elderly's standard of living has improved faster than that of younger people. Quite apart from the significant increase in Social Security benefits and their protection from erosion by inflation, the Supplemental Security Income in effect guarantees them a minimum income; national health insurance is provided through Medicare; and special tax privileges protect their assets in retirement. They even receive discounts on movie and bus tickets, and much more. All of these entitlements are available to the elderly regardless of need. And while claiming that their own benefits are beyond challenge, locally the old organize to oppose tax hikes to pay for school bonds and other desirable social policies.

The history of the Older Americans Act is instructive. This simple bill authorizing funds to state agencies for a few supportive and nutritional services was passed on the heels of Medicare in 1965. When Congress extended it for another four years in 1987 (a preface to the election), the services were generously expanded. The bill is still primarily addressed to the needy old, but within it are explicit assumptions that show how its provisions can be expanded. Take the definition of "elder abuse." When we hear of "child abuse," we think specifically of certain intolerable offenses: beatings and sexual molestations. However, in many state laws the definition of "elder abuse" is so wide as to include forms of neglect that may not be neglect at all—merely leaving the old to do for themselves what they wish to do, however slowly. This is only "abuse" in the eyes of the social workers and old people's organizations, who must justify their activities and funding.

MY OWN AGE gives me some standing in this matter. As I approach the arbitrary line of 65, which of course I do not consider aged, my first savoring of growing old seems to promise a time of great richness, contemplation, and absorbing interest. One not only has the years ahead, but begins to recapture the whole of one's life, in ways for which even one's middle years are unequipped. But most obviously it is less costly; one simply does not need so much. One's children are grown up and earning; one's grandchildren provide pleasure without much responsibility; mortgages are often paid off; and one need scarcely add to one's wardrobe. One is more content with simple fare in everything. It is less urgent to look for friends; one already has them, and new ones, often the young, keep turning up. In growing old, one has a stocked attic in which to rummage, and the still passing show and pageant of human life to observe, not only at a more leisurely pace, but with the convincing satisfaction and interest of having lived through many of the changes, even from their beginnings, that have brought us from there to here.

The elderly among whom I was raised did not withdraw. They may have retired from their jobs, but then they usually stayed where they were, assuming the responsibilities of a grandparent, and advising and encouraging the other young people they knew in the neighborhood. They also naturally assumed, not least in the working class and mainstream middle class, positions of leadership in the organizations, including the churches, that hold society together, so taking some of the pressure off the middle-aged and producers. They brought to them the wisdom of experience, and an unruffled, almost bustling, way of dealing with a crisis or emergency, because they had been through so many before. If I look back amazed at the time my elders found for me, then I also realize that they were not altogether selfless. I brought them news, kept them in touch, just as they brought me the otherwise inaccessible news from the immediate past. If this two-way transmission ceases, both the young and the elderly suffer.

But suppose the old, encouraged by federal programs, siphon themselves off to places where they congregate only with other aging people. A few years ago, when I traveled around the country for five months with a companion almost a third of my age as my driver, I bought a 338-page book called *Sunbelt Retirement: The Complete State Guide to Retiring in the South and West of the United States*. Partly guided by it, I went to see some of the retirement communities, resorts, call them what one wishes. Some of them, of course, are for the rich. La Jolla, just north of San Diego, had a population of 30,000 when I was there; it also had 400 doctors. One doctor for every 75 people who anyhow are about to be called to Abraham's bosom—cite that ratio in any inner city or small town in rural America, or even in the suburbs, where the middle-aged are terrified of the possible cost of medical care for their families. And how many of those doctors catering to the old are psychiatrists, therapists, and cosmeticians? (When I was in the hospital not long ago, the nurses told me that the medical care for many elderly patients was really cosmetic, to disguise the natural process of aging.) If one needs a psychiatrist by the time one is 65, one should take the quick way out—make a swallow dive from a high bridge to the tarmac, and go to meet the Great Therapist in the Sky.

Yet it is not the rich communities that are most alarming. The vast industry of "Sunbelt Retirement" is not built on the rich. It is built on federal programs for the elderly. (And of course even those doctors in La Jolla are sustained largely by Medicare.) Most of the communities composed solely of the old are for the retired mainstream Middle Americans from the Northeast and Midwest. These are not people who have accumulated exorbitant personal assets. As soon as I reached Arizona, I realized that the Southwest is living off, and ripping off, the very "government in Washington" that it always criticizes for taxing people too much for giveaway programs to the undeserving. Huge federal subsidies to the retirement industry have replaced the military establishments, defense industries, water subsidies, and the rest that have hitherto sustained the West.

All the way from the Pacific to the Atlantic you can see the old lined up in banks, feeding into their accounts the checks from a range of federal agencies. The pensions and other benefits from the Veterans Administration alone are not only generous but cumulatively indefensible, since the average age of today's 27 million living veterans is 62. Every month government benefits to 91 percent of those over the age of 65 total $13.6 billion; the $50 billion per year spent on medical care for the old when Reagan took office is expected to be four times as large 12 years from now. Senator Daniel Patrick Moynihan has dryly observed that the United States may be "the first society in history in which a person is more likely to be poor if young rather than old." Moynihan's point applies even to children, 20 percent of whom live in poverty, compared with 14 percent of the elderly. It is not something to be proud of. This coddling is not how the elderly are meant or should expect to live.

The pampered ones, increasingly numerous, are rather pathetic to observe, some riding around in gold carts even on the streets, instead of taking an invigorating walk—what used to be called a "constitutional." These are not

the infirm, only the naturally aging. There are no young where they live, no children, no bawling infants, no working, productive men or women. These communities frequently advertise the fact that they are "adults-only." They live with reflections of themselves. They are set apart, no longer of a piece with any larger society, with no obligations. Everything is provided. For the first time in their lives, in effect, they have servants. In vast Sun City outside Phoenix, which you reach by driving through the barrios, the legal and illegal Mexican immigrants attend to the needs of these white elders. Although they are tanned and imagine they are active, following their balls on the championship course in their carts, they in fact move as if in a mindless soft-shoe shuffle.

Of course there are millions of old people who do not live like this. Although the median income for people over 65 is now $22,000—a high figure for those who have few large purchases to make—there are still the third of the elderly blacks who live on less than $5,300. *That* is need. But the prominence of the resorts draws attention to the changed expectations of old age, among the elderly themselves, ourselves, and the society as a whole. And as in other areas, when such new expectations get lodged they take root, burgeon, and are hard to uproot, especially if they are stimulated and supported by programs that develop their own entrenched life. For it is a question not only of government, but as the gerontologist Carroll Estes has said, of "the aging establishment . . . the congeries of programs, organizations, bureaucracies, . . . providers, industries, and professionals that serve the old in one capacity or another." Even if an organization like the National Council of Senior Citizens concentrates on assisting the needy and helpless, it is trapped into supporting the fat in the entitlement programs that goes to those who are not the deserving poor.

The mischief must be halted and reversed, and not least in the interest of the elderly. For one thing, there is likely to be a revolt of the working members of society when the huge baby-boom generation reaches retirement age. And as the population comes to include ever-growing numbers of young Mexicans, Central Americans, South Americans, and Asians, they too are likely to rebel, especially since their own (nuclear *and* extended) families assume so many of the traditional responsibilities of caring for the old, even in their new environment. Why should they work to indulge the white elders so generously? The old might heed another of Moynihan's predictions: that quite early in the new century the American people will be markedly brown, Spanish-speaking, young, and Catholic.

Old age must be redefined, with the majority of benefits going only to the needy. We probably will have to make stern decisions. With the increasing number of people living beyond 85, we may even have to decide that today's costly medical technologies, such as transplants, should not be provided to truly elderly people. Early retirement, especially to a self-centered and soft existence, must be discouraged. Perhaps above all, we must shake off the peculiar notion, of only recent growth, that old age is a time in which people are entitled to be rewarded for no more than performing the accepted tasks of life, or fighting in the Second World War, as many of today's elderly bleat; that if they raise a family and contribute to society by working, then when they cease to be productive they have a right to live off the still-producing like the grasshopper in the fable; that because their needs diminish, their expectations are entitled to rise.

The old people's organizations sometimes work along these lines, as in resisting mandatory early retirement. Some have started and encouraged programs to stimulate the elderly to become productive again and remain an organic part of their society, such as working in schools as volunteers, or in special programs out of school; and of course old people are precisely those who should be well equipped to counter the basic illiteracy of even affluent children in the suburbs, the ignorance of any cultural heritage, and the decay of manners. But these efforts are marginal and sporadic, and are as nothing to the energy the lobby musters to protect the benefits for an entire class.

Meanwhile, by failing to define old age in a more limited way, by discouraging the elderly from remaining in their society, we are building a system of care that has one critical flaw. The sweeping claim of entitlements is the bubble in the whole glass house of federal assistance to the old that will eventually shatter it.

Credits/ Acknowledgments

Cover design by Charles Vitelli

1. The Phenomenon of Aging
Facing overview—United Nation photo by John Orr.

2. The Quality of Later Life
Facing overview—Colonial Penn Group, Inc.

3. Societal Attitudes Toward Old Age
Facing overview—United Nation photo by Jeffrey J. Foxx. 59—Susan Gilmore.

4. Problems and Potentials of Aging
Facing overview—United Nation photo by John Isaac. 111—Illustration by Juan Suarez Botas.

5. Retirement
Facing overview—United Nation photo by John Isaac.

6. The Experience of Dying
Facing overview—Middlesex Memorial Hospital. 145—EPA Documerica.

7. Living Environments in Later Life
Facing overview—United Nation photo by P. Sudhakaran. 163-164, 167—David Johnson. 182—United Nation photo by John Isaac.

8. Social Policies, Programs, and Services
Facing overview—United Nation photo by John Isaac.

ANNUAL EDITIONS ARTICLE REVIEW FORM

■ NAME: _____ DATE: _____

■ TITLE AND NUMBER OF ARTICLE: _____

■ BRIEFLY STATE THE MAIN IDEA OF THIS ARTICLE: _____

_____

_____

_____

_____

■ LIST THREE IMPORTANT FACTS THAT THE AUTHOR USES TO SUPPORT THE MAIN IDEA:

_____

_____

_____

_____

_____

■ WHAT INFORMATION OR IDEAS DISCUSSED IN THIS ARTICLE ARE ALSO DISCUSSED IN YOUR TEXTBOOK OR OTHER READING YOU HAVE DONE? LIST THE TEXTBOOK CHAPTERS AND PAGE NUMBERS:

_____

_____

_____

_____

_____

_____

■ LIST ANY EXAMPLES OF BIAS OR FAULTY REASONING THAT YOU FOUND IN THE ARTICLE:

_____

_____

_____

_____

■ LIST ANY NEW TERMS/CONCEPTS THAT WERE DISCUSSED IN THE ARTICLE AND WRITE A SHORT DEFINITION:

_____

_____

_____

_____

_____

*Your instructor may require you to use this Annual Editions Article Review Form in any number of ways:
for articles that are assigned, for extra credit, as a tool to assist in developing assigned papers, or simply
for your own reference. Even if it is not required, we encourage you to photocopy and use this page;
you'll find that reflecting on the articles will greatly enhance the information from your text.

ANNUAL EDITIONS:
Aging
Article Rating Form

Here is an opportunity for you to have direct input into the next revision of this volume. We would like you to rate each of the 40 articles listed below, using the following scale:

1. **Excellent: should definitely be retained**
2. **Above average: should probably be retained**
3. **Below average: should probably be deleted**
4. **Poor: should definitely be deleted**

Your ratings will play a vital part in the next revision. So please mail this prepaid form to us just as soon as you complete it.
Thanks for your help!

We Want Your Advice

Annual Editions revisions depend on two major opinion sources: one is our Advisory Board, listed in the front of this volume, which works with us in scanning the thousands of articles published in the public press each year; the other is you—the person actually using the book. Please help us and the users of the next edition by completing the prepaid article rating form on this page and returning it to us. Thank you.

Rating	Article	Rating	Article
	1. Why Do We Age?		24. Life-Care Contracts for the Elderly: A Risky Retirement?
	2. Meeting the Challenges of an Aging Nation		25. Participation in a Dual Economy and Adjustment to Retirement
	3. Old Age Is Not What It Used to Be		26. The Many Faces of Grief
	4. The Graying of America		27. Health Technology vs. Death: Should We Prolong the Inevitable?
	5. Human Aging: Usual and Successful		28. Euthanasia: The Time Is Now
	6. Older—But Coming on Strong		29. In Defense of the Humane and Dignified Death Act
	7. To Find a Way to Age in Health		30. A Theoretical Reassessment of the Applicability of Kübler-Ross's Stages of Dying
	8. Marriages in Later Life		31. Options for Aging
	9. Religiosity, Aging, and Life Satisfaction		32. Access to Health Care in a Black Urban Elderly Population
	10. Starting Over at Midlife: Why There's More Satisfaction to Life After 40		33. Aging, Generational Continuity, and Filial Support
	11. Meet the People Who Never Quit Learning		34. Family Caregivers: America's Primary Long-Term Care Resource
	12. Never Too Late		35. A New Look at Companies That Hire Experience
	13. Another Stereotype: Old Age as a Second Childhood		36. Staying in the Work Force
	14. Age Stereotyping		37. Process, Politics, & Policy
	15. The Vintage Years		38. Roles for Aged Individuals in Post-Industrial Societies
	16. Aging of the Brain: How Can We Prevent It?		39. Generational Equity and the Future of Generational Politics
	17. Minorities Face Stubborn Inequities		40. Talkin' 'Bout My Generation
	18. It's Never Too Late		
	19. Actions of Alcohol and Drugs in Older People		
	20. The Prevalence of Elder Abuse: A Random Sample Survey		
	21. Aging: Can It Be Slowed?		
	22. Productive Aging and the Future of Retirement		
	23. The "Unretired"—Seniors Are Returning To Work		

(Continued on next page)

ABOUT YOU

Name_____ Date_____

Are you a teacher? ☐ Or student? ☐

Your School Name _____

Department _____

Address _____

City _____ State _____ Zip _____

School Telephone # _____

YOUR COMMENTS ARE IMPORTANT TO US!

Please fill in the following information:

For which course did you use this book? _____

Did you use a text with this Annual Edition? ☐ yes ☐ no

The title of the text? _____

What are your general reactions to the Annual Editions concept?

Have you read any particular articles recently that you think should be included in the next edition?

Are there any articles you feel should be replaced in the next edition? Why?

Are there other areas that you feel would utilize an Annual Edition?

May we contact you for editorial input?

May we quote you from above?

ANNUAL EDITIONS: Aging 7th Edition

BUSINESS REPLY MAIL

First Class   Permit No. 84   Guilford, CT

Postage will be paid by addressee

The Dushkin Publishing Group, Inc.
Sluice Dock
DPG **Guilford, Connecticut 06437**